Be Our Guest 2005

IRISH HOTELS FEDERATION

13 Northbrook Road, Dublin 6, Ireland
Telephone +353 1 497 6459   Fax: +353 1 497 4613

Featuring over 1,000 Hotels & Guesthouses

as well as details on Golfing, Angling, Conference, Spa & Leisure Facilities and Touring Maps

irelandhotels.com
log on and book in

Republic of Ireland: 00 353 + local code (drop the 0)
Northern Ireland: 00 44 + local code (drop the 0)
If dialling Northern Ireland directly from the Republic of Ireland
replace the prefix code 028 with the code 048.

The Irish Hotels Federation does not accept any responsibility for errors, omissions or any information whatsoever in the Guide and members and users of the Guide are requested to consult page 399 hereof for further information.

CONTENTS

FACILITIES

🛏	Total number of rooms
	Number of rooms with bath/shower and toilet
☎	Direct dial facilities
📺	TV in all bedrooms
⬍	Elevator/Lift
T	Can be booked through travel agent / tourist office and commission paid
🛝	Childrens playground
🐎	Childrens playroom
C	Price reduction for children
	Babysitter service
CM	Childrens meals
CS	Crèche
❉	Garden for visitors use
	Indoor swimming pool
	Outdoor swimming pool
	Sauna
	Gym
	Leisure Complex (including sauna / swimming pool / gym)
⚲	Tennis court - hard / grass
	Games room
	Squash court
☡	Horse riding/pony trekking on site or nearby
⛳9	9-hole golf course on site
⛳18	18-hole golf course on site

	Angling on site or nearby
♫	Evening Entertainment
P	Car parking
	Facilities for pets
S	Price reduction for senior citizens excl. July/August and subject to availability
♀	Wine Licence
	Dispense Bar Service
	Licensed to sell all alcoholic drink
alc	À la carte meals provided
	Tea/coffee making facilities in bedroom
Inet	Modem access in room
WiFi	Wireless Internet Access
🐕	Guide Dogs welcome
🚶	**1.** Accessible to ambulant people capable of climbing flights of steps with a maximum height between landings of 1.8 metres.
	2. Accessible to ambulant people with mobility impairments but capable of climbing three steps.
♿	**3.** Accessible to wheelchair users including those who can transfer unaided to and from the wheelchair.
	4. Accessible to all wheelchair users including those requiring assistance to transfer to and from the wheelchair e.g. carer / partner.
☺	Special Offer

IRISH HOTELS FEDERATION	Denotes that premises are members of the *Irish Hotels Federation* as at 18 September 2004.	NIHF	Denotes that premises are members of the *Northern Ireland Hotels Federation* as at 18 September 2004.

ACTIVITY SECTIONS

Green symbols Illustrated below denote that the hotel or guesthouse is included in a particular activity section. Further details of the facilities available and the arrangements made on behalf of guests for participation in these activities are shown on pages 405 to 462.

 Golf Angling Conference 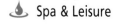 Spa & Leisure

GUINNESS

SELECTING YOUR HOTEL AND GUESTHOUSE

REGIONS

Begin by selecting the region(s) you wish to visit. This guide divides into eight separate Regions – South East, South West, Shannon, West, North West, North, Dublin & East Coast and Midlands & Lakelands – and they are represented in that order.

COUNTIES

Within each region, counties are presented alphabetically.

LOCATIONS – CITIES, TOWNS, VILLAGES

Within counties, locations are also presented alphabetically, see Index Pages 6 & 7.

PREMISES

Hotels and guesthouses are also presented in alphabetical order, see Index Pages 481 to 504.

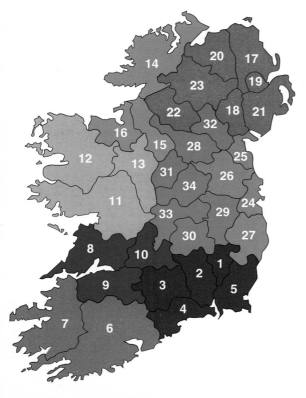

	COUNTIES	REGION	PAGES
1	CARLOW	South East	Page 22 to 25
2	KILKENNY	South East	Page 25 to 35
3	TIPPERARY SOUTH	South East	Page 35 to 43
4	WATERFORD	South East	Page 43 to 56
5	WEXFORD	South East	Page 56 to 69
6	CORK	South West	Page 72 to 108
7	KERRY	South West	Page 108 to 157
8	CLARE	Shannon	Page 160 to 180
9	LIMERICK	Shannon	Page 181 to 189
10	TIPPERARY NORTH	Shannon	Page 189 to 191
11	GALWAY	West	Page 194 to 229
12	MAYO	West	Page 229 to 241
13	ROSCOMMON	West	Page 241 to 243
14	DONEGAL	North West	Page 246 to 259
15	LEITRIM	North West	Page 260 to 262
16	SLIGO	North West	Page 263 to 267
17	ANTRIM	North	Page 269 to 272
18	ARMAGH	North	Page 273 to 273
19	BELFAST CITY	North	Page 274 to 278
20	DERRY	North	Page 279 to 281
21	DOWN	North	Page 282 to 284
22	FERMANAGH	North	Page 285 to 286
23	TYRONE	North	Page 286 to 287
24	DUBLIN	Dublin & East Coast	Page 290 to 348
25	LOUTH	Dublin & East Coast	Page 349 to 353
26	MEATH	Dublin & East Coast	Page 354 to 358
27	WICKLOW	Dublin & East Coast	Page 358 to 369
28	CAVAN	Midlands & Lakelands	Page 372 to 376
29	KILDARE	Midlands & Lakelands	Page 376 to 383
30	LAOIS	Midlands & Lakelands	Page 383 to 384
31	LONGFORD	Midlands & Lakelands	Page 385 to 386
32	MONAGHAN	Midlands & Lakelands	Page 386 to 387
33	OFFALY	Midlands & Lakelands	Page 387 to 391
34	WESTMEATH	Midlands & Lakelands	Page 391 to 396

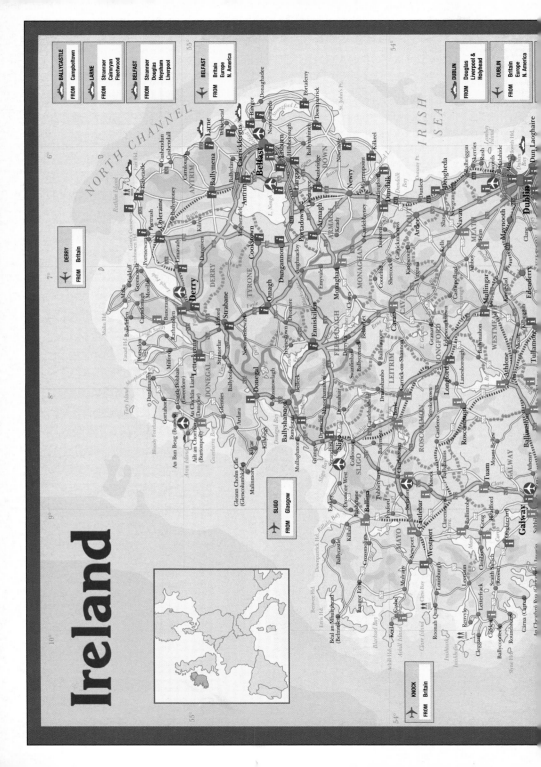

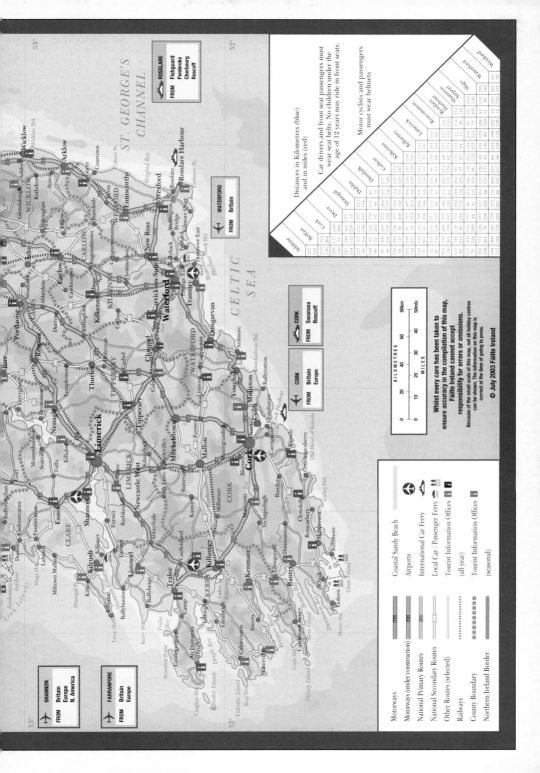

Dick Bourke
President, Irish Hotels Federation

Hotels and Guesthouses in Ireland are very special. The majority are family owned with the proprietor and members of the family there to welcome guests and to extend to them renowned Irish hospitality. Even when they are owned by a company, or are part of a group, they still retain the character and ambience of a family premises - a place where you will be truly welcome.

The Irish hotel is unique, in that more often than not, it acts as a social centre for the community. Hotels offer a lot more than just a bed and a meal - they are fully fledged social, leisure, business and community centres with every imaginable facility and amenity, providing food, accommodation, sports, leisure facilities, entertainment and other attractions.

If you are moving around the country, you'll find that "Be Our Guest" is an invaluable help in choosing your next location.

Ireland's hoteliers and guesthouse owners want to welcome you and want to play their part in ensuring that your stay in Ireland is a happy one. We hope that you will stay with us and that you will use this guide to select the hotel or guesthouse of your choice, so that we can personally invite you to -

Be Our Guest

Ní haon ní coitianta é an Óstlann nó an Teach Lóistín in Éirinn. Is i seilbh teaghlaigh iad a bhformhór acu agus bíonn an t-úinéir agus baill den teaghlach romhat chun fáilte Uí Cheallaigh a chur romhat. Fiú nuair is le comhlacht iad, nó is cuid de ghrúpa iad, baineann meon agus atmaisféar áitreabh teaghlaigh leo - áiteanna ina gcuirfí fíorchaoin fáilte romhat.

Rud ar leith is ea an óstlann in Éirinn agus is dócha ná a mhalairt go bhfeidhmíonn sí mar lárionad sóisialta don phobal. Cuireann an óstlann i bhfad níos mó ná leaba agus béile ar fáil - is lárionad sóisialta,a siamsaíochta, gnó agus pobail ar fheabhas í chomh maith agus gach aon áis faoin spéir aici, a chuireann bia, lóistín, imeachtaí spóirt, áiseanna siamsaíochta agus só agus tarraingtí nach iad ar fáil.

Agus tú ag taisteal timpeall na tíre gheobhaidh tú amach go mbeidh "Bí i d'Aoi Againn" an-áisiúil agus an chéad suíomh eile á roghnú agat.

Is mian le hóstlannaithe agus le lucht tithe lóistín na hÉireann fáilte a chur romhat agus a bheith in ann a dheimhniú go mbainfidh tú sult as do sheal in Éirinn. Tá súil againn go bhfanfaidh tú linn agus go mbainfidh tú leas as an treoir seo

chun do rogha óstlann nó teach lóistin a aimsiú, i dtreo is go mbeimid in ann a rá leat go pearsanta -

Be Our Guest

Les hôtels et les pensions en Irlande sont d'un caractère particulier.

Ils sont très souvent gérés par le propriétaire et des membres de sa famille, présents pour accueillir les visiteurs et leur faire découvrir la célèbre hospitalité irlandaise. Même s'ils appartiennent à une entreprise ou font partie d'un groupe de sociétés, ils possèdent toujours ce caractère et cette ambiance des lieux familiaux - un endroit où vous serez sincèrement bien accueillis.

L'hôtel irlandais est unique en ce qu'il joue très souvent le rôle de centre social pour la communauté. Les hôtels offrent beaucoup plus qu'un lit et un repas - ce sont, pour la communauté, de véritables centres sociaux, de loisirs et d'affaires, équipés de toutes les infrastructures et installations imaginables. Ils vous proposent le gîte et le couvert, mais aussi activités sportives et de loisir, divertissements et autres attractions.

Si vous voyagez dans le pays, vous trouverez que le guide "Be Our Guest"

est d'une aide précieuse pour vous aider à choisir votre prochaine destination.

Les hôteliers et les propriétaires de pensions irlandais veulent vous accueillir et être là pour vous assurer un séjour agréable en Irlande. Nous espérons que vous resterez avec nous et que vous utiliserez ce guide pour sélectionner l'hôtel ou la pension de votre choix, afin que nous ayons le plaisir de vous compter parmi nos visiteurs.

Be Our Guest

Die Hotels und Pensionen in Irland sind von ganz besonderer Art.

Zum größten Teil handelt es sich dabei um private Familienbetriebe, in denen der Besitzer und die Familienmitglieder ihre Gäste mit der vielgerühmten irischen Gastfreundschaft willkommen heißen. Aber auch wenn sich diese Häuser in Unternehmensbesitz befinden oder einer Kette angehören, strahlen sie dennoch den Charakter und die Atmosphäre von Familienbetrieben aus - ein Ort, an dem Sie immer herzlich willkommen sind.

Hotels in Irland sind einzig in ihrer Art und dienen oftmals als Mittelpunkt geselliger Treffen. Hotels haben viel mehr zu bieten als nur ein Bett und eine Mahlzeit - sie sind Gesellschafts-, Freizeit-, Geschäfts- und öffentlicher Treffpunkt mit allen nur erdenklichen Einrichtungen und Annehmlichkeiten, angefangen bei Essen, Unterkunft, Sport und Freizeitmöglichkeiten bis zur Unterhaltung und anderen Anziehungspunkten.

Auf Ihren Reisen im Land werden Sie feststellen, daß Ihnen der "Be Our Guest"-Führer eine wertvolle Hilfe bei der Suche nach der nächstgelegenen Unterkunft leistet.

Irlands Hotel- und Pensionsbesitzer heißen Sie gerne willkommen und möchten ihren Anteil dazu beitragen, daß Ihnen Ihr Aufenthalt in Irland in angenehmer Erinnerung bleibt. Wir hoffen, daß Sie uns besuchen werden und diesen Führer bei der Auswahl Ihres Hotels oder Ihrer Pension zu Rate ziehen, so daß wir Sie persönlich willkommen heißen können.

Be Our Guest

Los hoteles y las pensiones en Irlanda son muy especiales. La mayoría son propiedades familiares habitadas por el mismo propietario junto a los miembros de su familia que se encuentran predispuestos a dar la bienvenida a los huéspedes y, de este modo, contribuir a ampliar su reconocida hospitalidad irlandesa. Incluso si pertecen a una compañía o forman parte de un grupo, siempre mantendrán el carácter y ambiente de las propiedades familiares, un lugar donde siempre serás bienvenido de corazón. El hotel irlandés es único y se comporta bastante a menudo como el mismo centro social de la comunidad. Estos hoteles ofrecen algo más que una cama y comida, rebozan de centros sociales comunitarios de ocio y negocios con una amplia gama de servicios inimaginables. Ofrece comida, alojamiento, deportes, actividades de ocio, entretenimiento y todo tipo de atracciones.

Si te encuentras viajando por nuestro país, te darás cuenta que la ayuda que te ofrece "Be Our Guest", a la hora de elegir tu próximo destino, no tiene precio. Los hoteleros y propietarios de pensiones de Irlanda quieren darte la bienvenida y quieren contribuir a que tu estancia en Irlanda sea una estancia feliz. Esperamos que te quedes con nosotros y que utilices esta guía para elegir el hotel o pensión que tú elijas y para que nosotros podamos invitarte

personalmente a ser nuestro invitado, el invitado de "Be our Guest".

Be Our Guest

Gli hotel e le pensioni in Irlanda sono davvero speciali. Molti sono a conduzione familiare, e gli ospiti vengono accolti dai proprietari e le loro famiglie secondo le famose tradizioni di ospitalità irlandesi. Il calore e l'ambiente intimo e accogliente si ritrovano persino negli hotel delle grandi compagnie e catene alberghiere: avrete sempre la sensazione di essere ospiti graditi. Una caratteristica unica degli hotel irlandesi è che, molto spesso, fungono anche da centro di aggregazione della comunità. Gli alberghi offrono molto di più di un letto e dei pasti: sono centri per socializzare, divertirsi, fare affari e vivere la dimensione locale. Qui si può trovare ogni attrezzatura e comfort immaginabile: ristoranti, alloggi, impianti sportivi, attività ricreative, divertimento e tante altre attrazioni.

Se prevedete molti spostamenti, scoprirete in "Be Our Guest" uno strumento di valore inestimabile per la scelta delle prossime mete. Gli albergatori e i proprietari delle pensioni irlandesi vi aspettano per darvi il benvenuto e fare la loro parte per rendere piacevole il vostro soggiorno in Irlanda. Ci auguriamo che vogliate viaggiare con noi, usando la nostra guida per scegliere un hotel o una pensione di vostro gusto, così da potervi invitare personalmente a: "Be our Guest".

Be Our Guest

irelandhotels.com
log on and book in

FÁILTE IRELAND
NATIONAL TOURISM DEVELOPMENT AUTHORITY
www.ireland.travel.ie

IRELAND

Dublin
Fáilte Ireland,
Baggot Street Bridge, Dublin 2
Tel: 01 - 602 4000
Fax: 01 - 602 4100

NORTHERN IRELAND

Belfast
Fáilte Ireland,
53 Castle Street, Belfast BT1 1GH
Tel: 028 - 9026 5500
Fax: 028 - 9026 5515

Derry
Fáilte Ireland,
44 Foyle Street, Derry BT48 6AT
Tel: 028 - 7136 9501
Fax: 028 - 7136 9501

*If dialling Northern Ireland directly from the Republic of Ireland the code 048 followed by the telephone number is sufficient.

NORTHERN IRELAND TOURIST BOARD
www.discovernorthernireland.com

Belfast
Northern Ireland Tourist Board,
59 North Street, Belfast BT1 1NB
Tel: 028 - 9023 1221
Fax: 028 - 9024 0960

Dublin
Northern Ireland Tourist Board,
16 Nassau Street, Dublin 2
Tel: 01 - 679 1977
Fax: 01 - 679 1863

TOURISM IRELAND –
EUROPE
www.tourismireland.com

Austria
Tourism Ireland
Libellenweg 1, A-1140 Vienna
Tel: 01 - 501 596000
Email: info.at@tourismireland.com
Web: www.tourismireland.com

Belgium/Luxembourg
Tourism Ireland,
Avenue Louise 327, Louizalaan
1050 Brussels
Tel: 02 - 275 0171
E-mail: info.be@tourismireland.com
Web: www.ireland-tourism.be

Britain-London
Tourism Ireland, Nations House,
103 Wigmore Street,
London WIU 1QS
Tel: 0800-039 7000
Email: info.gb@tourismireland.com
Web: www.tourismireland.com

Britain-Glasgow
Tourism Ireland
James Miller House
98 West George Street (7th Floor)
Glasgow G2 1PJ
Tel: 0800 - 039 7000
Email: infoglasgow@tourismireland.com
Web: www.tourismireland.com

France
Office du Tourisme de l'île d'Irlande,
33 Rue de Miromesnil, 75008 Paris
Tel: 01 - 70 20 00 20
Email: info.fr@tourismireland.com
Web: www.irlande-tourisme.fr

Germany
Irland Information,
Gutleutstrasse 32,
D-60329 Frankfurt am Main
Tel: 069 668 00950
Email: info@tourismireland.de
Web: www.tourismireland.de

Italy
Turismo Irlandese,
Via Santa Maria Segreta 6,
20123 Milano
Tel: 02 - 4829 6060
Email: informazioni@tourismireland.com
Web: www.irlanda-travel.com

The Netherlands
Ierland Toerisme,
Spuistraat 104, 1012 VA Amsterdam
Tel: 020 - 504 0689
Email: info@ierland.nl
Web: www.ierland.nl

Nordic Region
Tourism Ireland
Nyhavn 16 (3rd Floor)
1051 Copenhagen K
Denmark
Tel: 33 15 80 45
Email: info@irland-turisme.dk
Web: www.irland-turisme.dk

info@irlanninmatkailu.com
www.irlanninmatkailu.com
info@visit-irland.com
www.visit-irland.com
info@irlandsinfo.com
www.irlandsinfo.com

Spain
Turismo de Irlanda,
Paseo de la Castellana 46,
3a Planta, 28046 Madrid
Tel: 91-7456 420
Email: info.sp@tourismireland.com
Web: www.turismodeirlanda.com

Switzerland
Tourism Ireland
Mettlenstrasse 22, CH-8142 Uitikon
Tel: 044-210 4153
Email: info.ch@tourismireland.com
Web: www.tourismireland.com

TOURISM IRELAND –
REST OF THE WORLD

USA
Tourism Ireland
345 Park Avenue, New York NY 10154
Tel: 1800-223 6470
Email: info.us@tourismireland.com
Web: www.tourismireland.com

Canada
Tourism Ireland
2 Bloor St. West, Suite 3403
Toronto, M4W 3E2
Tel: 1800 - 223 6470
Email:info.ca@tourismireland.com
Web: www.tourismireland.com

South Africa
Tourism Ireland,
c/o Development Promotions
Everite House, Level 7,
20 De Korte Street,
Braamfontein 2001, Gauteng
Tel: 011 - 339 48 65
Web: www.tourismireland.com

New Zealand
Tourism Ireland,
Level 6, 18 Shortland Street,
Private Bag, 92136, Auckland
Tel: 09 - 977 2255
Email: tourism@ireland.co.nz
Web: www.tourismireland.com

Australia
Tourism Ireland,
Level 5, 36 Carrington Street,
Sydney, NSW 2000
Tel: 02 - 9299 6177
Email: info@tourismireland.com.au
Web: www.tourismireland.com.au

Japan
Tourism Ireland, Woody 21,
23 Aizumi-cho, Shinjuku-ku,
Tokyo 160-0005
Tel: 03 - 5363 6515
Web: www.tourismireland.com

TWO OF THE
FINEST

THE GUINNESS IS GREAT

With over **1,000** Hotels & Guesthouses to choose from, Irelandhotels.com offers great value breaks to Ireland.

All the best from Ireland

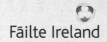

Fáilte Ireland

Optimus

Achieving Business Excellence

ooo
Award of Excellence
BUSINESS EXCELLENCE PROGRAMME

oo
Mark of Best Practice
BEST PRACTICE PROGRAMME

o
Ireland's Best
SERVICE EXCELLENCE PROGRAMME

Optimus helps tourism businesses achieve excellence in all aspects of their service to you, the customer.

Optimus – the brand of business excellence. Watch out for it in 2005

Fáilte Ireland
The National Tourism Development Authority
88 – 95 Amiens Street
Dublin 1

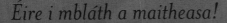

**DISCOVER
THE SKILLED
CRAFT OF
BARREL
MAKING**

We won't spoil your visit by giving away too many of our barrel-making secrets.
All will be revealed at Guinness Storehouse, Ireland's No.1 visitor attraction.

Located inside Arthur Guinness's original 1759 brewery, go on a surprising journey
into the heart of the world's greatest beer. And when you're done exploring, drink
in the view from Gravity, Dublin's highest bar, while enjoying a complimentary pint.

To book tickets for this unmissable experience visit us on-line at
www.guinness-storehouse.com. Open daily from 9.30am-5pm,
with last admission at 8pm during July and August.

DISCOVER THE VITAL INGREDIENT

**GUINNESS®
STOREHOUSE**

LORD BAGENAL INN

MAIN STREET,
LEIGHLINBRIDGE,
CO. CARLOW

TEL: 059-972 1668 FAX: 059-972 2629
EMAIL: info@lordbagenal.com
WEB: www.lordbagenal.com

HOTEL ★★★ MAP 7 M 8

Situated in the heritage village of
Leighlinbridge along the River Barrow,
with private marina and gardens, we
are ideally located to explore the
South East. Our en suite bedrooms
are luxuriously furnished to the
highest standards. Award winning
restaurant reputed for fine food and
excellent wines. Locals and visitors
frequent our bar where carvery lunch
and bar food are served daily.
Children always welcome. Weddings,
conferences, banquets catered for.
Gold Medal Entente Florale Floral
Pride.

B&B from €55.00 to €110.00

JAMES & MARY KEHOE

🛏🕯☎🖨🛎☕♿CMCS❄♪♫📠
12 12 🏠alc♿inet 🐕

MOUNT WOLSELEY COUNTRY RESORT

TULLOW,
CO. CARLOW

TEL: 059-915 1674 FAX: 059-915 2123
EMAIL: info@mountwolseley.ie
WEB: www.mountwolseley.ie

HOTEL U MAP 8 N 8

Opened in August 2004 the Mount
Wolseley Country Resort is designed
and built to international 4 star
specifications. Each of our 142
bedrooms have been carefully
designed in harmony with the
beautiful surrounding countryside and
the resort includes a championship
golf course designed by Christy
O'Connor Jnr. A luxurious spa
(opening early 2005) and a
children's activity centre. An
experience "in harmony with you".

B&B from €65.00 to €95.00

JOHN KEATING
GENERAL MANAGER

🛏🕯☎🖨🅿♿☕♿CM❄♿🖼
142 142 ♿🔍∪♿♪📠♿alc♿inet 🐕

HOTELS

WATERSIDE

THE QUAY,
GRAIGUENAMANAGH,
CO. KILKENNY

TEL: 059-972 4246 FAX: 059-972 4733
EMAIL: info@watersideguesthouse.com
WEB: www.watersideguesthouse.com

GUESTHOUSE ★★★ MAP 7 M 7

A beautifully restored 19th century
cornstore with feature wooden beams
and imposing granite exterior.
Riverside location, all rooms have a
view of the River Barrow. Excellent
base for boating, fishing, hillwalking.
16km from Mount Juliet for golf.
Nearby 13th century Duiske Abbey.
27km from historical Kilkenny.
Superb restaurant features continental
cuisine & international flavour wine
list. Relaxed & friendly approach.
Perfect for small groups. Guided
hillwalking for groups.

B&B from €39.00 to €52.50

BRIAN & BRIGID ROBERTS
MANAGERS

☺ Weekend specials from €119.00 pps

🛏🕯☎🖨T☕♿♿♪S🏠alc♿
10 10

HOTELS

B&B Rates are per Person Sharing per Night incl. Breakfast
Room Rates are per Room per Night

BERKERLEY HOUSE

5 LOWER PATRICK STREET,
KILKENNY

TEL: 056-776 4848 FAX: 056-776 4829
EMAIL: berkeleyhouse@eircom.net
WEB: www.berkeleyhousekilkenny.com

GUESTHOUSE ★★★ MAP 7 L 7

A warm and genuine welcome awaits
you here at this charming owner
operated period residence, uniquely
situated in the very heart of mediaeval
Kilkenny City. Berkerley House boasts
ample private car parking, 10
spacious & tastefully decorated
rooms, all en suite with multi channel
TV, direct dial phone & tea/coffee
facilities. We pride ourselves on a
dedicated and professional team and
ensure that every effort will be made
to make your stay with us a most
enjoyable one.

B&B from €35.00 to €55.00

VINCENT QUAN

10 10

Closed 23 - 28 December

BRANNIGANS GLENDINE INN

CASTLECOMER ROAD,
KILKENNY

TEL: 056-772 1069 FAX: 056-777 0714
EMAIL: branigan@iol.ie
WEB: www.kilkennyaccommodation.com

GUESTHOUSE ★★ MAP 7 L 7

The Glendine Inn has been a licensed
tavern for over 200 years. It consists
of 7 bedrooms (all en suite), a
residents' lounge, residents' dining
room, and public lounge and bars
serving snack or bar lunches. We are
ideally located for golf (course 200m
away), the railway station and the
historic city of Kilkenny are only
1.5km away. We assure you of a
friendly welcome.

B&B from €35.00 to €55.00

MICHAEL BRANNIGAN
PROPRIETOR

7 7

Open All Year

BRIDGECOURT HOUSE

GREENSBRIDGE,
KILKENNY

TEL: 056-776 2998 FAX: 056-776 2998
EMAIL: anegan@eircom.net
WEB: www.bridgecourtkilkenny.com

GUESTHOUSE ★★★ MAP 7 L 7

A 3 star family-run guesthouse
situated in a superb city centre
location with all facilities nearby. Our
impressive residence has en suite
rooms, colour TV, hairdryers etc. and
a cosy lounge where tea/coffee
making facilities are available. All our
bedrooms are beautifully decorated to
reach high standards. We offer all our
guests a warm welcome, tasty
breakfast and a friendly service all in
comfortable surroundings. Private car
parking.

B&B from €30.00 to €55.00

DON & NIAMH EGAN

Midweek specials from €99.00 pps

9 9

Open All Year

B&B Rates are per Person Sharing per Night incl. Breakfast
Room Rates are per Room per Night

BUTLER HOUSE

**PATRICK STREET,
KILKENNY**

TEL: 056-776 5707 FAX: 056-776 5626
EMAIL: res@butler.ie
WEB: www.butler.ie

GUESTHOUSE ★★★ MAP 7 L 7

Sweeping staircases, magnificent plastered ceilings & marble fireplaces are all features of this 16th century Dower House of Kilkenny Castle. The house is a combination of contemporary furnishings and period elegance. The larger superior rooms have graceful bow windows with lovely views of the walled Georgian garden and Kilkenny Castle. These rooms offer peace and tranquillity to the weary traveller, with the added advantage of being in the heart of the city. Conference facilities. AA ♦♦♦♦. Private car park.

B&B from €62.00 to €100.00

GABRIELLE HICKEY
MANAGER

☺ Midweek specials from €150.00 pps

13 13

Closed 24 - 29 December

CLUB HOUSE HOTEL

**PATRICK STREET,
KILKENNY**

TEL: 056-772 1994 FAX: 056-777 1920
EMAIL: clubhse@iol.ie
WEB: www.clubhousehotel.com

HOTEL ★★ MAP 7 L 7

Situated uniquely in a cultural & artistic centre & against the background of Kilkenny's medieval city, the magnificent 18th century Club House Hotel maintains a 200 year old tradition of effortless comfort, hospitality and efficiency. En suite rooms are decorated in both modern & period style with complimentary beverages, TV, hairdryer & phone. Food is locally sourced, cooked and presented to highest standards. Victors Bar has old world charm & luxury. Live music Saturday nights traditional Irish song & dance Tuesday nights July & August.

Member of MinOtel Ireland Hotel Group

B&B from €45.00 to €115.00

JAMES P. BRENNAN
MANAGING DIRECTOR

☺ Weekend specials from €165.00 pps

28 28

Closed 24 - 30 December

FANAD HOUSE

**CASTLE ROAD,
KILKENNY**

TEL: 056-776 4126 FAX: 056-775 6001
EMAIL: fanadhouse@hotmail.com
WEB: www.fanadhouse.com

GUESTHOUSE U MAP 7 L 7

Overlooking Kilkenny Castle Park, Fanad House is a five minute walk from the city centre. The newly built guesthouse offers all en suite rooms with complimentary beverages, multi-channel TV, hairdryer and direct dial phone. Extensive breakfast menu available. Private and secure parking provided. An ideal base for exploring the medieval city. We are adjacent to Kilkenny Tennis Club. Owner operated is your guarantee for an enjoyable stay.

B&B from €45.00 to €100.00

PAT WALLACE
PROPRIETOR

8 8

Open All Year

B&B Rates are per Person Sharing per Night incl. Breakfast
Room Rates are per Room per Night

HOTEL KILKENNY

COLLEGE ROAD,
KILKENNY

TEL: 056-776 2000 FAX: 056-776 5984
EMAIL: kilkenny@griffingroup.ie
WEB: www.griffingroup.ie

HOTEL ★★★ MAP 7 L 7

Hotel Kilkenny is situated in picturesque award - winning landscaped gardens, less than 10 minutes walk from medieval Kilkenny City. Facilities include 103 spacious bedrooms, the wonderful Broom's Bistro, relaxing Rosehill Bar and the superb 5 star Active Health + Fitness Club with 20m pool and spa area, excellent gymnasium, beauty treatment rooms and hairdressing salon. Excellent conference facilities available for 4-400 delegates. Why resort to less?

B&B from €60.00 to €130.00

RICHARD BUTLER
GENERAL MANAGER

103 103

Open All Year

KILFORD ARMS

JOHN STREET,
KILKENNY

TEL: 056-776 1018 FAX: 056-776 1128
EMAIL: kilfordarms@indigo.ie
WEB: www.kilfordarms.ie

HOTEL U MAP 7 L 7

Enviably located, just minutes walk from city centre and railway station, the Kilford Arms offers a personal service and great range of facilities. The White Oak Restaurant serves fresh local produce in comfortable surroundings. PV's traditional bar has entertainment nightly, with food served daily. O'Faoláin's Bar is Kilkenny's most vibrant bar, with 3 levels of stunning architecture, DJs and late bar nightly. Welcome to the Kilford Arms.

B&B from €45.00 to €115.00

PIUS PHELAN
OWNER

50 50

Open All Year

KILKENNY HIBERNIAN HOTEL

1 ORMONDE STREET,
KILKENNY CITY

TEL: 056-777 1888 FAX: 056-777 1877
EMAIL: info@kilkennyhibernianhotel.com
WEB: www.kilkennyhibernianhotel.com

HOTEL U MAP 7 L 7

The award-winning Kilkenny Hibernian Hotel, one of Kilkenny's finest boutique hotels, is located in the heart of the city. Experience an ambience of elegance and comfort, combined with a service that is hospitable, friendly and professional. The hotel offers 46 luxury bedrooms, incorporating Junior Suites and Penthouses, the classic Hibernian Bar, Morrissons - the city's leading contemporary bar and Jacobs Cottage - one of the region's leading restaurants.

B&B from €60.00 to €140.00

DAVID LAWLOR
GENERAL MANAGER/DIRECTOR

Weekend specials from €195.00 pps

46 46

Closed 24 - 26 December

B&B Rates are per Person Sharing per Night incl. Breakfast
Room Rates are per Room per Night

KILKENNY HOUSE

FRESHFORD ROAD,
KILKENNY

TEL: 056-777 0711 FAX: 056-777 0698
EMAIL: kilkennyhouse@eircom.net
WEB: www.kilkennyhouse.com

GUESTHOUSE ★★★ MAP 7 L 7

Kilkenny House is ideally located on the R.693 between the city's Saint Lukes and Aut Even Hospitals. Set in over 2 acres of mature gardens with secure private car parking. The Georgian style house was purpose built for guests and is long established. All rooms are en suite with power shower and some baths, TV, Hairdryer, Phone, Complimentary Beverages. The traditional hot and buffet breakfast is included in the price and served in the conservatory overlooking the rear gardens. Owner operated guarantees Kilkenny's best value accommodation and breakfast.

B&B from €30.00 to €40.00

MICHELENE AND TED DORE
PROPRIETORS

Midweek specials from €99.00 pps

10 10

Closed 21 - 28 December

KILKENNY ORMONDE HOTEL

ORMONDE STREET,
KILKENNY

TEL: 056-772 3900 FAX: 056-772 3977
EMAIL: info@kilkennyormonde.com
WEB: www.kilkennyormonde.com

HOTEL ★★★★ MAP 7 L 7

The new 4**** de luxe Kilkenny Ormonde Hotel is the most extensive hotel in the city, ideally situated just off the High Street with Kilkenny Castle on its doorstep. Complete with 118 of the largest bedrooms in Kilkenny, fully equipped leisure centre with 21 metre swimming pool & 2 award winning restaurants. Activity packed Kids Club open throughout midterm breaks & summer season, complimentary. Also offering complimentary parking, The Kilkenny Ormonde is the perfect choice for both corporate & leisure guests.

B&B from €64.00 to €130.00

PATRICK CURRAN
GENERAL MANAGER/DIRECTOR

2 nights B&B + 1 Dinner from €155.00 pps

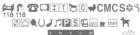
118 118

Closed 24 - 26 December

KILKENNY RIVER COURT

THE BRIDGE,
JOHN STREET,
KILKENNY

TEL: 056-772 3388 FAX: 056-772 3389
EMAIL: reservations@kilrivercourt.com
WEB: www.kilrivercourt.com

HOTEL ★★★★ MAP 7 L 7

Award winning RAC/AA 4**** hotel, leisure club and conference centre. City centre location, stunning views of Kilkenny Castle and the River Nore. Ideal as a conference venue or simply sheer relaxation. Leisure facilities, which include swimming pool, sauna, geyser pool, jacuzzi, fully equipped gymnasium and beauty salon. Limited free carparking. Within easy access of Dublin, Waterford and Cork.

Member of Select Hotels of Ireland

B&B from €45.00 to €160.00

PETER WILSON
GENERAL MANAGER

2 nights B&B + 1 Dinner from €155.00 pps

90 90

Closed 24 - 26 December

B&B Rates are per Person Sharing per Night incl. Breakfast
Room Rates are per Room per Night

LACKEN HOUSE

DUBLIN ROAD,
KILKENNY

TEL: 056-776 1085 FAX: 056-776 2435
EMAIL: info@lackenhouse.ie
WEB: www.lackenhouse.ie

GUESTHOUSE ★★★ MAP 7 L 7

Stay at Lacken House and enjoy high quality accommodation, superb food and a friendly welcome. We are a family-run guest house, situated in Kilkenny City, where you can enjoy exploring the medieval city. Superior & standard bedrooms available, all bedrooms are en suite with colour TV and tea/coffee facilities. Private car parking available for all residents. Our house features the home cooking of our award-winning chefs, where fresh food is cooked to perfection. Full bar service is also available.

Member of Best Loved Hotels

B&B from €55.00 to €99.00

JACKIE & TREVOR TONER
OWNERS

🛏️🏃☎️🖥️T☑CM✳️☀️✈️PS🔒alc
10 10

Closed 24 - 27 December

LANGTON HOUSE HOTEL

69 JOHN STREET,
KILKENNY

TEL: 056-776 5133 FAX: 056-776 3693
EMAIL: reservations@langtons.ie
WEB: www.langtons.ie

HOTEL ★★★ MAP 7 L 7

The Langton Group, incorporating Langtons Hotel; Bar & Restaurant; The Marble City Bar; Carrigans Liquor Bar, are all located in the heart of Kilkenny City. Langtons Hotel, complete with thirty bedrooms, incorporating executive, penthouse and art-deco suites. Having won "National Pub of the Year" a record 4 times, the Langton Bar, Garden Restaurant, (member of the Kilkenny Good Food Circle) and "Club Langton" disco complete the picture that is Langtons.

B&B from €55.00 to €120.00

PAUL MORRISSEY
MANAGER

✓

🛏️🏃☎️🖥️T☑C🐾CM✳️🎵P🔒alc▪️
30 30
🐕

Closed 25 December

LARAGH GUEST HOUSE

SMITHLAND NORTH,
WATERFORD ROAD,
KILKENNY CITY

TEL: 056-776 4674 FAX: 056-776 4674

WEB: www.laraghhouse.com

UNDER CONSTRUCTION · OPENING JANUARY 2005

GUESTHOUSE P MAP 7 L 7

Laragh House is a new attractive modern guesthouse offering luxury accommodation. Our bedrooms are en suite, spacious and well equipped with power showers and/or whirlpool baths, T.V., DD phones, internet, tea/coffee facilities, hairdryer etc. Guests can expect a warm welcome, comfort, and an appetising breakfast menu. Easy to find, we are on main route from city towards Waterford, but close to the by-pass and approx. 1km from the city centre's shops, restaurants, hotels and historic places. Parking.

B&B from €30.00 to €45.00

HELEN COONEY
MANAGER

😊 Details on request from Manager

🛏️🏃☎️🖥️T☑C✳️P▪️ Inet
8 8

Closed 24 - 30 December

B&B Rates are per Person Sharing per Night incl. Breakfast
Room Rates are per Room per Night

LAURELS

COLLEGE ROAD,
KILKENNY

TEL: 056-776 1501 FAX: 056-777 1334
EMAIL: laurels@eircom.net
WEB: www.thelaurelskilkenny.com

GUESTHOUSE ★★★ MAP 7 L 7

Purpose built townhouse 6-10 minutes walk from city centre and castle. Private car parking. All rooms en suite (some with whirlpool baths & super king sized beds). TV, Hairdryer, Tea/Coffee in all rooms. Some of the comments in Visitors Book: "Absolutely Wonderful", "Best B&B we had in Ireland", "First class & recommendable", "What more could one ask for, and a whirlpool bath too", "Wonderful". Opposite Hotel Kilkenny beside the famous Sceilp Pub.

Member of Premier Guesthouses

B&B from € 30.00 to €50.00

BRIAN AND BETTY MCHENRY

Inet

9   9

Inet

IRISH HOTELS FEDERATION

Open All Year

LAWLORS BAR & GUESTHOUSE

42/43 JOHN STREET,
KILKENNY

TEL: 056-772 1379 FAX: 056-776 1579
EMAIL: lawlors4243@eircom.net
WEB: www.lawlorsbarandguesthouse.ie

GUESTHOUSE P MAP 7 L 7

A luxurious Victorian bar and guesthouse within walking distance of Kilkenny's medieval city centre (opposite railway station). Stay and relax in one of our 10 luxurious bedrooms designed for a high quality of comfort. All rooms have satellite TV, computer ports, tea/coffee making facilities, hairdryer. Visit our newly refurbished Victorian bar which serves excellent food all day. A warm welcome awaits you.

B&B from €45.00 to €65.00

JOHN & MIRIAM LAWLOR

10   10

Closed 24 - 27 December

MCCOURTS

JOHN STREET (@ THE BRIDGE),
KILKENNY

TEL: 056-777 0844 FAX: 056-772 3389

HOTEL ★★ MAP 7 L 7

"McCourts" offering a contemporary modern bar and bistro with accommodation located in the city centre of Kilkenny just beyond John Street Bridge where spectacular views of Kilkenny Castle will impress you. Accommodation comprises fourteen functional bedrooms, all en-suite and simply furnished, including television and tea/coffee making facilities. Minutes away from the Railway Station, Castle, Theatre, High Street, Restaurants and Bars. Winner of the "Black & White 2003" and "Dining Pub 2004" award.

B&B from €45.00 to €65.00

PATRICK CRAWFORD

14   14

Closed 24 - 26 December

B&B Rates are per Person Sharing per Night incl. Breakfast
Room Rates are per Room per Night

METROPOLE HOTEL

HIGH STREET,
KILKENNY

TEL: 056-776 3778 FAX: 056-777 0232
EMAIL: info@metropolekilkenny.com
WEB: www.metropolekilkenny.com

HOTEL ★ MAP 7 L 7

The Metropole Hotel is situated in the heart of Kilkenny City. Occupies a dominant position in Kilkenny's main shopping area (High Street). Within walking distance of all the city's medieval buildings e.g. Kilkenny Castle, Roth House and St. Canice's Cathedral. All bedrooms are en suite with multi channel TV, direct dial telephone and tea/coffee facilities. Live entertainment. Failte Ireland approved.

B&B from €35.00 to €65.00

ROBERT DELANEY
PROPRIETOR

12 12

NEWPARK HOTEL

CASTLECOMER ROAD,
KILKENNY

TEL: 056-776 0500 FAX: 056-776 0555
EMAIL: info@newparkhotel.com
WEB: www.newparkhotel.com

HOTEL ★★★ MAP 7 L 7

The newly extended and luxurious Newpark Hotel (3***, AA***), set in 40 acres of parkland in Ireland's Mediaeval City, boasts a total of 130 superior bedrooms en suite, with TV, hairdryer, telephone, trouser press and tea/coffee making facilities. Our extended Leisure Centre w/52ft Pool, Sauna, Jacuzzi, Steamroom, Gym and new Health & Beauty Spa. Scott Dove Bar serves carvery lunch/evening meals. Enjoy fine dining in Gullivers Restaurant. Live entertainment most nights. State of the art conference and banqueting facilities.

Member of Best Western Hotels

B&B from €60.00 to €130.00

DAVID O'SULLIVAN
MANAGING DIRECTOR

130 130

O'MALLEYS GUESTHOUSE

ORMONDE COURT,
ORMONDE ROAD,
KILKENNY

TEL: 056-777 1003 FAX: 056-777 1577

WEB: www.o'malleys.com

GUESTHOUSE ★★ MAP 7 L 7

A beautiful guesthouse ideally situated on a quiet road in the lovely medieval city of Kilkenny. Two minutes walk to Kilkenny Castle, The Design Centre, Rothe House, high street shopping and numerous restaurants, pubs and entertainment venues to suit all tastes. All rooms are en-suite with multi-channel T.V., hairdryer and complimentary tea/coffee tray. Private car parking. When staying at O'Malleys you are assured a warm welcome and comfortable stay

B&B from €30.00 to €60.00

EIMER CROGHAN

☺ Midweek special from €50.00 per room per night

8 8

Open All Year

Open All Year

Open All Year

B&B Rates are per Person Sharing per Night incl. Breakfast
Room Rates are per Room per Night

SAN ANTONIO

CASTLECOMER ROAD, KILKENNY

TEL: 056-777 1834 FAX: 056-775 6393
EMAIL: sanantonio@eircom.net
WEB: www.sanantonio.kilkenny.20m.com

GUESTHOUSE ★★ MAP 7 L 7

San Antonio is a family-run guesthouse. Just a 10 minute walk to Kilkenny City centre. All our rooms are en suite with tea/coffee making facilities, multi channel TV, hairdryers and telephones. Private car parking available for all residents. Ideally located to explore the Mediaeval City and South East area. You are assured a warm and friendly welcome.

B&B from €35.00 to €50.00

MARIE ROCHE
OWNER

8   8

Open All Year

SPRINGHILL COURT HOTEL, SPA & LEISURE CLUB

WATERFORD ROAD, KILKENNY

TEL: 056-772 1122 FAX: 056-776 1600
EMAIL: reservations@springhillcourt.com
WEB: www.springhillcourt.com

HOTEL ★★★ MAP 7 L 7

Located only minutes from the bustling centre of " the Marble City". We boast one of Kilkenny's most modern leisure clubs. Our facilities include a 19m deck level pool, sauna, jacuzzi, steam room and fully equipped gymnasium. Unwind in "AquaSpa" offering 7 treatment rooms including floatation therapy. This compliments our superb restaurant, friendly bar, conference centre and 85 well appointed bedrooms. Sister hotel: The Arklow Bay Conference & Leisure Hotel, Co. Wicklow.

Member of Chara Hotel Group

B&B from €55.00 to €99.00

JOHN HICKEY
GENERAL MANAGER

 Midweek special 2 nights B&B + 1 Dinner from €99.00 pps

85   85

HOTELS
FEDERATION

Open All Year

ZUNI RESTAURANT & TOWNHOUSE

26 PATRICK STREET, KILKENNY

TEL: 056-772 3999 FAX: 056-775 6400
EMAIL: info@zuni.ie
WEB: www.zuni.ie

HOTEL U MAP 7 L 7

A family-run business in operation for five years, Zuni has earned its reputation as one of the best places to stay & eat in Ireland. Ideally located in the heart of the mediaeval city with private parking and within walking distance of all that Kilkenny has to offer.

B&B from €45.00 to €85.00

PAUL BYRNE
PROPRIETOR

Midweek specials from €135.00 pps
2 nights B&B + 1 Dinner

13   13

HOTELS
FEDERATION

Closed 23 - 27 December

B&B Rates are per Person Sharing per Night incl. Breakfast
Room Rates are per Room per Night

CARROLLS HOTEL

KNOCKTOPHER,
CO. KILKENNY

TEL: 056-776 8082 FAX: 056-776 8290
EMAIL: info@carrollshotel.com
WEB: www.carrollshotel.com

HOTEL ★★ MAP 7 L 6

Situated on the N10 between Kilkenny and Waterford. Enjoy the excellent service, warmth and luxury of our newly opened family-run hotel. All rooms are en suite with TV and direct dial phone. Our Sionnach Síoc Restaurant has an excellent reputation for good food. The hotel provides live music 2 nights a week. Golfing, karting, fishing, horseriding and shooting are available nearby.

B&B from €45.00 to €100.00

PÁDRAIG CARROLL
GENERAL MANAGER

10 10

Closed 24 - 26 December

RISING SUN

MULLINAVAT,
VIA WATERFORD,
CO. KILKENNY

TEL: 051-898173 FAX: 051-898435
EMAIL: info@therisingsun.ie
WEB: www.therisingsun.ie

GUESTHOUSE ★★★ MAP 4 L 6

A family-run guesthouse, 14km from Waterford City on the main Waterford-Dublin road. It has 10 luxurious bedrooms all en suite with D/D telephone, TV and Tea/Coffee making facilities. The Rising Sun Guesthouse is an ideal base for sports enthusiasts, surrounded by some beautiful golf courses within 15-30 minutes drive. The old world charm of stone and timberwork sets the tone of comfort and relaxation in the bar and lounge. Traditional home cooked lunches and bar food served daily. The Restaurant offers full à la carte menu and wine list.

B&B from €40.00 to €60.00

CLAIRE PHELAN
MANAGER

10 10

Closed 23 - 27 December

MOUNT JULIET CONRAD

THOMASTOWN,
CO. KILKENNY

TEL: 056-777 3000 FAX: 056-777 3019
EMAIL: mountjulietinfo@conradhotels.com
WEB: www.conradhotels.com

HOTEL ★★★★ MAP 7 L 6

At 1500 acres, Mount Juliet is one of the oldest surviving walled estates in the world. Guests can chose from accommodation in the carefully refurbished 18th century manor house overlooking the meandering waters of the River Nore, or in the Club Rooms at the estate's old stable yards, restored just over a decade ago. For longer stays, The Rose Garden Lodges offer privacy, flexibility & comfort. On site activities include horseriding, fishing, clay shooting & archery, golf on the 18 hole Nicklaus course or the 18 hole putting course & a luxurious spa & leisure centre.

Member of Conrad Group of Hotels

Room Rate from € 175.00 to € 265.00

ANTONY TRESTON
GENERAL MANAGER

58 58

Open All Year

B&B Rates are per Person Sharing per Night incl. Breakfast
Room Rates are per Room per Night

RAMADA ENCORE - URLINGFORD

URLINGFORD,
CO. KILKENNY

TEL: 056-883 8880 FAX: 056-883 8866
EMAIL: urlingford@ramadaireland.com
WEB: www.ramadaireland.com

UNDER CONSTRUCTION - OPENING JULY 2005

HOTEL P   MAP 7 K 7

Perfectly located on the main Dublin / Cork road (N8), half way from either city. This is the first of a new, innovative & contempory brand in Ireland. All of the 76 rooms will offer modern facilities along with free unlimited broadband internet access and in-room movies. The emphasis is on quality and service while offering exceptional value for money. A great location from which to tour many of the local points of interest.

Member of Ramada International

B&B from €35.00 to €55.00

MICHEAL KNOX JOHNSTON
MANAGING DIRECTOR

☺ Weekend specials from €115.00 pps

76   76

Open all Year

CAHIR HOUSE HOTEL

THE SQUARE,
CAHIR,
CO. TIPPERARY

TEL: 052-43000 FAX: 052-42728
EMAIL: info@cahirhousehotel.ie
WEB: www.cahirhousehotel.ie

HOTEL ★★★   MAP 3 J 6

New Health & Beauty Spa opened. Featuring the finest pampering facilities & treatments available. Specialty weekends. Ideal location for touring, situated where N8 meets N24. Town Centre location. Golf breaks a specialty 8 courses close by. Carvery lunch daily. Bar food available all day. À la Carte menu served in our Butler's Pantry Restaurant. As part of the Féile Bia promotion of Irish food we serve only the finest locally produced food.

B&B from €45.00 to €70.00

CAROL O'BRIEN

☺ Weekend specials from €90.00 pps

42   42

IRISH
HOTELS
FEDERATION

Open all year

CASTLE COURT HOTEL

CASHEL ROAD,
CAHIR,
CO. TIPPERARY

TEL: 052-43955 FAX: 052-45130
EMAIL: info@castlecourthotelcahir.com
WEB: www.castlecourthotelcahir.com

HOTEL P   MAP 3 J 6

This charming family-run hotel is perfect for either business or a short break away. The newly refurbished Castle Court Hotel boasts 18 en suite air conditioned bedrooms. Being centrally located, the Castle Court Hotel is the perfect base for touring the South East. Enjoy your food or a pint on our Roof Garden with a view of The Granary and Cahir Castle. Full bar and à la carte menu. Enjoy a relaxing meal in our Cream Room Restaurant.

B&B from €49.00 to €69.00

KEVIN CURRY
OWNER/DIRECTOR

☺ Weekend specials from €100.00 pps

18   18

IRISH
HOTELS
FEDERATION

Open All Year

B&B Rates are per Person Sharing per Night incl. Breakfast
Room Rates are per Room per Night

CO. TIPPERARY SOUTH
CAHIR / CARRICK-ON-SUIR / CASHEL

KILCORAN LODGE HOTEL

CAHIR,
CO. TIPPERARY

TEL: 052-41288 FAX: 052-41994
EMAIL: kilcoran@eircom.net
WEB: www.kilcoranlodgehotel.com

HOTEL ★★★ MAP 3 J 6

Kilcoran, a former hunting lodge set in spacious grounds overlooking beautiful countryside. An ideal holiday base located equal distance (15 min drive) between Tipperary, Cashel, Clonmel & Mitchelstown & 45 mins drive from Cork, Kilkenny & Limerick on the main Cork-Dublin road. The hotel has the charm of bygone days yet all the modern facilities of a 3 star hotel. Guests have free access to Shapes Leisure Centre with indoor pool etc. There are also ten luxury detached holiday lodges, self-catering for up to 6 persons, ideal for golf, walking and fishing breaks.

B&B from €60.00 to €75.00

JACQUELINE MULLEN
MANAGING DIRECTOR

Midweek 2 B&B and 1 Dinner from €125.00 pps

22 22

Open All Year

CARRAIG HOTEL

MAIN STREET,
CARRICK-ON-SUIR,
CO. TIPPERARY

TEL: 051-641455 FAX: 051-641604
EMAIL: info@carraighotel.com
WEB: www.carraighotel.com

HOTEL R MAP 3 K 5

The Carraig Hotel is the focal point of the town of Carrick-on-Suir. The recently refurbished and extended hotel offers well appointed en suite bedrooms with DD telephone, TV, tea/coffee making facilities, bar and residents lounge, carvery lounge and bar menu served daily. Restaurant serving Irish and International cuisine, conference meeting facilities, functions and banqueting. New fitness centre from Spring 2005. Weekend entertainment. Ideal base for golf, angling, walking and cycling.

B&B from €65.00 to €75.00

PAT POWER
GENERAL MANAGER

24 24

Closed 24 - 26 December

AULBER HOUSE

DEERPARK,
GOLDEN ROAD, CASHEL,
CO. TIPPERARY

TEL: 062-63713 FAX: 062-63715
EMAIL: beralley@eircom.net
WEB: www.aulberhouse.com

GUESTHOUSE ★★★ MAP 3 J 6

Aulber House - newly built luxury guesthouse. Ideally located on the outskirts of the historic town of Cashel. Home away from home. Perfect base for touring the South. Beautiful views of the Rock of Cashel and Hoare Abbey from some rooms and lobby. All rooms are spacious with en suite, power showers, direct dial phones, TV, hairdryers and computer modems. Non-smoking guesthouse. Golf and angling facilities available locally. AA ◆◆◆◆.

B&B from €40.00 to €65.00

BERNICE & SEÁN ALLEY

12 12

Closed 24 - 28 December

36 **SOUTH EAST**

B&B Rates are per Person Sharing per Night incl. Breakfast
Room Rates are per Room per Night

BAILEYS OF CASHEL

MAIN STREET,
CASHEL,
CO. TIPPERARY
TEL: 062-61937 FAX: 062-63957
EMAIL: info@baileys-ireland.com
WEB: www.baileys-ireland.com

GUESTHOUSE ★★★ **MAP 3 J 6**

Baileys is a beautifully restored listed Georgian house ideally situated right in the town centre with private parking available. With en suite bedrooms individually and tastefully decorated, Baileys is perfect for an overnight stop or a relaxing weekend stay. The fully licenced Cellar Restaurant, with its open fire and cosy atmosphere, is a wonderful place to enjoy excellent food and wine with friendly and attentive service. AA rated 4 ◆◆◆◆.

B&B from €45.00 to €50.00

PHIL DELANEY
MANAGER

Closed 24 - 28 December

CASHEL PALACE HOTEL

MAIN STREET,
CASHEL,
CO. TIPPERARY
TEL: 062-62707 FAX: 062-61521
EMAIL: reception@cashel-palace.ie
WEB: www.cashel-palace.ie

HOTEL ★★★★ **MAP 3 J 6**

Built in 1730 as an Archbishop's Palace, the Cashel Palace is complemented by tranquil walled gardens and a private walk to the famous Rock of Cashel. Our 23 bedrooms are all en suite with TV, phone & trouser press. Our Bishop's Buttery Restaurant is open for lunch & dinner, while the Guinness Bar is open for light snacks daily. The hotel has recently been completely restored & guests can now enjoy the finest furnishings, fabrics, art & antiques in the most elegant surroundings. AA 4★★★★ hotel. AA Rosette Award for Culinary Excellence 2003/2004.

B&B from €97.50 to €137.50

SUSAN & PATRICK MURPHY
PROPRIETORS

Closed 24 - 26 December

DUNDRUM HOUSE HOTEL

DUNDRUM,
CASHEL,
CO. TIPPERARY
TEL: 062-71116 FAX: 062-71366
EMAIL: dundrumh@iol.ie
WEB: www.dundrumhousehotel.com

HOTEL ★★★ **MAP 3 1 7**

One of Ireland's best inland resort hotels, Dundrum House Hotel is surrounded by the manicured fairways of its own 18-hole Championship course designed by Ryder Cup hero Philip Walton. The Country Club features the Venue Clubhouse Bar/Restaurant, 'White-Flag' award-winning Health & Leisure Centre with 20m indoor pool, gym, jacuzzi, sauna and steamroom. Beauty treatments/massage by appointment. Eighty four elegant bedrooms with antiques, two penthouse suites and seven apartments.

Member of Manor House Hotels

B&B from €85.00 to €125.00

AUSTIN & MARY CROWE
PROPRIETORS

☺ Midweek specials from €155.00 pps

Closed 24 - 26 December

B&B Rates are per Person Sharing per Night incl. Breakfast
Room Rates are per Room per Night

HILL HOUSE

PALMER'S HILL,
CASHEL,
CO. TIPPERARY
TEL: 062-61277
EMAIL: hillhouse1@eircom.net
WEB: www.hillhousecashel.com

GUESTHOUSE P   MAP 3 J 6

Hill House is one of Ireland's most historic Georgian homes. Constructed in 1710, Hill House is overlooking the Rock of Cashel, with private car park. We are 3 minutes walk from the town centre. The house has been extensively refurbished incorporating family heirlooms and antiques. The stylish elegance in the guest bedrooms is individual, some of our rooms have 4-poster king-size beds with all modern comforts, all rooms have DD phones and computer modems. Recommended by leading guides such as Friendly Homes of Ireland and Hidden Places of Ireland.

B&B from €40.00 to €50.00

CARMEL PURCELL
PROPRIETOR

♿🛏☎🖥🗖C➜❄♿P🚶 Inet
5   5

HOTELS

Closed 24 - 28 December

LEGENDS TOWNHOUSE & RESTAURANT

THE KILN,
CASHEL,
CO. TIPPERARY
TEL: 062-61292
EMAIL: info@legendsguesthouse.com
WEB: www.legendsguesthouse.com

GUESTHOUSE ★★★   MAP 3 J 6

Legends is your home from home, a place to relax and unwind after your day's travelling. You can enjoy your breakfast, lunch or dinner in our comfortable surroundings with spectacular views of the Rock of Cashel. Recommended consistently by leading guides such as AA Hotel Guide, Michelin, Karen Brown & Bridgestone 100 Best. An ideal base to explore Kilkenny, Waterford and Limerick or simply sit back and be inspired by the historical monument that is the Rock of Cashel. Unmissable!

B&B from €40.00 to €60.00

GRAZIELLE & JOHN QUINLAN

☺ Weekend specials from €120.00 pps

♿🛏☎🖥T C♿♪P🖥 a/c
7   7

HOTELS

Open All Year

BRIGHTON HOUSE

1 BRIGHTON PLACE,
CLONMEL,
CO. TIPPERARY
TEL: 052-23665 FAX: 052-23665
EMAIL: brighton@iol.ie
WEB: www.tipp.ie/brighton.htm

GUESTHOUSE ★★   MAP 3 K 5

Family-run 3 storey Georgian guest house, with a hotel ambience and antique furnishings. Clonmel Town centre - the largest inland town in Ireland bridging Rosslare Harbour (132km) with Killarney (160km) and the South West. Host to Fleadh Cheoil na hEireann 1993/94. Visit the Rock of Cashel, Mitchelstown Caves, Cahir Castle etc. Golf, fishing and pony trekking arranged locally. All rooms have direct dial phones, TV, radio, hairdryer and tea/coffee making facilities.

B&B from €35.00 to €50.00

BERNIE MORRIS
PROPRIETOR

♿🛏☎T P S
6   5

HOTELS

Closed 24 - 29 December

B&B Rates are per Person Sharing per Night incl. Breakfast
Room Rates are per Room per Night

FENNESSY'S HOTEL

GLADSTONE STREET,
CLONMEL,
CO. TIPPERARY
TEL: 052-23680 FAX: 052-23783
EMAIL: info@fennessyshotel.com
WEB: www.fennessyshotel.com

HOTEL ★★ MAP 3 K 5

This beautiful Georgian building is newly restored and refurbished. Right in the centre of Clonmel, it is easily located opposite the town's main church. All bedrooms are en suite, have direct dial phone, multi channel TV, hairdryer, tea/coffee facilities, and some have jacuzzis. Family-run hotel. Elegant ambience throughout. Main shopping area, swimming pool, leisure centre, riverside walks are a stone's throw from our front door. Golf, hill walking, fishing, ponytrekking. After your visit, you will wish to return.

B&B from €35.00 to €55.00

RICHARD AND ESTHER FENNESSY
PROPRIETORS

10 10

Open All Year

HOTEL MINELLA & LEISURE CENTRE

CLONMEL,
CO. TIPPERARY
TEL: 052-22388 FAX: 052-24381
EMAIL: frontdesk@hotelminella.ie
WEB: www.hotelminella.ie

HOTEL ★★★ MAP 3 K 5

Situated on the banks of the River Suir, & set amidst 9 acres of landscaped grounds, we offer a friendly welcome, warmth & hospitality. High quality bedrooms include superior rooms with spacious accommodation & either a steamroom or jacuzzi. "Club Minella" has a 20m swimming pool, fully equipped gym, outdoor hot tub & tennis court. Massage and beauty treatments can be prebooked. Newly refurbished public areas include conference facilities, the bar & restaurants. 2 RAC Dining Awards 04/05. Family run & managed by the Nallens.

Member of Irish Country Hotels

B&B from €90.00 to €150.00

JOHN NALLEN
MANAGING DIRECTOR

70 70

Closed 23 - 29 December

MEADOWVALE FARM GUESTHOUSE

MEADOWVALE FARM,
DERRYGRATH, CLONMEL,
CO. TIPPERARY
TEL: 052-38914 FAX: 052-38875
EMAIL: info@meadowvaleguesthouse.com
WEB: www.meadowvaleguesthouse.com

GUESTHOUSE P MAP 3 J 6

This family-run purpose built guesthouse provides luxury accommodation from the super king sized beds and power showers to the chesterfield leather suites and log fires, perfect for the quiet family getaway, romantic break or the nature lover alike. Set in a stud farm, the views are magic, with mountains on all sides. Centrally located within 1 hour of 3 Airports, 10 minutes from Cashel, Cahir & Clonmel, yet is quiet and peaceful. Mobile number: 087 2768188

B&B from €35.00 to €50.00

EITHNE MAHER

Weekend specials from €95.00 pps

10 10

Open all Year

B&B Rates are per Person Sharing per Night incl. Breakfast
Room Rates are per Room per Night

MULCAHYS

47 GLADSTONE STREET,
CLONMEL,
CO. TIPPERARY
TEL: 052-25054 FAX: 052-24544
EMAIL: info@mulcahys.ie
WEB: www.mulcahys.ie

GUESTHOUSE ★★ MAP 3 K 5

Mulcahys is run by the Higgins family. Our bedrooms are tastefully designed, all en suite with tea/coffee making facilities, multi channel TV and hairdryer. The carvery opens for lunch from 12pm and our "East Lane" menu is served from 6pm which includes lobsters and oysters from our fish tank. "Dance the night away" at our award winning nightclub "Dannos". Some of Ireland's best golf courses are within easy reach of Clonmel and the River Suir has been described as an "angler's paradise".

B&B from €35.00 to €65.00

CLAIRE HARRIS

10 10

Closed 24 - 28 December

AHERLOW HOUSE HOTEL

GLEN OF AHERLOW,
CO. TIPPERARY

TEL: 062-56153 FAX: 062-56212
EMAIL: reservations@aherlowhouse.ie
WEB: www.aherlowhouse.ie

HOTEL ★★★ MAP 3 I 6

Aherlow House Hotel and 4**** de luxe holiday homes. The Hotel & Lodges are set in the middle of a coniferous forest just 4 miles from Tipperary Town. Originally a hunting lodge now converted into an exquisitely furnished hotel. Aherlow House welcomes you to its peaceful atmosphere, enhanced by a fine reputation for hospitality, excellent cuisine and good wines. Overlooks the Glen of Aherlow and has beautiful views of the Galtee Mountains. Activities can be arranged.

B&B from €65.00 to €82.00

FERGHAL & HELEN PURCELL
OWNER

29 29

Open All Year

GLEN HOTEL

GLEN OF AHERLOW,
CO. TIPPERARY

TEL: 062-56146 FAX: 062-56152

HOTEL ★★ MAP 3 I 6

The Glen Hotel set in the shadows of the majestic Galtee Mountains, amidst the splendour of the Aherlow Valley is just 5 miles from Tipperary Town. To relax, dream, reminisce or plan - this is the ideal haven. Our bedrooms are all en suite. This family owned and operated hotel has built up a fine reputation for excellent cuisine and offers friendly and efficient service. Hill walking, horseriding, fishing and golf.

B&B from €49.00 to €69.00

MARGOT AND JAMES COUGHLAN
PROPRIETORS

Weekend specials from €115.00 pps

22 22

Open All Year

B&B Rates are per Person Sharing per Night incl. Breakfast
Room Rates are per Room per Night

HORSE AND JOCKEY INN

HORSE AND JOCKEY,
(NEAR CASHEL),
CO. TIPPERARY
TEL: 0504-44192 FAX: 0504-44747
EMAIL: horseandjockeyinn@eircom.net
WEB: www.horseandjockeyinn.com

HOTEL ★★★ MAP 7 J 7

The Horse and Jockey Inn, located at the heartland of County Tipperary, midway between Cork and Dublin on the N8 holds great association with people from sporting, cultural and political walks of life. Our modern refurbishment includes spacious lounge and bar facilities, a high quality restaurant, de luxe accommodation and a modern conference centre. Experience the atmosphere that's steeped in tradition and share with us the real Ireland, in the comfort of our new inn. New leisure and conference facilities due for completion Autumn 2005.

B&B from €80.00 to €80.00

TOM EGAN
PROPRIETOR

30 30

Inet

Open All Year

ARDAGH HOUSE

KILLENAULE,
CO. TIPPERARY

TEL: 052-56224 FAX: 052-56224
EMAIL: ahouse@iol.ie
WEB: www.ardaghhouse.ie

GUESTHOUSE ★ MAP 3 K 7

Fully licensed family guesthouse, piano lounge bar, residents' lounge, rooms en suite, home cooking. Set in the shadow of romantic Slievenamon, in the area of the Derrynaflan Chalice, the famous Coolmore Stud, in the heart of the Golden Vale. Near Holycross Abbey, Cashel and Kilkenny. Central for hunting, fishing, shooting, golf, horseriding and less strenuous walks through the hills of Killenaule. Finally, just one hour from the sea.

B&B from €35.00 to €37.00

MARY & MICHAEL McCORMACK
MANAGERS

6 6

Closed 24 - 27 December

ACH NA SHEEN GUESTHOUSE

CLONMEL ROAD,
TIPPERARY TOWN,
CO. TIPPERARY
TEL: 062-51298 FAX: 062-80467
EMAIL: gernoonan@eircom.net
WEB: www.achnasheen.net

GUESTHOUSE ★★ MAP 3 I 6

Family-run guesthouse, 5 minutes from the town centre with a spacious sun lounge and diningroom overlooking gardens and the beautiful Galtee Mountains. Our 10 rooms are all en suite, equipped with TV and tea/coffee making facilities. Ach-na-Sheen is adjacent to the picturesque Glen of Aherlow where fishing and hill walking can be arranged. Golf can be enjoyed at any number of nearby championship courses. G & S Noonan offer you the utmost in Irish hospitality.

B&B from €38.00 to €45.00

SYLVIA & GER NOONAN
PROPRIETORS

9 9

Closed 18 December - 06 January

B&B Rates are per Person Sharing per Night incl. Breakfast
Room Rates are per Room per Night

BALLYGLASS COUNTRY HOUSE

GLEN OF AHERLOW ROAD,
BALLYGLASS,
TIPPERARY TOWN
TEL: 062-52104 FAX: 062-52229
EMAIL: info@ballyglasshouse.com
WEB: www.ballyglasshouse.com

HOTEL U MAP 316

Ballyglass Country House is an 18th century country residence set in its own grounds on the outskirts of Tipperary and just 2km from the beautiful Glen of Aherlow. Here at this family run hotel you can enjoy the best of local produce in our "Colonel's Restaurant" and relax in front of a real coal fire in our "Forge Bar". Ballyglass Country House is perfectly situated for touring Munster. Golfing, fishing, hillwalking & horseriding are all available locally.

B&B from €47.50 to €62.50

JOAN AND BILL BYRNE
PROPRIETORS

🛏️🔥☎️🖥️◻️T C CM✻♨️J P ⸱🍴S🔇
10 10
    alc ▪ 🐕

IRISH HOTELS FEDERATION

Closed 24 - 26 December

RAMADA HOTEL & SUITES AT BALLYKISTEEN

LIMERICK JUCTION,
NEAR TIPPERARY TOWN,
CO. TIPPERARY
TEL: 062-33333 FAX: 062-33333
EMAIL: ballykisteen@ramadaireland.com
WEB: www.ramadaireland.com

UNDER CONTRUCTION - OPENING JUNE 2005

HOTEL P MAP 316

The hotel is beautifully located at Ballykisteen Golf & Country Club, at Limerick Junction, on the main Limerick / Tipperary road. Easy access by car, train and plane. An oasis of tranquillity with emphasis on quality food, friendly staff and great facillities. Rejuvenate with one of the wellness treatments. Enjoy some of the many outdoor activities including Tipperary Racecourse. Geared for corporate and leisure travellers - with in-house movies.

Member of Ramada International

B&B from €45.00 to €87.50

MICHAEL KNOX JOHNSTON
MANAGING DIRECTOR

🍴💧

😊 Midweek specials from €110.00 pps

🛏️🔥☎️🖥️◻️▪T C ✻CM✻♨️📷🔍
85 85
U⸱🎵J P S🔇 alc ▪ Inet WiFi 🐕

Open all Year

ROYAL HOTEL TIPPERARY

BRIDGE STREET,
TIPPERARY TOWN,
CO. TIPPERARY
TEL: 062-33244 FAX: 062-33596

WEB: www.royalhoteltipperary.com

HOTEL ★★ MAP 316

Situated in Tipperary Town, a familiar meeting place serving excellent food from 8am to 10pm daily, using finest quality local produce. Tastefully decorated rooms with all amenities. Just a few minutes from Tipperary Racecourse, 3 outstanding golf clubs (special arrangements & packages available to the hotel for Tipperary, Dundrum & Ballykisteen clubs). Sport & Leisure Complex 3 minutes from the hotel and The Excel Theatre within a short walking distance. So if it's business or pleasure, a warm welcome awaits you.

B&B from €35.00 to €55.00

JEREMIAH IVESON
PROPRIETOR

🛏️🔥☎️🖥️◻️T C CM P🔇 alc ▪ Inet 🐕 🐎
16 16

Open All Year

B&B Rates are per Person Sharing per Night incl. Breakfast
Room Rates are per Room per Night

TIMES HOTEL

BANK PLACE,
TIPPERARY TOWN

TEL: 062-31111 FAX: 062-31255
EMAIL: judynolan@eircom.net

HOTEL ★ MAP 6 I 6

Times Hotel is an historic Georgian building which has acted as an hotel since 1847. Our bedrooms, all of which are en suite, still retain many of the original historic features. Our residents' lounge is intimate and relaxing for guests, a combination of old and contemporary. At night there's ballroom dancing, traditional or contemporary music sessions & plenty of 'craic' in our main ballroom & attached Black Sheep Bar. The new Excel Centre offers a choice of cinema or theatre by night & houses a heritage centre & tourist office. Can be contacted on 087 2059247.

B&B from €45.00 to €50.00

ALBERT NOLAN

10 10

Open All Year

NEWTOWN FARM GUESTHOUSE

GRANGE,
ARDMORE, VIA YOUGHAL,
CO. WATERFORD

TEL: 024-94143 FAX: 024-94054
EMAIL: newtownfarm@eircom.net
WEB: www.newtownfarm.com

GUESTHOUSE ★★★ MAP 3 K 3

Family-run farm guesthouse in scenic location, surrounded by its own farmlands with dairying as the main enterprise, with views of the Atlantic Ocean, hills and cliff walks. All bedrooms en suite with tea/coffee making facilities, TV, DD phone and hairdryer. Grange is 6 minutes from the beach and Ardmore Round Tower and Cathedral, built in the 12th century, raises its heights to 97 feet. 2 hours drive from Port of Rosslare. Signposted on N25 turn left at Flemings Pub, 200m.

Member of Premier Guesthouses

B&B from €35.00 to €40.00

TERESA O'CONNOR
PROPRIETOR

7 7

7 Inet

Closed 31 October - 01 March

ROUND TOWER HOTEL

COLLEGE ROAD,
ARDMORE,
CO. WATERFORD

TEL: 024-94494 FAX: 024-94254
EMAIL: rth@eircom.net

HOTEL U MAP 3 K 3

Situated within walking distance of Ardmore's award-winning beach, the Round Tower Hotel offers 12 well appointed en suite bedrooms. Fresh local produce feature prominently on both the bar and restaurant menus. The ancient monastic settlement of St. Declan & the Round Tower are situated behind the hotel. Ardmore also boasts some world famous cliff walks and breathtaking scenery. Ardmore is 21kms from Dungarvan & a 2 hour drive from the port of Rosslare on the Primary N25 route.

B&B from €40.00 to €55.00

AIDAN QUIRKE
PROPRIETOR

12 12

Closed 21 - 28 December

B&B Rates are per Person Sharing per Night incl. Breakfast
Room Rates are per Room per Night

HANORAS COTTAGE

NIRE VALLEY,
BALLYMACARBRY,
CO. WATERFORD
TEL: 052-36134 FAX: 052-36540
EMAIL: hanorascottage@eircom.net
WEB: www.hanorascottage.com

GUESTHOUSE ★★★★ MAP 3 K 5

A haven of peace and tranquillity in the Comeragh Mountains, Hanoras has everything for discerning guests. Relax in the sheer bliss of an adult only house with the soothing sounds of the Nire River running by. Spacious rooms with jacuzzi tubs. Superior rooms for that special occasion! Enjoy excellent cuisine from our Ballymaloe School chefs who cater for all diets. AA and RAC ◆◆◆◆◆ recommended in Bridgestone Guide 100 Best Places in Ireland. National award winners Guesthouse Of The Year and Breakfast Of The Year. The Wall Family welcome you.

B&B from €80.00 to €125.00

THE WALL FAMILY
PROPRIETORS

🛏🐾☎🖵T❄🍴P🍷▪
10   10

Closed 20 - 28 December

RICHMOND HOUSE

CAPPOQUIN,
CO. WATERFORD
TEL: 058-54278 FAX: 058-54988
EMAIL: info@richmondhouse.net
WEB: www.richmond.house.net

GUESTHOUSE ★★★★ MAP 3 J 4

Delightful 18th century Georgian country house and fully licenced award winning restaurant set in private grounds. Relax in total peace and tranquillity in front of log fires. Each room is a perfect blend of Georgian splendour combined with all modern comforts for the discerning guest. AA ◆◆◆◆◆. Recommended in the Bridgestone Guides; 100 Best Places to Stay, 100 Best Restaurants in Ireland and all leading guides. Ideal location for a short break.

B&B from €65.00 to €125.00

PAUL & CLAIRE DEEVY
PROPRIETORS

🛏🐾☎🖵TCCM❄🍴P🖳alc
9   9

Closed 23 December - 10 January

THREE RIVERS GUEST HOUSE

CHEEKPOINT,
CO. WATERFORD
TEL: 051-382520 FAX: 051-382542
EMAIL: mail@threerivers.ie
WEB: www.threerivers.ie

GUESTHOUSE ★★★ MAP 4 M 5

3* award winning guesthouse, a haven of peace and tranquillity with magnificent views of Waterford Estuary. Situated on the outskirts of the historic village Cheekpoint, with its award winning pubs and seafood restaurants. Sample the delights of breakfast in our Estuary view dining room or relax over coffee in our spacious lounge. Ideal base for touring sunny South East. Close to Waterford, Dunmore East, Tramore and 2km from Faithlegg Golf Course. All rooms en suite.

B&B from €36.00 to €50.00

THERESA & BRIAN JOYCE

🛏🐾☎TC🍴❄🍴P S 🐴
14   14

Closed 20 December - 7 January

B&B Rates are per Person Sharing per Night incl. Breakfast
Room Rates are per Room per Night

BARNAWEE BRIDGE GUESTHOUSE

KILMINION,
DUNGARVAN,
CO. WATERFORD
TEL: 058-42074
EMAIL: michelle@barnawee.com
WEB: www.barnawee.com

GUESTHOUSE ★★★ MAP 3 K 4

Our newly built guesthouse with fabulous sea and mountain views near all local amenities including three 18 hole golf courses, indoor swimming, sea angling, tennis, fishing and bird watching. Also various countryside walks. Food & drinks available locally, also a kitchennette for tea/coffee and snacks available for all our customers. All rooms are very spacious with en suite and color T.V., making for a very enjoyable stay. Mobile number: 087 2620269.

B&B from €35.00 to €50.00

MICHELLE DWANE/GARY TREEN
PROPRIETORS

Midweek specials from €100.00 pps

6   6

Open All Year

CLONEA STRAND HOTEL, GOLF & LEISURE

CLONEA,
DUNGARVAN,
CO. WATERFORD
TEL: 058-45555 FAX: 058-42880
EMAIL: info@clonea.com
WEB: www.clonea.com

HOTEL ★★★ MAP 3 K 4

Clonea Strand Hotel overlooking Clonea Beach. Family-run by John and Ann McGrath. All rooms en suite with tea/coffee making facilities, hairdryer and colour TV. Indoor leisure centre with heated pool, jacuzzi, sauna, Turkish bath, gymnasium and ten pin bowling alley. Situated close by is our 18 hole golf course bordering on the Atlantic Ocean with a scenic background of Dungarvan Bay and Comeragh Mountains. Our Bay Restaurant specialises in locally caught seafood.

B&B from €49.50 to €95.00

MARK KNOWLES
GEN.MGR.GROUP/MARKETING

Midweek specials from €104.50 pps

58   58

Open All Year

LAWLORS HOTEL

BRIDGE STREET,
DUNGARVAN,
CO. WATERFORD
TEL: 058-41122 FAX: 058-41000
EMAIL: info@lawlorshotel.com
WEB: www.lawlorshotel.com

HOTEL ★★★ MAP 3 K 4

Lawlors Hotel is family-run with 89 bedrooms, all en suite with tea/coffee making facilities, TV and direct dial phone. Lawlors is the ideal choice for your stay in the beautiful West Waterford countryside. Conferences, Weddings, Parties, Seminars are especially catered for. Good food is a speciality at Lawlors and the friendly atmosphere of Dungarvan Town is brought to life in the Old Worlde bar surroundings.

B&B from €49.00 to €80.00

MICHAEL BURKE
PROPRIETOR

Weekend specials from €165.00 pps

89   89

Closed 24 - 26 December

B&B Rates are per Person Sharing per Night incl. Breakfast
Room Rates are per Room per Night

PARK HOTEL

DUNGARVAN,
CO. WATERFORD

TEL: 058-42899 FAX: 058-42969
EMAIL: photel@indigo.ie
WEB: www.flynnhotels.com

HOTEL ★★★ MAP 3 K 4

Overlooking the Colligan River Estuary, owned and run by the Flynn Family, whose experience in the hotel business is your best guarantee of an enjoyable and memorable stay. The hotel's spacious and comfortable bedrooms have been furnished with flair and imagination. All have private bathroom, direct dial telephone, 16 channel satellite TV. The hotel's leisure centre has a 20m swimming pool, sauna, steamroom & gym.

B&B from € 60.00 to € 80.00

PIERCE FLYNN
MANAGER

29 29

Closed 24 - 28 December

POWERSFIELD HOUSE

BALLINAMUCK,
DUNGARVAN,
CO. WATERFORD

TEL: 058-45594 FAX: 058-45550
EMAIL: powersfieldhouse@cablesurf.com
WEB: www.powersfield.com

GUESTHOUSE ★★★ MAP 3 K 4

Powersfield House is situated just outside Dungarvan on the R672. Ideally located for the three 18-hole golf courses and beautiful beaches. The six bedrooms are all en suite with pressure showers. Each room is individually decorated using antique furniture, crisp linens and fresh flowers. Enjoy our award winning breakfast. Dinner is served to residents - advance booking required. AA 5 Diamonds, Bridgestone Guide 100 Best Places To Stay, Georgina Campbell's Guides.

Member of Premier Guesthouses

B&B from € 50.00 to € 65.00

EUNICE & EDMUND POWER

☺ Midweek specials from €145.00 pps

6 6

Inet

Closed 24 - 26 December

SEAVIEW

WINDGAP,
N25/YOUGHAL ROAD, DUNGARVAN,
CO. WATERFORD

TEL: 058-41583 FAX: 058-41679
EMAIL: faheyn@gofree.indigo.ie
WEB: www.amireland.com/seaview/

GUESTHOUSE ★★★ MAP 3 K 4

Want your vacation to never stop being a vacation? Enjoy breakfast overlooking the sea? Play one of Dungarvan's three 18 hole golf courses or take a bus tour of the area and let someone else do the driving. How about dinner, entertained by traditional Irish musicians, at the nearby Marine Bar? Make every ounce of your vacation count. Try Seaview on N25 5km west of Dungarvan. Fax and e-mail facilities available. Continental and Full Irish breakfast served. Laundry service available.

Member of Premier Guesthouses

B&B from € 30.00 to € 40.00

NORA & MARTIN & MEALLA FAHEY

☺ Midweek specials from €80.00 pps

8 8

Open All Year

B&B Rates are per Person Sharing per Night incl. Breakfast
Room Rates are per Room per Night

BELFRY HOTEL

CONDUIT LANE,
WATERFORD

TEL: 051-844800 FAX: 051-844814
EMAIL: info@belfryhotel.ie
WEB: www.belfryhotel.ie

HOTEL ★★★ MAP 4 L 5

The Belfry is a family-run hotel that
has a special ambience, combining
traditional charm with superb modern
amenities. Bedrooms are spacious
and luxurious. Riada's Restaurant
offers a well chosen and varied à la
carte menu for dinner, while an
extensive bar menu is available daily
in the popular and stylish Chapter
House Bar. City centre location, close
to bus and rail station. Superb range
of golf courses nearby. Golf packages
available.

B&B from €55.00 to €95.00

SHARON MANSFIELD
GENERAL MANAGER

☺ Special offers available throughout
the year

49 49

inet

HOTELS

Closed 24 - 30 December

BRIDGE HOTEL

NO 1 THE QUAY,
WATERFORD

TEL: 051-877222 FAX: 051-877229
EMAIL: info@bridgehotelwaterford.com
WEB: www.bridgehotelwaterford.com

HOTEL ★★★ MAP 4 L 5

Whether your stay in Waterford's
Viking City is one of business or
pleasure, you will quickly find that the
Bridge Hotel, situated in the heart of
this vibrant & exciting city, is exactly
where you will want to stay. This 133
en suite bedroom hotel offers the
finest traditions of quality & service
expected from a modern 3*** hotel.
Our restaurants specialise in local
seafood & succulent steaks. Relax &
enjoy a drink in our Timbertoes Bar. 2
minutes walk from bus & rail stations.
Entertainment 5 nights a week. The
Bridge Hotel for excellence in
customer care. AA ***.

Member of MinOtel Ireland Hotel Group

B&B from €49.00 to €99.00

BRIDGET & JIM TREACY
PROPRIETORS

☺ Weekend specials from €125.00 pps

133 133

inet

HOTELS

Closed 03 - 14 January

COACH HOUSE

BUTLERSTOWN CASTLE,
BUTLERSTOWN, CORK ROAD,
WATERFORD

TEL: 051-384656 FAX: 051-384751
EMAIL: coachhse@iol.ie
WEB: www.iol.ie/~coachhse

GUESTHOUSE ★★★ MAP 4 L 5

Surround yourself with comfort in this
elegantly restored 19th century house.
Situated 3 miles from Waterford City
(Waterford Crystal 5 mins away) in
an historic, tranquil, romantic setting
(13th century castle in grounds). All
rooms en suite. Private sauna
available. 5 golf courses within 6
miles radius. Excellent pubs,
restaurants nearby. 3*** Irish Tourist
Board, AA ◆◆◆◆, Michelin
recommended, Best Magazine's No.1
in Ireland. `Crackling log fires and
personal attention'.

B&B from €38.50 to €55.00

DES O'KEEFFE
PROPRIETOR

7 7

HOTELS

Closed 20 December - 20 January

B&B Rates are per Person Sharing per Night incl. Breakfast
Room Rates are per Room per Night

DIAMOND HILL COUNTRY HOUSE

SLIEVERUE,
WATERFORD

TEL: 051-832855 FAX: 051-832254
EMAIL: diamondhill29@hotmail.com
WEB: www.diamondhillhouse.com

GUESTHOUSE ★★★ MAP 4 L 5

Situated 2km from Waterford City off the Rosslare Waterford Road N25. Convenient to ferrys. A long established guesthouse of considerable charm and friendliness, set in its own national award winning gardens. The house has been extensively refurbished incorporating family heirlooms and antiques resulting in a countryside oasis, a haven of luxury and tranquillity, yet only minutes from the bustling city of Waterford. Recommended by Frommers, Foders, Michelin, AA ◆◆◆◆. Member of Premier Guesthouses.

Member of Premier Guesthouses
B&B from €35.00 to €45.00

SMITH/LEHANE FAMILY
OWNERS

17 17

IRISH HOTELS FEDERATION

Closed 20 - 26 December

DOOLEY'S HOTEL

THE QUAY,
WATERFORD

TEL: 051-873531 FAX: 051-870262
EMAIL: hotel@dooleys-hotel.ie
WEB: www.dooleys-hotel.ie

HOTEL ★★★ MAP 4 L 5

The waters of the River Suir swirl past the door of this renowned hotel, which is situated on The Quay in Waterford. Dooley's is an ideal choice for a centrally located hotel, close to all amenities, cultural & business centres. This family-run hotel caters for the corporate/leisure traveller. The hotel has a purpose-built conference centre with full facilities - The Rita Nolan Conference & Banqueting Suite. Enjoy the style & comfort of The New Ship Restaurant & Dry Dock Bar. Ireland's Best Service Excellence Award 2003/04. 24 hour online booking: www.dooleys-hotel.ie

Member of Holiday Ireland Hotels
B&B from €50.00 to €100.00

MARGARET & TINA DARRER
DIRECTORS

113 113

IRISH HOTELS FEDERATION

Closed 25 - 27 December

GRANVILLE HOTEL

MEAGHER QUAY,
WATERFORD

TEL: 051-305555 FAX: 051-305566
EMAIL: stay@granville-hotel.ie
WEB: www.granville-hotel.ie

HOTEL ★★★ MAP 4 L 5

One of Waterford's most prestigious city centre hotels, RAC★★★★ overlooking the River Suir. This family-run hotel is one of Ireland's oldest with significant historical connections. Justly proud of the Granville's heritage, owners Liam and Ann Cusack today vigorously pursue the Granville's long tradition of hospitality, friendliness and comfort. It has been elegantly refurbished, retaining its old world Georgian character. Award-winning Bianconi Restaurant, Thomas Francis Meagher Bar.

Member of Best Western Hotels
B&B from €70.00 to €100.00

ANN AND LIAM CUSACK
MANAGERS/PROPRIETORS

Weekend specials from €140.00 pps

98 98

IRISH HOTELS FEDERATION

Closed 24 - 27 December

B&B Rates are per Person Sharing per Night incl. Breakfast
Room Rates are per Room per Night

IVORY'S HOTEL

TRAMORE ROAD,
WATERFORD

TEL: 051-358888 FAX: 051-358899
EMAIL: info@ivoryshotel.ie
WEB: www.ivoryshotel.ie

HOTEL ★★★ MAP 4 L 5

A ten minute walk from Tramore's beaches, a short walk from Waterford Crystal and City Centre, Ivory's is ideal whatever your needs. Whether it's enjoying good food and great value at McGinty's Bistro our Pub/Carvery or unwinding on the sun terrace, Ivory's offers a relaxing atmosphere and we're happy to organise any of the attractions the county has to offer. Complimentary parking and a pet-friendly policy make Ivory's perfect for business or family breaks.

B&B from €55.00 to €95.00

NATALIE & DECLAN IVORY
MANAGING PROPRIETORS

Weekend specials from €125.00 pps

40 40

Closed 24 - 27 December

MCENIFF ARD RÍ HOTEL

FERRYBANK,
WATERFORD

TEL: 051-832111 FAX: 051-832863
EMAIL: reservations@ardri.org
WEB: www.ardri.org

HOTEL ★★★ MAP 4 L 5

The McEniff Ard Rí Hotel is newly refurbished and set on 10 acres of parkland grounds. It commands a stunning view of the River Suir and the historical Waterford City, which lies literally at its feet. Enjoy excellent cuisine in Bardens Restaurant, state of the art conference facilities and superior leisure centre. Enjoy Waterford Crystal, Reginald's Tower, the Dunbrody Famine Ship, golf, Dunmore & Tramore beaches plus lots more locally.

Member of McEniff Hotels

B&B from €55.00 to €99.00

ROBERT MCCARTHY
GENERAL MANAGER

100 100

Closed 24 - 28 December

QUALITY HOTEL WATERFORD

CANADA STREET,
THE QUAYS,
WATERFORD

TEL: 1850-746 8357 FAX: 021-427 1489
EMAIL: info@qualityhotelwaterford.com
WEB: www.qualityhotelwaterford.com

HOTEL U MAP 4 L 5

The Quality Hotel is ideally located on the banks of the River Suir just minutes walk from the bustling city centre. Featuring generously appointed en suite guestrooms and executive suites, the hotel is your ideal base for touring the South East. Relax by the river in Lannigans Restaurant & Bar and enjoy our international menus. Complimentary secure car park. Conference facilities for up to 50 delegates. Call the hotel direct at 051 856600.

Member of Quality Hotels

B&B from €40.00 to €120.00

NANCY GALLAGHER
GENERAL MANAGER

Weekend specials from €90.00 pps

81 81

Closed 21 - 26 December

B&B Rates are per Person Sharing per Night incl. Breakfast
Room Rates are per Room per Night

CO. WATERFORD
WATERFORD CITY

RHU GLENN COUNTRY CLUB HOTEL

LUFFANY,
SLIEVERUE,
WATERFORD

TEL: 051-832242 FAX: 051-832242
EMAIL: info@rhuglennhotel.com
WEB: www.rhuglennhotel.com

HOTEL ★★ MAP 4 L 5

Built within its own grounds with parking for cars, coaches, etc., the hotel is family-run. Situated on the N25 Rosslare to Waterford Road, convenient to ferries, it offers a superb location whether your pleasure be golfing, fishing, or simply exploring the South East. All rooms are en suite with direct dial phone and multi-channel TV. The restaurant is renowned for its service of fine food. Relax and enjoy our lounge bars and ballroom with live entertainment provided by Ireland's top artistes.

B&B from €40.00 to €55.00

LIAM MOONEY
PROPRIETOR

🛏️📞📺TC CM❄️♪PS
30 30
ald

IRISH HOTELS FEDERATION

Closed 24 - 25 December

RICE GUESTHOUSE & BATTERBERRY'S BAR

35 & 36 BARRACK STREET,
WATERFORD

TEL: 051-371606 FAX: 051-357013
EMAIL: info@riceguesthouse.com
WEB: www.riceguesthouse.com

GUESTHOUSE U MAP 4 L 5

Waterford's premier city centre guesthouse, located 2 minutes from Waterford's City Square Shopping Centre and Waterford Crystal Gallery. Offering our customers hotel accommodation at guesthouse prices. Purpose built in 1997, all rooms en suite with cable TV, direct dial phones & tea/coffee facilities. Full bar and resident's bar, Batterberry's Bar offers ceol & craic with live music 5 nights a week, bar food and the finest Irish hospitality. Tee times arranged for golfers. Midweek and weekend break specials available.

Member of Premier Guesthouses

B&B from €35.00 to €55.00

JOHN & JIMMY FITZGERALD

🛏️📞📺TC CMU♪S
20 20

IRISH HOTELS FEDERATION

Closed 23 - 27 December

ST. ALBANS GUESTHOUSE

CORK ROAD,
WATERFORD

TEL: 051-358171 FAX: 051-358171
EMAIL: stalbansbandb@yahoo.com
WEB: www.stalbanswaterford.com

GUESTHOUSE ★★ MAP 4 L 5

St. Albans is a well established family-run guesthouse. Ideally located minutes walk from Waterford City Centre and Waterford Crystal. Our very spacious superbly appointed rooms are all en suite with multi-channel TV, tea/coffee facilities and hairdryer. Secure parking at rear of premises. 4 championship golf courses in vicinity. Horseriding 3km. Tennis courts, swimming pool 2 minutes. Several local beaches and breathtaking scenery. Bus and train station a short distance. Freephone: UK: 0800 912 3910 USA: 0877 207 3910

B&B from €33.00 to €45.00

TOM & HELEN MULLALLY
PROPRIETORS

🛏️📺TCUP
8 8

IRISH HOTELS FEDERATION

Closed 18 - 28 December

B&B Rates are per Person Sharing per Night incl. Breakfast
Room Rates are per Room per Night

TOWER HOTEL & LEISURE CENTRE

**THE MALL,
WATERFORD**

**TEL: 051-875801 FAX: 051-870129
EMAIL: reservations@thw.ie
WEB: www.towerhotelwaterford.com**

HOTEL ★★★ MAP 4 L 5

A Tower Group Hotel - with its riverside location in the heart of Waterford City and 141 guest bedrooms offering every modern amenity. The Tower Hotel is the flagship hotel of the Tower Hotel Group. The Tower Hotel is the ideal base to discover this wonderful city and county, with two restaurants - Traditional carvery and award-winning Bistro, Riverside Bar, leisure centre with 20m pool, extensive conference facilities and private guest car park. Special online offers available on www.towerhotelgroup.com

Member of Tower Hotel Group

B&B from €70.00 to €110.00

MICHAEL SKEHAN
GENERAL MANAGER

Weekend specials from €135.00 pps

141 141

Closed 24 - 28 December

VIKING HOTEL

**CORK ROAD,
WATERFORD**

**TEL: 051-876 133 FAX: 051-876 144
EMAIL: info@vikinghotel.ie
WEB: www.vikinghotel.ie**

UNDER CONSTRUCTION - OPENING APRIL 2005

HOTEL P MAP 4 L 5

Waterford's newest hotel, on the N25, Rosslare to Cork route, 2 miles from Waterford City, minutes from Waterford Crystal and Waterford Industrial Estate, and close to all the local beaches and golf courses. Spotlessly clean, our friendly staff's mission is to provide the best sleep in town, accompanied by an invigorating shower and a great breakfast. We provide state-of-the-art meeting facilities, free broadband, a lively bar, regular enterainment and gym.

B&B from €45.00 to €90.00

MARGUERITE FITZGERALD

Weekend specials from €115.00 pps

100 100

Open all Year

WATERFORD CASTLE HOTEL & GOLF CLUB

**THE ISLAND,
BALLINAKILL,
WATERFORD**

**TEL: 051-878203 FAX: 051-879316
EMAIL: info@waterfordcastle.com
WEB: www.waterfordcastle.com**

HOTEL U MAP 4 L 5

Waterford Castle Hotel & Golf Club is uniquely situated on a 310 acre island overlooking the estuary of the River Suir, 3 miles from Waterford City. Access to the island is by a chain linked car ferry. Furnished with antiques and open fireplaces. The 15th century castle combines gracious living of an elegant past with every modern comfort, service and convenience. Own 18 hole championship golf course. Excellent dining experience.

Member of Best Loved Hotels

Room Rate from €195.00 to €450.00

GILLIAN BUTLER
GENERAL MANAGER

19 19

Closed 06 January - 06 February

**B&B Rates are per Person Sharing per Night incl. Breakfast
Room Rates are per Room per Night**

WATERFORD MANOR HOTEL

KILLOTTERAN,
WATERFORD

TEL: 051-377 814 FAX: 051-354 545
EMAIL: sales@waterfordmanorhotel.ie
WEB: www.waterfordmanorhotel.ie

HOTEL U MAP 4 L 5

Situated just 3 miles from Waterford City and located on 16 acres of gardens, the Waterford Manor Hotel is the ideal venue for a quiet relaxing break. It is the perfect setting for private parties and weddings and with its purpose built conference centre, it is the most sought after Manor hotel in the South-East.

B&B from €65.00 to €75.00

PAT & KATE COUGHLAN

☺ Midweek specials from €145 pps
(3 nights B&B, 2 dinners)

20 20

Closed 31 December - 02 January

WOODLANDS HOTEL

DUNMORE ROAD,
WATERFORD

TEL: 051-304574 FAX: 051-304575
EMAIL: info@woodlandshotel.ie
WEB: www.woodlandshotel.ie

HOTEL ★★★ MAP 4 L 5

This contemporary hotel offers 46 stylish bedrooms, modern leisure centre (pool, sauna, jacuzzi, steamroom, gym), lively bar with regular entertainment, stylish Arbutus Restaurant and air-conditioned conference and banqueting facilities. Our new addition for 2005 is Caroline's Hair & Beauty Salon offering a wide variety of hair and beauty treatments. Just 3 miles from Waterford's City Centre and a short drive from local golf courses and sandy beaches.

Member of Select Hotels of Ireland

B&B from €55.00 to €95.00

DEREK ANDREWS

☺ Weekend specials from €125.00 pps

46 46

Open All Year

DUNBRODY COUNTRY HOUSE HOTEL & COOKERY SCHOOL

ARTHURSTOWN,
CO. WEXFORD

TEL: 051-389600 FAX: 051-389601
EMAIL: dunbrody@indigo.ie
WEB: www.dunbrodyhouse.com

HOTEL ★★★★ MAP 4 M 5

Dunbrody Country House Hotel & Cookery School is regarded as one of Ireland's top country retreats. Offering unrivalled cuisine with a wonderfully relaxed ambience, guests return again and again. Member of both Small Luxury Hotels of the World and Ireland's Blue Book. Dunbrody is also recommended by numerous guides and is the recipient of "Restaurant of the year 2004".

Member of Ireland's Blue Book

B&B from €110.00 to €210.00

KEVIN & CATHERINE DUNDON
OWNERS

22 22

Closed 22 - 27 December

B&B Rates are per Person Sharing per Night incl. Breakfast
Room Rates are per Room per Night

STANVILLE LODGE WEXFORD

BARNTOWN,
CO. WEXFORD

TEL: 053-34300 FAX: 053-34989
EMAIL: info@stanville.ie
WEB: www.stanville.ie

HOTEL N MAP 4 N 6

Stanville Lodge is positioned in the picturesque countryside, just minutes from Wexford Town. Offering 32 finely appointed bedrooms, junior suites and executive rooms. Comprising of state of the art conference and banqueting facilities for up to 200 delegates. For the ultimate dining experience, quality & service are assured in our O' Nuaills Bistro Restaurant, lounge, daily carvery and bar. "Relish the experience".

B&B from €49.00 to €75.00

SHANE CARROLL
GENERAL MANAGER

Weekend specials from €89.00pps

32 32

Closed 25 - 27 December

MILLRACE HOTEL (THE)

CARRIGDUFF,
BUNCLODY,
CO. WEXFORD

TEL: 054-75100 FAX: 054-75124
EMAIL: info@millrace.ie
WEB: www.millrace.ie

HOTEL P MAP 8 N 7

Newly built luxury hotel designed to 4**** standards with 60 well appointed bedrooms, 12 family apartments and Lady Lucy's fine dining rooftop restaurant. The Millrace Spa with 7 treatment suites and dedicated relaxation room and leisure club. Located on the edge of the Hall-Dare Estate and on the banks of the Clody River. Bunclody is a beautiful picturesque town situated on the N80 between Carlow and Enniscorthy. 80 minutes drive from Dublin, 50 minutes from Rosslare.

B&B from €85.00 to €110.00

RICHARD ADRIANO
GENERAL MANAGER

Weekend specials from €129.00 pps

60 60

Closed 24 - 27 December

BAYVIEW HOTEL

COURTOWN HARBOUR,
GOREY,
CO. WEXFORD

TEL: 055-25307 FAX: 055-25576
EMAIL: bayview@iol.ie
WEB: www.bayview.ie

HOTEL ★★ MAP 8 O 7

The Bayview is owned and run by the McGarry Family. The hotel is overlooking the marina at Courtown Harbour. It is renowned for its good food and friendly atmosphere. All rooms are en suite with TV, video channel and direct dial telephone. Self catering apartments in hotel. Courtown's 18 hole golf course 2km. It is an ideal setting for weddings and parties. Nearby is the Courtown superb indoor 25m pool and Forest Park Woodland Walks.

B&B from €68.00 to €78.00

BRIAN MCGARRY
MANAGER

Midweek specials from €190.00 pps

13 13

Closed 01 November - 01 March

B&B Rates are per Person Sharing per Night incl. Breakfast
Room Rates are per Room per Night

CO. WEXFORD
COURTOWN HARBOUR / CURRACLOE

COURTOWN HOTEL

COURTOWN HARBOUR,
GOREY,
CO. WEXFORD
TEL: 055-25210 FAX: 055-25304
EMAIL: reservations@courtownhotel.com
WEB: www.courtownhotel.com

HOTEL ★★ MAP 8 O 7

The family-run Courtown Hotel &
Leisure Centre is renowned for its
friendly atmosphere and excellent
cuisine. This is an AA 3*** hotel and
features the AA award-winning
"Bradley's" Restaurant and a selection
of lounge bars and beer garden. All
rooms are en suite with T.V. and
direct dial telephone. Residents enjoy
complimentary use of our leisure
facilities which include an indoor
heated swimming pool, sauna,
jacuzzi & steamroom. Weddings and
parties a speciality.

B&B from €50.00 to €90.00

MARLENE DURKIN
GENERAL MANAGER

☺ Weekend specials from €99.00 pps

22 22

Closed 10 November - 07 March

HARBOUR HOUSE GUESTHOUSE

COURTOWN HARBOUR,
COURTOWN, GOREY,
CO. WEXFORD
TEL: 055-25117 FAX: 055-25117
EMAIL: stay@harbourhouseguesthouse.com
WEB: www.harbourhouseguesthouse.com

GUESTHOUSE ★★ MAP 8 O 7

Harbour House just off the main
Rosslare/Dublin N11 route and only
6km from Gorey is ideally located in
the renowned seaside resort of
Courtown Harbour. Harbour House is
the ideal base for both business and
holiday travellers and is central to all
amenities and only three minutes
from Courtown's sandy beaches. All
rooms are en suite. Private car park.
Come and enjoy Courtown's new
25m swimming pool. 2 kiddies pools
and a 65m water slide all set within
63 acres of woodland with beautiful
river walks.

B&B from €35.00 to €40.00

DONAL & MARGARET O'GORMAN
PROPRIETORS

13 13

Closed 31 October - 10 April

HOTEL CURRACLOE

CURRACLOE,
CO. WEXFORD

TEL: 053-37308 FAX: 053-37587
EMAIL: hotelcurracloe@eircom.net
WEB: www.hotelcurracloe.com

HOTEL ★★ MAP 4 O 6

Hotel Curracloe is ideally situated,
only five miles from Wexford Town,
minutes from Blue/Green Flag
beaches and central to golfing,
angling, bird-watching, hill walking
and horseriding amenities. Our 29
rooms are en suite with modern
facilities and our award-winning
Blake Restaurant and Tavern Pub
serve the best of home produce. The
Brent Banqueting Room will cater for
every special occasion. Our friendly
staff will ensure that Hotel Curracloe
is the perfect base for your leisure
time in the sunny South East.

B&B from €40.00 to €50.00

JOHN & MARGARET HANRAHAN
OWNERS

29 29

Open All Year

B&B Rates are per Person Sharing per Night incl. Breakfast
Room Rates are per Room per Night

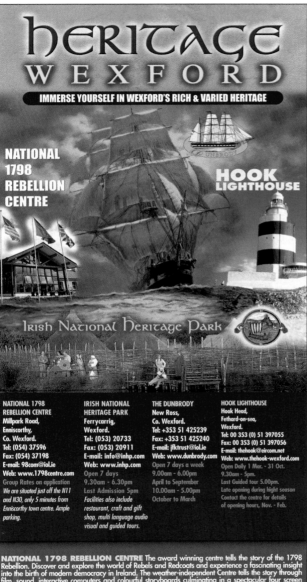

HERITAGE WEXFORD

IMMERSE YOURSELF IN WEXFORD'S RICH & VARIED HERITAGE

NATIONAL 1798 REBELLION CENTRE

HOOK LIGHTHOUSE

Irish National Heritage Park

NATIONAL 1798 REBELLION CENTRE
Millpark Road,
Enniscorthy,
Co. Wexford.
Tel: (054) 37596
Fax: (054) 37198
E-mail: 98com@iol.ie
Web: www.1798centre.com
Group Rates on application
We are situated just off the N11
and N30, only 5 minutes from
Enniscorthy town centre. Ample
parking.

IRISH NATIONAL HERITAGE PARK
Ferrycarrig,
Wexford.
Tel: (053) 20733
Fax: (053) 20911
E-mail: info@inhp.com
Web: www.inhp.com
Open 7 days
9.30am - 6.30pm
April to September
Last Admission 5pm
Facilities also include
restaurant, craft and gift
shop, multi language audio
visual and guided tours.

THE DUNBRODY
New Ross,
Co. Wexford.
Tel: +353 51 425239
Fax: +353 51 425240
E-mail: jfktrust@iol.ie
Web: www.dunbrody.com
Open 7 days a week
9.00am - 6.00pm
April to September
10.00am - 5.00pm
October to March

HOOK LIGHTHOUSE
Hook Head,
Fethard-on-sea,
Wexford.
Tel: 00 353 (0) 51 397055
Fax: 00 353 (0) 51 397056
E-mail: thehook@eircom.net
Web: www.thehook-wexford.com
Open Daily 1 Mar. - 31 Oct.
9.30am - 5pm.
Last Guided tour 5.00pm.
Late opening during high season
Contact the centre for details
of opening hours, Nov. - Feb.

NATIONAL 1798 REBELLION CENTRE The award winning centre tells the story of the 1798 Rebellion. Discover and explore the world of Rebels and Redcoats and experience a fascinating insight into the birth of modern democracy in Ireland. The weather-independent Centre tells the story through film, sound, interactive computers and colourful storyboards culminating in a spectacular four screen reenactment of the Battle of Vinegar Hill. After your tour, relax in our bright, restaurant or browse in the craft shop.

IRISH NATIONAL HERITAGE PARK Stroll through the park with it's homesteads, places of ritual and burial modes. Your sences come alive with sights and sounds stretching back almost nine thousand years.

DUNBRODY Visit Ireland's unique emigrant ship. The Dunbrody is a full scale reconstruction of a 19th century Famine ship, an authentic replica of the Three Masted Barque built in Quebec in 1845 for the Graves family of New Ross.

HOOK LIGHTHOUSE Visit one of the Oldest Operational Lighthouses in the World. "By hooke or by Crooke" you will be enthralled. Guided tours of the lighthouse, Multi-lingual Literature, Café, Craft Shop, Car and Coach Parking.

B&B Rates are per Person Sharing per Night incl. Breakfast
Room Rates are per Room per Night

LEMONGROVE HOUSE

BLACKSTOOPS,
ENNISCORTHY,
CO. WEXFORD
TEL: 054-36115 FAX: 054-36115
EMAIL: lemongrovehouse@iolfree.ie
WEB: www.euroka.com/lemongrove

GUESTHOUSE ★★★ MAP 4 N 6

Elegant country house 1km north of Enniscorthy just off roundabout on Dublin/Rosslare Road (N11). Lemongrove House is set in mature gardens with private parking. All rooms en suite with direct dial phone, TV, hairdryer and tea/coffee making facilities. Recommended by Guide du Routard, AA and other leading guides. Within walking distance of a choice of restaurants, pubs and new pool and leisure centre. Locally we have beaches, golf, horseriding, walking and quad track.

B&B from €33.00 to €40.00

COLM & ANN MCGIBNEY
OWNERS

9 9

Closed 20 - 29 December

PINES COUNTRY HOUSE HOTEL

CAMOLIN,
ENNISCORTHY,
CO. WEXFORD
TEL: 054-83600 FAX: 054-83588
EMAIL: thepines@eircom.net
WEB: www.pinescountryhousehotel.com

HOTEL ★★ MAP 4 N 6

Family-run hotel with award-winning resturant, European and real Indian food. Top class accommodation, state of the art gym, sauna, steamroom, plunge pool, pony trekking, hill walking, birdwatching. Nearby Courtown and Curracloe beaches, historic Ferns, heritage park, quad trekking, fishing, music and on-site Bouncy Castle/slide, horseriding, trampolines and sunshine. Music on Saturdays.

B&B from €45.00 to €75.00

FRANK MURHILL
DIRECTOR MANAGER

Weekend specials from €115.00 pps

11 11

Open All Year

RIVERSIDE PARK HOTEL AND LEISURE CLUB

THE PROMENADE,
ENNISCORTHY,
CO. WEXFORD
TEL: 054-37800 FAX: 054-37900
EMAIL: info@riversideparkhotel.com
WEB: www.riversideparkhotel.com

HOTEL ★★★ MAP 4 N 6

Nestling along the scenic banks of the River Slaney, the Riverside Park Hotel and Leisure Club is an ideal base for touring the treasures of the sunny South East. With a choice of two superb restaurants, The Moorings and The Alamo, Tex-Mex at its best. A luxurious bar with spectacular views. Relax and unwind with our 15m indoor swimming pool, sauna, steamroom and gym.

B&B from €63.50 to €87.50

JIM MAHER
GENERAL MANAGER

2 B&B + 1D from €89.00 pps

60 60

Closed 24 - 26 December

TREACY'S HOTEL

TEMPLESHANNON,
ENNISCORTHY,
CO. WEXFORD
TEL: 054-37798 FAX: 054-37733
EMAIL: info@treacyshotel.com
WEB: www.treacyshotel.com

HOTEL ★★★ MAP 4 N 6

Situated in the heart of beautiful Enniscorthy, Treacy's Hotel is in the ideal location for both excitement and relaxation. Whether it's sport, music, fine dining or a memorable night life you desire, you need look no further. A world of choice is available including; Chang Thai - our authentic Thai resturant, Bagenai Harvey - European Continental style cuisine & in our Temple Bar we have an Italian style Bistro menu. Temple Bar & Benedicts superpub provide top Irish entertainment & our new Heated all-weather beer garden is pure relaxation.

B&B from €70.00 to €120.00

ANTON TREACY

Weekend specials from €119.00 pps

48 48

Closed 24 - 26 December

B&B Rates are per Person Sharing per Night incl. Breakfast
Room Rates are per Room per Night

HORSE AND HOUND INN

BALLINABOOLA,
FOULKSMILLS,
CO. WEXFORD
TEL: 051-428323 FAX: 051-428471
EMAIL: info@horseandhound.net
WEB: www.horseandhound.net

GUESTHOUSE ★★★ MAP 4 N 5

The Horse and Hound Inn, Ballinaboola, Co. Wexford is owned and run by the Murphy Family. Situated six miles from New Ross on the N25 from Rosslare. It is a convenient venue for a meal and a rest. Best Irish produce is used in preparing specialities of fish and beef dishes. There are twelve bedrooms should you wish to stay. Catering for all needs - from private parties, weddings to conferences.

B&B from €45.00 to €60.00

CHRISTY MURPHY

27 27

Open All Year

ASHDOWN PARK HOTEL CONFERENCE & LEISURE CENTRE

COACH ROAD,
GOREY,
CO. WEXFORD
TEL: 055-80500 FAX: 055-80777
EMAIL: info@ashdownparkhotel.com
WEB: www.ashdownparkhotel.com

HOTEL ★★★★ MAP 8 O 7

Enjoy a well-earned leisure break in this stylish, friendly 4**** de luxe hotel, located on its own private grounds just a 3 minute stroll from Gorey town. All 60 splendid bedrooms, 6 of which are executive suites are modern classical in style, offering the highest level of comfort, with all conveniences. State of the art leisure facilities offer all guests the perfect way of unwinding after a long day touring the quaint seaside towns and historic sites of Wexford. Centrally located close to Dublin and Rosslare.

B&B from €70.00 to €130.00

LIAM MORAN
GENERAL MANAGER

60 60

IRISH
HOTELS
FEDERATION

Closed 24 - 26 December

MARLFIELD HOUSE HOTEL

GOREY,
CO. WEXFORD

TEL: 055-21124 FAX: 055-21572
EMAIL: info@marlfieldhouse.ie
WEB: www.marlfieldhouse.com

HOTEL ★★★★ MAP 8 O 7

This fine Regency period house is set in 36 acres of grounds and filled with antiques. The Bowe family opened its doors to guests in 1978 and has maintained an outstanding reputation for food, comfort and service ever since. The 20 bedrooms are filled with antiques, paintings and flowers and all have marble bathrooms. There are six sumptuous state rooms overlooking the lake. Member of Relais & Châteaux, Ireland's Blue Book, AA Red Star and RAC Gold Ribbon. Highly acclaimed conservatory restaurant.

Member of Relais Et Châteaux

B&B from €128.00 to €138.00

MARY BOWE
PROPRIETOR

20 20

Closed 15 December - 25 January

B&B Rates are per Person Sharing per Night incl. Breakfast
Room Rates are per Room per Night

HOTEL SALTEES

**KILMORE QUAY,
CO. WEXFORD**

TEL: 053-29601 FAX: 053-29602

HOTEL ★★ MAP 4 N 5

Hotel Saltees is situated in the picturesque fishing village of Kilmore Quay. Renowned for its thatched cottages and maritime flavour, it is located just 22km from Wexford Town and 19km from the international port of Rosslare. Offering excellent value accommodation, with all rooms en suite, TV, telephone and all well designed to cater for families. The Coningbeg Seafood Restaurant specialises in serving the freshest seafood. Shore and deep-sea fishing available locally.

B&B from €45.00 to €53.00

NED BYRNE
PROPRIETOR

☺ Weekend specials from €127.00 pps

Open All Year

QUAY HOUSE

**KILMORE QUAY,
CO. WEXFORD**

TEL: 053-29988 FAX: 053-29808
EMAIL: quayhome@eircom.net
WEB: www.kilmorequay.net

GUESTHOUSE ★★★ MAP 4 N 5

Quay House is a family-run bed and breakfast guest house. Deep sea fishing, miles of nature trails, sandy beaches, bird sanctuaries, near to Kilmore Quay, good position in centre of village, private car park. All facilities in rooms, ensuite, TV, tea/coffee service in rooms, full Irish breakfast, guest lounge, early ferry breakfasts, 14 miles from Ferry Port. Spacious rooms, marina, harbour, bars, restaurants, public transport to Wexford Town daily.

B&B from €40.00 to €50.00

SIOBHAN MCDONNELL
PROPRIETOR

Closed 25 December

BRANDON HOUSE HOTEL, HEALTH CLUB & SPA

**NEW ROSS,
CO. WEXFORD**

TEL: 051-421703 FAX: 051-421567
EMAIL: brandonhouse@eircom.net
WEB: www.brandonhousehotel.ie

HOTEL ★★★ MAP 4 M 6

A de luxe country manor house set in landscaped grounds with panoramic views overlooking the River Barrow. Dine in the Gallery Restaurant or relax in the Library Bar. All rooms are elegantly furnished. Luxurious health & leisure club with 20m pool, sauna, steamroom, jacuzzi, fully equipped gym, kiddies pool, hydrotherapy grotto and thalasso treatment room. Nearby golf, angling, beaches, horseriding & gardens. An ideal base for touring the sunny South East. Creche available. Conference and banqueting for up to 400 people.

B&B from €68.00 to €85.00

GRACE MCPHILLIPS
GENERAL MANAGER

☺ Midweek specials from €135.00 pps

Closed 24 - 27 December

B&B Rates are per Person Sharing per Night incl. Breakfast
Room Rates are per Room per Night

BLARNEY PARK HOTEL AND LEISURE CENTRE

**BLARNEY,
CO. CORK**

TEL: 021-438 5281 FAX: 021-438 1506
EMAIL: info@blarneypark.com
WEB: www.blarneypark.com

HOTEL ★★★ MAP 2 H 3

Set on 12 acres in the picturesque village of Blarney with Cork City just 10 minutes away. From the moment you arrive, you can be certain of a uniquely warm welcome and pampering. Savour our superb cuisine and relax in the comfort of our residents' lounge. With our excellent supervised playroom and leisure centre with 20m pool, 40m slide, hotrooms and holistic treatment, it makes a short break seem like a holiday.

Member of The Blarney Group Hotels

B&B from €60.00 to €105.00

CONOR BUTLER
GENERAL MANAGER

☺ Weekend specials from €130.00 pps

91 91

Closed 24 - 26 December

BLARNEY WOOLLEN MILLS HOTEL

**BLARNEY,
CO. CORK**

TEL: 021-438 5011 FAX: 021-438 5350
EMAIL: info@blarneywoollenmillshotel.com
WEB: www.blarneywoollenmillshotel.com

HOTEL ★★★ MAP 2 H 3

Blarney Woollen Mills 3*** Hotel with 45 beautifully appointed superior rooms & 3 executive suites. Many of the rooms have spectacular views of the famous Blarney Castle. All rooms have been tastefully decorated in the traditional style. All day dining in our self service restaurant & evening dining in Christys Grill Bar. The hotel boasts one of the finest fitness centres in the area. Located within the old Mill buildings in the famous Blarney Woollen Mills complex where you can enjoy a relaxing drink & experience some Irish hospitality in Christy's Pub.

B&B from €60.00 to €70.00

DOMINIC HEANEY
GENERAL MANAGER

✓

48 48

Closed 20 December - 02 January

MUSKERRY ARMS

**BLARNEY,
CO. CORK**

TEL: 021-438 5200 FAX: 021-438 1013
EMAIL: info@muskerryarms.com
WEB: www.muskerrys.com

GUESTHOUSE ★★★ MAP 2 H 3

There in the very centre of Blarney the biggest little village in Ireland, just 5 miles from Cork City you will find the Muskerry Arms personally managed by Nell O' Connor and her family. All our comfortable bedrooms have power showers, central heating, hairdryers, colour televisions, direct dial telephone, internet and fax systems. They also enjoy a stunning view of Blarney Village and the Castle.

B&B from €40.00 to €65.00

NELL O' CONNOR

✓

11 11

Closed 24 - 26 December

B&B Rates are per Person Sharing per Night incl. Breakfast
Room Rates are per Room per Night

CARRIGALINE COURT HOTEL & LEISURE CENTRE

CARRIGALINE,
CO. CORK

TEL: 021-485 2100 FAX: 021-437 1103
EMAIL: reception@carrigcourt.com
WEB: www.carrigcourt.com

HOTEL U MAP 3 H 3

Luxury RAC 4**** hotel, located just minutes from city centre, airport and ferry terminal. Spacious bedrooms with satellite TV, tea/coffee facilities, ISDN line and all modern comforts as standard. Superb restaurant and traditional Irish bar. Exquisite leisure centre incl. 20m pool, sauna, jacuzzi, steamroom and gym. Golf arranged at Cork's best courses. Local activities include sailing, angling, horseriding and a host of other activities in this beautiful area.

B&B from € 90.00 to € 110.00

JOHN O'FLYNN
GENERAL MANAGER

😊 Weekend specials from €140.00 pps

9 9

Closed 25 December

FERNHILL GOLF & COUNTRY CLUB

FERNHILL,
CARRIGALINE,
CO. CORK

TEL: 021-437 2226 FAX: 021-437 1011
EMAIL: fernhill@iol.ie
WEB: www.fernhillcountryclub.com

GUESTHOUSE ★★★ MAP 3 H 3

The guesthouse is situated in a unique location, on its own private 18 hole golf course. 8km from Cork Airport and City, 5 minutes from Ringaskiddy Ferryport and 21km to Kinsale makes Fernhill Golf and Country Club the ideal venue for any type of break. Facilities include indoor swimming pool, sauna, gym and tennis court with horseriding and sea angling nearby. Guests can also use the facilities of our excellent Country Club with its restaurant, bar, beer garden/BBQ area and live music at weekends. All rooms en suite, TV, direct dial phone, tea/coffee.

B&B from € 45.00 to € 85.00

ALAN BOWES
GENERAL MANAGER

😊 Weekend specials including golf from €140.00 pps

40 40

Closed 25 - 26 December

GLENWOOD HOUSE

BALLINREA ROAD,
CARRIGALINE,
CO. CORK

TEL: 021-437 3878 FAX: 021-437 3878
EMAIL: info@glenwoodguesthouse.com
WEB: www.glenwoodguesthouse.com

GUESTHOUSE ★★★★ MAP 3 H 3

Glenwood House is a purpose built, self contained guesthouse, designed with all guest requirements in mind. The rooms are large and spacious, offering similar facilities to those of quality hotels, firm orthopaedic beds, heated towel rails, complimentary beverages, trouser press, satellite TV, power shower and many more. Located close to Ringaskiddy Ferry Port (5mins), Cork City (7mins), Kinsale (15mins), Crosshaven (5mins), Airport (5mins). We offer secure car parking, and have facilities to look after disabled guests. All accommodation is of hotel quality.

Member of Premier Guesthouses

B&B from € 45.00 to € 75.00

ADRIAN SHEEDY
PROPRIETOR

10 10

Closed 09 December - 06 January

B&B Rates are per Person Sharing per Night incl. Breakfast
Room Rates are per Room per Night

CASTLE (THE)

CASTLETOWNSHEND,
NEAR SKIBBEREEN,
CO CORK

TEL: 028-36100 FAX: 028-36166
EMAIL: castle_townshend@hotmail.com
WEB: www.castle-townshend.com

GUESTHOUSE ★ MAP 2 F 1

18th century Townshend family home overlooking Castlehaven Harbour. Set in its own grounds at water's edge with access to small beach and woods. Most bedrooms en suite on second floor with excellent sea views. Panelled hall/sitting room with TV and open fire. Breakfast in elegant dining room. Mary Ann's Restaurant close by. Ideal for touring Cork and Kerry. Also self-catering apartments and cottages. For illustrated brochure please apply.

B&B from €45.00 to €75.00

ANNE AND MALCOLM COCHRANE
TOWNSHEND

7   7

Closed 15 December - 15 January

DUNMORE HOUSE HOTEL

MUCKROSS,
CLONAKILTY,
CO. CORK

TEL: 023-33352 FAX: 023-34686
EMAIL: enquiries@dunmorehousehotel.ie
WEB: www.dunmorehousehotel.com

HOTEL ★★★ MAP 2 G 2

Situated on the South West coast of Ireland, Dunmore House Hotel is family owned. Rooms are beautifully decorated, all with spectacular views of the Atlantic Ocean. Sample a true taste of West Cork with our home-cooked local produce and seafood. Private foreshore available for sea angling. Green fees at the on-site golf club are free to residents. Horseriding available by arrangement. Interesting collection of local and modern Irish art.

B&B from €70.00 to €80.00

DERRY & MARY O'DONOVAN
PROPRIETORS

Midweek specials from €210.00 pps

29   29

alc

Closed 23 January - 01 March

B&B Rates are per Person Sharing per Night incl. Breakfast
Room Rates are per Room per Night

EMMET HOTEL

EMMET SQUARE,
CLONAKILTY,
CO. CORK

TEL: 023-33394 FAX: 023-35058
EMAIL: emmethotel@eircom.net
WEB: www.emmethotel.com

HOTEL U MAP 2 G 2

The Emmet offers its guests an uncompromising level of service, personal yet efficient. O'Keeffes of Clonakility Restaurant has established itself as one of the leading restaurants in West Cork, offering innovative menus at very reasonable prices. Facilities in the hotel include restaurant, function facilities, bars, garden patio, and the Bubble Lounge night club.There are 20 bedrooms, all en suite with TV, direct dial telephone and tea/coffee making facilities.

B&B from €45.00 to €75.00

THE O'KEEFFE FAMILY
PROPRIETORS

😊 Midweek specials from €120.00 pps

20 20

Closed 24 - 26 December

FERNHILL HOUSE HOTEL

CLONAKILTY,
CO. CORK

TEL: 023-33258 FAX: 023-34003
EMAIL: info@fernhillhousehotel.com
WEB: www.fernhillhousehotel.com

HOTEL ★★ MAP 2 G 2

Fernhill House is a family-run old Georgian style hotel located on picturesque grounds 0.8km from Clonakilty. All bedrooms en suite with tea/coffee making facilities, phone, TV and hairdryer. Conference and function facilities available, Par 3 golf on-site and 18 hole Pitch & Putt course. Our hotel offers an intimate homely atmosphere, excellent food and a comfortable bar. Holiday with us and enjoy scenic West Cork from centrally situated Fernhill House Hotel.

B&B from €55.00 to €60.00

MICHAEL & TERESA O'NEILL
PROPRIETORS

15 15

Closed 23 December - 01 January

INCHYDONEY ISLAND LODGE & SPA

CLONAKILTY,
WEST CORK

TEL: 023-33143 FAX: 023-35229
EMAIL: reservations@inchydoneyisland.com
WEB: www.inchydoneyisland.com

HOTEL ★★★★ MAP 2 G 2

Situated on the idyllic island of Inchydoney, between two EU Blue Flag beaches, this luxurious hotel offers de luxe rooms, a fully equipped thalassotherapy (seawater) spa, award-winning restaurant, Dunes Pub and function and meeting facilities. Within a short distance guests can enjoy sailing, golf at the Old Head of Kinsale, riding and deep sea fishing, whale watching and surfing. The style of cooking in the Gulfstream Restaurant reflects the wide availability of fresh seafood and organically grown vegetables.

B&B from €154.00 to €165.00

ROBERT DELAHUNTY
GENERAL MANAGER

😊 Weekend specials from €310.00 pps

67 67

Closed 24 - 27 December

B&B Rates are per Person Sharing per Night incl. Breakfast
Room Rates are per Room per Night

O'DONOVAN'S HOTEL

PEARSE STREET,
CLONAKILTY,
WEST CORK

TEL: 023-33250 FAX: 023-33250
EMAIL: odhotel@iol.ie
WEB: www.odonovanshotel.com

HOTEL ★★ MAP 2 G 2

Charles Stewart Parnell, Marconi and Gen. Michael Collins found time to stop here. This fifth generation, family-run hotel is located in the heart of Clonakilty Town. Abounding in history, the old world charm has been retained whilst still providing the guest with facilities such as bath/shower en suite, TV etc. Our restaurant provides snacks and full meals and is open to non-residents. Ideal for conferences, private functions, meetings etc., with lock up car park.

B&B from €50.00 to €60.00

O'DONOVAN FAMILY PROPRIETORS

26 26

alc inet

IRISH HOTELS FEDERATION

Closed 25 - 28 December

QUALITY HOTEL AND LEISURE CENTRE

CLONAKILTY,
CO. CORK

TEL: 1850-746 8357 FAX: 021-427 1489
EMAIL: info@qualityhotelclonakilty.com
WEB: www.qualityhotelclonakilty.com

HOTEL ★★★ MAP 2 G 2

Clonakilty is a thriving and busy attractive town with a wealth of musical and artistic cultural activities. This unique hotel complex which opened in July 1999 offers the following excellent facilities, 80 en suite bedrooms, 5 executive holiday homes, Lannigans Restaurant, Oscars Bar with regular entertainment, an award-winning leisure centre, and our new adventure three screen multiplex cinema complete the complex. The ideal destination for your breakaway. Telephone hotel direct at 023 36400.

Member of Quality Hotels

B&B from €39.00 to €119.00

DAVID HENRY GENERAL MANAGER

☺ Weekend specials from €90.00 pps

80 80

IRISH HOTELS FEDERATION

Closed 20 - 26 December

Titanic Trail
Cobh, Co. Cork

ExploreCobh's Fascinating history and the towns' direct links with Titanic! The original Titanic Trail guided walking tour takes place every day all year. Leaving at **11am daily** from the Commodore Hotel this famous tour is educational, interesting and fun. Cost is €7.50 which includes a complimentary glass of Guinness in Jack Doyle's Bar. Duration is approximately 75 minutes.

In June, July, and August additional tours also run at 11am, 2pm and 4pm

Contact: Michael Martin
Author and Creator Titanic Trail

Tel: + 353 (21) 4815211
Mobile: +353 (87) 276 7218
Email: info@titanic-trail.com
URL www.titanic-trail.com

RANDLES CLONAKILTY HOTEL

WOLFE TONE STREET,
CLONAKILTY,
WEST CORK

TEL: 023-34749 FAX: 023-35035
EMAIL: clonakilty@randleshotels.com
WEB: www.randleshotels.com

HOTEL ★★★ MAP 2 G 2

Nestled in the beauty and tranquillity of glorious West Cork stands the Randles Clonakilty Hotel. This boutique style hotel is both charming and elegant which is evident in the exquisite furnishings of the lobby. With only 30 bedrooms one can enjoy the intimacy of a smaller hotel backed by a professional team. Maxwell Irwins Bar & Bistro with its wood panelled interior offers traditional and local fayre in attractive surroundings.

B&B from €50.00 to €100.00

EMMA MCCARTHY
GENERAL MANAGER

☺ 2 nights B&B at weekends from €99.00 pps

30 30

Closed 21 - 27 December

COMMODORE HOTEL

COBH,
CO. CORK

TEL: 021-481 1277 FAX: 021-481 1672
EMAIL: commodorehotel@eircom.net
WEB: www.commodorehotel.ie

HOTEL ★★ MAP 3 1 3

The Commodore Hotel, owned and managed by the O'Shea family for 35 years overlooks Cork Harbour. 25 minutes from city centre. Facilities: indoor swimming pool, sauna, snooker - entertainment and roof garden. Locally (subject to availability at clubs) free golf and pitch & putt. Ideal location for visiting Fota Wildlife Park, Fota Golf Course, Blarney etc, The Jameson and Queenstown Heritage Centres. All 42 rooms have full facilities, (21 overlook Cork Harbour supplement applies). Ringaskiddy Ferryport 15 mins via river car ferry.

B&B from €57.00 to €70.00

PATRICK O'SHEA
GENERAL MANAGER

☺ Weekend specials from €125.00 pps

42 42

Closed 24 - 27 December

RUSHBROOKE HOTEL

COBH,
CO CORK

TEL: 021-481 2242 FAX: 021-481 2245
EMAIL: info@rushbrookehotel.ie
WEB: www.rushbrookehotel.ie

HOTEL U MAP 3 1 3

The Rushbrooke Hotel, located on the banks of the River Lee, with a magical marine view is an ideal base for touring East, West Cork and Kerry. Visit Fota Wildlife Park or The Hamlet Town of Cobh with the famous Titanic Trail. Enjoy a mouth watering-meal, an evening's entertainment in the bar and wake up to a spectacular view overlooking the harbour. Cork International Airport 20Km.

Member of Irish Court Hotels

B&B from €30.00 to €95.00

PAUL COUGHLAN
GENERAL MANAGER

☺ Weekend specials from €79.00 pps

39 39

Closed 25 December

B&B Rates are per Person Sharing per Night incl. Breakfast
Room Rates are per Room per Night

LOUGH MAHON HOUSE

TIVOLI,
CORK

TEL: 021-450 2142 FAX: 021-450 1804
EMAIL: info@loughmahon.com
WEB: www.loughmahon.com

GUESTHOUSE ★★★ MAP 3 H 3

Luxurious Georgian house with private parking. Convenient to city centre, bus & rail station.100 metres from Silver Springs Moran Hotel. En suite bedrooms with cable TV, DD phone, hairdryer, tea/coffee making facilities. We offer in-house holistic treatments (integrated energy therapy, reiki, massage, la stone therapy & face & body treatments etc.). Close to Fota Wildlife Park, Cobh Heritage Centre, Blarney Castle, golf glubs & ferry terminals. Renowned for our fresh orange juice & extensive breakfast menu, it amounts to a great place to stay.

Member of Premier Guesthouses

B&B from €38.00 to €44.50

PETE & LISA
PROPRIETORS

6 6

Open all year

MARYBOROUGH HOUSE HOTEL

MARYBOROUGH HILL,
DOUGLAS,
CORK

TEL: 021-436 5555 FAX: 021-436 5662
EMAIL: info@maryborough.ie
WEB: www.maryborough.com

HOTEL ★★★★ MAP 3 H 3

Distinctive, delightful and different. Maryborough is set on 24 acres of listed gardens and woodland, located only 10 minutes from Cork City. This charming 18th century house, with its creatively designed extension, features exquisite conference, banqueting and leisure facilities. 79 spacious rooms, some with balconies overlooking the magnificent gardens and orchards. Zing's Restaurant, in contemporary relaxed design, is an exciting mix of modern flavours and styles. 4 minutes from Lee Tunnel. Wheelchair friendly.

B&B from €85.00 to €125.00

JUSTIN MCCARTHY
GENERAL MANAGER

☺ Weekend specials from €165.00 pps

79 79

Closed 24 - 26 December

QUALITY HOTEL & LEISURE CENTRE, CORK

JOHN REDMOND STREET,
CORK

TEL: 1850-746 8357 FAX: 021-452 9222
EMAIL: info@qualityhotelcork.com
WEB: www.qualityhotelcork.com

HOTEL U MAP 2 H 3

A great location for a city break. This city centre hotel now exudes a modern, contemporary experience. Spacious guest rooms, relaxing surroundings and imaginative menu choices available at Lannigans Restaurant are to be enjoyed. Club Vitae boasts a superb 20m pool, gym, jacuzzi, steamroom and treatment room. Limited car parking. Telephone hotel direct at 021- 452 9200.

Member of Quality Hotels

B&B from €40.00 to €120.00

AIDAN MOYNIHAN
GENERAL MANAGER

☺ Weekend specials from €90.00 pps

101 101

Open All Year

B&B Rates are per Person Sharing per Night incl. Breakfast
Room Rates are per Room per Night

SOUTH WEST   91

REDCLYFFE GUEST HOUSE

WESTERN ROAD,
CORK

TEL: 021-427 3220 FAX: 021-427 8382
EMAIL: redclyffe@eircom.net
WEB: www.redclyffe.com

GUESTHOUSE U MAP 2 H 3

Redclyffe is a charming Victorian red brick guesthouse, combining olde world charm with modern elegance. Opposite University College Cork, museum, consultant's clinic and Jurys Hotel. All rooms en suite with TV, hairdryer, direct dial phone, tea & coffee making facilities. Close to city centre, No. 8 bus at door. Easy drive to airport and car ferry. Spacious car park. Be assured of a warm welcome at this family-run guesthouse. Additional email: info@redclyffe.com

B&B from €30.00 to €40.00

MICHAEL & MAURA SHEEHAN
PROPRIETORS

🛏🏃☎🖥TCPS🛗
13 13

Open All Year

ROCHESTOWN PARK HOTEL

ROCHESTOWN ROAD,
DOUGLAS,
CORK

TEL: 021-489 0800 FAX: 021-489 2178
EMAIL: info@rochestownpark.com
WEB: www.rochestownpark.com

HOTEL ★★★★ MAP 3 H 3

The Rochestown Park Hotel is a manor style hotel set in mature gardens. Facilities include an award-winning leisure centre and Ireland's premier Thalasso Therapy Centre. A large proportion of our 163 bedrooms are air-conditioned and overlook our gardens and Mahon Golf Club. We cater for weekend breaks, conferences, meetings, as well as groups, families and weddings.

Member of Select Hotels

B&B from €60.00 to €110.00

LIAM LALLY
GENERAL MANAGER

😊 Weekend specials from €145.00 pps

🛏🏃☎🖥🖥TC🖊CM❄🔾🖥🏠🔾
163 163
🎵PS🖥aid🔲WiFi🐎🎿

T R I S H
HOTELS
FEDERATION

Open all year

ROSE LODGE GUEST HOUSE

MARDYKE WALK,
OFF WESTERN ROAD,
CORK

TEL: 021-427 2958 FAX: 021-427 4087
EMAIL: info@roselodge.net
WEB: www.roselodge.net

GUESTHOUSE ★★★ MAP 2 H 3

Rose Lodge is a 10 minute walk from city centre and close to bus and train stations. 16 en suite bedrooms (jacuzzi optional) with direct dial telephone, TV, tea/coffee making facilities, hairdryer and ironing facilities. An ideal base for the busy executive or holidaymaker to explore the South West. Airport and ferry 15 minutes drive. Golf, tennis, cricket, fishing nearby and just minutes from University College Cork.

B&B from €40.00 to €60.00

PADDY MURPHY
PROPRIETOR

🛏🏃☎🔲CPS🛗
16 16

Open All Year

B&B Rates are per Person Sharing per Night incl. Breakfast
Room Rates are per Room per Night

SILVER SPRINGS MORAN HOTEL

**TIVOLI,
CORK**

TEL: 021-450 7533 FAX: 021-450 7641
EMAIL: silversprings@moranhotels.com
WEB: www.moranhotels.com

HOTEL ★★★★ MAP 3 H 3

This 4**** hotel has been completely redesigned and re-furbished. The hotel is located only minutes from Cork City. 109 bedrooms including 5 de luxe suites all with cable TV, trouser press and tea/coffee facitlities. Centrally located only 5 minutes from the city centre and 7 miles from Cork Intenational Airport. Excellent base for touring Cork's many visitor attractions. Full leisure facilities available include 25m pool. Free parking. A Moran Hotel.

Member of Moran Hotel Group

B&B from €60.00 to €120.00

TOM & SHEILA MORAN
PROPRIETORS

☺ Weekend specials from €120.00 pps

109 109

IRISH HOTELS FEDERATION

Closed 24 - 27 December

VICTORIA HOTEL

**PATRICK STREET,
COOK STREET,
CORK**

TEL: 021-427 8788 FAX: 021-427 8790
EMAIL: info@thevictoriahotel.com
WEB: www.thevictoriahotel.com

HOTEL ★★ MAP 3 H 3

The Victoria Hotel is situated in Cork City centre. All rooms have bath & shower, direct dial phone, TV and hairdryer. Family suites available. Built in 1810, it was frequented by European Royalty and was home to some of our own great political leaders, including Charles Stewart Parnell who made his major speeches from its upper balcony. James Joyce recounts his stay in Portrait of an Artist. Conference room available.

Member of MinOtel Hotel Group

B&B from €45.00 to €90.00

PAUL KING
MANAGER

29 29

IRISH HOTELS FEDERATION

Closed 24 - 26 December

VIENNA WOODS HOTEL

**GLANMIRE,
CORK**

TEL: 021-482 1146 FAX: 021-482 1120
EMAIL: info@viennawoodshotel.com
WEB: www.viennawoodshotel.com

HOTEL ★★★ MAP 3 H 3

This unique country house hotel set in 20 acres of woodland 7 minutes from Cork City centre. All 50 bedrooms have been decorated to offer a high standard of comfort. Food is available throughout the day, casual dining in the Conservatory Bar and in the Blue Room. Ideally placed close to Munster's finest golf courses, Cobh Titanic Heritage centre, Fota Wildlife Park & Kinsale. Leisure Centre due for completion Summer 2005.

B&B from €65.00 to €80.00

JOHN MURRAY/JOHN & DARINA GATELY

☺ Midweek specials from €210.00 pps

50 50

IRISH HOTELS FEDERATION

Closed 24 - 26 December

B&B Rates are per Person Sharing per Night incl. Breakfast
Room Rates are per Room per Night

WHISPERING PINES HOTEL

CROSSHAVEN,
CO. CORK

TEL: 021-483 1843 FAX: 021-483 1679
EMAIL: reservations@whisperingpineshotel.com
WEB: www.whisperingpineshotel.com

HOTEL ★★ MAP 313

Whispering Pines, personally run by the Twomey Family, is a charming hotel sheltered by surrounding woodland and overlooking the Owenabue River. In this idyllic setting one can enjoy good company, quality homecooked food and a host of amenities to ensure your stay is a restful and memorable experience. All rooms with direct dial phone, tea/coffee facilities and TV. Our 3 angling boats fish daily from April-October. Ideal base for touring Cork/Kerry Region. Cork Airport 12km and Cork City 19km. AA approved.

B&B from €40.00 to €60.00

NORMA TWOMEY
PROPRIETOR

15 15

IRISH HOTELS FEDERATION

Closed 01 December - 28 Feburary

CASTLEHYDE HOTEL

CASTLEHYDE,
FERMOY,
CO. CORK

TEL: 025-31865 FAX: 025-31485
EMAIL: kate.cashyde@iol.ie
WEB: www.castlehydehotel.ie

HOTEL U MAP 314

Country house hotel accommodation in a fully restored Georgian house and courtyard. Gracious hospitality in luxurious surroundings. Only 30 minutes from Cork but a world apart from its bustle. Many outdoor pursuits available locally. Exquisite cuisine, perfect peace and luxury in one. The ideal base for exploring the beautiful North Cork region whether your trip is for leisure or for business.

B&B from €65.00 to €75.00

MICHAEL O'DWYER
MANAGER

☺ Weekend specials from €160.00 pps

14 14

inet

IRISH HOTELS FEDERATION

Closed 24 - 27 December

GLANWORTH MILL COUNTRY INN

GLANWORTH (NEAR FERMOY),
CO. CORK

TEL: 025-38555 FAX: 025-38560
EMAIL: enquiries@glanworthmill.ie
WEB: www.glanworthmill.ie

GUESTHOUSE ★★★★ MAP 314

A water mill, a Norman castle, a river, an ancient bridge, attractive rooms, à la carte restaurant, guest library/lounge, a courtyard garden and river walk... you'll find it here at Glanworth Mill. Unwind in this 1790 water mill with its sense of history. There is a wealth of activities nearby - fishing, horseriding, golf, hill walking, historic trails, houses and gardens to visit. Hidden Gem Award 2000. AA guest accommodation for Ireland 2001/2002. All in the lush Blackwater Valley of North Cork. T.V in all rooms.

B&B from €70.00 to €155.00

MICHAEL & MARGARET COOKE
PROPRIETORS

10 10

IRISH HOTELS FEDERATION

Closed 24 December - 03 January

B&B Rates are per Person Sharing per Night incl. Breakfast
Room Rates are per Room per Night

LONG QUAY HOUSE

LONG QUAY,
KINSALE,
CO. CORK
TEL: 021-477 4563 FAX: 021-477 4563
EMAIL: longquayhouse@eircom.net
WEB: www.longquayhousekinsale.com

GUESTHOUSE ★★★ MAP 2 H 2

Long Quay House is a Georgian residence which typifies its era with rooms of splendid dimensions, furnished to afford the greatest possible guest comfort. Bedrooms are en suite (majority with bath), TV, direct dial phone, tea-making facilities and hairdryer. Located centrally overlooking inner harbour, yacht marina and within walking distance of all Kinsale's gourmet restaurants and many tourist attractions. Sea angling trips by local skippers arranged. AA and RAC recognised establishment ♦♦♦♦.

B&B from €35.00 to €65.00

JIM & PETER DEASY
HOSTS

7 7 ☎ ▢ ▢ C ✱ CM ☞ S ▪ inet

Closed 15 November - 27 December

OLD BANK HOUSE

11 PEARSE STREET,
NEXT TO POST OFFICE, KINSALE,
CO. CORK
TEL: 021-477 4075 FAX: 021-477 4296
EMAIL: oldbank@indigo.ie
WEB: www.oldbankhousekinsale.com

GUESTHOUSE ★★★★ MAP 2 H 2

The Old Bank House is a Georgian residence of great character & charm providing luxurious accommodation in the historic harbour town of Kinsale. Each bedroom has super king or twin beds, antique furniture and original art, whilst bathrooms are beautifully appointed with tub and shower, top quality toiletries and Egyptian cotton towels and bathrobes. Gourmet breakfast by award-winning Master Chef Michael Riese. Golf friendly and tee times arranged. Voted one of the "Top 100 Places to Stay in Ireland" every year since 1993. RAC ♦♦♦♦♦, AA ♦♦♦♦♦.

Member of Hidden Ireland

B&B from €85.00 to €125.00

MICHAEL & MARIE RIESE
PROPRIETORS

17 17 ☎ ▢ ▢ ✱ T U ☺ ⚲

IRISH
HOTELS
FEDERATION

Closed 01 - 28 December

QUAYSIDE HOUSE

PIER ROAD,
KINSALE,
CO. CORK
TEL: 021-477 2188 FAX: 021-477 2664
EMAIL: quaysidehouse@eircom.net
WEB: www.euroka.com/quayside

GUESTHOUSE ★★★ MAP 2 H 2

A family-run guesthouse ideally located in a picturesque setting overlooking Kinsale Harbour adjacent to town centre, yachting marina and all amenities. All bedrooms are en suite with direct dial telephone, TV and tea/coffee making facilities. Kinsale's famous gourmet restaurants are all within walking distance and Kinsale Golf Club is just a five minute drive. Sea angling trips can be arranged.

B&B from €32.00 to €50.00

MARY COTTER

6 6 ☎ ▢ ▢ C ✱ ✱ U ☞ ⚲ ▪

IRISH
HOTELS
FEDERATION

Open All Year

B&B Rates are per Person Sharing per Night incl. Breakfast
Room Rates are per Room per Night

TIERNEY'S GUEST HOUSE

MAIN STREET,
KINSALE,
CO. CORK
TEL: 021-477 2205 FAX: 021-477 4363
EMAIL: mtierney@indigo.ie
WEB: www.tierneys-kinsale.com

GUESTHOUSE ★★ MAP 2 H 2

Tierney's Guest House. A well established guest house perfectly situated in the heart of magnificent award-winning Kinsale. Our guest house offers all amenities, TV, en suite, hairdryers, tea/coffee on request. Tastefully decorated and a warm welcome guaranteed. Stay in Tierney's and be in the centre of Kinsale and enjoy the gourmet restaurants, various bars & music lounges, breathtaking scenery, water sports, golf, etc.

B&B from €33.00 to €36.00

MAUREEN TIERNEY
OWNER

9 9

Closed 23 - 27 December

TRIDENT HOTEL

WORLD'S END,
KINSALE,
CO. CORK
TEL: 021-477 9300 FAX: 021-477 4173
EMAIL: info@tridenthotel.com
WEB: www.tridenthotel.com

HOTEL U MAP 2 H 2

The Trident enjoys a spectacular location on the shores of Kinsale Harbour offering guests unrivaled views and award-winning cuisine. Exciting new €8 million development sees the upgrade of facilities and new executive bedrooms and luxury suites. The Savannah Waterfront Restaurant - a member of Kinsale Good Food Circle - is one of the finest restaurants in Kinsale. Enjoy scenic walks, explore Kinsale or unwind in the Trident's sauna, steamroom or jacuzzi.

B&B from €55.00 to €110.00

HAL MCELROY
MANAGING DIRECTOR

☺ Weekend specials from €110.00 pps

66 66

Closed 24 - 26 December

WHITE HOUSE

PEARSE ST. & THE GLEN,
KINSALE,
CO. CORK
TEL: 021-477 2125 FAX: 021-477 2045
EMAIL: whitehse@indigo.ie
WEB: www.whitehouse-kinsale.ie

GUESTHOUSE ★★★ MAP 2 H 2

The White House epitomises Kinsale hospitality with 3*** accommodation, Le Restaurant D'Antibes and a thoroughly modern bar and bistro where all the old values of guest satisfaction, comfort and value for money prevail. We have welcomed both visitors and locals since the 1850s and from its earliest days it has enjoyed a reputation for fine food, drinks of good cheer and indulgent service. Today we pride ourselves on enhancing that tradition. A member of Kinsale's Good Food Circle.

Member of Premier Guesthouses

B&B from €47.50 to €80.00

MICHAEL & ROSE FRAWLEY
PROPRIETORS

10 10

Closed 24 - 25 December

B&B Rates are per Person Sharing per Night incl. Breakfast
Room Rates are per Room per Night

CASTLE HOTEL & LEISURE CENTRE

MAIN STREET,
MACROOM,
CO. CORK
TEL: 026-41074 FAX: 026-41505
EMAIL: castlehotel@eircom.net
WEB: www.castlehotel.ie

HOTEL ★★★   MAP 2 F 3

Experience an intimate welcome to the spectacular South West from the Buckleys, proprietors for 50 years. Exciting new €5 million development features superior bedrooms & suites, "B's" award-winning restaurant (AA Rosette 92-04), "Dan Buckleys" Bar (The Black & White Munster Hotel Bar of The Year 02/03), and "The Ardilaun" Conference and Banqueting Centre . Relax in our extensive health and leisure centre, avail of our Pamper Treatment Room, or enjoy reduced green fees on Macroom's 18 hole golf course and free pitch & putt. RAC ★★★★.

Member of Irish Country Hotels

B&B from €64.50 to €82.50

DON & GERARD BUCKLEY
PROPRIETORS

60 60

Closed 24 - 28 December

B&B Rates are per Person Sharing per Night incl. Breakfast
Room Rates are per Room per Night

COOLCOWER HOUSE

COOLCOWER,
MACROOM,
CO. CORK
TEL: 026-41695 FAX: 026-42119
EMAIL: coolcowerhouse@eircom.net

GUESTHOUSE ★★   MAP 2 F 3

Coolcower House is a large country residence on picturesque grounds. The house is ideally located within easy driving distance of all the tourist attractions in the Cork-Kerry region including Killarney, Kenmare, Kinsale, Blarney and Bantry. Located on the river's edge for coarse fishing and boating. Also outdoor tennis court. The restaurant offers the best of home produce on its à la carte and dinner menus. Fully licensed bar. TVs and tea/coffee making facilities, also direct dial telephones and hairdryers in all bedrooms.

B&B from €35.00 to €40.00

EVELYN CASEY

☺ Midweek specials from €95.00 pps

12 12

Closed 07 December - 07 March

CORTIGAN HOUSE

GOLF COURSE ROAD,
MALLOW,
CO. CORK
TEL: 022-22770 FAX: 022-22732
EMAIL: info@cortiganhouse.com
WEB: www.cortiganhouse.com

GUESTHOUSE ★★★ MAP 2 G 4

A warm welcome awaits you at our 18th century home, overlooking Mallow Castle & River Blackwater, renowned for salmon & trout angling. Just a 25 minute drive from Cork City & Blarney. Cortigan House is ideally based for touring Kinsale, Killarney and South West. We are adjacent to Mallow Golf Club and within easy drive of ten other courses. 5 minutes walk to excellent restaurants, traditional pubs and genealogy centre. Recommended by Le Guide du Routard. AA Selected ♦♦♦♦.

B&B from €35.00 to €45.00

SHEILA & LIONEL BUCKLEY
PROPRIETORS

🛏️ 📞 🖵 T C ❄ ♻ U 🅿 ▪
9   9

IRISH HOTELS FEDERATION

Closed 01 December - 01 March

HIBERNIAN HOTEL AND LEISURE CENTRE

MAIN STREET,
MALLOW,
CO. CORK
TEL: 022-21588 FAX: 022-22632
EMAIL: info@hibhotel.com
WEB: www.hibhotel.com

HOTEL ★★★ MAP 2 G 4

The Hibernian Hotel and Leisure Centre is located at the heart of the Munster region within easy access of Cork, Killarney and Blarney. The hotel has a beautiful Tudor style frontage and the interior is also tastefully decorated and the open fires create a wonderful atmosphere. All rooms are en suite and equipped to modern day standards. A choice of two bars provides excellent variety. Modern leisure facilities are available to guests.

B&B from €60.00 to €78.00

CATHERINE GYVES
GENERAL MANAGER

🛏️ 📞 🖵 T C CM ❄ 🐴 U J
54   54

IRISH HOTELS FEDERATION

Closed 25 December

SPRINGFORT HALL HOTEL

MALLOW,
CO. CORK

TEL: 022-21278 FAX: 022-21557
EMAIL: stay@springfort-hall.com
WEB: www.springfort-hall.com

HOTEL ★★★ MAP 2 G 4

Springfort Hall 18th century Georgian manor house, owned by the Walsh Family. Highly recommended restaurant, fully licensed bar, bedrooms en suite, colour TV and direct outside dial. 6km from Mallow off the Limerick Road, N20. Ideal for touring the South West, Blarney, Killarney, Ring of Kerry. Local amenities, 18-hole golf course, horseriding, angling on River Blackwater. Gulliver Central Reservations.

B&B from €55.00 to €85.00

WALSH FAMILY
PROPRIETORS

☺ Midweek specials from €180.00 pps

🛏️ 📞 🖵 T C CM ❄ U J P S
49   49

Closed 24 December - 26 December

B&B Rates are per Person Sharing per Night incl. Breakfast
Room Rates are per Room per Night

AHERNE'S TOWNHOUSE & SEAFOOD RESTAURANT

163 NORTH MAIN STREET,
YOUGHAL,
CO. CORK
TEL: 024-92424 FAX: 024-93633
EMAIL: ahernes@eircom.net
WEB: www.ahernes.com

GUESTHOUSE ★★★★ MAP 3 J 3

Open turf fires and the warmest of welcomes await you in this family-run guesthouse in the historic walled port of Youghal. Our rooms exude comfort and luxury, stylishly furnished with antiques and paintings. Our restaurant and bar food menus specialise in the freshest of locally landed seafood. Youghal is on the N25, 35 minutes from Cork Airport and is a golfer's paradise. There are 18 golf courses within 1 hour's drive. Find us in Ireland's Blue Book and other leading guides. Old Head of Kinsale 50 minutes drive.

Member of Ireland's Blue Book

B&B from €80.00 to €115.00

THE FITZGIBBON FAMILY

🐴🐾☎️🖥️ⓣ©✎CM♪🅿️🅂🔒alc
13 13

IRISH
HOTELS
FEDERATION

Closed 23 - 29 December

QUALITY HOTEL AND LEISURE CENTRE YOUGHAL

REDBARN,
YOUGHAL,
CO. CORK
TEL: 1850-746 8357 FAX: 021-427 1489
EMAIL: info@qualityhotelyoughal.com
WEB: www.qualityhotelyoughal.com

HOTEL P MAP 3 J 3

Commanding the perfect location on the Blue Flag Beach at Redbarn, Youghal, with breathtaking views of the Atlantic Ocean. Facilities include Club Vitae leisure centre with 4 treatment and therapy rooms, 2 outdoor floodlit pitches, childrens' playground, Lannigans Restaurant and Bar with superb sea views. The resort offers a range of different room types including double en suite, family rooms and apartments with special family facilities. Demand is expected to be especially high for the sea view rooms. Call the hotel direct on 024 93050.

Member of Quality Hotels

B&B from €39.00 to €119.00

RAYMOND KELLEHER
SALES MANAGER

😊 Weekend specials from €90.00 pps

🐴🐾☎️🖥️⬇️Ⓣ🅰️🐾©✎CMCS❖
🔥🖼️🍴♪♫🅿️🅂🔒🐕🐓
24 24

Closed 18 - 27 December

Skibbereen Heritage Centre

The Great Famine Commemoration Exhibition uses today's multimedia to bring this period of Irish history to life.

Lough Hyne Visitor Centre reveals the unique nature of Ireland's first Marine Nature Reserve.

GENEALOGY INFORMATION

All situated in a beautifully restored historic riverside building with features on the Old Gasworks and it's history

Open: 10am to 6pm, with last admission at 5.15pm 7 day opening during high season (Mid May to Mid September)

Tuesday to Saturday Mid March to Mid may and Mid September to the end of October.

Winter opening by appointment

Old Gas Works Building, Upper Bridge Street, Skibbereen, West Cork.

Telephone: 028 40900
info@skibbheritage.com
www.skibbheritage.com

B&B Rates are per Person Sharing per Night incl. Breakfast
Room Rates are per Room per Night

WALTER RALEIGH HOTEL

O'BRIEN PLACE,
YOUGHAL,
CO. CORK

TEL: 024-92011 FAX: 024-93560
EMAIL: walterraleighhotel@eircom.net
WEB: www.walterraleighhotel.com

HOTEL ★★★ MAP 3 J 3

A warm and friendly welcome awaits you at the Walter Raleigh Hotel. Situated overlooking a green park and Youghal's five miles of Blue Flag beaches. The hotel is the perfect base for exploring nationally known attractions such as Fota Wildlife Park, Cobh Heritage Centre and the tranquility of ancient Lismore. Services include 38 en suite bedrooms, the Walter Bar, the Parkview Restaurant, the Adelphi Ballroom and the Blackwater Conference Centre. Golf packages a speciality.

B&B from €55.00 to €79.00

THERESE DONNELLY
MANAGER

☺ Weekend specials from €125.00 pps

38 38

Closed 24 - 25 December

BALLINSKELLIGS INN

BALLINSKELLIGS,
CO. KERRY

TEL: 066-947 9104 FAX: 066-947 9418
EMAIL: ballinskelligsinn@eircom.net
WEB: www.ballinskelligsinn.com

GUESTHOUSE P MAP 1 B 3

The Ballinskelligs Inn has hosted visitors for over 100 years. Located on one of Ireland's premier Blue Flag beaches, awaken to the sound of gentle surf rolling along the beautiful sandy beach at the end of the gardens. Stroll to the castle or perhaps further to the 12th century abbey. Breathtaking scenery will allow you to relax, have a drink and eat at your leisure. So many places to go and see.

B&B from €30.00 to €45.00

RICHARD SWARBRICK
GENERAL MANAGER

14 14

Open All Year

19TH LODGE (THE)

GOLF LINKS ROAD,
BALLYBUNION,
CO. KERRY

TEL: 068-27592 FAX: 068-27830
EMAIL: the19thlodge@eircom.net
WEB: www.the19thlodgeballybunion.com

GUESTHOUSE N MAP 5 D 6

Ballybunion's 19th Lodge is a golfer's paradise. Aptly named for its enviable location, directly opposite Ballybunion's famous links. Good five iron to first tee. Purpose built to suit our golfing clientéle. With stunning views of the course from bedrooms. Enjoy your breakfast in our dining room overlooking the course, while you watch others tee-off. Breakfast menu available from 6 am. Golf storage & drying room & green-fee concessions for our guests. Air-conditioned rooms. Tee-times available for the Old and Cashen Courses.

B&B from €50.00 to €85.00

MARY & JAMES BEASLEY
OWNERS

12 12

Open All Year

B&B Rates are per Person Sharing per Night incl. Breakfast
Room Rates are per Room per Night

CASHEN COURSE HOUSE

GOLF LINKS,
BALLYBUNION,
CO. KERRY

TEL: 068-27351 FAX: 068-28934
EMAIL: golfstay@eircom.net
WEB: www.playballybunion.com

GUESTHOUSE ★★★★ MAP 5 D 6

Welcome to our luxury guesthouse overlooking Ballybunion's famous golf courses with panoramic views of golf links, Cashen River & countryside. After a day's golf, relax in our magnificent rooms & enjoy a jacuzzi bath in one of our luxurious bathrooms. Air-con, DD phone, computer access, trouser press. Small groups welcome for conference/ golfing breaks. Beside Clubhouse. Private parking for buses & cars. Concession green fees October to June incl. Golf packages for Ballybunion Old Course & Cashen Course. Drying room. AA ◆◆◆◆◆.

B&B from €50.00 to €90.00

DEIRDRE O'BRIEN
OWNER/MANAGER

🏨 🦮 ☎ 🖵 T C 🖊 C M ☼ ∪ ∫ P S 🌣 ▪
9 9
inet 🐎

HOTELS
IRISH FEDERATION

Closed 01 November - 01 March

EAGLE LODGE

BALLYBUNION,
CO. KERRY

TEL: 068-27224

GUESTHOUSE U MAP 5 D 6

Owner managed, delightful guesthouse situated in town centre. All bedrooms with bathrooms and central heating throughout. A beautiful lounge and private car park for guests. Local amenities include two championship golf courses, sea fishing, tennis, pitch and putt, swimming and boating. Extra value reduced green fees at Ballybunion Golf Club. Cliff walks and surfing also available.

B&B from €35.00 to €60.00

MILDRED GLEASURE

🏨 🦮 ☎ 🖵 T C C M ∫ P S
8 8

HOTELS
IRISH FEDERATION

Open All Year

HARTY COSTELLO TOWN HOUSE

MAIN STREET,
BALLYBUNION,
CO. KERRY

TEL: 068-27129 FAX: 068-27489
EMAIL: hartycostello@eircom.net
WEB: www.hartycostello.com

GUESTHOUSE ★★★★ MAP 5 D 6

Four star townhouse with traditional bar & seafood restaurant, in the centre of Ballybunion just a short walk from the beach. The en suite bedrooms are spacious & have been refurbished in a refreshing modern style with satellite TV & direct dial phone. The townhouse has an informal atmosphere & is a charming base from which to enjoy links golf & the beauty of Kerry. Local amenities, two championship golf links, cliff walks, hot seaweed baths, fishing, four golden beaches, bird watching & pony trekking. Tee times available for Old Course & Cashen.

Member of Ballybunion Marketing Group

B&B from €60.00 to €85.00

DAVNET & JACKIE HOURIGAN
OWNERS

 Weekend specials from €130.00 pps

🏨 🦮 ☎ 🖵 T ∪ J S 🔒 alc ▪
8 8

HOTELS
IRISH FEDERATION

Closed 30 October - 01 April

B&B Rates are per Person Sharing per Night incl. Breakfast
Room Rates are per Room per Night

IRAGH TI CONNOR

MAIN STREET,
BALLYBUNION,
CO. KERRY
TEL: 068-27112 FAX: 068-27787
EMAIL: iraghticonnor@eircom.net
WEB: www.golfballybunion.com

GUESTHOUSE P   MAP 5 D 6

Iragh Ti Connor is a 19th century luxury country house recently completely restored. It contains 14 spacious bedrooms & 3 mini-suites, all filled with antique furniture, power showers, DD phone, satellite TV. Same day laundry facilities. The restaurant speciality is lobster straight from the sea tank. Full bar facilities offering guests a choice of mingling with the locals or relaxing by the fireside in the private drawing room. Tee times can be reserved on request. Ideal base for golfers with easy access to Lahinch, Doonbeg, Tralee, Waterville & Dooks Golf Club.

B&B from € 95.00 to € 140.00

JOAN & JOHN O'CONNOR
PROPRIETORS

🛏🏌☎🖥Ⓣ C M✲♪🅟♿aⓒ 🛢
17 17

IRISH HOTELS FEDERATION

Closed 01 December - 01 Feburary

MANOR INN

DOON EAST,
BALLYBUNION,
CO. KERRY
TEL: 068-27577 FAX: 068-27757
EMAIL: drao@eircom.net
WEB: www.ballybunion-manorinn.com

GUESTHOUSE ★★★   MAP 5 D 6

Manor Inn has a lot to offer holiday-makers, especially golfers who will appreciate its tranquility & high standard. The purpose built guest house at the mouth of the River Shannon, caters for nature lovers, with a veiw of the Atlantic Ocean from most of the rooms. It is .5km away from the natural habitat of the dolphins in the Atlantic Ocean. Bedrooms all en suite, TV, alarm radio, DD phone, computer port, hairdryer, tea/coffee facilities, central heating. Car parking. Tee times can be reserved. Every aspect of your golfing vacation is catered for.

B&B from € 33.00 to € 58.00

RAO
PROPRIETOR

🛏🏌☎🖥Ⓣ C✲♿🅟♿ inet
8   8

Closed 15 November - 14 March

MARINE LINKS HOTEL

SANDHILL ROAD,
BALLYBUNION,
CO. KERRY
TEL: 068-27139 FAX: 068-27666
EMAIL: info@marinelinkshotel.com
WEB: www.marinelinkshotel.com

HOTEL ★★   MAP 5 D 6

Overlooking the mouth of the River Shannon and the Atlantic Ocean, a warm welcome awaits you at the Marine Links Hotel from the Nagle Family and all the staff. Our hotel is committed to providing excellent food and good service and we have been awarded the RAC Merit Award for hospitality for the past number of years.

B&B from € 40.00 to € 65.00

DEREK NAGLE
PROPRIETOR/GENERAL MANAGER

🛏🏌☎🖥Ⓣ C♿CM♪🎵🅟Ⓢ♿aⓒ
11 11
♿🐕

IRISH HOTELS FEDERATION

Closed 31 October - 01 April

B&B Rates are per Person Sharing per Night incl. Breakfast
Room Rates are per Room per Night

TEACH DE BROC

**LINK ROAD,
BALLYBUNION,
CO. KERRY**

TEL: 068-27581 FAX: 068-27919
EMAIL: teachdebroc@eircom.net
WEB: www.ballybuniongolf.com

GUESTHOUSE ★★★★ MAP 5 D 6

Tea to tee in 2 minutes is a reality when you stay at the 4**** accommodation offered at Teach de Broc. With its enviable location directly opposite the entrance gates to Ballybunion Golf Club, you can enjoy the personal attention that is synonymous with this golfer's haven. Tee times are available through Teach de Broc which is an ideal base for golfers with ease of access to Lahinch, Doonbeg and Tralee. Visit our website at www.ballybuniongolf.com

B&B from €60.00 to €85.00

SEAMUS AND AOIFE BROCK
OWNERS

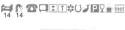
14 14

Closed 15 December - 15 March

DERRYNANE HOTEL

**CAHERDANIEL,
RING OF KERRY,
CO. KERRY**

TEL: 066-947 5136 FAX: 066-947 5160
EMAIL: info@derrynane.com
WEB: www.derrynane.com

HOTEL ★★★ MAP 1 C 2

Amidst the most spectacular scenery in Ireland, halfway round the famous Ring of Kerry (on the N70) lies the Derrynane Hotel . 70 en suite bedrooms. Facilities include 15m outdoor heated pool, steamroom, sauna, gym, luxurious seaweed bath suite, childrens' games room, tennis court & gardens. We are surrounded by beautiful beaches and hills, lovely walks and Derrynane House and National Park. Deep sea angling, lake fishing, golf, horseriding, seasports, boat trips to Skellig Rock all within a short distance. Newly published hotel walking guide with maps to the area.

B&B from €75.00 to €95.00

MARY O'CONNOR
MANAGER/DIRECTOR

Weekend specials from €159.00 pps

70 70

Closed 03 October - 15 April

SCARRIFF INN

**CAHERDANIEL,
CO. KERRY**

TEL: 066-947 5132 FAX: 066-947 5425
EMAIL: scarriff1@aol.com
WEB: www.caherdaniel.net

GUESTHOUSE ★★ MAP 1 C 3

This family-run guesthouse overlooks the best view in Ireland, with majestic views of Derrynane, Kenmare and Bantry Bay, situated halfway round the Ring of Kerry. All our rooms have sea views. Dine in our seafood restaurant and enjoy outstanding cuisine as recommended by Sir Andrew Lloyd Webber or relax in our Vista Bar and enjoy scenery and ambience. The area is varied in activities with, the Kerry Way and several beautiful beaches within walking distance. Day trips to Skellig Rocks.

B&B from €35.00 to €50.00

KATIE O'CARROLL
PROPRIETOR

6 6

Closed 01 November - 15 March

B&B Rates are per Person Sharing per Night incl. Breakfast
Room Rates are per Room per Night

ARD-NA-SIDHE

CARAGH LAKE,
KILLORGLIN,
CO. KERRY

TEL: 066-976 9105 FAX: 066-976 9282
EMAIL: sales@kih.liebherr.com
WEB: www.killarneyhotels.ie

HOTEL ★★★★ MAP 1 D 4

18 bedroom 4★★★★ de luxe Victorian mansion delightfully located in its own park on Caragh Lake. Tastefully furnished with antiques and open fireplaces. Luxurious lounges and restaurant. Free boating, fishing and facilities of sister hotels - Hotel Europe and Hotel Dunloe Castle - available to guests. 10 major golf courses nearby. Special green fees. Central Reservations Tel: 064-71350 Fax: 064-37900.

Member of Killarney Hotels Ltd

B&B from €75.00 to €105.00

ADRIAN O'SULLIVAN

☺ Weekend specials from €200.00 pps

18 18

Closed 03 October - 01 May

CARAGH LODGE

CARAGH LAKE,
CO. KERRY

TEL: 066-976 9115 FAX: 066-976 9316
EMAIL: caraghl@iol.ie
WEB: www.caraghlodge.com

GUESTHOUSE ★★★★ MAP 1 D 4

A Victorian fishing lodge standing in 7.5 acres of parkland containing many rare and subtropical trees and shrubs. Winner of the National Garden Award. The gardens sweep down to Caragh Lake, ideal for trout fishing. The lounges and dining room are very comfortably furnished and overlook the gardens and lake. Excellent cuisine includes local lamb and wild salmon. Golf and beaches within 5 minutes. RAC Gold Ribbon 2000, 2001, 2002 and 2003.

Member of Ireland's Blue Book

B&B from €92.50 to €162.50

MARY GAUNT
OWNER

15 15

Closed 13 October - 23 April

CARRIG HOUSE

CARAGH LAKE,
KILLORGLIN,
CO. KERRY

TEL: 066-976 9100 FAX: 066-976 9166
EMAIL: info@carrighouse.com
WEB: www.carrighouse.com

GUESTHOUSE ★★★★ MAP 1 D 4

Charming Victorian Manor on acres of woodlands & gardens (935 plant species) running down to the lake shore. Furnished in period style with antique furniture. Central to 12 superb golf courses, fishing, shooting, hillwalking or just lazing by the fireside with a good book. Critically acclaimed restaurant (open to non residents). Ideal for touring the Ring of Kerry, Dingle & Killarney. Recommended by Bridgestone Guide, 100 Best Places to Stay in Ireland 2004, Georgina Campbell's Jameson Guide, AA Guest Accommodation of the Year Ireland 2003/4.

B&B from €70.00 to €135.00

FRANK & MARY SLATTERY
HOSTS/PROPRIETORS

☺ Special packages available
on request

16 16

Closed 01 December - 01 March

B&B Rates are per Person Sharing per Night incl. Breakfast
Room Rates are per Room per Night

CRUTCH'S HILLVILLE HOUSE HOTEL

CONOR PASS ROAD, CASTLEGREGORY,
DINGLE PENINSULA,
CO. KERRY
TEL: 066-713 8118 FAX: 066-713 8159
EMAIL: macshome@iol.ie
WEB: www.dinglehotel.com

HOTEL ★★ MAP 1 C 5

Step back in time at this delightful country house hotel situated near Fermoyle Beach on the scenic Dingle Peninsula. The main house has been upgraded and most of our bedrooms have 4 poster beds, some with sea views. All rooms with private bathrooms. We have a number of ground floor rooms offering easy access. Our restaurant offers a varied choice using local fresh produce, special diets catered for upon request.

Member of Irish Country Hotels

B&B from €45.00 to €75.00

RON & SANDRA
PROPRIETORS

3 Dinners & 3 B&B from €225.00 pps

19 19

Open All Year

HARBOUR HOUSE & LEISURE CENTRE

SCRAGGANE PIER,
CASTLEGREGORY,
CO. KERRY
TEL: 066-713 9292 FAX: 066-713 9557
EMAIL: stay@iol.ie
WEB: www.maharees.ie

GUESTHOUSE N MAP 1 C 5

The family-run Harbour House is superbly located on the tip of the Maharees Peninsula and has its own indoor heated swimming pool, sauna and gym. Its Islands Restaurant has panoramic views of the breathtaking scenery of the Maharees Islands and offers an excellent range of locally caught seafood, prime steak, meat and vegetarian dishes. If you want tranquillity, serenity, charm and true Irish hospitality, this is the place for you. Local amenities include golf, walking, scuba diving, windsurfing, surfing, fishing, horseriding, cycling etc.

B&B from €32.00 to €35.00

RONNIE & PAT FITZGIBBON

Special offers available

15 15

IRISH
HOTELS
FEDERATION

Closed 15 December - 03 January

O'CONNOR'S GUESTHOUSE

CLOGHANE,
DINGLE PENINSULA,
CO. KERRY
TEL: 066-713 8113 FAX: 066-713 8270
EMAIL: oconnorsguesthouse@eircom.net
WEB: www.cloghane.com

GUESTHOUSE ★★ MAP 1 B 5

A long established, spacious country home with spectacular views of sea and mountains, overlooking Brandon Bay and within easy reach of Dingle on the Dingle Way. Private car park, guest lounge, open fire, home cooked meals, pub and a warm welcome are just some of the things awaiting our guests.

B&B from €30.00 to €60.00

MICHEAL & ELIZABETH O'DOWD
OWNERS

Weekly partial board from €350.00 pps

9 9

IRISH
HOTELS
FEDERATION

Closed 01 November - 28 February

B&B Rates are per Person Sharing per Night incl. Breakfast
Room Rates are per Room per Night

ALPINE HOUSE

MAIL ROAD,
DINGLE,
CO. KERRY

TEL: 066-915 1250 FAX: 066-915 1966
EMAIL: alpinedingle@eircom.net
WEB: www.alpineguesthouse.com

GUESTHOUSE ★★★ MAP 1 B 4

Superb guesthouse run by the O'Shea Family. AA ◆◆◆◆ and RAC ◆◆◆◆ highly acclaimed. Elegant en suite bedrooms with TV, direct dial phone, hairdryers, central heating and tea/coffee facilities. Spacious dining room with choice of breakfast. Delightful guest lounge. 2 minutes walk to town centre, restaurants, harbour and bus stop. Local amenities include Slea Head Drive and Blasket Islands, also pony trekking, angling and boat trips to Fungi the dolphin. Non-smoking premises.

B&B from €33.00 to €47.50

PAUL O'SHEA
MANAGER

🐴🛏☎️🖥TC❄️⏱♪PS🔋
10 10

HOTELS

Open All Year

AN BOTHAR GUESTHOUSE, RESTAURANT & BAR

CUAS, BALLYDAVID,
DINGLE PENINSULA, TRALEE,
CO KERRY

TEL: 066-915 5342
EMAIL: botharpub@eircom.net
WEB: www.botharpub.com

GUESTHOUSE N MAP 1 B 5

An Bothar Guesthouse Restaurant and Bar is a family-run guesthouse and pub situated at the foot of Mount Brandon just 7 miles from Dingle. An ideal base for a walking holiday close to beaches fishing and golf. In the heart of the Gaeltacht, gaelic is the first language of the house. À la carte menu and bar food available during season, March to September. Meals arranged by request out of season. Home baking and local produce on menu.

B&B from €35.00 to €35.00

MAURICE WALSH
OWNER

🐴🛏☎️🖥CCM❄️♪♫PS🔋🔋
7 7
🐕

Closed 24 - 25 December

BAMBURY'S GUEST HOUSE

MAIL ROAD,
DINGLE,
CO. KERRY

TEL: 066-915 1244 FAX: 066-915 1786
EMAIL: info@bamburysguesthouse.com
WEB: www.bamburysguesthouse.com

GUESTHOUSE ★★★ MAP 1 B 4

AA Selected ◆◆◆◆, new house, excellent location, 2 minutes walk to town centre. Offering peaceful accommodation in spacious, double, twin or triple rooms all en suite with direct dial telephone and satellite TV. Attractive guest lounge to relax in. Private car parking, choice of breakfast in spacious dining room. Local attractions, Dingle Peninsula, horseriding, angling and golf on local 18 hole golf links. Reduced green fees can be arranged. Listed in all leading guides.

B&B from €35.00 to €60.00

BERNIE BAMBURY
PROPRIETOR

🐴🛏☎️🖥U P
12 12

HOTELS

Open All Year

B&B Rates are per Person Sharing per Night incl. Breakfast
Room Rates are per Room per Night

BARR NA SRAIDE INN

UPPER MAIN STREET,
DINGLE,
CO. KERRY
TEL: 066-915 1331 FAX: 066-915 1446
EMAIL: barrnasraide@eircom.net
WEB: www.barrnasraide.com

GUESTHOUSE ★★★ MAP 1 B 4

Family-run guesthouse and bar. Located in the town centre. The Barr na Sraide Inn has been recently refurbished to a very high standard. An extensive menu awaits our guests for breakfast. End each day with a relaxing drink in our comfortable bar amongst the locals. Private enclosed car park. Ideal base for your stay in the South West. Golf, fishing, sailing, cycling, horseriding and trips to Fungi the dolphin available nearby.

B&B from €40.00 to €60.00

PATRICIA GEANEY

22 22

Closed 13 - 26 December

BOLAND'S GUESTHOUSE

UPPER MAIN STREET,
DINGLE,
CO. KERRY
TEL: 066-915 1426
EMAIL: bolanddingle@eircom.net
WEB: www.dingle-region.com/bolands.htm

GUESTHOUSE ★★ MAP 1 B 4

Welcome to Boland's purpose built guest house situated on Upper Main Street overlooking Dingle Bay. All bedrooms en suite with direct dial phone, TV, hairdryers, tea/coffee making facilities. Full breakfast menu in our conservatory dining room. Relax in our guest lounge.

B&B from €30.00 to €45.00

BREDA BOLAND
OWNER

8 8

Closed 20 - 31 December

CASTLEWOOD HOUSE

THE WOOD,
DINGLE,
CO. KERRY
TEL: 066-915 2788
EMAIL: castlewoodhouse@eircom.net
WEB: www.castlewooddingle.com

UNDER CONSTRUCTION · OPENING APRIL 2005

GUESTHOUSE P MAP 1 B 4

At Castlewood House a warm welcome awaits you. Luxurious new guesthouse located on the shores of Dingle Bay offering de luxe and superior rooms. All rooms are spacious and individually styled to a very high standard. Facilities include en suite bathrooms, pressure showers, TV, DD phone, internet access and hospitality tray. Elevator access. Speciality breakfast served in our dining room with its collection of Irish art, or relax in our drawing room with spectacular views of Dingle Bay.

B&B from €50.00 to €75.00

HELEN WOODS HEATON & BRIAN HEATON

12 12

Closed 10 January - 14 February

B&B Rates are per Person Sharing per Night incl. Breakfast
Room Rates are per Room per Night

CLEEVAUN COUNTRY HOUSE

LADYS CROSS,
MILLTOWN, DINGLE,
CO. KERRY

TEL: 066-915 1108 FAX: 066-915 2228
EMAIL: cleevaun@iol.ie
WEB: www.cleevaun.com

GUESTHOUSE ★★★ MAP 1 B 4

Cleevaun AA/RAC ◆◆◆◆. Galtee Regional Breakfast Winner. Cleevaun is set in landscaped gardens, beautifully perched overlooking Dingle Bay. All rooms with private bathrooms, satellite TV, DD phones, hairdryer, tea/coffee facilities. Relax and enjoy the magnificent views of Dingle Bay from our lounge or breakfast room while you choose from our award-winning breakfast menu. Cleevaun is often described as an oasis of peace and tranquillity. Recommend by Karen Browne's, AA/RAC etc. Local amenities 18 hole golf links, angling, pony trekking.

B&B from €40.00 to €50.00

CHARLOTTE CLUSKEY
HOST

🐾🔥☎️🖥️✳️⛵️🎵🅿️🆂️🔌
8   8

HOTELS

Closed 15 November - 15 March

COASTLINE GUESTHOUSE

THE WOOD,
DINGLE,
CO. KERRY

TEL: 066-915 2494 FAX: 066-915 2493
EMAIL: coastlinedingle@eircom.net
WEB: www.coastlinedingle.com

GUESTHOUSE ★★★ MAP 1 B 4

Beautiful new guesthouse on the water's edge of Dingle Bay. All rooms are en suite with direct dial phone, TV, hairdryer, tea/coffee making facilities and all have panoramic views of the harbour. Ground floor rooms available. Enjoy our excellent breakfast and relax in our sitting room and watch the local fishing fleet return with their catch. Private car park. 5 minute walk to town centre. Ideal base to enjoy all Dingle has to offer - excellent restaurants and pubs.

B&B from €32.00 to €45.00

VIVIENNE O'SHEA
PROPRIETOR

🔥☎️🖥️🅣️✳️🎵🅿️🆂️🔌
7   7

HOTELS

Closed 18 November - 10 February

DINGLE BAY HOTEL

STRAND STREET,
DINGLE,
CO KERRY

TEL: 066-915 1231 FAX: 066-915 2740
EMAIL: info@dinglebayhotel.com
WEB: www.dinglebayhotel.com

HOTEL P MAP 1 B 4

Newly built luxury hotel situated by the pier/marina in Dingle town. The hotel has been designed to the highest standards, from its stylish bar to its tastefully furnished bedrooms. Paudie's Bar, exceptional food, outstanding service and friendly atmosphere. Long's Restaurant offers a superb à la carte menu with sea food a speciality. Guests receive a discount at the nearby Harmony Health Club, featuring gym, pool, sauna and steamroom.

B&B from €60.00 to €105.00

KATHLEEN SHEEHY
GENERAL MANAGER

😊 Midweek specials available

🐾🔥☎️🖥️🅘️🅒️CM🎵🅿️🆘️🔌
25   25
🔌 🐕

Closed 18 - 26 December

B&B Rates are per Person Sharing per Night incl. Breakfast
Room Rates are per Room per Night

DINGLE BENNERS HOTEL

MAIN STREET,
DINGLE,
CO. KERRY

TEL: 066-915 1638 FAX: 066-915 1412
EMAIL: info@dinglebenners.com
WEB: www.dinglebenners.com

HOTEL U   MAP 1 B 4

Located in the heart of Dingle Town, the hotel is favoured for its old world charm and style. Luxuriously appointed bedrooms provide an intimate cosy atmosphere complemented with authentic Irish antique furnishings. Mrs Benner's Bar & Lounges will captivate you on arrival, have a warm friendly welcome and will fill you with a sense of yesteryear. Special weekend and midweek packages available.

Member of Manor House Hotels

B&B from €79.00 to €125.00

MUIREANN NIC GIOLLA RUAIDH
GENERAL MANAGER

Midweek specials from €132.00 pps

52   52

Closed 24 - 26 December

DINGLE SKELLIG HOTEL

DINGLE,
CO. KERRY

TEL: 066-915 0200 FAX: 066-915 1501
EMAIL: reservations@dingleskellig.com
WEB: www.dingleskellig.com

HOTEL ★★★★   MAP 1 B 4

Renowned hotel situated on the beautiful harbour of Dingle Bay. Luxurious leisure club & pool. Fungi Kids Club & Creche on weekends & holidays. Excellent cuisine in our Coastguard Restaurant. Established conference & banqueting centre with stunning views for up to 250 people. New Peninsula Spa features Yon-Ka face & body treatments, hydrotherapy, wraps, hot stone massage, holistic & sports massage, tanning & beauty. Relaxation suite, outdoor hot tub with stunning views, sauna and steamroom.

B&B from €60.00 to €115.00

GRAHAM FITZGERALD
GENERAL MANAGER

Weekend specials from €140.00 pps

110   110

Closed 19 - 27 December

DOYLES SEAFOOD BAR & TOWN HOUSE

JOHN STREET,
DINGLE,
CO. KERRY

TEL: 066-915 1174 FAX: 066-915 1816
EMAIL: cdoyles@iol.ie
WEB: www.doylesofdingle.com

GUESTHOUSE ★★★★   MAP 1 B 4

The Town House has some of the most delightful rooms in Dingle. All 8 spacious rooms with full bathrooms have recently been refurbished in a most comfortable style. Satellite TV, phone, trouser press/iron, tea/coffee facilities. The world renowned restaurant has an old range & sugán chairs. Natural stone & wood combination gives Doyles a cosy country atmosphere. The menu consists only of fresh food and is chosen on a daily basis from the fish landed on Dingle boats. AA♦♦♦♦ RAC♦♦♦♦ Les Routiers "Restaurant of the Year" 2002.

B&B from €45.00 to €75.00

SEÁN CLUSKEY
HOST

8   8

Closed 15 November - 14 February

B&B Rates are per Person Sharing per Night incl. Breakfast
Room Rates are per Room per Night

EMLAGH HOUSE

DINGLE,
CO. KERRY

TEL: 066-915 2345 FAX: 066-915 2369
EMAIL: info@emlaghhouse.com
WEB: www.emlaghhouse.com

GUESTHOUSE ★★★★ MAP 1 B 4

Welcome to Emlagh House a Georgian style family-run home, overlooking Dingle Harbour. Relax in our calm and gracious drawing room and library. Spacious individually themed rooms offer every modern convenience from CD players to air conditioning. A short stroll will take you to Dingle Town centre. AA ◆◆◆◆◆, RAC Sparkling Diamond Award, Warm Welcome and Little Gem Awards. Bridgestone Top 100.

B&B from €80.00 to €130.00

GRAINNE & MARION KAVANAGH

10 10

Closed 01 November - 01 March

GORMAN'S CLIFFTOP HOUSE AND RESTAURANT

GLAISE BHEAG, BALLYDAVID,
DINGLE PENINSULA, TRALEE,
CO. KERRY

TEL: 066-915 5162 FAX: 066-915 5003
EMAIL: info@gormans-clifftophouse.com
WEB: www.gormans-clifftophouse.com

GUESTHOUSE ★★★★ MAP 1 B 5

A welcoming cliff-top refuge on the western edge of the Dingle Peninsula. All rooms pay homage to the landscape, offering breathtaking views of the ocean and mountains. Our emphasis is on comfort, mini suites boasting king size beds and jacuzzi baths. Downstairs guests can gather around the fire to read or chat, dine handsomely in our fully licensed restaurant. AA ◆◆◆◆ premier select. Les Routiers "Hidden Gem Ireland" 2001. Georgina Campbell 'Guesthouse of the Year' 2002 (Jameson Guide) - Les Routiers 'Hotel of the Year 2001'.

B&B from €50.00 to €80.00

VINCENT AND SILE O'GORMAIN
PROPRIETORS

9 9

Closed 24 - 26 December

GREENMOUNT HOUSE

UPPER JOHN STREET,
DINGLE,
CO. KERRY

TEL: 066-915 1414 FAX: 066-915 1974
EMAIL: greenmounthouse@eircom.net
WEB: www.greenmount-house.com

GUESTHOUSE ★★★★ MAP 1 B 4

Greenmount House is the proud recipient of the 1997 RAC Guest House of the Year for Ireland. A charming 4**** country house yet centrally located. Spacious lounges to relax in and take advantage of its magnificent scenic location overlooking Dingle Town & Harbour. Each bedroom has private bathroom, TV / radio & direct dial phone. Award-winning buffet breakfasts served in conservatory with commanding views of Dingle. Luxurious, peaceful retreat. Recognised by all leading guides.

B&B from €50.00 to €75.00

JOHN & MARY CURRAN
OWNERS

9 9

Closed 10 December - 04 January

B&B Rates are per Person Sharing per Night incl. Breakfast
Room Rates are per Room per Night

HEATON'S GUESTHOUSE

THE WOOD,
DINGLE,
CO. KERRY
TEL: 066-915 2288 FAX: 066-915 2324
EMAIL: heatons@iol.ie
WEB: www.heatonsdingle.com

GUESTHOUSE ★★★★ MAP 1 B 4

Superb 4**** family-run guesthouse situated on the shore of Dingle Bay with spectacular views, 5 minutes walk from the town. All rooms are en suite (pressure shower and bath), with TV, DD phone and tea/coffee welcome tray. Breakfast is our speciality. Luxury junior suites and de luxe rooms recently opened (rates available on request). Local amenities include golf, sailing, fishing, surfing, cycling, walking, horseriding and the renowned gourmet restaurants. Awarded Guest House of the Year for Ireland 2002 - Les Routiers.

B&B from €43.00 to €64.00

NUALA & CAMERON HEATON
PROPRIETORS

16 16

IRISH HOTELS FEDERATION

Closed 02 January - 04 February

HILLGROVE INN

SPA ROAD,
DINGLE,
CO. KERRY
TEL: 066-915 1131 FAX: 066-915 1441
EMAIL: hillgrovedingle@eircom.net
WEB: www.hillgroveinn.com

GUESTHOUSE N MAP 1 B 4

The Hillgrove is family owned and managed. Located 5 minutes walk from Dingle's main street. Our rooms are all en suite, with DD phone, TV and tea/coffee making facilities. Our private lounge is the ideal place to relax with full bar facilities available. The Hillgrove offers a perfect combination of professional service with cheerful and helpful staff. We will ensure that your stay is the highlight of your visit to our beautiful town.

B&B from €35.00 to €70.00

SANDRA KENNEDY

☺ Midweek specials from €99.00 pps

12 12

IRISH HOTELS FEDERATION

Closed 01 October - 01 May

MAINSTAY GUESTHOUSE (THE)

DYKEGATE STREET,
DINGLE,
CO. KERRY
TEL: 066-915 1598 FAX: 066-915 2376
EMAIL: info@mainstaydingle.com
WEB: www.mainstaydingle.com

GUESTHOUSE U MAP 1 B 4

Located on a quiet street in the heart of Dingle this is a charming guesthouse of character and distinction. All rooms are en suite with satellite TV, in-room coffee and tea, hairdryer and direct telephone. Breakfast here is an indulgence, served in our well appointed open hearth dining room. Our landscaped garden and cozy lounge provide a restful retreat after a day's adventure in Kerry.

B&B from €38.00 to €48.00

RUTH & GUS CERO
PROPRIETORS

14 14

IRISH HOTELS FEDERATION

Open All Year

B&B Rates are per Person Sharing per Night incl. Breakfast
Room Rates are per Room per Night

MILLTOWN HOUSE

DINGLE,
CO. KERRY

TEL: 066-915 1372 FAX: 066-915 1095
EMAIL: info@milltownhousedingle.com
WEB: http://milltownhousedingle.com/

GUESTHOUSE ★★★★ MAP 1 B 4

Award-winning family-run Milltown House is ideally located overlooking Dingle Bay and Town from our private gardens. All rooms which retain the character of the 130 year old house are en suite, have tea/coffee making facilities, direct dial phone, TV, trouser press, hairdryer and safety deposit box. The house was home to Robert Mitchum during the making of David Lean's epic movie "Ryan's Daughter". Assistance in planning your day. One of the most scenic and quiet locations in the town area, less than 15 minutes walk or 2 minutes drive!

B&B from €55.00 to €75.00

TARA KERRY

10 10

Closed 30 October - 25 April

OLD PIER, RESTAURANT AND GUESTHOUSE

AN FHEOTHANACH,
BALLYDAVID, DINGLE,
CO. KERRY

TEL: 066-915 5242
EMAIL: info@oldpier.com
WEB: www.oldpier.com

GUESTHOUSE ★★★ MAP 1 B 4

Situated in the heart of the West Kerry Gaeltacht on the Dingle Peninsula overlooking beautiful Smerwick Harbour and the Atlantic Ocean. This family-run establishment offers 3*** accommodation with beautiful sea and mountain vistas. The Old Pier Restaurant offers a broad range of locally caught seafood, prime steak and meat dishes. Adjacent activities include 18 hole golf course, deep sea angling, mountain walking and archaeology sites. A warm welcome awaits you.

B&B from €50.00 to €50.00

JACQUI & PÁDRAIG O CONNOR

6   6

Open All Year

PAX HOUSE

UPPER JOHN STREET,
DINGLE,
CO. KERRY

TEL: 066-915 1518 FAX: 066-915 2461
EMAIL: paxhouse@iol.ie
WEB: www.pax-house.com

GUESTHOUSE ★★★★ MAP 1 B 4

Superb 4**** AA 5♦♦♦♦♦ family-run guesthouse. Voted one of the top ten places to stay in Ireland. Pax House has undeniably one of the most spectacular views in the peninsula. All rooms including suites (rates on request) are beautifully appointed & include a fridge & safe. Enjoy our award-winning breakfast we offer guests. Charm, tranquillity & unequaled hospitality. Sit on the balcony & watch the activity in the bay & a sighting of "Fungi" the dolphin. Golf nearby reduced fees & tee times arranged. Pax House is 1km from Dingle Town.

Member of Premier Guesthouses

B&B from €50.00 to €70.00

RON & JOAN BROSNAN WRIGHT
OWNERS

12 12

Closed 01 November - 01 April

B&B Rates are per Person Sharing per Night incl. Breakfast
Room Rates are per Room per Night

EVISTON HOUSE HOTEL

NEW STREET,
KILLARNEY,
CO. KERRY

TEL: 064-31640 FAX: 064-33685
EMAIL: evishtl@eircom.net
WEB: www.killarney-hotel.com

HOTEL ★★★ MAP 2 E 4

Located in the town centre yet only minutes from the National Park and championship golf. Our luxurious bedrooms are newly decorated with all modern amenities. Dining options feature the Colleen Bawn restaurant for candlelit dinner and the luxurious Ivy Lounge for light snacks. Alternatively, dine in our famous pub "The Danny Mann" while enjoying the best in traditional music and a lively atmosphere. For the healthy minded try our new fitness suite with sauna and hot tub. A warm welcome awaits you at the Eviston House.

Member of Best Western Hotels

B&B from €39.00 to €79.00

EDWARD EVISTON
PROPRIETOR

Weekend specials from €129.00 pps

75 75

Open All Year

B&B Rates are per Person Sharing per Night incl. Breakfast
Room Rates are per Room per Night

FAILTE HOTEL

COLLEGE STREET,
KILLARNEY,
CO. KERRY

TEL: 064-33404 FAX: 064-36599
EMAIL: failtehotel@eircom.net

HOTEL ★★ MAP 2 E 4

The Failte Hotel, furbished to a very high standard, is owned and managed by the O'Callaghan family. It is internationally known for its high standard of cuisine. Paudie supervises the award winning bar. It is situated in the town centre, adjacent to railway station, new factory outlet, shopping complex. Also close by are many local cabarets & night clubs. Local amenities include golfing, fishing, walking.

B&B from €45.00 to €75.00

DERMOT & EILEEN O'CALLAGHAN
PROPRIETORS

15 15

Closed 24 - 26 December

FAIRVIEW GUESTHOUSE

MICHAEL COLLINS PLACE,
COLLEGE STREET, KILLARNEY,
CO. KERRY
TEL: 064-34164 FAX: 064-71777
EMAIL: info@fairviewkillarney.com
WEB: www.fairviewkillarney.com

GUESTHOUSE ★★★★ MAP 2 E 4

This purpose built 4 star guesthouse stands proudly in the heart of Killarney, yet in a quiet location. Convenient to bus & rail stations. Parking, spacious rooms. Optional jacuzzi suites, & all modern amenities incl. lift & wheelchair facilities. A deluxe base from which to tour, golf or socialise. Privately owned & managed we ensure a memorable & exceptional stay. Awards include AA & RAC 5 ◆◆◆◆◆, sparkling diamond & Warm Welcome Award, Killarney Best New Development, & the prestigious Little Gem 2004/2005 Award.

B&B from €39.00 to €65.00

JAMES & SHELLEY O' NEILL
PROPRIETORS

18 18

HOTELS

Closed 24 - 25 December

FOLEY'S TOWNHOUSE

23 HIGH STREET,
KILLARNEY,
CO. KERRY
TEL: 064-31217 FAX: 064-34683
EMAIL: info@foleystownhouse.com
WEB: www.foleystownhouse.com

GUESTHOUSE ★★★★ MAP 2 E 4

Originally a 19th C Coaching Inn, this old house has hosted generations of travellers. Newly refurbished, this is a 4★★★★ family-run town centre guesthouse. Luxury bedrooms are individually designed for comfort with every modern amenity, including lift wheelchair access & 2 de luxe suites. Downstairs is our award-winning seafood & steak restaurant. Chef/Owner Carol provides meals from fresh local produce. Choose from approx 300 wines. Personal supervision. Private parking. Awarded AA ◆◆◆◆◆, RAC Highly Acclaimed.

B&B from €58.75 to €65.00

CAROL HARTNETT
PROPRIETOR

28 28

Inet

HOTELS

Closed 15 November - 01 March

FRIARS GLEN

MANGERTON ROAD,
MUCKROSS, KILLARNEY,
CO. KERRY
TEL: 064-37500 FAX: 064-37388
EMAIL: fullerj@indigo.ie
WEB: www.friarsglen.ie

GUESTHOUSE ★★★★ MAP 2 E 4

This 4★★★★ guesthouse, built in a traditional style, offers a haven of peace and tranquillity. Set in its own 28 acres of wood and pastureland and located in the heart of Killarney National Park. Reception rooms have a rustic feel, with a warm and friendly atmosphere, finished in stone and wood with open fires and antiques. Bedrooms & bathrooms are finished to the highest standards. The dining room, patio & garden have a terrific mountain view. An ideal base in the South West. Highly recommended by Michelin.

B&B from €45.00 to €60.00

MARY FULLER
PROPRIETOR

10 10

HOTELS

Closed 30 November - 01 March

B&B Rates are per Person Sharing per Night incl. Breakfast
Room Rates are per Room per Night

KILLARNEY AVENUE HOTEL

KENMARE PLACE,
KILLARNEY,
CO. KERRY

TEL: 064-32522 FAX: 064-33707
EMAIL: kavenue@odonoghue-ring-hotels.com
WEB: www.odonoghue-ring-hotels.com

HOTEL ★★★★ MAP 2 E 4

This boutique 4**** hotel has an idyllic setting in the heart of Killarney. Well appointed air-conditioned guestrooms provide guests with every care and comfort. Druids Restaurant provides a perfect blend of local and classical cuisine. The Kenmare Rooms is a distinctly different hotel bar. Guests are welcome to use the leisure facilities of our sister hotel (Killarney Towers Hotel), 100m away. Underground garage parking available. Close to shopping, vistor attractions and Kerry's premier golf courses.

B&B from €55.00 to €75.00

DENIS MCCARTHY
GENERAL MANAGER

66 66

Closed 01 November - 14 March

KILLARNEY GREAT SOUTHERN HOTEL

KILLARNEY,
CO. KERRY

TEL: 064-38000 FAX: 064-31642
EMAIL: res@killarney-gsh.com
WEB: www.gshotels.com

HOTEL ★★★★ MAP 2 E 4

The Great Southern Hotel Killarney combines old world charm and modern elegance. Originally built in 1854 this Victorian hotel was extensively renovated in 2002. Facilities include Garden Room Restaurant, Peppers à la carte restaurant, Innisfallen Spa with swimming pool, steamroom, monsoon shower, hydrotherapy bath, beauty treatments. Conference facilities for 800. Bookable worldwide through UTELL Int'l or Central Reservations Tel: 01-214 4800

Room Rate from € 132.00 to € 260.00

CONOR HENNIGAN
GENERAL MANAGER

☺ Weekend specials from €242.00 pps

172 172

Open All Year

B&B Rates are per Person Sharing per Night incl. Breakfast
Room Rates are per Room per Night

KILLARNEY HEIGHTS HOTEL

CORK ROAD,
KILLARNEY,
CO. KERRY
TEL: 064-31158 FAX: 064-35198
EMAIL: khh@iol.ie

HOTEL U   MAP 2 E 4

Situated 1km from Killarney Town Centre on the Cork Road, this beautiful 70 bedroomed hotel overlooks the majestic Torc & Mangerton Mountains. Open fires, olde world flagstone floors and pitch pine furnishings create a unique nostalgic atmosphere in the bars, restaurants and bistro. The hotel is easily accessed by mainline rail or by flying into Kerry Airport, just 14km away. The Killarney Heights Hotel, the perfect venue for the perfect holiday, to begin your tour of our beautiful scenic countryside.

B&B from € 63.50 to € 86.50

BERNARD O'RIORDAN

70 70

Closed 24 - 25 December

KILLARNEY LODGE

COUNTESS ROAD,
KILLARNEY,
CO. KERRY
TEL: 064-36499 FAX: 064-31070
EMAIL: klylodge@iol.ie
WEB: www.killarneylodge.net

GUESTHOUSE ★★★★   MAP 2 E 4

Welcome to Killarney Lodge, a purpose built four star guesthouse set in private walled-in gardens, yet only 2 minutes walk from Killarney Town Centre. The Lodge provides private parking, spacious en suite air conditioned bedrooms with all modern amenities including wheelchair facilities. Enjoy an extensive breakfast menu, relax in comfortable lounges with open fires where traditional home baking is served. The Lodge has justifiably earned an outstanding reputation for quality of service, relaxed atmosphere and friendliness.

B&B from € 45.00 to € 70.00

CATHERINE TREACY
OWNER

16 16

Closed 15 November - 14 February

KILLARNEY OAKS

MUCKROSS ROAD,
KILLARNEY,
CO. KERRY
TEL: 064-37600 FAX: 064-37619
EMAIL: info@killarneyoaks.com
WEB: www.killarneyoaks.com

HOTEL P   MAP 2 E 4

Set in the picturesque area of Killarney, 69 bedrooms, offering every modern amenity. On the edge of Killarney National Park and convenient to town centre. There is an excellent bar, with music most nights during season. Our restaurant offers superb local food. Activities can be arranged. Local amenities include golf, angling, horseriding, sandy beaches and hill walking. Private car park.

B&B from € 50.00 to € 90.00

EAMON COURTNEY
PROPRIETOR

69 69

Closed 31 October - 01 February

B&B Rates are per Person Sharing per Night incl. Breakfast
Room Rates are per Room per Night

KILLARNEY PARK HOTEL

TOWN CENTRE,
KILLARNEY,
CO. KERRY
TEL: 064-35555 FAX: 064-35266
EMAIL: info@killarneyparkhotel.ie
WEB: www.killarneyparkhotel.ie

HOTEL ★★★★★ MAP 2 E 4

Superbly located in the heart of Killarney Town on its own grounds , this family owned hotel is renowned as a place of elegance laced with warmth and hospitality. The hotel offers 72 beautifully appointed guest rooms and suites complemented by a luxurious full service spa. Other hotel features include a 20m swimming pool, outdoor hot-tub, jacuzzi, library, drawing room, billiards room, games room, golf locker and drying room. Conference facilities for up to 150 delegates. A warm welcome awaits you.

Member of Leading Small Hotels of the World.

B&B from € 130.00 to € 192.50

PÁDRAIG & JANET TREACY
PROPRIETORS

☺ Weekend specials from €260.00 pps

72 72

Closed 18 - 26 December

KILLARNEY PLAZA HOTEL & SPA

KENMARE PLACE,
KILLARNEY,
CO. KERRY
TEL: 064-21100 FAX: 064-21190
EMAIL: info@killarneyplaza.com
WEB: www.killarneyplaza.com

HOTEL U MAP 2 E 4

The Killarney Plaza successfully blends gracious hospitality, quality service and amenities in such a way guests using the hotel for business or pleasure feel at ease. This elegant hotel enjoys a wonderful location in Killarney. The leisure area and Molton Brown Spa allow guests to unwind and relax in luxurious surroundings. All bedrooms and suites are luxuriously furnished and air conditioned. The Killarney Plaza is a "must see, must stay" rendezvous.

B&B from € 85.00 to € 250.00

JAMES TYNAN
GENERAL MANAGER

198 198

Open All Year

KILLARNEY ROYAL

COLLEGE STREET,
KILLARNEY,
CO. KERRY
TEL: 064-31853 FAX: 064-34001
EMAIL: royalhot@iol.ie
WEB: www.killarneyroyal.ie

HOTEL U MAP 2 E 4

Privately owned by the Scally family & located in the heart of Killarney, the Killarney Royal is the perfect base for walking, golfing, & touring the Southwest of Ireland. Air conditioned throughout, this 4 star standard boutique property boasts 24 deluxe rooms also 5 junior suites tastefully designed by the proprietor Mrs. Scally, who modestly uses a country classical design at the Killarney Royal Hotel. "Overall, outstanding service with a positive attitude. I would recommend it to anyone looking for a small hotel with charm & loads of hospitality" - Peter Zummo.

B&B from € 75.00 to € 160.00

NICOLA DUGGAN
GENERAL MANAGER

☺ Weekend specials from €159.00 pps

29 29

Closed 23 - 26 December

B&B Rates are per Person Sharing per Night incl. Breakfast
Room Rates are per Room per Night

KILLEEN HOUSE HOTEL

AGHADOE,
LAKES OF KILLARNEY,
CO. KERRY
TEL: 064-31711 FAX: 064-31811
EMAIL: charming@indigo.ie
WEB: www.killeenhousehotel.com

HOTEL ★★★ MAP 2 E 4

The Killeen House is truly a charming little hotel. With only 23 rooms, 8 of them de luxe, it is the ideal base for touring 'God's own country', the magical Kingdom of Kerry. With our DIY Golf Pub and Rozzers elegant dining room you are assured a memorable experience. Go on, do the smart thing and call us now! We look forward to extending the 'hostility of the house' to you!

B&B from €70.00 to €120.00

GERALDINE & MICHAEL ROSNEY
OWNERS

☺ Weekend specials from €180.00 pps

 23 23

Closed 01 November - 10 April

KINGFISHER LODGE GUESTHOUSE

LEWIS ROAD,
KILLARNEY,
CO. KERRY
TEL: 064-37131 FAX: 064-39871
EMAIL: kingfisherguesthouse@eircom.net
WEB: www.kingfisherkillarney.com

GUESTHOUSE ★★★ MAP 2 E 4

A warm welcome awaits you at Kingfisher Lodge, a family-run luxury Irish Tourist Board registered guesthouse, AA ◆◆◆◆. 3 minute walk from the town centre with its excellent pubs, restaurants, entertainment and shopping. Our spacious bedrooms are beautifully decorated with TV, phone , hairdryer, tea/coffee. Relaxing guest lounge, varied breakfast menu. Private parking. Garden. Tackle, drying rooms. Tours, golfing, walking, angling arranged with host Donal, a qualified guide. Non-smoking guesthouse.

B&B from €30.00 to €50.00

ANN & DONAL CARROLL
PROPRIETORS

10 10

Closed 14 December - 01 February

LAKE HOTEL

ON LAKE SHORE,
MUCKROSS ROAD, KILLARNEY,
CO. KERRY
TEL: 064-31035 FAX: 064-31902
EMAIL: lakehotel@eircom.net
WEB: www.lakehotel.com

HOTEL ★★★ MAP 2 E 4

Refurbished to a 4 star standard for the 2005 session! Now completed. The most beautiful location in Ireland. Set on Killarney's lake shore, open log fires, double height ceilings, relaxed & friendly atmosphere. Standard rooms, luxury lakeside suites with jacuzzi, balcony & some four poster beds. Spa sensations with outdoor hot tub on the lakeshore, sauna, steamroom, gym and treatment rooms. New resident's library. The Lake Hotel - "A little bit of heaven on earth." See www.lakehotel.com

B&B from €50.00 to €170.00

TONY HUGGARD
MANAGING DIRECTOR

 84 84

Closed 11 December - 27 January

B&B Rates are per Person Sharing per Night incl. Breakfast
Room Rates are per Room per Night

VICTORIA HOUSE HOTEL

MUCKROSS ROAD,
KILLARNEY,
CO. KERRY
TEL: 064-35430 FAX: 064-35439
EMAIL: info@victoriahousehotel.com
WEB: www.victoriahousehotel.com

HOTEL ★★★ MAP 2 E 4

Set at the gateway to Killarney's National Park, this charming and cosy boutique hotel, family owned, and managed, offers the ambience of a country house, with first class personal and friendly staff. Our 35 bedrooms offer comfort and luxury, and are decorated and maintained to an exceptionally high standard. Frequent live music and traditional sessions in "The Ivy Room Bar" add to the ambience of this unique hotel. Private parking available.

B&B from €50.00 to €90.00

JOHN COURTNEY
PROPRIETOR

😊 Weekend specials from €125.00 pps

35   35

Closed 01 December - 01 February

WOODLAWN HOUSE

WOODLAWN ROAD,
KILLARNEY,
CO. KERRY
TEL: 064-37844 FAX: 064-36116
EMAIL: woodlawn@ie-post.com
WEB: www.woodlawn-house.com

GUESTHOUSE ★★★ MAP 2 E 4

Old style charm and hospitality. Family-run. Relaxed atmosphere. All modern conveniences. Ideally located 5 minutes walk from town centre. Near leisure centre, lakes and golf courses. Tours arranged. Private parking. Decorated with natural pine wood. Orthopaedic beds dressed in white cotton and linen. Irish and vegetarian menus. Our wholesome breakfasts include freshly squeezed orange juice, homemade preserves and bread. Early bird breakfast also available. A warm welcome assured.

B&B from €45.00 to €55.00

JAMES & ANNE WRENN

10   10

Closed 23 - 30 December

BIANCONI

KILLORGLIN,
RING OF KERRY,
CO. KERRY
TEL: 066-976 1146 FAX: 066-976 1950
EMAIL: bianconi1@iol.ie
WEB: www.bianconi.ie

GUESTHOUSE ★★★ MAP 1 D 4

Family-run inn on The Ring of Kerry. Gateway to Dingle Peninsula, Killarney 18km. On the road to Glencar - famous for its scenery, lakes, hill walking and mountain climbing. Famous for its table. High standard of food in bar. Table d'hôte and à la carte available. 50 minutes to Waterville, Tralee & Ballybunion golf courses. 15 minutes to Dooks & Beaufort courses. 5 minutes to Killorglin course. 15 mins to Killarney course. Private access to Caragh Lake. Own boat. Mentioned by many guides.

B&B from €45.00 to €55.00

RAY SHEEHY
OWNER

15   15

Closed 24 - 29 December

B&B Rates are per Person Sharing per Night incl. Breakfast
Room Rates are per Room per Night

GROVE LODGE RIVERSIDE GUESTHOUSE

KILLARNEY ROAD,
KILLORGLIN,
CO. KERRY

TEL: 066-976 1157 FAX: 066-976 2330
EMAIL: info@grovelodge.com
WEB: www.grovelodge.com

GUESTHOUSE ★★★ MAP 1 D 4

Ideally located for all your holiday activities; golfing, fishing, hill walking, sightseeing, beaches, Ring of Kerry, Dingle, with local gourmet restaurants & pub entertainment. (5 minutes walk from town centre). We invite you to share your holiday with us in our newly refurbished, spacious & luxurious accommodation, situated on 3 acres of mature gardens & woodlands, fronted by the River Laune & McGillycuddy Reeks Mountains & savour our speciality gourmet breakfasts. RAC, AA ◆◆◆◆.

B&B from € 45.00 to € 65.00

DELIA & FERGUS FOLEY
OWNERS & MANAGERS

Closed 01 - 31 December

WESTFIELD HOUSE

KILLORGLIN,
CO. KERRY

TEL: 066-976 1909 FAX: 066-976 1996
EMAIL: westhse@iol.ie
WEB: www.westfieldhse.com

GUESTHOUSE ★★★ MAP 1 D 4

Westfield House is a family-run guesthouse. All rooms are bright & spacious en suite, orthopaedic beds, direct dial telephone, TV, tea/coffee maker. Extra large family room available. We are situated on the Ring of Kerry in a quiet peaceful location only 5 minutes walk from town with panoramic views of McGillycuddy Reeks. There are five 18 hole golf courses within 20 minutes drive. Recognised stop for many weary cyclists. Ideal location for the hillwalker and climber.

B&B from € 35.00 to € 35.00

MARIE & LEONARD CLIFFORD
PROPRIETORS

IRISH
HOTELS
FEDERATION

Closed 01 November - 01 March

MOORINGS (THE)

PORTMAGEE,
CO. KERRY

TEL: 066-947 7108 FAX: 066-947 7220
EMAIL: moorings@iol.ie
WEB: www.moorings.ie

GUESTHOUSE ★★★ MAP 1 B 3

The Moorings is a family owned guesthouse & restaurant overlooking the picturesque fishing port in Portmagee. Excellent cuisine, specialising in locally caught seafood. Adjacent to the Moorings is the Bridge Bar, also run by the family, where you can enjoy a wonderful night of music, song & dance. The Moorings is central to all local amenities including angling, diving, watersports, 18 hole golf course etc. Trips to Skellig Michael can be arranged. RAC ◆◆◆◆, BIM Seafood Award 2004.

B&B from € 40.00 to € 55.00

GERARD & PATRICIA KENNEDY
PROPRIETORS

inet

IRISH
HOTELS
FEDERATION

Closed 01 November - 01 March

B&B Rates are per Person Sharing per Night incl. Breakfast
Room Rates are per Room per Night

PARKNASILLA GREAT SOUTHERN HOTEL

SNEEM,
CO. KERRY

TEL: 064-45122 FAX: 064-45323
EMAIL: res@parknasilla-gsh.com
WEB: www.gshotels.com

HOTEL ★★★★ MAP 1 C 3

Acknowledged as one of Ireland's finest hotels, Parknasilla is a 19th century house set in 300 acres of grounds. A classically individual hotel with 83 bedrooms equipped with every modern amenity. Leisure facilities include indoor heated swimming pool, sauna, steamroom, jacuzzi, hydrotherapy baths, outdoor hot tub, clay pigeon shooting, horseriding, archery, private 12 hole golf course - special green fees for guests, and guided walks. UTELL International or Central Reservations Tel: 01-214 4800.

Room Rate from €132.00 to €260.00

PAT CUSSEN
GENERAL MANAGER

☺ Weekend specials from €247.00 pps

83 83

Open All Year

TAHILLA COVE COUNTRY HOUSE

TAHILLA,
NEAR SNEEM,
CO. KERRY

TEL: 064-45204 FAX: 064-45104
EMAIL: tahillacove@eircom.net
WEB: www.tahillacove.com

GUESTHOUSE ★★★ MAP 1 D 3

Travel writers have described this family-run, fully licensed seashore guesthouse as the most idyllic spot in Ireland - the haunt of Irish/British dignitaries. Located on The Ring of Kerry seashore. 14 acre estate boasts mature gardens & private pier. Ideal place for a relaxing holiday/touring centre. Each room has en suite facilities, phone, TV, radio, hairdryer, iron and tea/coffee facilities. Log fires, superb views, home cooking. Take Sneem Road from Kenmare (N70).

B&B from €50.00 to €65.00

JAMES/DEIRDRE/CHAS WATERHOUSE
OWNERS

☺ 7 nights B&B + 5 Dinners from €550.00 pps

9   9

Closed 15 October - 26 April

KIRBY'S LANTERNS HOTEL

GLIN/TARBERT COAST ROAD,
TARBERT,
CO. KERRY

TEL: 068-36210 FAX: 068-36553
EMAIL: reservations@thelanternshotel.ie
WEB: www.thelanternshotel.ie

HOTEL ★★ MAP 5 E 7

The Kirby family of Kirby's Brogue Inn Tralee are the new owners of Kirby's Lanterns Hotel. Overlooking the majestic Shannon Estuary Kirby's Lanterns Hotel is an ideal tourist base for Kerry, Limerick and Clare. Central to world famous Golf Courses at Ballybunion, Tralee, Killarney, Adare, Doonbeg & Lahinch. Enjoy a stay at Kirby's Lanterns Hotel. Superb accommodation, great food & friendly service. Food served from 6.30a.m. to 10.00p.m. daily. Music sessions every weekend. Call to Kirby's Lanterns Hotel where a warm Kirby welcome awaits you.

B&B from €45.00 to €60.00

MARIE KIRBY
MANAGER

22 22

Closed 25 December

B&B Rates are per Person Sharing per Night incl. Breakfast
Room Rates are per Room per Night

ABBEY GATE HOTEL

MAINE STREET,
TRALEE,
CO. KERRY
TEL: 066-712 9888 FAX: 066-712 9821
EMAIL: info@abbeygate-hotel.com
WEB: www.abbeygate-hotel.com

HOTEL ★★★ MAP 1 D 5

Welcome, the Abbey Gate Hotel is located in the heart of Tralee. All 100 rooms are spacious with full facilities. The Old Market Place Pub is Tralee's liveliest venue with great pub grub served all day and casual dining in our Bistro at night. Or try our fabulous Toscana Ristorante Italiano for the best in authentic Italian cuisine. The Abbey Gate Hotel is your gateway to the delights of Kerry.

B&B from €65.00 to €99.95

PATRICK DILLON
GENERAL MANAGER

100 100

Closed 24 - 26 December

BALLYGARRY HOUSE HOTEL

KILLARNEY ROAD,
TRALEE,
CO. KERRY
TEL: 066-712 3322 FAX: 066-712 7630
EMAIL: info@ballygarryhouse.com
WEB: www.ballygarryhouse.com

HOTEL ★★★★ MAP 1 D 5

Set at the foot of the Kerry Mountains on 4 acres of mature themed gardens, Ballygarry House is a newly refurbished country manor with all the treasures associated of times past. Traditional design & contemporary twists lend itself to that home away from home air of well being. With 40 luxurious guestrooms,one master suite & five junior suites, library, drawing room, resident's lounge, renowned restaurant, old world pub & numerous landscaped walkways it is a haven for relaxation. 1.5km from Tralee & 6km from Kerry Airport, an ideal location for golfing or touring.

B&B from €80.00 to €125.00

PÁDRAIG MCGILLICUDDY
GENERAL MANAGER

Weekend specials from €139.00 pps

46   46

Closed 20 - 26 December

BALLYROE HEIGHTS HOTEL

BALLYROE,
TRALEE,
CO. KERRY
TEL: 066-712 6796 FAX: 066-712 5066
EMAIL: info@ballyroe.com
WEB: www.ballyroe.com

HOTEL ★★★ MAP 1 D 5

A modern luxurious hotel set in six and a half acres of woodland and sloping gardens. Situated 3km from Tralee Town it is the ideal base for touring, golfing or just relaxing. The views of the Sliabh Mish Mountains and Tralee Bay are breathtaking. Relax in our spectacular Summit Restaurant or Palace Bar while enjoying the view. All en suite bedrooms have satellite TV, hairdryer and tea/coffee making facilities.

B&B from €60.00 to €80.00

MARK SULLIVAN
GENERAL MANAGER

Midweek specials, 3 nights B&B & 2 Dinners from €135.00 pps

25   25

Open All Year

B&B Rates are per Person Sharing per Night incl. Breakfast
Room Rates are per Room per Night

BALLYSEEDE CASTLE HOTEL

BALLYSEEDE,
TRALEE,
CO. KERRY
TEL: 066-712 5799 FAX: 066-712 5287
EMAIL: ballyseede@eircom.net
WEB: www.ballyseedecastle.com

HOTEL ★★★ MAP 1 D 5

Ballyseede Castle Hotel is a casual, almost cosy 15th century castle on 35 hectares of parkland. The castle boasts fine continental cuisine as well as many traditional Irish dishes. Located on the main Tralee/Killarney Road, within easy reach of Kerry's five magnificent golf courses - Ballybunion, Waterville, Killarney, Dooks and Barrow, the course for Tralee recently designed by Arnold Palmer. Ideally situated for touring the Ring of Kerry and Dingle Peninsula. Sister hotel of Cabra Castle, Co. Cavan.

B&B from €75.00 to €150.00

MARNIE CORSCADDEN
GENERAL MANAGER

12 12

ālC ▪ Inet ▪

IRISH HOTELS FEDERATION

Closed 24 - 26 December

BARROW COUNTRY HOUSE

WEST BARROW,
ARDFERT, TRALEE,
CO. KERRY
TEL: 066-713 6437 FAX: 066-713 6402
EMAIL: info@barrowhouse.com
WEB: www.barrowhouse.com

GUESTHOUSE ★★★★ MAP 1 D 5

Built in 1723 & former home to the Knight of Kerry. The house is located on Barrow Harbour next to the Slieve Mish Mountains & the Dingle Peninsula. This period house has been elegantly renovated & refurbished to provide a combination of luxurious suites & de luxe rooms. Each bedroom enjoys the comfort of modern day living in a unique & tranquil setting. Golf, angling, golden beaches, sailing, award-winning restaurants & pubs close by. Tralee's Arnold Palmer designed golf course is nearby. Ballybunion 35 mins & Killarney 50 mins.

Member of Spectra Hotel Group

B&B from €50.00 to €85.00

LORRAINE WALSH
MANAGER

☺ Midweek specials from €150.00 pps

16 16

IRISH HOTELS FEDERATION

Closed 01 November- 14 February

B&B Rates are per Person Sharing per Night incl. Breakfast
Room Rates are per Room per Night

BRANDON HOTEL CONFERENCE AND LEISURE CENTRE

PRINCES STREET,
TRALEE,
CO. KERRY
TEL: 066-712 3333 FAX: 066-712 5019
EMAIL: sales@brandonhotel.ie
WEB: www.brandonhotel.ie

HOTEL ★★★ MAP 1 D 5

Renowned, privately owned premises ideally located in the heart of Tralee Town, close to shopping and visitor attractions. The hotel offers a range of accommodation - standard rooms, de luxe rooms and suites, and a choice of bars and restaurants. It is also equipped with full leisure centre incorporating swimming pool, sauna, steamroom, jacuzzi, gymnasium and beauty treatment rooms, as well as extensive conference and banqueting facilities. Private Parking available. Tralee is accessible by mainline rail and air with Kerry Airport just 10 miles away.

B&B from €55.00 to €120.00

SHAY LIVINGSTONE
GENERAL MANAGER

Midweek specials 3BB + 3 Dinners from €149.00 pps

183 183

Closed 23 - 29 December

BRANDON INN

JAMES STREET,
TRALEE,
CO. KERRY
TEL: 066-712 9666 FAX: 066-712 5019
EMAIL: sales@brandonhotel.ie
WEB: www.brandonhotel.ie

HOTEL U MAP 1 D 5

The concept - quality at a fixed price. Located in Tralee Town centre. Bright, modern and spacious rooms, each en suite with tea/coffee making facilities. The room only price remains fixed whether the room is occupied by 1, 2 or 3 adults or 2 adults and 2 children. Guests at The Brandon Inn have full use of facilities at our sister hotel, Brandon Hotel, which is located a stone throw away. Private parking available for guests.

Room Rate from €79.00 to €99.00

SHAY LIVINGSTONE
GENERAL MANAGER

49 49

Closed 01 December - 29 January

BROOK MANOR LODGE

FENIT ROAD,
TRALEE,
CO. KERRY
TEL: 066-712 0406 FAX: 066-712 7552
EMAIL: brookmanor@eircom.net
WEB: www.brookmanorlodge.com

GUESTHOUSE ★★★★ MAP 1 D 5

A warm welcome awaits you at our new 4**** luxurious, family-run lodge. Only minutes drive from Tralee, golden beaches and Arnold Palmer designed golf course. 30 minutes from Killarney. 40 minutes from Ballybunion. The Lodge is situated in acres of meadowlands and surrounded by a babbling brook. All our rooms are en suite with full facilities. Brook Manor Lodge is the ideal place for the perfect holiday.

B&B from €55.00 to €70.00

MARGARET & VINCENT O'SULLIVAN
OWNERS

8 8

Open All Year

B&B Rates are per Person Sharing per Night incl. Breakfast
Room Rates are per Room per Night

COMFORT INN TRALEE

CASTLE STREET,
TRALEE,
CO. KERRY

TEL: 1850-266 3678 FAX: 021-427 1489
EMAIL: info@comfortinntralee.com
WEB: www.comfortinntralee.com

HOTEL ★★★ MAP 1 D 5

Situated in the heart of bustling Tralee. The Comfort Inn Tralee exudes an air of hospitality that appeals to young and old. All rooms are en suite with multi-channel TV, DD phone and tea/coffee making facilities. Enjoy live entertainment in McDades Bar and dance away in the Courthouse Nite Club. 2 minutes from the train and bus station. 15 minutes from Kerry Airport. Telephone hotel directly on 066 712 1877.

Member of Comfort Inns

Room Rate from €49.00 to €139.00

ADRIAN MURPHY
HOTEL MANAGER

☺ Weekend specials from €90.00 pps

45 45

Closed 20 - 26 December

GLENDUFF HOUSE

KIELDUFF,
TRALEE,
CO. KERRY

TEL: 066-713 7105 FAX: 066-713 7099
EMAIL: glenduffhouse@eircom.net
WEB: www.glenduff-house.com

GUESTHOUSE ★★★ MAP 1 D 5

Enter the old world charm of the 19th century in our family-run period house set on 6 acres with mature gardens. Refurbished to give the comforts of the modern day, yet keeping its original character with antiques & paintings. Personal attention assured. Relax & enjoy a drink in our friendly bar. Also self catering cottages in the courtyard. Ideally situated for golf and sports amenities. From Tralee take route to racecourse off N21 at Joe Keohane Roundabout. Continue for 4.5 miles and turn right at large sign on right.

Member of Premier Guesthouses

B&B from €38.00 to €55.00

JAMES & LESLEY SUGRUE
OWNERS

5 5

Closed 18 December - 06 January

B&B Rates are per Person Sharing per Night incl. Breakfast
Room Rates are per Room per Night

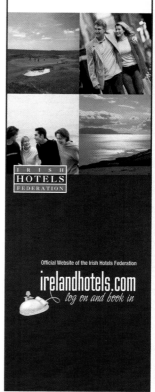

GRAND HOTEL

DENNY STREET,
TRALEE,
CO. KERRY
TEL: 066-712 1499 FAX: 066-712 2877
EMAIL: info@grandhoteltralee.com
WEB: www.grandhoteltralee.com

HOTEL ★★★ MAP 1 D 5

The Grand Hotel is a 3*** hotel situated in Tralee Town Centre. Established in 1928, its open fires, ornate ceilings & mahogany furnishings offer guests old world charm in comfortable surroundings. All our rooms are equipped with direct dial phone, computer point, satellite TV and tea/coffee welcoming trays. Residents can avail of green fee reductions at Tralee Golf Club. Also reduced rates to the fabulous Aqua Dome Waterworld complex. Family rooms are available at discounted rates. Limited parking available.

B&B from €45.00 to €75.00

DICK BOYLE
GENERAL MANAGER

Weekend specials from €150.00 pps

44 44

Closed 24 - 27 December

MANOR WEST HOTEL

MANORWEST,
TRALEE,
CO. KERRY
TEL: 066-7118 382 FAX: 066-7126 783
EMAIL: manorwesthotel@eircom.net

UNDER CONSTRUCTION · OPENING MAY 2005

HOTEL P MAP 1 D 5

Tralee's latest addition, with 70 bedrooms, 10 of which will be suites, is being built with the discerning 4 star client in mind and is due to open in May 2005. Situated on the main Limerick / Killarney road, just a mile from the town centre, it will provide all the facilities you would associate with a new de luxe development. A visit to our Spa/Leisure/Gym area is a must.

B&B from €75.00 to €160.00

JIM FEENEY
GENERAL MANAGER

Weekend specials from €155.00 pps

70 70

Open all Year

MEADOWLANDS HOTEL

OAKPARK,
TRALEE,
CO. KERRY
TEL: 066-718 0444 FAX: 066-718 0964
EMAIL: medlands@iol.ie
WEB: www.meadowlands-hotel.com

HOTEL ★★★★ MAP 1 D 5

A charming and intimate hotel, set in a tranquil corner of Tralee, on its own beautiful landscaped gardens. This luxurious hotel comprises 58 superbly appointed rooms, including suites. Our award winning restaurant specialises in the freshest of locally-caught seafood and shellfish cuisine. State of the art conference centre. Ideal base for golfing enthusiasts and touring the Dingle Peninsula, The Ring of Kerry. Experience an experience.

B&B from €70.00 to €150.00

PÁDRAIG & PEIGI O' MATHUNA
OWNERS

58 58

Closed 24 - 26 December

B&B Rates are per Person Sharing per Night incl. Breakfast
Room Rates are per Room per Night

GREGANS CASTLE HOTEL

THE BURREN,
BALLYVAUGHAN,
CO. CLARE
TEL: 065-707 7005 FAX: 065-707 7111
EMAIL: stay@gregans.ie
WEB: www.gregans.ie

HOTEL ★★★★ MAP 6 F 10

4 star luxury hotel amid splendid Burren mountain scenery, overlooking Galway Bay. Country house comforts, turf fires, tranquillity, no TV in rooms. Award winning gardens, food, service, accommodations. Individually decorated rooms/suites. Nearby ocean swimming, horse-riding, hillwalking. Golf at Lahinch and Doonbeg. Halfway between Kerry and Connemara using ferry. RAC Blue Ribbon winner. AA Red Stars award. 1 hour to Shannon and Galway Airports. Excellence through family ownership for 29 years. On-line booking available at www.gregans.ie

Member of Ireland's Blue Book

B&B from €85.00 to €105.00

SIMON HADEN
MANAGING DIRECTOR

☺ 3 days half board from €399.50 pps

🛏🛌☎🖥TC🍴CM❄☽♪♫🅿🔌alc
21 21

Closed 25 October - 23 March

HYLAND'S BURREN HOTEL

BALLYVAUGHAN,
CO. CLARE
TEL: 065-707 7037 FAX: 065-707 7131
EMAIL: hylandsburren@eircom.net
WEB: www.hylandsburren.com

HOTEL ★★★ MAP 6 F 10

Hyland's Burren Hotel is a charming hotel, dating back to the 18th century and now tastefully modernised. It is located in the picturesque village of Ballyvaughan, nestling in the unique Burren landscape of County Clare. Experience bygone charm with the best of modern facilities, open turf fires, informal bars and restaurants specialising in the finest local seafood. An ideal base for golfing and walking enthusiasts and truly an artist's haven.

Member of Irish Country Hotels

B&B from €45.00 to €65.00

DOROTHY COSTELLO
MANAGER

🛏🛌☎🖥TC🍴CM❄☽♪♫📺
29 29
S🅂🔌alc▮🐴

Closed 01 November - 31 January

RUSHEEN LODGE

BALLYVAUGHAN,
CO. CLARE
TEL: 065-707 7092 FAX: 065-707 7152
EMAIL: rusheen@iol.ie
WEB: www.rusheenlodge.com

GUESTHOUSE ★★★★ MAP 6 F 10

Rusheen Lodge is a 4****, AA ♦♦♦♦♦, RAC ♦♦♦♦♦ luxury guest house nestling in the Burren Mountains, providing elegant tastefully designed en suite bedrooms, suites, dining room and resident's lounge, ensuring a comfortable and relaxing stay. Previous winner Jameson Guide and RAC Guest House of the Year. RAC Sparkling Diamond and Warm Welcome Award. Ideally located for touring the Shannon region, Aran Islands and Connemara. Non-smoking.

B&B from €38.00 to €48.00

KAREN McGANN
PROPRIETOR

🛏🛌☎🖥TC❄☽♪♫🅿S▮♞
9 9

Closed 18 November - 10 February

B&B Rates are per Person Sharing per Night incl. Breakfast
Room Rates are per Room per Night

BUNRATTY CASTLE HOTEL

BUNRATTY,
CO. CLARE

TEL: 061-478700 FAX: 061-364891
EMAIL: info@bunrattycastlehotel.com
WEB: www.bunrattycastlehotel.com

HOTEL ★★★ MAP 6 G 7

The new Bunratty Castle Hotel is a 3*** Georgian hotel. Situated in the centre of Bunratty Village overlooking the historic Bunratty Castle and just across the road from Ireland's oldest pub, Durty Nellies. The rooms have been tastefully decorated in the traditional style. All rooms have air conditioning, satellite TV and have every modern comfort. Relax in Kathleens Pub and Restaurant and enjoy great food. We welcome you to experience the warmth and hospitality here.

B&B from €68.00 to €90.00

DEIRDRE WELCH
GENERAL MANAGER

79 79

Closed 24 - 25 December

BUNRATTY GROVE

CASTLE ROAD,
BUNRATTY,
CO. CLARE

TEL: 061-369579 FAX: 061-369561
EMAIL: bunrattygrove@eircom.net
WEB: http://homepage.eircom.net/~bunrattygrove

GUESTHOUSE ★★★ MAP 6 G 7

Bunratty Grove is a purpose built luxurious guesthouse. This guesthouse is located within 3 minutes drive of Bunratty Castle and Folk Park and is 10 minutes from Shannon Airport. Fishing, golfing, historical interests within a short distance. Ideally located for tourists arriving or departing Shannon Airport. Bookings for Bunratty and Knappogue Banquets taken on request. All rooms en suite with multi-channel TV, hairdryer, tea/coffee facilities and direct dial phone.

B&B from €30.00 to €40.00

JOE & MAURA BRODIE
PROPRIETORS

9 9

Open All Year

BUNRATTY MANOR HOTEL

BUNRATTY,
CO. CLARE

TEL: 061-707984 FAX: 061-360588
EMAIL: bunrattymanor@eircom.net
WEB: www.bunrattymanor.net

HOTEL ★★★ MAP 6 G 7

Bunratty Manor is a "home from home" style relaxed intimate family run hotel renowned for friendliness and hospitality. Just two minutes walk from the mediaeval banquets of Bunratty Castle and Folk Park, it serves as an ideal touring base for the Cliffs of Moher, the Burren and numerous championship golf courses. Our intimate restaurant has a delicately selective menu with locally sourced seafood and meats. All rooms tastefully decorated. Tea/coffee, ice, TV, ISDN. Recommended by Les Routiers Guide 2005.

B&B from €57.50 to €67.50

FIONA & NOEL WALLACE
OWNERS

14 14

Closed 20 December - 31 January

B&B Rates are per Person Sharing per Night incl. Breakfast
Room Rates are per Room per Night

BUNRATTY WOODS COUNTRY HOUSE

LOW ROAD,
BUNRATTY,
CO. CLARE
TEL: 061-369689 FAX: 061-369454
EMAIL: bunratty@iol.ie
WEB: www.bunrattywoods.com

GUESTHOUSE ★★★ MAP 6 G 7

Bunratty Woods is wonderful 'old world' style guesthouse, all rooms en suite. TV, telephone, hairdryer. At Bunratty Castle turn sharp left on to LOW ROAD, we are the 5th house on left side. 5 miles to Shannon Airport and half a mile to Bunratty Castle/Folk Park, Duty Free shops, pubs and restaurants. Breakfast menu: Our pancakes are famous!! Recommended by Frommer, Michelin, Don McClelland and Fodor Guide Books. Closed mid November to mid March but available for telephone, fax, email bookings for 2005.

B&B from €35.00 to €60.00

MAUREEN & PADDY O'DONOVAN
OWNERS

🔧 📞 💻 TC ✳ J P
14   14

Closed 10 November - 15 March

FITZPATRICK BUNRATTY

BUNRATTY,
CO. CLARE
TEL: 061-361177 FAX: 061-471252
EMAIL: info@bunratty.fitzpatricks.com
WEB: www.fitzpatrickhotels.com

HOTEL U MAP 6 G 7

Located in the picturesque village of Bunratty, neighbouring Bunratty Castle, Folk Park & Durty Nellies. 10 minutes from Shannon International Airport & 10 minutes from Limerick City. Hotel's facilities include excellent leisure facilities & Ravens Hair and Beauty Salon. There are 9 dining options in the village, shopping at Meadows & Byrne and Avoca Handweavers. With so much to offer "Destination Bunratty" has all you need for an exciting stay without ever having to leave the village.

B&B from €60.00 to €90.00

KATE O'CONNOR
REVENUE MANAGER

✓ ✗
😊 Midweek specials from €135.00 pps
(3 nights B&B & 1 dinner)
🔧 📞 💻 TC ✓ CMCS ✳ 🗑 🏠 J
J P 🔋 a/c ⚡ Inet WiFi 🐴

Closed 24 - 26 December

B&B Rates are per Person Sharing per Night incl. Breakfast
Room Rates are per Room per Night

ARAN VIEW HOUSE HOTEL & RESTAURANT

COAST ROAD,
DOOLIN,
CO. CLARE
TEL: 065-707 4061 FAX: 065-707 4540
EMAIL: bookings@aranview.com
WEB: www.aranview.com

HOTEL ★★★ MAP 5 E 9

A Georgian house built in 1736, it has a unique position commanding panoramic views of the Aran Islands, the Burren region and the Cliffs of Moher. Situated on 100 acres of farmland, Aran View echoes spaciousness, comfort and atmosphere in its restaurant and bar. Menus are based on the best of local produce, fish being a speciality. All rooms with private bathroom, colour TV and direct dial phone. Visitors are assured of a warm and embracing welcome at the Aran View House Hotel.

B&B from €50.00 to €80.00

THERESA & JOHN LINNANE
PROPRIETORS

Closed 31 October - 18 April

BALLINALACKEN CASTLE COUNTRY HOUSE & RESTAURANT

COAST ROAD,
DOOLIN,
CO. CLARE
TEL: 065-707 4025 FAX: 065-707 4025
EMAIL: ballinalackencastle@eircom.net
WEB: www.ballinalackencastle.com

HOTEL ★★★ MAP 5 E 9

A romantic peaceful oasis steeped in history and ambience offering the most spectacular views of the Cliffs of Moher, Aran Islands, Atlantic Ocean & Connemara Hills. Built in 1840 as the home of Lord O'Brien. Family members radiate a warm friendly welcome. Award winning chef Frank Sheedy (son-in-law) makes dining here an experience to remember. Peat and log fires add to the cosy atmosphere. Ideal base for exploring Clare. Recommended by Egon Ronay, Michelin, Fodor, Frommer, Charming Hotels of Ireland, New York Times, Washington Post & London Times.

B&B from €60.00 to €95.00

MARY AND DENIS O'CALLAGHAN
PROPRIETORS

Closed 31 October - 22 April

BALLYVARA HOUSE

BALLYVARA,
DOOLIN,
CO. CLARE
TEL: 065-707 4467 FAX: 065-707 4868
EMAIL: bvara@iol.ie
WEB: www.ballyvarahouse.com

GUESTHOUSE P MAP 5 E 9

Luxury accommodation and exceptional service await you at Ballyvara House. Renovated to 4 star standards with nothing spared regarding guests' comfort: all the spacious rooms have at least a queen-size bed with our luxurious suites boasting king-size sleigh beds. Every bath is either a jacuzzi or spa bath. Relax and unwind in our lounge bar which serves wine and beer or courtyard garden over a glass of fine wine after a day of exploring the Aran Islands, Burren or Cliffs of Moher.

B&B from €35.00 to €75.00

JOHN FLANAGAN & BECKY BRANNON
HOSTS

Closed 22 - 28 December

B&B Rates are per Person Sharing per Night incl. Breakfast
Room Rates are per Room per Night

WESTBROOK HOUSE

GALWAY ROAD,
ENNIS,
CO. CLARE

TEL: 065-684 0173 FAX: 065-686 7777
EMAIL: westbrook.ennis@eircom.net
WEB: www.westbrookhouse.net

GUESTHOUSE ★★★ MAP 6 F 8

Westbrook House is a recently built luxury guesthouse in Ennis. All rooms are fitted to exceptionally high standards. Within walking distance of the centre of historic Ennis, with its friendly traditional pubs and fantastic shopping. Ideal base for golfing holidays, special discounts with local golf courses. A short drive to the majestic Cliffs of Moher, The Burren or Bunratty Castle and Folk Park. Only 15 minutes from Shannon Airport.

B&B from €35.00 to €45.00

SHEELAGH & DOMHNALL LYNCH
PROPRIETORS

🛏️🔥☎️🖥️TC✻U♩PS♀☕inet
10   10

IRISH
HOTELS
FEDERATION

Closed 23 - 26 December

FALLS HOTEL

ENNISTYMON, NEAR LAHINCH,
CO. CLARE

TEL: 065-707 1004 FAX: 065-707 1367
EMAIL: sales@fallshotel.ie
WEB: www.fallshotel.ie

HOTEL ★★★ MAP 5 E 9

The Falls Hotel is conveniently located for touring The Burren & The Cliffs of Moher & for the golfer The Ch'ship Lahinch Golf Course is a mere 3 kms, with Doonbeg only a 20 mins drive. The Hotel itself is surrounded by 50 acres of woodland and riverside walks. The Falls Hotel exudes warmth & atmosphere which pervades throughout - The Georgian manor entrance, 140 spacious bedrooms, The Dylan Thomas Bar, An Teach Mor Bistro, Cascades Restaurant & Conference/Banqueting facilities for 350 people. A Céad Míle Fáilte awaits you at the Falls Hotel.

B&B from €45.00 to €75.00

JAMES O'BRIEN
MANAGER

✓🍴

☺ Weekend specials from €109.00 pps

🛏️🔥☎️🖥️📺TC✻C♥CM✻U♩
140 140

♩PS©alc📠

IRISH
HOTELS
FEDERATION

Open All Year

B&B Rates are per Person Sharing per Night incl. Breakfast
Room Rates are per Room per Night

GROVEMOUNT HOUSE

LAHINCH ROAD,
ENNISTYMON,
CO. CLARE
TEL: 065-707 1431 FAX: 065-707 1823
EMAIL: grovmnt@gofree.indigo.ie
WEB: www.grovemount.com

GUESTHOUSE ★★★ MAP 5 E 9

Grovemount House is a family-run guesthouse situated on the outskirts of Ennistymon Town. From here you can access with ease the renowned Cliffs of Moher and the spectacular and unique Burren. Just 5 minutes drive away is Lahinch championship golf links and Blue Flag Beach. Whatever is your pleasure: fishing, golfing, sightseeing, horseriding or the best traditional music, enjoy and then return to luxurious tranquillity in Grovemount House.

Member of Premier Guesthouses

B&B from €32.00 to €40.00

SHEILA LINNANE
OWNER

☺ Midweek specials from €85.00 pps

7   7

Closed 26 October - 30 April

HALPIN'S TOWNHOUSE HOTEL

ERIN STREET,
KILKEE,
CO. CLARE
TEL: 065-905 6032 FAX: 065-905 6317
EMAIL: halpinshotel@iol.ie
WEB: www.halpinsprivatehotels.com

HOTEL ★★★ MAP 5 D 7

Highly acclaimed 3*** town house hotel. Combination of old world charm, fine food, vintage wines & modern comforts - overlooking old Victorian Kilkee, near Shannon Airport & Killimer car ferry. Ideal base for touring - Cliffs of Moher, Bunratty, The Burren & Loop drive. Nearby golf courses - Lahinch, Doonbeg & Ballybunion. Accolades- RAC, AA, Times, Best Loved Hotels, Johansens. Sister property of Aberdeen Lodge and Merrion Hall.
USA toll free 1800 617 3178.
UK free phone 0800 096 4748.
Direct Dial 353 65 905 6032.

Member of Best Loved Hotels of the World

B&B from €40.00 to €60.00

PAT HALPIN
PROPRIETOR

12   12

Closed 15 November - 15 March

KILKEE BAY HOTEL

KILRUSH ROAD,
KILKEE,
CO. CLARE
TEL: 065-906 0060 FAX: 065-906 0062
EMAIL: info@kilkee-bay.com
WEB: www.kilkee-bay.com

HOTEL ★★★ MAP 5 D 7

A superb location - 3 minutes walk from Kilkee's renowned Blue Flag beach and town centre. This modern hotel has 41 spacious en suite bedrooms with direct dial phone, tea/coffee facilities and TV. On site tennis court, bar and bistro. The perfect base for touring the Cliffs of Moher, Burren and Ailwee Caves. Shannon Airport/Limerick City within an hour's drive. Reduced rates at local dolphin watching, golf, diving centre, thalassotherapy and pony trekking.

B&B from €40.00 to €65.00

MARIE SPICER
GENERAL MANAGER

☺ Weekend specials from €110.00 pps

41   41

Closed 26 October - 11 March

B&B Rates are per Person Sharing per Night incl. Breakfast
Room Rates are per Room per Night

STRAND GUEST HOUSE

THE STRAND LINE,
KILKEE,
CO. CLARE
TEL: 065-905 6177 FAX: 065-905 6177
EMAIL: thestrandkilkee@eircom.net
WEB: www.clareguesthouse.com

GUESTHOUSE ★★★ MAP 5 O 7

Situated on the seafront in Kilkee, one of the most westerly seaside resorts in Europe. Kilkee is built around a 1.5km beach, considered one of the best and safest bathing places in the west with breathtaking coastal walks. The Strand makes an ideal touring base - visit The Burren, Cliffs of Moher, Ailwee Caves. For golf enthusiasts there is a local 18 hole course, Kilrush 13km, Lahinch 42km or Ballybunion 40km (via car ferry). Restaurant fully licenced, specialises in local seafood.

B&B from €34.00 to €45.00

JOHNNY & CAROLINE REDMOND

🛏️🐾☎️⬜ⓉⒸ☕🔌🅱️abc♿
6 6

Open All Year

THOMOND GUESTHOUSE & KILKEE THALASSOTHERAPY CENTRE

GRATTAN STREET,
KILKEE,
CO. CLARE
TEL: 065-905 6742 FAX: 065-905 6762
EMAIL: info@kilkeethalasso.com
WEB: www.kilkeethalasso.com

GUESTHOUSE ★★★ MAP 5 D 7

Thomond Guesthouse is a magnificent premises with 5 en suite rooms coupled with Kilkee Thalassotherapy Centre, offering natural seaweed baths, algae body wraps, beauty salon & other thalassotherapy treatments. Non-smoking. Children over 16 welcome. Ideal for those looking for a totally unique & relaxing break. Situated in beautiful Kilkee with golfing, scuba diving, deep sea angling, dolphin watching, swimming, pony trekking & spectacular cliff walks, nearby. Private Car Parking. Winner Best Day Spa 2004/ Irish Beauty Industry

B&B from €35.00 to €45.00

EILEEN MULCAHY
PROPRIETOR

💧

😊 Midweek special 2 nights B&B + 6 Treatments from €300.00 pps

🛏️🐾☎️⬜ⓉⒸ☕🅿️Ⓢ Inet
5 5

Closed 20 December - 10 January

Clare Museum

Arthur's Row, Ennis
Tel: 065 6823382
Fax: 065 6842119
Email: claremuseum@clarecoco.ie
Web: www.clarelibrary.ie

RICHES of **CLARE**
CLARE MUSEUM

Clare is a remarkable county and the story of its people stretches back 6,000 years. Its incredible history is excitingly captured at the Clare Museum. Beautifully displayed artifacts, original works of art, enthralling audio visual and interactive experiences and dramatic images all combine to provide an exciting glimpse into rich history and heritage of Clare.

Location
Centre of Ennis, off O'Connell square. Car parking is adjacent to the Temple Gate.

Opening Times
Oct - May: 9.30 - 5.30 Tues-Sat
Jun - Sept: 9.30 - 5.30 Mon-Sat
Closed 1-2pm. Sun 2pm-5pm
Last Adm: 4.30pm

Free Admission

Facilities
Gift Shop

Parking
Parking for cars and buses 100 yards.

Your Host
John Rattigan (Curator)

B&B Rates are per Person Sharing per Night incl. Breakfast
Room Rates are per Room per Night

KINCORA HALL HOTEL

ON THE LAKE,
KILLALOE,
CO. CLARE
TEL: 061-376000 FAX: 061-376665
EMAIL: info@kincorahall.com
WEB: www.kincorahall.com

HOTEL U   MAP 6 H 8

Beautifully situated, overlooking our own picturesque Harbour & Yachting Marina on the shores of Lough Derg. This friendly, family run hotel exudes a warmth from the minute you enter and view the blazing open hearth fire, and the welcoming smile of the reception staff, you are assured of a memorable visit. Peaceful, relaxing, luxurious bedrooms with modern day facilities, many with views of River Shannon. Enjoy lunch time carvery and candlelight dining. Scenic walks & nature trails, fishing, horseriding, watersports & golf, all within minutes. Conference facilities are available.

B&B from €55.00 to €95.00

MATT SHERLOCK
GENERAL MANAGER

30 30

Open All Year

LAKESIDE HOTEL & LEISURE CENTRE

KILLALOE,
CO. CLARE
TEL: 061-376122 FAX: 061-376431
EMAIL: lakesidehotelkilaloe@eircom.net
WEB: www.lakeside-killaloe.com

HOTEL ★★★   MAP 6 H 8

On the banks of the River Shannon, overlooking Lough Derg, the Lakeside is the ideal base for touring Counties Clare, Limerick and Tipperary. Enjoy our fabulous indoor leisure centre with its 40 metre water-slide, swimming pools, sauna and steamrooms, jacuzzi, gym, snooker and creche rooms. Our 3*** hotel has 46 en suite bedrooms. Fully licensed restaurant and conference facilities available.

B&B from €55.00 to €75.00

CHRISTOPHER BYRNES
GENERAL MANAGER

46 46

IRISH
HOTELS
FEDERATION

Closed 23 - 26 December

LANTERN HOUSE

OGONNELLOE,
KILLALOE,
CO. CLARE
TEL: 061-923034 FAX: 061-923139
EMAIL: phil@lanternhouse.com
WEB: www.lanternhouse.com

GUESTHOUSE ★★★   MAP 6 H 8

Ideally situated overlooking Lough Derg in a beautiful part of East Clare, 6 miles north of historic Killaloe and 45 minutes drive from Shannon Airport. Our en suite rooms are non-smoking, have semi-orthopaedic beds, direct dial phone, TV and radio. Residents' lounge, homely atmosphere and safe car parking. Enjoy the wonderful views from our fully licenced restaurant. Owner chef. Local activities include golf, watersports, fishing, pony trekking and walking.

B&B from €36.00 to €40.00

ELIZABETH COPPEN/PHILIP HOGAN
OWNERS

6   6

Closed 01 November - 01 March

B&B Rates are per Person Sharing per Night incl. Breakfast
Room Rates are per Room per Night

ADARE MANOR HOTEL & GOLF RESORT

ADARE,
CO. LIMERICK

TEL: 061-396566 FAX: 061-396124
EMAIL: reservations@adaremanor.com
WEB: www.adaremanor.com

HOTEL ★★★★★ MAP 6 G 7

Located 20 miles from Shannon Airport. Adare Manor Hotel & Golf Resort, set on the banks of the River Maigue, boasts splendour in its luxuriously finished rooms. The Oak Room Restaurant provides haute cuisine laced with Irish charm. Indoor heated pool, fitness room, spa. Outdoor pursuits include fishing, laser shooting, horseriding, and the Robert Trent Jones Senior championship golf course. An ideal venue for a romantic getaway or group event.

Member of Leading Small Hotels of the World

Room Rate from €225.00 to €395.00

ANITA CAREY
GENERAL MANAGER

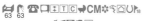
63 63

Open All Year

CARRABAWN HOUSE

KILLARNEY ROAD (N21),
ADARE,
CO. LIMERICK

TEL: 061-396067 FAX: 061-396925
EMAIL: bridget@carrabawnhouseadare.com
WEB: www.carrabawnhouseadare.com

GUESTHOUSE ★★★ MAP 6 G 7

Only 20 miles from Shannon Airport, beside Adare Manor Golf Resort. This superior quality guest accommodation is a must for the weary traveller. We take pride in caring for you as though you were a member of our family. Tastefully decorated, Carrabawn House is ideally located within a few minutes walk of the village centre. Set among award-winning gardens, a delight in all seasons, your stay is assured of being memorable indeed. Many of our guests return from year to year, such is our friendly service. So come stay a while and "be our guest".

Member of Premier Guesthouses

B&B from €35.00 to €65.00

BRIDGET LOHAN
PROPRIETOR

☺ Midweek specials from €90.00pps

8 8

Closed 24 - 26 December

B&B Rates are per Person Sharing per Night incl. Breakfast
Room Rates are per Room per Night

DUNRAVEN ARMS HOTEL

ADARE,
CO. LIMERICK

TEL: 061-396633 FAX: 061-396541
EMAIL: reservations@dunravenhotel.com
WEB: www.dunravenhotel.com

HOTEL ★★★★ MAP 6 G 7

Established in 1792 a 4**** old world hotel surrounded by ornate thatched cottages, in Ireland's prettiest village. Each bedroom, including twelve suites, is beautifully appointed with antique furniture, dressing room and bathroom en suite. Award-winning restaurant, AA Three Red Rosettes. Leisure centre comprised of a 17m pool, steam room and gym studio. Equestrian and golf holidays a speciality. 30 minutes from Shannon Airport. Hotel of the Year 2004 - Georgina Campbell Jameson Guide.

Member of Small Luxury Hotels of the World

Room Rate from € 130.00 to € 195.00

LOUIS MURPHY
PROPRIETOR

 76 76

Open All Year

FITZGERALDS WOODLANDS HOUSE HOTEL, HEALTH AND LEISURE SPA

KNOCKANES,
ADARE,
CO. LIMERICK

TEL: 061-605100 FAX: 061-396073
EMAIL: reception@woodlands-hotel.ie
WEB: www.woodlands-hotel.ie

HOTEL ★★★ MAP 6 G 7

Luxurious 94 bedroom hotel located in the splendour of Adare, on its own grounds of 44 acres, the gateway to the scenic south west. Superior and executive suites available boasting jacuzzi baths. Brennan Room Restaurant, Timmy Mac's Traditional Bar and Bistro, trad sessions. Reva's Hair, Beauty & Relaxation Spa boasting Balneotherapy spa baths & Stone therapy massage. State of the art Health & Leisure Spa. Golf & health spa breaks a speciality. Excellent Wedding and Conference Facilities.

Member of Irish Country Hotels

B&B from € 56.00 to € 109.00

DICK, MARY & DAVID FITZGERALD
HOSTS

 94 94

Closed 24 - 25 December

CASTLE OAKS HOUSE HOTEL & COUNTRY CLUB

CASTLECONNELL,
CO. LIMERICK

TEL: 061-377666 FAX: 061-377717
EMAIL: info@castleoaks.ie
WEB: www.castleoaks.ie

HOTEL ★★★ MAP 6 H 7

Experience our casual country elegance. Located 10 minutes from Limerick City, just off the new Limerick by-pass. The Castle Oaks House Hotel and Leisure Club is situated on 26 acres of mature gardens. The hotel boasts 20 lavishly appointed bedrooms and 22 (2 bed roomed) suites with individual private lounges, 19 4**** self-catering homes and new day spa. Extensive conference and banqueting facilities. Award-winning Acorn Restaurant. Fishing on site. Golf, equestrian facilities nearby. Shannon Airport 40 minutes away.

Member of Great Fishing Houses of Ireland

B&B from € 59.00 to € 100.00

TOM WALSH
GENERAL MANAGER/PROPRIETOR

 64 64

Closed 24 - 26 December

B&B Rates are per Person Sharing per Night incl. Breakfast
Room Rates are per Room per Night

CASTLETROY PARK HOTEL

DUBLIN ROAD,
LIMERICK

TEL: 061-335566 FAX: 061-331117
EMAIL: sales@castletroy-park.ie
WEB: www.castletroy-park.ie

HOTEL ★★★★ MAP 6 H 7

Limerick's finest 4 star hotel offering the ultimate in comfort & luxury. The Castletroy Park Hotel, stands on 14 acres of beautifully landscaped gardens overlooking the Clare Hills & is a short stroll from the River Shannon & the entrance to the 500 acres of Plassey Park, home to University of Limerick. This elegant hotel offers the McLaughlin's award winning restaurant, the Merry Pedlar Irish Pub & Bistro with a superb fitness & leisure centre. The 101 rooms & 6 suites are equipped to the highest standards offering high-speed broadband Internet access.

B&B from €67.50 to €120.00

BRIAN HARRINGTON
GENERAL MANAGER

Weekend specials from €179.00 pps

107 107

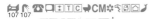

Open All Year

B&B Rates are per Person Sharing per Night incl. Breakfast
Room Rates are per Room per Night

With over **1,000** Hotels & Guesthouses to choose from, Irelandhotels.com offers great value breaks to Ireland.

IRISH
HOTELS
FEDERATION

Official Website of the Irish Hotels Federation

irelandhotels.com
log on and book in

CLARION HOTEL LIMERICK

STEAMBOAT QUAY,
LIMERICK

TEL: 061-444 100 FAX: 061-444 101
EMAIL: info@clarionhotellimerick.com
WEB: www.clarionhotellimerick.com

HOTEL ★★★★ MAP 6 H 7

This 17 storey oval shaped hotel, the tallest hotel in Ireland, boasts a spectacular riverside location just minutes walk from city centre & has magnificent views of the River Shannon. Standard, executive, de luxe & serviced suite accommodation - all equipped with the latest technology. The Waterfornt Sinergie Restaurant & Kudos Bar offer a choice of exemplary cuisine. Health & leisure club includes swimming pool, gym, sauna, steamroom & jacuzzi. European Clarion Hotel of the Year, 2003. Call direct at 061- 444100.

Member of Choice Hotels Ireland

B&B from €60.00 to €125.00

SEÁN LALLY
MANAGING PARTNER

93 93

Closed 24 - 26 December

CLIFTON HOUSE GUEST HOUSE

ENNIS ROAD,
LIMERICK

TEL: 061-451166 FAX: 061-451224
EMAIL: cliftonhouse@eircom.net

GUESTHOUSE ★★★ MAP 6 H 7

Set in 1 acre of landscaped gardens. All sixteen rooms en suite, with multi-channel TV, trouser press, hair dryers, direct dial telephone. Complimentary tea/coffee available in our spacious TV lounge. We are situated on the main Limerick/ Shannon Road. Within 15 minutes walk of city centre. 22 space car park. AA listed. Friendly welcome awaits you.

Member of Premier Guesthouses

B&B from €35.00 to €40.00

MICHAEL & MARY POWELL
PROPRIETOR

16 16

Closed 19 December - 05 January

CLONMACKEN HOUSE GUEST HOUSE

CLONMACKEN,
OFF ENNIS ROAD (AT IVANS),
LIMERICK

TEL: 061-327007 FAX: 061-327785
EMAIL: clonmac@indigo.ie
WEB: www.euroka.com/clonmacken

GUESTHOUSE ★★★ MAP 6 H 7

A purpose built family-run guesthouse all with en suite rooms, with T.V., telephone, tea/coffee and hairdryer in all 10 rooms. We are within 15 minutes walk of the city centre and King John's Castle, 5 minutes walk of the G.A.A. stadium and 5 minutes walk of the famous Munster Rugby Grounds. Bunratty Castle and Shannon Airport are only 15 minutes drive. We have ample car and bus parking as we are situated on 1 acre site.

Member of Premier Guesthouses

B&B from €35.00 to €40.00

BRID AND GERRY MCDONALD
PROPRIETORS

10 10

Closed 22 December - 05 January

B&B Rates are per Person Sharing per Night incl. Breakfast
Room Rates are per Room per Night

GREENHILLS HOTEL CONFERENCE/LEISURE

ENNIS ROAD,
LIMERICK

TEL: 061-453 033 FAX: 061-453 307
EMAIL: info@greenhillsgroup.com
WEB: www.greenhillsgroup.com

HOTEL ★★★ MAP 6 H 7

The newly refurbished Greenhills Hotel, set in 3.5 acres of tended gardens offers a superb base to explore the attractions of the South West. 5 minutes from Limerick City and 15 minutes from Shannon Airport. Enjoy "Bryan's" Bar and "Hughs on the Greene" Restaurant. Relax in our award-winning Leisure Centre, which includes an 18m pool. State of the art conference and banqueting facilities catering for up to 400. Lots of local attractions and amenities.

B&B from €65.00 to €90.00

DAPHNE GREENE
SALES & MARKETING MGR

59 59

Closed 24 - 26 December

JURYS INN LIMERICK

LOWER MALLOW STREET,
LIMERICK

TEL: 061-207000 FAX: 061-400966
EMAIL: jurysinnlimerick@jurysdoyle.com
WEB: www.jurysinns.com

HOTEL ★★★ MAP 6 H 7

Set in the heart of the city along the banks of the Shannon and just a two minute stroll from the shopping and cultural centre of Limerick. This very welcoming Inn provides an excellent base from which to explore many scenic delights in Limerick City, Co. Limerick and Co. Clare.

Member of Jurys Doyle Hotel Group

Room Rate from €79.00 to €85.00

AILEEN PHELAN
GENERAL MANAGER

151 151

Closed 23 - 28 December

LIMERICK STRAND HOTEL

ENNIS ROAD,
LIMERICK

TEL: 061-327777 FAX: 061-326400
EMAIL: stay@limerickstrand.com
WEB: www.limerickstrand.com

HOTEL ★★★★ MAP 6 H 7

Located in the heart of the city and just 15 minutes from Shannon Airport, the hotel is an ideal base for both the corporate and leisure guests. The contemporary style hotel offers 95 bedrooms, the stylish Sorrels Restaurant and Limerick's Bar.The hotel boasts a full leisure centre with an 18 metre pool, jacuzzi, steamroom, full gymnasium and outdoor tennis court. Free on-site parking available to all guests.

B&B from €60.00 to €90.00

PAUL FLAVIN
GENERAL MANAGER

95 95

Closed 24 - 27 December

B&B Rates are per Person Sharing per Night incl. Breakfast
Room Rates are per Room per Night

OLD QUARTER LODGE

DENMARK STREET,
LIMERICK

TEL: 061-315320 FAX: 061-316995
EMAIL: lodge@oldquarter.ie
WEB: www.oldquarter.ie

GUESTHOUSE ★★★ MAP 6 H 7

Old Quarter Lodge, formerly known as Cruises House. Newly refurbished, luxurious en suite rooms, situated in the heart of Limerick City centre, convenient to our finest shops & tourist attractions. All rooms en suite with DD telephone, hairdryer, tea/coffee making facilities, satellite TV. Additional facilities include room service, selection of suites, conference rooms, guest lounge, wireless internet access, fax/photocopying & bureau de change. Old Quarter Bar & Café also located within the building. A warm & friendly welcome awaits you. AA ♦♦♦ recognition.

B&B from €40.00 to €50.00

CAROLE KELLY
LODGE MANAGER

☺ Midweek specials from €99.00 pps

26 26

Closed 24 December - 02 January

PERY'S HOTEL

GLENTWORTH STREET,
LIMERICK

TEL: 061-413822 FAX: 061-413073
EMAIL: info@perys.ie
WEB: www.perys.ie

HOTEL ★★★ MAP 6 H 7

Formerly known as The Glentworth Hotel, this historic city centre hotel is located in the heart of Georgian Limerick. Pery's has been completely refurbished throughout and now offers a striking yet warm, stylish and intimate ambience. Choice of menus and dining options. Excellent wedding and conference facilities. Gym, sauna and private car park. Railway station, shops, theatres, museums, art galleries within minutes. Shannon Airport 20 minutes drive.

Member of Best Western

B&B from €50.00 to €90.00

BARRY DEANE
GENERAL MANAGER

☺ Weekend specials from €125.00 pps

62 62

Closed 25 - 26 December

RADISSON SAS HOTEL

ENNIS ROAD,
LIMERICK

TEL: 061-326666 FAX: 061-327418
EMAIL: sales.limerick@radissonsas.com
WEB: www.radissonsas.ie

HOTEL ★★★★ MAP 6 H 7

The Radisson SAS Hotel, Limerick is strategically located on the Ennis Road (N18) just 5 minutes drive from Limerick City and 15 minutes from Shannon Airport. Set in landscaped gardens, the hotel boasts 154 de luxe bedrooms including luxurious suites. Enjoy our Porters Restaurant or Heron's Irish Pub. Leisure club with swimming pool, sauna, steam room, gymnasium, solarium and beauty salon. Outdoor tennis courts, childrens' playground and complimentary parking.

Member of Radisson SAS Hotels & Resorts

B&B from €80.00 to €150.00

EIVIND DALVANG
GENERAL MANAGER

154 154

Open All Year

B&B Rates are per Person Sharing per Night incl. Breakfast
Room Rates are per Room per Night

RAILWAY HOTEL

**PARNELL STREET,
LIMERICK**

TEL: 061-413653 FAX: 061-419762
EMAIL: sales@railwayhotel.ie
WEB: www.railwayhotel.ie

HOTEL ★★ MAP 6 H 7

Family-run hotel, owned and managed by the McEnery/Collins Family, this hotel offers Irish hospitality at its best. Personal attention is a way of life, along with an attractive lounge/bar, comfortable en suite accommodation and good home cooked food, one can't ask for more. Ideally situated, opposite rail/bus station, convenient to city centre, it is the perfect stop for the tourist and business person alike. All major credit cards accepted.

B&B from €35.00 to €45.00

PAT & MICHELE MCENERY
OWNERS/MANAGERS

30 25

Closed 24 - 26 December

RAMADA KILMURRY

**CASTLETROY,
LIMERICK**

TEL: 061-331133 FAX: 061-330011
EMAIL: kilmurry.reservations@ramadaireland.com
WEB: www.kilmurrylodge.com

HOTEL ★★★ MAP 6 H 7

This newly refurbished hotel set among four acres of landscaped gardens is perfectly located adjacent to the University of Limerick on the Dublin road (N7), whilst still only minutes from the thriving city centre. The business and conference services (1 - 600 people) exceed the highest of expectations and the hotel's "Olde World" character and charm is complemented by the latest in technology including free broadband access in all guest bedrooms.

Member of Ramada International

B&B from €42.00 to €60.00

DARAGH MURPHY
GENERAL MANAGER

100 100

Inet WiFi

Closed 24 - 27 December

SARSFIELD BRIDGE HOTEL

**SARSFIELD BRIDGE,
LIMERICK CITY**

TEL: 061-317179 FAX: 061-317182
EMAIL: info@tsbh.ie
WEB: www.tsbh.ie

HOTEL N MAP 6 H 7

The Sarsfield Bridge Hotel located in the heart of Limerick City beside the River Shannon. Ease of access for sightseeing, shopping, sports events or business makes our hotel the perfect city centre location. All 55 en suite bedrooms are bright, comfortable and relaxing. On the ground floor, our very attractive Pier One Bar & Restaurant overlooking the Shannon offers excellent cuisine. 20 minutes from Shannon Airport. GDS Access Code UI.

B&B from €45.00 to €55.00

DARAGH O'NEILL
PROPRIETOR

55 55

Open All Year

B&B Rates are per Person Sharing per Night incl. Breakfast
Room Rates are per Room per Night

WOODFIELD HOUSE HOTEL

ENNIS ROAD,
LIMERICK

TEL: 061-453022 FAX: 061-326755
EMAIL: woodfieldhotel@eircom.net
WEB: www.woodfieldhousehotel.com

HOTEL ★★★ MAP 6 H 7

Woodfield House Hotel ideally located within strolling distance of Limerick City Centre, Georgian streets, lovely quays, along the Shannon and King John's Castle, St. Mary's Cathedral and the Hunt Museum. Complete your evening in our Bistro where fine cuisine and attentive service create a special dining experience. Our Lansdowne Bar offers a welcoming retreat for both locals and visitors alike.

Member of MinOtel Ireland Hotel Group

B&B from €55.00 to €75.00

KEN & MAJELLA MASTERSON
PROPRIETORS

26 26
Inet

IRISH HOTELS FEDERATION

Closed 24 - 26 December

COURTENAY LODGE HOTEL

NEWCASTLE WEST,
CO. LIMERICK

TEL: 069-62244 FAX: 069-77184
EMAIL: res@courtenaylodge.iol.ie
WEB: www.courtenaylodgehotel.com

HOTEL ★★★ MAP 2 F 6

A warm welcome awaits you at the Courtenay Lodge Hotel situated on the main Limerick to Killarney Road and only 15 minutes from the picturesque village of Adare. The newly-built, tastefully decorated, en suite rooms complete with TV, direct dial phone, power showers, trouser press, tea/coffee facilities, etc. ensure a level of comfort second to none. The ideal base for touring the Shannon and South West regions and the perfect location for golfers to enjoy some of the most renowned courses.

B&B from €45.00 to €75.00

DECLAN O'GRADY
GENERAL MANAGER

39 39
alc

IRISH HOTELS FEDERATION

Closed 25 December

SUNVILLE COUNTRY HOUSE & RESTAURANT

SUNVILLE,
PALLASGREEN,
CO. LIMERICK

TEL: 061-384822 FAX: 061-384823
EMAIL: amgarvey@eircom.net
WEB: www.sunvillehouse.com

GUESTHOUSE P MAP 6 H 7

Elegant Georgian country house, set on 7 acres of gardens, walks & woodland, outside the village of Pallasgreen (N24, 11 miles from Tipperary & 14 miles from Limerick) in the heart of The Golden Vale. Built in 1826, with an original walled kitchen garden & stone courtyard with its old Belltower. Beautifully and sensitively refurbished with features and antiques, once home to relatives of the Duke of Wellington. It now plays host to guests who relax in its splendour and dine on the excellent cuisine of organic produce.

B&B from €58.00 to €115.00

GERRY & ANNE GARVEY

Weekend specials from €145.00 pps

6 6
P
alc

IRISH HOTELS FEDERATION

Closed 16 Febuary - 01 March

B&B Rates are per Person Sharing per Night incl. Breakfast
Room Rates are per Room per Night

RATHKEALE HOUSE HOTEL

RATHKEALE,
CO. LIMERICK

TEL: 069-63333 FAX: 069-63300
EMAIL: info@rathkealehousehotel.com
WEB: www.rathkealehousehotel.com

HOTEL ★★★ MAP 6 G 6

Rathkeale House Hotel, located just off the N21 Limerick to Killarney route and 4 miles west of Ireland's prettiest village, Adare. 26 superior en suite rooms, O'Deas Bistro open each evening 6-9.30pm. Chestnut Tree Bar where carvery lunch is available each day. Conference & banqueting facilities for 300 guests. Golf packages a speciality. Local courses, Adare, Adare Manor, Newcastle West (Ardagh), Charleville. Spacious gardens for your relaxation. A warm welcome awaits you.

Member of Lynch Associates Hotels

B&B from € 50.00 to € 80.00

GERRY O'CONNOR
GENERAL MANAGER

Closed 25 December

ABBEY COURT HOTEL AND TRINITY LEISURE CLUB

DUBLIN ROAD,
NENAGH,
CO. TIPPERARY

TEL: 067-41111 FAX: 067-41022
EMAIL: info@abbeycourt.ie
WEB: www.abbeycourt.ie

HOTEL ★★★ MAP 6 I 8

Situated in the historic town of Nenagh, the Abbey Court is the ideal gateway to Lough Derg. Just off the Dublin to Limerick Road (N7). Hotel presents 82 tastefully & thoughtfully decorated superior bedrooms, exclusive conference & banqueting facilities, award-winning Cloisters Restaurant, Abbots Bar, coupled with a 20m indoor pool, techno gym, Rugrats kiddies club, crêche, hair salon, a spa & beauty centre with balneotherapy unit. A genuine Cead Mile Failte awaits, whether you are on business or taking that long promised & well deserved break.

Member of Best Western Hotels

B&B from € 55.00 to € 110.00

PAT GALVIN
GENERAL MANAGER

Closed 24 - 27 December

GRANT'S HOTEL

CASTLE STREET,
ROSCREA,
CO. TIPPERARY

TEL: 0505-23300 FAX: 0505-23209
EMAIL: grantshotel@eircom.net
WEB: www.grantshotel.com

HOTEL ★★★ MAP 7 J 9

Located on the main link road from Dublin to Kerry, Limerick and Clare (N7). Visit 3*** Grant's Hotel, in the heart of the heritage town of Roscrea. The hotel features 25 en suite bedrooms pleasantly furnished in warm-toned colours. Lunch and evening meals served in Kitty's Tavern daily. The award-winning Lemon Tree Restaurant is the ideal place to relax after a day's golfing, fishing or exploring Ely O'Carroll country. Special golf, hillwalking, river adventure and canoeing packages available.

Room Rate from € 49.00 to € 89.00

CHARLIE HORAN
GENERAL MANAGER

☺ Weekend specials from € 99.00 pps

Closed 25 December

B&B Rates are per Person Sharing per Night incl. Breakfast
Room Rates are per Room per Night

RACKET HALL COUNTRY HOUSE GOLF & CONFERENCE HOTEL

DUBLIN ROAD,
ROSCREA,
CO. TIPPERARY
TEL: 0505-21748 FAX: 0505-23701
EMAIL: racketh@iol.ie
WEB: www.rackethallhotel.com

HOTEL U   MAP 7 J 9

Located on the main N7 just outside the Heritage Town of Roscrea and set in the heart of the monastic Midlands beneath the Slieve Bloom Mountains, this charming family run olde world residence boasts 40 new luxurious guest rooms. The ideal location for the avid golfer, hill walking, fishing enthusiast or history buff. An extremely convenient stopping off point from Dublin to Limerick, Shannon, Clare or Kerry. Award-winning Lily Bridges Steakhouse Bar and Willow Tree Restaurant. Fully wheelchair accessible.

B&B from €49.00 to €79.00

EAMONN CUNNINGHAM
GENERAL MANAGER

40 40

Open All Year

TOWER GUESTHOUSE, BAR & RESTAURANT

CHURCH STREET,
ROSCREA,
CO. TIPPERARY
TEL: 0505-21774 FAX: 0505-22425
EMAIL: thetower@eircom.net

GUESTHOUSE ★★★ MAP 7 J 9

Tucked away on the side of the road beside a mediaeval Round Tower this is a wonderful combination of a guesthouse, restaurant & bar. Situated in the centre of the town, with ample car parking, this is an ideal touring base with golfing, hill walking, horse riding and fishing all within close proximity. The en suite bedrooms are beautifully appointed and tastefully decorated. Overall this establishment has everything for lovers of good food, quality accommodation and classical bars.

Member of Premier Guesthouses

B&B from €35.00 to €45.00

BRIDIE & GERARD COUGHLAN
PROPRIETORS

10 10

Closed 25 - 26 December

TEMPLEMORE ARMS HOTEL

MAIN STREET,
TEMPLEMORE,
CO. TIPPERARY
TEL: 0504-31423 FAX: 0504-31343
EMAIL: info@templemorearmshotel.com
WEB: www.templemorearmshotel.com

HOTEL ★★ MAP 7 J 8

The Templemore Arms Hotel is located in the shadow of one of Ireland's most prominent landmarks, The Devil's Bit, in the centre of the town of Templemore. Recently rebuilt to match the demands of the most discerning guests, it boasts lounge bars, carvery, restaurant, banqueting suite and conference room, providing first class service. Visit the Templemore Arms Hotel and experience an enjoyable getaway.

B&B from €50.00 to €80.00

DAN WARD

☺ 3 Nights B&B + 2 Dinners from €149.95 pps

15 15

Closed 25 December

B&B Rates are per Person Sharing per Night incl. Breakfast
Room Rates are per Room per Night

PIER HOUSE GUESTHOUSE

LOWER KILRONAN,
ARAN ISLANDS,
CO. GALWAY
TEL: 099-61417 FAX: 099-61122
EMAIL: pierh@iol.ie

GUESTHOUSE ★★★ MAP 5 D 10

Pier House is perfectly located less than 100m from Kilronan Harbour and Village, within walking distance of sandy beaches, pubs, restaurants and historical remains. This modern house is finished to a very high standard, has a private gym for guest use and many other extra facilities. Its bedrooms are well appointed and have perfect sea and landscape views. If it is comfort and old fashioned warmth and hospitality you expect, then Pier House is the perfect location to enjoy it.

B&B from €35.00 to €60.00

MAURA JOYCE
PROPRIETOR

12 12

HOTELS

Closed 01 November - 01 March

B&B Rates are per Person Sharing per Night incl. Breakfast
Room Rates are per Room per Night

TIGH FITZ

KILLEANY, KILRONAN,
INISHMORE, ARAN ISLANDS,
CO. GALWAY
TEL: 099-61213 FAX: 099-61386
EMAIL: penny@tighfitz.com
WEB: www.tighfitz.com

GUESTHOUSE ★★★ MAP 5 D 10

Tigh Fitz, a family-run guest house, bar, lounge, is in Killeany, Inishmore. Offering luxurious accommodation in this unspoilt area of the Aran Isles. Tigh Fitz is unique in its situation, in its spaciousness and proximity to beaches and areas of archaeological and historical remains. In this area are the tall cliffs of Aran and the magnificent pre-historic forts. Tigh Fitz is 1.6km from the island capital Kilronan and close to the Aer Arann Airstrip.

B&B from €45.00 to €90.00

PENNY FITZPATRICK
PROPRIETOR

11 11

HOTELS

Closed 01 - 28 December

CASTLEGATE HOTEL

**NORTHGATE STREET,
ATHENRY,
CO. GALWAY**
TEL: 091-845111 FAX: 091-845154
EMAIL: info@castlegatehotel.com
WEB: www.castlegatehotel.com

HOTEL ★★ MAP 6 G 10

Small family-run hotel situated in the heart of mediaeval Athenry, a heritage status town with 14 well appointed comfortable en suite bedrooms with TV. 15 minutes from Galway City in close proximity to the train station. Hot food served daily 9.30am to 9.30pm. Live traditional music four nights a week.

B&B from €40.00 to €60.00

ANDREW KELLY
PROPRIETOR

14 14

Closed 31 October - 01 March

BALLYNAHINCH CASTLE HOTEL

**BALLYNAHINCH,
RECESS, CONNEMARA,
CO. GALWAY**
TEL: 095-31006 FAX: 095-31085
EMAIL: bhinch@iol.ie
WEB: www.ballynahinch-castle.com

HOTEL ★★★★ MAP 5 D 11

Once home to the O'Flaherty Chieftains, pirate queen Grace O'Malley, Humanity Dick Martin & Maharajah Ranjitsinji, Ballynahinch is now a 4**** hotel. With casual country elegance, overlooking both river & mountains, offering an unpretentious service & an ideal centre from which to tour the West. Log fires & a friendly fisherman's pub complement a restaurant offering the best in fresh game, fish & produce. Voted in the top 20 hotels in the world by Fodor's, it is the jewel in Connemara's crown. RAC 2 Dining Award.

Member of Great Fishing Houses of Ireland
B&B from €105.00 to €130.00

PATRICK O'FLAHERTY
GENERAL MANAGER

40 40

alc Inet

Closed Christmas Week & February

CARNA BAY HOTEL

**CARNA,
CONNEMARA,
CO. GALWAY**
TEL: 095-32255 FAX: 095-32530
EMAIL: carnabay@iol.ie
WEB: www.carnabay.com

HOTEL ★★★ MAP 9 D 11

Are you looking for somewhere special? Allow us to plan your carefree days in the most magical scenery in Ireland. Connemara, unique landscape, flora and fauna, unspoilt beaches, mountain ranges. Beautiful Western Way walking routes. Cycling, bicycles provided free. Our kitchen offers the finest fresh Irish produce. 26 well appointed rooms, most with scenic views. Locally: St. McDara's Island, Connemara National Park, Kylemore Abbey, Aran and Inisbofin Ferry 40 minutes drive.

Member of Irish Country Hotels
B&B from €45.00 to €75.00

MICHAEL & SHEAMUS CLOHERTY
PROPRIETORS

26 26

Closed 23 -27 December

B&B Rates are per Person Sharing per Night incl. Breakfast
Room Rates are per Room per Night

HOTEL CARRAROE

CARRAROE,
CO. GALWAY

TEL: 091-595116 FAX: 091-595187
EMAIL: hotelcarraroe@eircom.net
WEB: www.hotelcarraroe.com

HOTEL U   MAP 5 D 10

The Hotel Carraroe is a 25 bedroomed en suite family-run hotel situated in the heart of the Connemara Gaeltacht. The village of Carraroe itself is renowned for its traditional values and music. Daily boat trips to the Aran Islands are from nearby Rossaveal Harbour. Our local friendly staff will provide information on where to fish, play golf, horse ride or tour beautiful Connemara. Enjoy our new Irish Themed Bar.

B&B from € 50.00 to € 100.00

SEOSAMH Ó LOIDEÁIN

☺ Weekend specials from €90.00 pps

25 25

Open All Year

CASHEL HOUSE HOTEL

CASHEL,
CO. GALWAY

TEL: 095-31001 FAX: 095-31077
EMAIL: info@cashel-house-hotel.com
WEB: www.cashel-house-hotel.com

HOTEL ★★★★   MAP 5 D 11

Elegance in a wilderness on the shores of the Atlantic. It is set amidst the most beautiful gardens in Ireland. Enjoy long walks, cycling and fishing. Later, relax in front of a peat fire in this elegant residence appointed with antique furniture and period paintings. Most guestrooms look onto the gardens and some onto the sea. Dine on bounty from the sea and garden - enjoy vintage wine.

Member of Relais et Châteaux

B&B from € 96.00 to € 141.00

MCEVILLY FAMILY
PROPRIETORS

32 32

Inet

Closed 05 January - 05 February

ZETLAND COUNTRY HOUSE HOTEL

CASHEL BAY,
CONNEMARA,
CO. GALWAY
TEL: 095-31111 FAX: 095-31117
EMAIL: zetland@iol.ie
WEB: www.zetland.com

HOTEL ★★★★   MAP 5 D 11

Overlooking Cashel Bay this 19th century manor house is renowned for its peace and commanding views. The bedrooms and superb seafood restaurant overlook the gardens and Cashel Bay. Facilities include tennis court and billiard room and there are many activities, hill walking and golf in the surrounding area. Good Hotel Guide recommended, AA Courtesy of Care Award and Gilbeys Gold Medal Winner. 4**** Manor House Hotel.

Member of Manor House Hotels

B&B from € 95.00 to € 110.00

JOHN & MONA PRENDERGAST
PROPRIETORS

☺ Midweek specials from €180.00 pps

20 20

Closed 01 December - 01 February

B&B Rates are per Person Sharing per Night incl. Breakfast
Room Rates are per Room per Night

CLAREGALWAY HOTEL

CLAREGALWAY,
CO. GALWAY

TEL: 091-738 200 FAX: 091-738 211
EMAIL: stay@claregalwayhotel.ie
WEB: www.claregalwayhotel.ie

HOTEL P   MAP 6 11 G

The new Claregalway Hotel is a privately owned state of the art hotel, leisure club & conference centre located just ten minutes from Galway City in the picturesque village of Claregalway. The hotel is designed in a contemporary Irish style featuring all the facilities one would expect from a de luxe hotel. Extensive conference and banqueting facilities in the luxurious Waterdale Suite, Escape Health and Leisure Club, Tí Cusack's Public House & Café Bar and the highly acclaimed River Bistro.

B&B from €60.00 to €120.00

PAUL GILL
PROPRIETOR

CMCS
48 48
alc   Inet

HOTELS
IRISH
FEDERATION

Closed 23 - 27 December

ABBEYGLEN CASTLE HOTEL

SKY ROAD,
CLIFDEN,
CO. GALWAY

TEL: 095-22832 FAX: 095-21797
EMAIL: info@abbeyglen.ie
WEB: www.abbeyglen.ie

HOTEL ★★★★   MAP 9 C 12

Abbeyglen Castle Hotel was built in 1832 in the heart of Connemara by John D'Arcy of Clifden Castle. It is romantically set in beautiful gardens with waterfalls and streams, has a panoramic view of Clifden and the bay with a backdrop of the Twelve Bens. Abbeyglen provides a long list of indoor/outdoor facilities, cuisine of international fame, unique qualities of peace, serenity and ambience. Complimentary afternoon tea a speciality. AA 1 rosette for good food and service. Reservations from USA 011 353 95 22832, from Europe 00 353 95 22832.

Member of Manor House Hotels

B&B from €89.00 to €110.00

BRIAN/PAUL HUGHES
MANAGER/PROPRIETOR

45 45
alc

HOTELS
IRISH
FEDERATION

Closed 02 January - 04 February

ALCOCK AND BROWN HOTEL

CLIFDEN,
CONNEMARA,
CO. GALWAY

TEL: 095-21206 FAX: 095-21842
EMAIL: alcockandbrown@eircom.net
WEB: www.alcockandbrown-hotel.com

HOTEL ★★★   MAP 9 C 12

Alcock and Brown Hotel is family owned and operated. Situated in the centre of Clifden Village, featuring Brownes Restaurant with AA Rosette and 2 RAC ribbons for food and service. Ideal base for touring Connemara. Pursuits to be enjoyed are pony trekking, golfing on Connemara championship links course. Sea angling, guided heritage walks and mountain climbing. Numerous sandy beaches nearby. Member of Best Western Hotels - Central Reservations 01-6766776.

Member of Best Western Hotels

B&B from €55.00 to €80.00

DEIRDRE KEOGH
MANAGER

 Weekend specials from €126.00 pps

TCCMU S alc Inet
19 19

HOTELS
IRISH
FEDERATION

Closed 22 - 27 December

B&B Rates are per Person Sharing per Night incl. Breakfast
Room Rates are per Room per Night

ARDAGH HOTEL & RESTAURANT

**BALLYCONNEELY ROAD,
CLIFDEN,
CO. GALWAY**
TEL: 095-21384 FAX: 095-21314
EMAIL: ardaghhotel@eircom.net
WEB: www.ardaghhotel.com

HOTEL ★★★   MAP 9 C 12

A quiet family-run 3*** hotel, 2km from Clifden on Ardbear Bay, AA and RAC recommended. Bedrooms individually decorated with television, telephone and tea/coffee facilities. Award-winning restaurant, 2 AA rosettes & 3 dining seals by RAC. Specialises in lobsters, salmon, oysters and Connemara lamb with homegrown vegetables and a wide selection of wines. Local amenities: golf, fishing and beaches. Reservations by post, phone, fax, email and website. Superior suites with bay view available.

Member of Irish Country Hotels

B&B from €75.00 to €95.00

STEPHANE & MONIQUE BAUVET
PROPRIETOR/MANAGER/CHEF

Weekend specials from €89.00pps

17 17

Closed 27 October - 25 March

BEN VIEW HOUSE

**BRIDGE STREET,
CLIFDEN, CONNEMARA,
CO. GALWAY**
TEL: 095-21256 FAX: 095-21226
EMAIL: benviewhouse@ireland.com
WEB: www.connemara-tourism.org

GUESTHOUSE ★★   MAP 9 C 12

Dating from 1848 Benview has been owned and managed by our family since 1926. See our history on web site. Recommended by Frommer and Le Petit Fute Guides. RAC ◆◆◆ and AA ◆◆◆ approved. Enjoy all the modern comforts of this elegant guesthouse, surrounded by antiques and old world atmosphere. Walking distance to all amenities, harbour and seaside. Free on street parking. Lock-up garage available for motorcycles and bicycles. Your hostess Eileen wishes everyone a safe and pleasant journey.

B&B from €27.00 to €38.00

EILEEN MORRIS
PROPRIETOR

Midweek specials from €90.00 pps

9 9

IRISH
HOTELS
FEDERATION

Closed 24 - 26 December

Kylemore Abbey & Garden

Neo-Gothic Castle and Church

Abbey Exhibition Rooms
(Under Restoration)
Neo-Gothic Church
(Under Restoration)
"Cathedral in miniature"
• Lake Walk • Video • Craft Shop
• Pottery Studio • Restaurant

A '*Great Garden of Ireland*'

**6-Acre Victorian
Walled Garden**
(Under Restoration)
**featuring Formal Flower
& Kitchen Garden**
• Woodland Walk
• Exhibition • Museum

Opening Times:

Abbey, Craft Shop & Restaurant
Mar - Nov: 9.30am - 5.30pm
Nov - Mar: 10.30am - 4.00pm
(except Christmas week & Good Friday)
Garden
Easter - October: 10.30am - 4.30pm

**Kylemore Abbey & Garden,
Kylemore, Connemara,
Co. Galway, Ireland**

Tel: +353 95 41146
Fax: +353 95 41440
Email: info@kylemoreabbey.ie
www.kylemoreabbey.com

B&B Rates are per Person Sharing per Night incl. Breakfast
Room Rates are per Room per Night

BENBAUN HOUSE

LYDONS,
WESTPORT ROAD, CLIFDEN,
CO. GALWAY
TEL: 095-21462 FAX: 095-21462
EMAIL: benbaunhouse@eircom.net
WEB: www.benbaunhouse.com

GUESTHOUSE ★★★ MAP 9 C 12

We invite you to enjoy the affordable luxury of Benbaun, set well back from the road in mature, leafy gardens, 2 minutes walk from Clifden Town Centre. Newly refurbished to a very high standard. We offer a variety of en suite rooms with TV, DD phone, hairdryers and a hospitality trolley in the study. Breakfast is special, a feast offering tempting choices. Whether you're sightseeing, fishing, rambling or golfing Benbaun House is where you'll find a home away from home.

B&B from €30.00 to €40.00

DR BRENDAN LYDON
PROPRIETOR

🛏 🅰 ☎ 🖵 T Ⓐ C ↩ CM ✻ ⊍ J P S
14 14

🖵 Inet

IRISH
HOTELS
FEDERATION

Closed 30 September - 01 May

BUTTERMILK LODGE

WESTPORT ROAD,
CLIFDEN,
CO. GALWAY
TEL: 095-21951 FAX: 095-21953
EMAIL: buttermilklodge@eircom.net
WEB: www.buttermilklodge.com

GUESTHOUSE ★★★ MAP 9 C 12

A warm friendly home from home, 400m from Clifden Town Centre. Spacious bedrooms each with multi-channel TV, DD phone, personal toiletries, hairdryer, ironing facilities and private bath/shower room. Your warm welcome includes tea/coffee and home baking by the turf fire where there is always a cuppa available. Our breakfast options, tasteful décor, interesting cow collection, stunning mountain views, friendly Connemara Ponies and many extra touches ensure return visits. Irish Tourist Board 3***, RAC ◆◆◆◆◆, AA ◆◆◆◆.

B&B from €35.00 to €50.00

CATHRIONA & PATRICK O'TOOLE
PROPRIETORS/HOSTS

☺ Midweek specials from €95.00 pps

🛏 🅰 ☎ 🖵 T C ✻ ⊍ J P S Inet
11 11

IRISH
HOTELS
FEDERATION

Closed 03 January - 10 February

BYRNE MAL DUA HOUSE AND RESTAURANT

GALWAY ROAD,
CLIFDEN, CONNEMARA,
CO. GALWAY
TEL: 095-21171 FAX: 095-21739
EMAIL: info@maldua.com
WEB: www.maldua.com

GUESTHOUSE ★★★★ MAP 9 C 12

The 4**** award-winning Byrne Mal Dua House & Restaurant offers luxury and personalized hospitality in a relaxed friendly atmosphere, all one expects of a private hotel. Enjoy dinner in our award-winning Fuchsia Restaurant or just relax in our landscaped gardens. Winners of the RAC Little Gem Award 2004 and Property of the Year by Les Routiers. RAC ◆◆◆◆◆, AA ◆◆◆◆◆, Karen Brown's guide and other publications. Internet Access. Use of nearby Leisure Centre. USA Toll Free 1 866 891 9420 & UK Free Phone 0800 904 7532.

B&B from €50.00 to €85.00

THE BYRNE FAMILY

☺ Special offers available on our website.

🛏 🅰 ☎ 🖵 T C ↩ CM ✻ ⊍ J P S Ⓨ alc
14 14

🖵 Inet 🛍

IRISH
HOTELS
FEDERATION

Open All Year

B&B Rates are per Person Sharing per Night incl. Breakfast
Room Rates are per Room per Night

GLENLO ABBEY HOTEL

**BUSHYPARK,
GALWAY**

TEL: 091-526666 FAX: 091-527800
EMAIL: info@glenloabbey.ie
WEB: www.glenlo.com

HOTEL ★★★★★ MAP 6 F 10

Glenlo Abbey Hotel - an 18th century country residence, is located on a 138 acre lakeside golf estate just 4km from Galway City. A Failte Ireland rated 5***** hotel, Glenlo Abbey is a haven for all discerning travellers. All 46 rooms have a marbled bathroom, personal safe, direct dial phone, trouser press, cable TV, radio and 24 hour room service. The Pullman Restaurant, two unique Orient Express carriages, offers a totally new dining experience. Other activities include fishing, etc.

Member of Small Luxury Hotels

Room Rate from €199.00 to €314.00

PEGGY & JOHN BOURKE
PROPRIETORS

Midweek specials from €214.00 pps

46 46

Open All Year

HARBOUR HOTEL

**NEW DOCK ROAD,
GALWAY**

TEL: 091-569466 FAX: 091-569455
EMAIL: stay@harbour.ie
WEB: www.harbour.ie

HOTEL U MAP 6 F 10

The Harbour is located in the city centre adjacent to the waterfront area. This contemporary style hotel offers 96 spacious rooms, a chic bar and restaurant along with "state of the art" meeting rooms to cater for up to 75 people. The Harbour also boasts an exclusive leisure suite which includes a gym, steamroom, jacuzzi and treatment rooms. The Harbour prides itself on its outstanding levels of service and quality in refreshingly unique surroundings.

B&B from €59.00 to €170.00

SINEAD O'REILLY
GENERAL MANAGER

Weekend specials from €159.00 pps

96 96

Closed 23 - 28 December

HOTEL SACRE COEUR

**LENABOY GARDENS,
SALTHILL,
GALWAY**

TEL: 091-523355 FAX: 091-523553
EMAIL: info@sacrecoeurhotel.com
WEB: www.sacrecoeurhotel.com

HOTEL ★★ MAP 6 F 10

Hotel Sacre Coeur is a family owned and managed hotel where a Céad Míle Fáilte awaits you. All of our 40 rooms are en suite, have direct dial telephone, with colour TV and tea/coffee making facilities. Within five minutes walk of the hotel we have Salthill's magnificent promenade, a tennis club and a wonderful 18 hole golf course. Renowned for its friendly service and excellent food you will enjoy your stay at the Sacre Coeur.

B&B from €49.00 to €56.00

SEÁN OG DUNLEAVY
MANAGER

40 40

Closed 22 - 31 December

B&B Rates are per Person Sharing per Night incl. Breakfast
Room Rates are per Room per Night

HOTEL SPANISH ARCH

**QUAY STREET,
GALWAY**

TEL: 091-569600 FAX: 091-569191
EMAIL: info@spanisharchhotel.ie
WEB: www.spanisharchhotel.ie

HOTEL U MAP 6 F 10

Situated in Galway City centre. 20 superbly appointed en suite bedrooms with bath & shower, direct dial telephone, TV, hairdryer, tea & coffee making facilities. Ideally located for shopping, theatres, art galleries, museums, pubs, restaurants and clubs. Bar food served daily in the Spanish Arch Bar and an à la carte menu is available in the evening. Live entertainment weekly including Trad and Jazz sessions. Our team of friendly, professional staff will do everything to make your stay a relaxing and enjoyable one.

B&B from €45.00 to €130.00

AIDAN & MARTINA MCINTYRE
GENERAL MANAGER

20 20

HOTELS FEDERATION

Closed 25 - 26 December

IMPERIAL HOTEL

**EYRE SQUARE,
GALWAY**

TEL: 091-563033 FAX: 091-568410
EMAIL: imperialhtl@hotmail.com
WEB: www.imperialhotelgalway.ie

HOTEL ★★★ MAP 6 F 10

A bustling hotel in the centre of Galway City with modern comfortable 3 star bedrooms. Located in the main shopping area surrounded by a large choice of restaurants, pubs and quality shops. Five minutes walk from the new Galway Theatre, main bus and rail terminals. Beside main taxi rank with multi storey parking nearby. Full service hotel; friendly and informative staff. No service charge. RAC 3 ***.

B&B from €50.00 to €100.00

JOHN KELLEHER
GENERAL MANAGER

84 84

HOTELS FEDERATION

Closed 24 - 27 December

INISHMORE GUESTHOUSE

**109 FR. GRIFFIN ROAD,
LOWER SALTHILL,
GALWAY**

TEL: 091-582639 FAX: 091-589311
EMAIL: inishmorehouse@eircom.net
WEB: www.galwaybaygolfholidays.com

GUESTHOUSE ★★★ MAP 6 F 10

A charming family residence with secure carpark within 5 minutes walk of city and beach. All rooms contain direct dial phone, multi-channel TV and hairdryers. Tea/coffee and ironing facilities available. German spoken. An ideal base for touring the Aran Islands, Burren and Connemara. All day tours can be organised. Golf holidays, sea angling trips and coarse or game fishing arranged. Recommended by many leading travel guides. Specialise in Golf Package Holidays.

B&B from €30.00 to €60.00

MARIE & PETER
PROPRIETORS

Midweek specials from €90.00 pps

8 8

HOTELS FEDERATION

Closed 23 December - 07 January

B&B Rates are per Person Sharing per Night incl. Breakfast
Room Rates are per Room per Night

PORTFINN LODGE

**LEENANE,
CO. GALWAY**

TEL: 095-42265 FAX: 095-42315
EMAIL: rorydaly@anu.ie
WEB: www.portfinn.com

GUESTHOUSE ★★ MAP 9 D 12

Portfinn Lodge is a family-run guest house offering 8 comfortable rooms en suite including double and triple bedrooms, a guest lounge and a restaurant which has an international reputation for its fresh seafood. Rory and Brid Daly will be delighted to make you feel welcome. An ideal centre from which beaches, walking, angling, watersports etc. are within easy reach. When in Connemara, stay at Portfinn. Member of Premier Guesthouses.

Member of Premier Guesthouses of Ireland

B&B from €34.00 to €45.00

BRID & RORY DALY
OWNERS

Closed 01 November - 31 March

B&B Rates are per Person Sharing per Night incl. Breakfast
Room Rates are per Room per Night

ROSLEAGUE MANOR HOTEL

**LETTERFRACK,
CONNEMARA,
CO. GALWAY**

TEL: 095-41101 FAX: 095-41168
EMAIL: info@rosleague.com
WEB: www.rosleague.com

HOTEL ★★★★ MAP 9 C 12

Rosleague is a Regency manor now run as a first class country house hotel by Mark Foyle and Eddie Foyle. It lies 7 miles north west of Clifden on the coast overlooking a sheltered bay and surrounded by the Connemara Mountains, beside the National Park. It is renowned for its superb cuisine personally supervised by the owners with all the amenities expected by today's discerning guest. Also a member of Ireland's Blue Book.

Member of I.C.H.R.A. (Blue Book)

B&B from €80.00 to €110.00

EDDIE FOYLE/MARK FOYLE
OWNER/MANAGER

Closed 17 November - 14 March

MEADOW COURT HOTEL

CLOSTOKEN,
LOUGHREA,
CO. GALWAY
TEL: 091-841051 FAX: 091-842406
EMAIL: meadowcourthotel@eircom.net
WEB: www.meadowcourthotel.com

HOTEL ★★★ MAP 6 H 10

Newly extended and refurbished the Meadow Court Hotel's en suite rooms have full facilities, multi channel TV, hairdryer and garment press. Superb dining is on offer in our award-winning restaurant renowned for its outstanding cuisine. Enjoy after dinner drinks in our Derby Bar. Situated on the main Galway Dublin Road 2 miles from Loughrea, 18 miles from Galway, convenient to all local 18-hole golf courses, angling, horseriding, water sports. Banqueting & conference facilities. Carpark.

B&B from €50.00 to €100.00

TOM & DAVID CORBETT
DIRECTORS

21 21

Closed 23 - 26 December

O'DEAS HOTEL

BRIDE STREET,
LOUGHREA,
CO. GALWAY
TEL: 091-841611 FAX: 091-842635
EMAIL: odeashotel@eircom.net
WEB: www.odeashotel.com

HOTEL ★★★ MAP 6 H 10

O'Deas Hotel is a family hotel, a Georgian town house hotel of character, with open fires and within walking distance of Loughrea's game fishing lake. It is an ideal touring base situated on the N6 (exactly halfway between Clonmacnoise, 35 miles to the east and the Cliffs of Moher, 35 miles to the west). The start of the Burren country is just 12 miles away. Galway City 20 miles.

Member of MinOtel of Ireland

B&B from €55.00 to €55.00

MARY O'NEILL
PROPRIETOR/MANAGER

32 32

Closed 24 - 26 December

PEACOCKES HOTEL & COMPLEX

MAAM CROSS,
CONNEMARA,
CO. GALWAY
TEL: 091-552306 FAX: 091-552216
EMAIL: peacockes@eircom.net
WEB: www.peacockeshotel.com

HOTEL ★★★ MAP 6 F 10

Newly built, nestling between the lakes and mountains at the crossroads to Connemara. Peacockes Hotel is the ideal base for hillwalking, cycling, golfing, fishing, horseriding or watersports. After a day's travel, relax with a drink by the open turf fire in the Bogdale Bar or enjoy a sumptuous meal in our Quiet Man Restaurant. Visit our 20m high viewing tower, extensive craft shop and replica Quiet Man cottage.

B&B from €50.00 to €100.00

EIMEAR KILLIAN
GENERAL MANAGER

Weekend specials from €99.00 pps

25 25

Closed 23 - 26 December

B&B Rates are per Person Sharing per Night incl. Breakfast
Room Rates are per Room per Night

ORANMORE LODGE HOTEL, CONFERENCE & LEISURE CENTRE

ORANMORE,
CO. GALWAY

TEL: 091-794400 FAX: 091-790227
EMAIL: orlodge@eircom.net
WEB: www.oranmorelodge.com

HOTEL ★★★ MAP 6 G 10

This manor house hotel 5 minutes from Galway city, 3 Kms from Galway Airpport. Located in the picturesque village of Oranmore, overlooking Galway Bay. Rooms consisting of 2 queen size beds and luxury executive suites, swimming pool, sauna, steamroom, jacuzzi, gym. New conference rooms with a.c., plasma screens and up-to-date communications technology. Your host and the friendly staff look forward to welcoming you.

B&B from €50.00 to €150.00

BRIAN J. O'HIGGINS
MANAGING DIRECTOR

😊 Weekend specials from €99.00 pps

60   60

Closed 22 - 27 December

QUALITY HOTEL AND LEISURE CENTRE GALWAY

ORANMORE,
CO. GALWAY

TEL: 1850-746 8357 FAX: 021-427 1489
EMAIL: res@qualityhotelgalway.com
WEB: www.qualityhotelgalway.com

HOTEL ★★★ MAP 6 G 10

This luxury hotel is ideally located on the N6 approach to Galway, adjacent to the picturesque village of Oranmore, 5 mins drive from Galway. Facilities include 113 spacious & contemporary bedrooms, a lively pub with regular entertainment & all day menu, Lannigans Restaurant, residents' lounge & a superb leisure centre with 20m pool, jacuzzi, hi-tech gym, steamroom, sauna, therapy suite & solarium. Rooms to accommodate up to 2 adults & 3 children. Golf, karting, horseriding nearby, adjacent to bowling, cinema & kids playcentre. Direct tel: 091-792244.

Member of Quality Hotels

B&B from €40.00 to €120.00

DERMOT COMERFORD
GENERAL MANAGER

😊 Weekend specials from €100.00 pps

113 113

Closed 24 - 27 December

BOAT INN (THE)

THE SQUARE,
OUGHTERARD,
CO. GALWAY

TEL: 091-552196 FAX: 091-552694
EMAIL: info@theboatinn.com
WEB: www.theboatinn.com

GUESTHOUSE ★★★ MAP 5 E 11

3*** guesthouse in the heart of Oughterard, just 25 minutes from Galway. 5 minutes to Lough Corrib and redesigned 18 hole golf course. Ideal base to explore Connemara. The Boat Bar and Restaurant offer an imaginative choice of food, drink and wine. Enjoy the continental feel of our terrace and rear gardens. Live music in the bar. All bedrooms en suite with TV, radio, phone and tea & coffee making facilities.

B&B from €35.00 to €40.00

JOE WALSH & ANNETTE WRAFTER
PROPRIETORS

😊 Weekend specials from €95.00 pps

10   10

Closed 25 December

B&B Rates are per Person Sharing per Night incl. Breakfast
Room Rates are per Room per Night

CARROWN TOBER HOUSE

ARVARNA,
OUGHTERARD,
CO. GALWAY

TEL: 091-552166 FAX: 091-866 8981
EMAIL: info@carrowntober.com
WEB: www.carrowntober.com

GUESTHOUSE P   MAP 5 E 11

Carrown Tober House, situated just off the N59 and within walking distance of Oughterard. Family-run guesthouse with all rooms en suite, with TVs and direct dial telephones. Within easy access of the Connemara Mountains and the famous Lough Corrib. Choice of 4 championship golf courses and numerous fishing lakes.

B&B from € 30.00 to € 35.00

MCDONNELL FAMILY

7   7

Open All Year

CONNEMARA GATEWAY HOTEL

OUGHTERARD,
CO. GALWAY

TEL: 091-552328 FAX: 091-552332
EMAIL: gateway@iol.ie
WEB: www.connemaragateway.com

HOTEL ★★★   MAP 5 E 11

You will find this hotel located just 16 miles outside Galway City in the picturesque location of Oughterard known as "The Gateway to Connemara". Surrounded by well maintained mature grounds, you will be able to relax in front of the welcoming turf fire in the pine panelled lobby. With entertainment in O'Nuallains Bar, attractive restaurant menus, indoor heated swimming pool & sauna this is an ideal place to enjoy true Irish hospitality. All rooms are en suite & enjoy views overlooking the gardens. Conference facilities for corporate events.

B&B from € 50.00 to € 125.00

MICHELLE AND DENIS DOHERTY
MANAGERS

☺ Weekend specials from €99.00 pps

62   62

IRISH
HOTELS
FEDERATION

Closed 21 - 27 December

CORRIB WAVE GUEST HOUSE

PORTACARRON,
OUGHTERARD, CONNEMARA,
CO. GALWAY

TEL: 091-552147 FAX: 091-552736
EMAIL: cwh@gofree.indigo.ie
WEB: www.corribwave.com

GUESTHOUSE ★★★   MAP 5 E 11

Panoramic lakeside guest house - the home of Michael & Maria Healy. As our guests, you are assured of a warm welcome to a family home with every comfort and Irish hospitality, superb home cooking, excellent wines, beautiful en suite bedrooms (all with double and single beds), TVs, hairdryers. Spectacular views, turf fire, peace & tranquillity. Angling specialists, boats, engines. Boatmen for hire. Wild brown trout, salmon, pike, lakeside walks. 18 hole golf 1km. Colour brochure on request. For more information contact us direct.

B&B from € 35.00 to € 40.00

MARIA & MICHAEL HEALY
PROPRIETORS

☺ 3 day special €165.00 - €180.00
3 nights B&B and 3 dinners.

10   10

IRISH
HOTELS
FEDERATION

Closed 01 December - 01 February

B&B Rates are per Person Sharing per Night incl. Breakfast
Room Rates are per Room per Night

CURRAREVAGH HOUSE

OUGHTERARD,
CONNEMARA,
CO. GALWAY
TEL: 091-552312 FAX: 091-552731
EMAIL: mail@currarevagh.com
WEB: www.currarevagh.com

GUESTHOUSE ★★★★ MAP 5 E 11

A charming country mansion, built in 1842, romantically situated beside Lough Corrib in 60 ha. of private woodlands. The relaxing atmosphere & classically simple menus receive much international praise. Own fishing, boats, tennis court, with golf & riding locally. Recommendations: Egon Ronay, Guide Michelin, Footprint Guide, Lonely Planet, Karen Brown's Irish Country Inns, Good Food Guide, Good Hotel Guide & many other intl. hotel & food guides. They suggest that you stay at least 3 nights to absorb the atmosphere & gently explore Connemara.

Member of Ireland's Blue Book

B&B from €75.00 to €110.00

HARRY & JUNE HODGSON
PROPRIETORS

☺ 3-6 days half board from €115.00 pp per day + S.C.

🛏 🐕 ☀ 🎣 🎱 🐎
15 15

Closed 20 October - 24 March

LAKE HOTEL

OUGHTERARD,
CO. GALWAY
TEL: 091-552275 FAX: 091-552794

HOTEL ★★ MAP 5 E 11

Family-run hotel under the personal supervision of Frank & Mary O' Meara. There are 4 championship golf courses - Oughterard, Connemara, Barna, Galway Bay Golf & Country Club close by. Oughterard is within easy access of Connemara's rugged hills and hidden lakes, only 20 minutes drive to Galway City. Wild Brown Trout, Salmon in the beautiful Lough Corrib. We cater for shooting groups. Special group rates. All rooms en suite with TV and phone.

B&B from €40.00 to €45.00

FRANK & MARY O'MEARA
PROPRIETORS

🛏 🐕 ☎ 🖵 T C CM 🎣 🎵 S 🔒 🆎 🐕
18 18

Open All Year

MOUNTAIN VIEW GUEST HOUSE

AUGHNANURE,
OUGHTERARD,
CO. GALWAY
TEL: 091-550306 FAX: 091-550133
EMAIL: tricia.oconnor@eircom.net

GUESTHOUSE ★★★ MAP 5 E 11

Situated just off the N59, 24kms from Galway City and within 2-4 km of Oughterard, with the Connemara mountains in the distance and Lough Corrib nearby. Leisure activities include; Golf at the renowned Oughterard Golf Club, established walks along scenic routes, boating or fishing on Lough Corrib. All bedrooms en suite, with TV, direct dial phones, tea/coffee making facilities and hairdryers.

B&B from €30.00 to €35.00

RICHARD & PATRICIA O'CONNOR
PROPRIETORS

☺ Midweek specials from €85.00 pps

🛏 🐕 ☎ 🖵 T C ⛵ CM ☀ ∪ 🎣 🔒 🐕
10 10

Closed 23 - 28 December

B&B Rates are per Person Sharing per Night incl. Breakfast
Room Rates are per Room per Night

ROSS LAKE HOUSE HOTEL

ROSSCAHILL,
OUGHTERARD,
CO. GALWAY

TEL: 091-550109 FAX: 091-550184
EMAIL: rosslake@iol.ie
WEB: www.rosslakehotel.com

HOTEL ★★★ MAP 5 E 11

Ross Lake House is a wonderful Georgian house set in the magnificent wilderness of Connemara. Six acres of mature gardens surround the house creating an air of peace and tranquillity. Hosts Henry and Elaine Reid have beautifully restored this manor house to its former glory. A high quality Irish menu is prepared daily featuring a tempting variety of fresh produce from nearby Connemara hills, streams and lakes as well as fish straight from the Atlantic.

Member of Green Book of Ireland

B&B from €75.00 to €85.00

ELAINE & HENRY REID
PROPRIETORS

☺ Midweek specials from €325.00 pps
(3 nights B&B + 3 Dinner)

13 13

Closed 01 November - 14 March

SHANNON OAKS HOTEL & COUNTRY CLUB

PORTUMNA,
CO. GALWAY

TEL: 090-974 1777 FAX: 090-974 1357
EMAIL: sales@shannonoaks.ie
WEB: www.shannonoaks.ie

HOTEL ★★★ MAP 6 I 9

Shannon Oaks Hotel & Country Club lies adjacent to the 17th century Portumna Castle and estate, by the shores of Lough Derg. All our rooms have satellite television, DD phone and an en suite bathroom. A distinguished menu of classic and fusion Irish dishes are available each evening. Our leisure centre, with its indoor heated swimming pool, sauna, steamroom and gymnasium provides the stress free atmosphere in which to relax and unwind.

Member of Irish Country Hotels

B&B from €50.00 to €75.00

PAUL ADAMS
GENERAL MANAGER

63 63

Open All Year

LOUGH INAGH LODGE

RECESS,
CONNEMARA,
CO. GALWAY

TEL: 095-34706 FAX: 095-34708
EMAIL: inagh@iol.ie
WEB: www.loughinaghlodgehotel.ie

HOTEL ★★★★ MAP 5 D 11

Lough Inagh Lodge was built in 1880. It offers all the comforts of an elegant modern hotel in an old world atmosphere, open log fires in the library and oak panelled bar symbolises the warmth of Inagh hospitality. The lodge is surrounded by famous beauty spots including the Twelve Bens Mountain Range and the Connemara National Park. Kylemore Abbey is also nearby.

Member of Manor House Hotels

B&B from €89.00 to €107.00

MAIRE O'CONNOR
PROPRIETOR

☺ Weekend specials from €187.00 pps

12 12

Closed 08 December - 12 March

B&B Rates are per Person Sharing per Night incl. Breakfast
Room Rates are per Room per Night

MAOL REIDH LODGE

TULLYCROSS,
RENVYLE,
CO. GALWAY
TEL: 095-43844 FAX: 095-43784
EMAIL: maolreidhhotel@eircom.net
WEB: www.maolreidhhotel.com

HOTEL N MAP 9 C 12

Situated in the delightful village of Tullycross, Renvyle the new Maol Reidh Lodge offers guests a high standard of luxury. We are close to Connemara National Park and Kylemore Abbey. For the active guest, we are nestled in the Twelve Bens and Maamturk Mountains, and only a few minutes drive from Scuba-Dive West and Oceans Alive sealife centre. A perfect place to enjoy the natural paradise of Connemara.

B&B from €45.00 to €65.00

JACK & MONICA LYDON
PROPRIETORS

🏨 🛏 ☎ 🖥 🅃 🅃 CM ♪ PS 🚶 alc
12 12
🖥 inet

Open All Year

RENVYLE HOUSE HOTEL

RENVYLE,
CONNEMARA,
CO. GALWAY
TEL: 095-43511 FAX: 095-43515
EMAIL: info@renvyle.com
WEB: www.renvyle.com

HOTEL ★★★ MAP 9 C 12

Historic coastal hotel set amid the magical beauty of sea, lake and mountains, the keynotes are warmth and comfort with award winning fine fare. Turf fires and cosy lounges make you relax and feel at home. Golf, tennis, horseriding, swimming pool, snooker, boating, fishing are the facilities to name but a few. Wonderful walking and cycling routes throughout an area that hosts a vast National Park. Additional facilities include claypigeon shooting.

B&B from €30.00 to €125.00

ZOE COYLE
SALES & MARKETING MANAGER

🏨 🛏 ☎ 🖥 T 🅰 ⚲ C 🔌 CMCS ❄ ⚲
⚲ 🚶 ♪ 🎵 PS 🔌 alc 🐴 🎣

IRISH
HOTELS
FEDERATION

Closed 03 January - 12 February

ELDONS HOTEL

ROUNDSTONE,
CONNEMARA,
CO. GALWAY
TEL: 095-35933 FAX: 095-35722
EMAIL: eldonshotel@eircom.net
WEB: www.eldonshotel.com

HOTEL ★★ MAP 9 C 11

Situated in the village of Roundstone, has a view of the harbour and Twelve Bens mountain range. We are a newly built, family-run hotel, offering all bedrooms with private bathrooms, colour TV and D.D. phones. Locally; 18 hole golf course and sea angling. Our Beola Restaurant has been operating successfully for many years and is renowned for its fine food, with lobster being its speciality. Credit cards taken. New annexe consisting of 6 superior rooms with a lift.

B&B from €50.00 to €80.00

ANN & NOLEEN CONNEELY
OWNER/CHEF

☺ Weekend specials from €145.00 pps

🏨 🛏 ☎ 🖥 🅃 🅃 🔌 CM ❄ ⚲ ∪ 🅿
S 🔌 alc

IRISH
HOTELS
FEDERATION

Closed 01 November - 14 March

B&B Rates are per Person Sharing per Night incl. Breakfast
Room Rates are per Room per Night

ROUNDSTONE HOUSE HOTEL

ROUNDSTONE,
CONNEMARA,
CO. GALWAY

TEL: 095-35864 FAX: 095-35944
EMAIL: vaughanshotel@eircom.net
WEB: www.irishcountryhotels.com

HOTEL ★★ MAP 9 C 11

Roundstone House Hotel is a family hotel situated in the picturesque village of Roundstone. Roundstone is a fascinating place for a holiday offering a wide range of interests for the holidaymakers. Many outdoor activities are available locally including sea angling, watersports, hillwalking, pony trekking and a championship 18 hole golf course nearby. Come to beautiful Roundstone for a holiday to remember.

Member of Irish Country Hotels

B&B from €47.50 to €52.50

MAUREEN VAUGHAN
PROPRIETOR

🐎 🦮 ☎ 🖥 T C 🛒 CM ❄ ⚲ ∪ 🎵 P S
13 13
🏠 alc 🛒 🐕

IRISH
HOTELS
FEDERATION

Closed 01 November - 24 March

AN CRUISCIN LAN HOTEL

SPIDDAL,
CO. GALWAY

TEL: 091-553148 FAX: 091-553712
EMAIL: info@cruiscinlanhotel.com
WEB: www.cruiscinlanhotel.com

HOTEL ★★ MAP 5 E 10

An Cruiscin Lan Hotel is located in the heart of Irish speaking Spiddal Village at the gateway to the Gaeltacht, Connemara and the Aran Islands. All rooms are en suite with a colour TV and direct dial telephone. The hotel offers a snug bar, lounge bar, dining conservatory and beer garden with spectacular views of Galway Bay. Our restaurant is renowned locally for quality, value and a commitment to service. Our meeting room is suitable for up to 20 delegates.

B&B from €40.00 to €80.00

JOHN FOYE

🐎 🦮 ☎ 🖥 C CM ∪ 🎵 🎶 alc 🛒
14 14

IRISH
HOTELS
FEDERATION

Closed 25 December

PARK LODGE HOTEL

PARK,
SPIDDAL,
CO. GALWAY

TEL: 091-553159 FAX: 091-553494
EMAIL: parklodgehotel@eircom.net
WEB: www.parklodgehotelandrentacottage.com

HOTEL U MAP 5 E 10

The Park Lodge Hotel is owned and run by the Foyle Family. It is situated on the coast road from Galway to Connemara, 16km west of Galway City and just east of Spiddal Village. Most of the 23 bedrooms have a view of Galway Bay. There are also seven detached cottages on the grounds, each self-catering and fully equipped for 5 persons. Cottages open all year.

B&B from €47.50 to €60.00

JANE MARIE FOYLE
MANAGER

🐎 🦮 ☎ 🖥 🚗 ⚠ 🛒 C 🛒 CM ❄ ∪ 🎵 P S
23 23
🏠 🛒

IRISH
HOTELS
FEDERATION

Closed 01 October - 31 May

B&B Rates are per Person Sharing per Night incl. Breakfast
Room Rates are per Room per Night

TIGH CHUALAIN

**KILROE EAST,
SPIDDAL,
CO. GALWAY**
TEL: 091-553609 FAX: 091-553049
EMAIL: tighchualain@eircom.net

GUESTHOUSE ★★★ MAP 5 E 10

Tigh Chualain is a charming, family-run 3*** guesthouse, 16km west of Galway City and 2km west of Spiddal Village, en route to the Aran Islands' Ferry. Overlooking Galway Bay, with a nearby Blue Flag beach, it is in the heart of the Connemara Gaeltacht. An obvious starting point for exploring the rugged beauty of Connemara with its manifold attractions. All bedrooms are en suite with direct dial telephone and colour TV.

B&B from €30.00 to €35.00

**COLM & NORA FOLAN
PROPRIETORS**

Midweek specials from €85.00 pps

9   9

Closed 31 October - 31 March

ACHILL CLIFF HOUSE HOTEL

**KEEL,
ACHILL ISLAND,
CO. MAYO**
TEL: 098-43400 FAX: 098-43007
EMAIL: info@achillcliff.com
WEB: www.achillcliff.com

HOTEL ★★★ MAP 9 C 14

New family-run smoke free hotel in a superb location. Keel beach, ideal for walking is only 2 minutes away. The hotel commanding magnificent views offers excellent home made food, comfortable accommodation and good value. Fine wines and an extensive breakfast menu are available. All facilities are nearby, fishing, horseriding, golf, walking, painting, photography. The Deserted Village and House of Prayer.There is no nightclub. Check out our web-site for last minute special offers.

B&B from €40.00 to €80.00

**JJ & TERESA MCNAMARA
PROPRIETORS**

Midweek specials from €99.00 pps

10   10

Closed 23 -27 December

GRAYS GUEST HOUSE

**DUGORT,
ACHILL ISLAND,
CO. MAYO**
TEL: 098-43244

GUESTHOUSE ★★★ MAP 9 C 14

Vi McDowell welcomes you to Grays where you are assured of a restful holiday, with good food, comfort and personal attention. Turf fires and electric blankets. Late dinner is served at 7pm. There are three lounges, colour TV, table tennis room and croquet lawn and swings in an enclosed garden. Art Gallery for use of artists staying in guesthouse.

B&B from €45.00 to €55.00

**VI MCDOWELL
OWNER/MANAGER**

15   15

Closed 24 - 26 December

**B&B Rates are per Person Sharing per Night incl. Breakfast
Room Rates are per Room per Night**

MCDOWELL'S HOTEL

SLIEVEMORE ROAD,
DUGORT,
ACHILL, CO.MAYO
TEL: 098-43148
EMAIL: mcdowellshotel@eircom.net
WEB: www.achill-leisure.ie

HOTEL ★★ MAP 9 C 14

Family-run hotel, nestled at the base of the Slievemore Mountain, offering a warm welcome and a friendly service. Cuisine is the best of home cooked local fresh produce - à la carte, barfood, seafood, childrens' choice. Our restaurant overlooks the majestic Minaun Heights. Relax in our cosy turf fire bar. Adventure and leisure activity facilities.

B&B from €50.00 to €60.00

RICHARD & TINA O'HARA
PROPRIETORS

10 9

ÓSTÁN OILEÁN ACLA

ACHILL SOUND,
CO. MAYO

TEL: 098-45138 FAX: 098-45198
EMAIL: reservations@achillislandhotel.com
WEB: www.achillislandhotel.com

HOTEL U MAP 9 C 14

Enjoy the panoramic views of Achill Island from our new luxury hotel situated at the gateway to Achill Island. In our elegant Seafood Restaurant choose from a wide range of local produce. Relax and enjoy a drink in our friendly traditional bar. Convenient to 5 Blue Flag beaches, the highest cliffs in Europe, golf courses, pitch and putt course, outdoor activities. A warm friendly welcome awaits you at Óstán Oileán Acla.

B&B from €45.00 to €80.00

MICHAEL & UNA MCLOUGHLIN
PROPRIETORS

26 26

BELLEEK CASTLE

BELLEEK,
BALLINA,
CO. MAYO
TEL: 096-22400 FAX: 096-71750
EMAIL: belleekcastlehotel@eircom.net
WEB: www.belleekcastle.com

HOTEL U MAP 10 F 15

Historic, romantic, set in 1000 acres of woodland on banks of River Moy - wine/dine till midnight - Gourmet organic food enthusiasts welcomed - 'Perchance to Dream' in a four poster. For your added pleasure: tour of 16th century castle armoury, giant fossil exhibits, Spanish Armada Bar, dramatic artefacts and timbers salvaged from Galleons wrecked off the Irish West Coast 1588. Sporting: international surfing, golf, fishing, tennis, riding, ten stables in castle.

B&B from €70.00 to €120.00

MARSHALL & JACQUELINE DORAN

15 15

B&B Rates are per Person Sharing per Night incl. Breakfast
Room Rates are per Room per Night

CILL AODAIN HOTEL

MAIN STREET,
KILTIMAGH,
CO. MAYO

TEL: 094-938 1761 FAX: 094-938 1838
EMAIL: cillaodain@eircom.net
WEB: www.cillaodainhotel.com

HOTEL ★★ MAP 10 F 14

This RAC 2** hotel is set in the centre of historic Kiltimagh. Furnished with flair and imagination, panelled lounges and open fires. The restaurant which has received many accolades is open each evening. The rooms, with all amenities, are individually furnished and decorated. Kiltimagh is one of Ireland's most famous small towns. 5km off Galway to Sligo Road. Ideally situated for visiting Knock Village. Member of Irish Country Hotels.

Member of Irish Country Hotels

B&B from €40.00 to €60.00

MARY HALLIGAN
PROPRIETOR

12 12

Closed 24 - 26 December

BELMONT HOTEL

KNOCK,
CO. MAYO

TEL: 094-938 8122 FAX: 094-938 8532
EMAIL: reception@belmonthotel.ie
WEB: www.belmonthotel.ie

HOTEL ★★★ MAP 10 G 13

A haven of hospitality nestled at the rear entrance to Knock Shrine off N17. The hotel radiates Old Country Warmth from the moment you arrive. RAC 3***, Fáilte Ireland 3*** and AA 3*** status. Daily carvery and sumptuous bar food menu complement our award-winning Bialann Restaurant. Our specially developed Natural Health Therapy packages are very professional and attractive. Tastefully furnished bedrooms with facilities.

B&B from €40.00 to €70.00

ANNEMARIE KELLY
GENERAL MANAGER

63 63

Open all year

KNOCK HOUSE HOTEL

BALLYHAUNIS ROAD,
KNOCK,
CO. MAYO

TEL: 094-938 8088 FAX: 094-938 8044
EMAIL: info@knockhousehotel.ie
WEB: www.knockhousehotel.ie

HOTEL ★★★ MAP 10 G 13

Located in over 100 acres of parkland and nestling behind the Basilica, this 5 year old hotel is a gem! With 68 comfortable bedrooms, of which 6 are designed for wheelchair users, every need is catered for. The superb Four Seasons Restaurant - open all day - and the glazed reception and lounge areas, surrounded by local limestone, overlook countryside. This well run, tranquil hotel will be hard to leave.

B&B from €53.00 to €69.00

BRIAN CROWLEY
GENERAL MANAGER

68 68

Open All Year

B&B Rates are per Person Sharing per Night incl. Breakfast
Room Rates are per Room per Night

HEALYS RESTAURANT & COUNTRY HOUSE HOTEL

PONTOON,
FOXFORD,
CO. MAYO

TEL: 094-925 6443 FAX: 094-925 6572
EMAIL: info@healyspontoon.com
WEB: www.healyspontoon.com

HOTEL ★★ MAP 9 F 14

Dining room with lake view, restaurant/bar, extensive wine cellar. Bar food served from 12.30 to 21.30. Breakfast for non-residents. Dining pub of the year 03 & 04. Georgina Campbell Guide. Recommended by 'Trout & Salmon Magazine' Great Fishing Houses of Ireland. BIM Seafood Circle. Minutes from River Moy for salmon, Lough Conn for salmon & trout. Boats, Ghillies arranged. Enniscrone Golf Links 30 mins. Westport championship parkland 45 mins. 10 courses nearby. Walking, riding, shooting can also be arranged.

B&B from €45.00 to €55.00

JOHN DEVER & JOSETTE MAURER
PROPRIETORS

14 14

Closed 24 - 25 December

PONTOON BRIDGE HOTEL

PONTOON,
FOXFORD,
CO. MAYO

TEL: 094-925 6120 FAX: 094-925 6688
EMAIL: relax@pontoonbridge.com
WEB: www.pontoonbridge.com

HOTEL ★★★ MAP 10 F 14

Family managed hotel on the shores of Lough Conn & Cullin in the centre of Mayo. Famous for trout & salmon fishing - River Moy, golf, horseriding, scenery, central for touring. Twin Lakes Restaurant boasts the best food in Mayo. Geary's Waterfront Bar & Bistro with seasonal live music. New panoramic terrace restaurant on water's edge. Tennis court, sandy beaches, archery school locally, conference facilities. Families welcome. School of fly fishing, landscape painting & cookery. Bedrooms with panoramic views of the lakes. Warm friendly welcome.

Member of Great Fishing Houses of Ireland

B&B from €70.00 to €100.00

BRETA GEARY
GENERAL MANAGER

Midweek specials from €160.00 pps
(2 nights B&B + 2 Dinners)

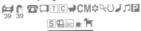
39 39

Closed 24 - 26 December

ARDMORE COUNTRY HOUSE HOTEL AND RESTAURANT

THE QUAY,
WESTPORT,
CO. MAYO

TEL: 098-25994 FAX: 098-27795
EMAIL: ardmorehotel@eircom.net
WEB: www.ardmorecountryhouse.com

HOTEL ★★★★ MAP 9 E 13

Ardmore Country House and Restaurant is a small luxurious 4★★★★ hotel, owned and managed by Pat and Noreen Hoban and family, offering warm hospitality. Ardmore House is idyllically situated overlooking Clew Bay with breathtaking sunsets, in the shadow of Croagh Patrick. The restaurant offers the best of local produce, including fresh fish from Clew Bay, organic vegetables and herbs from local producers and a selection of Irish farmhouse cheeses. All bedrooms are non-smoking.

B&B from €75.00 to €120.00

NOREEN & PAT HOBAN

13 13

Closed 01 January - 15 March

B&B Rates are per Person Sharing per Night incl. Breakfast
Room Rates are per Room per Night

DOHERTY'S POLLAN BEACH HOTEL

ARDAGH,
BALLYLIFFIN,
CO. DONEGAL

TEL: 074-937 8840 FAX: 074-937 8844
EMAIL: pollanbeachhotel@eircom.net
WEB: www.pollanbeachhotel.com

HOTEL ★★★ MAP 14 K 21

Doherty's Pollan Beach Hotel is situated 100 yds from sandy beach with childrens' playground. All bedrooms are en suite, equipped with modern facilities. Most bedrooms have sea views. Spacious dining room and bar overlooking the beach and Atlantic Ocean. The hotel overlooks the two 18 hole golf courses in Ballyliffin, the Classic Old Links and the New Glasheady Links. Ideal for: golf, fishing, cycling and walking. 40 minutes drive from City of Derry Airport, 2 hours drive from Belfast International. Perfect retreat for short break.

B&B from €35.00 to €65.00

KATHLEEN AND VINCENT DOHERTY
PROPRIETORS

Midweek specials from €120.00 pps

21 21
alc Inet

Open All Year

CREEVY PIER HOTEL

CREEVY,
BALLYSHANNON,
CO. DONEGAL

TEL: 071-985 8355 FAX: 071-985 8356

WEB: www.creevypierhotel.com

HOTEL ★ MAP 13 I 17

Creevy Pier Hotel has a breathtaking view overlooking Donegal Bay. This is a small friendly family-run hotel. Local activities include scuba diving, swimming, pony trekking, seashore and deep sea angling, and two 18 hole golf courses. Our restaurant specialises in modern French/Irish cuisine with an emphasis on local seafood. Tranquil, peaceful and traditional are but a few words to describe this hotel.

B&B from €35.00 to €49.00

PAT COYLE
PROPRIETOR

Weekend specials from €89.00 pps

10 10
alc

Open All Year

B&B Rates are per Person Sharing per Night incl. Breakfast
Room Rates are per Room per Night

DORRIANS IMPERIAL HOTEL

MAIN STREET,
BALLYSHANNON,
CO. DONEGAL

TEL: 071-985 1147 FAX: 071-985 1001
EMAIL: info@dorriansimperialhotel.com
WEB: www.dorriansimperialhotel.com

HOTEL ★★★ MAP 13 1 17

Town centre family-run hotel (built 1781). All rooms en suite, TV, telephone, tea/coffee facilities. Private car park. Open fire. Hotel recently renovated, embracing old and new décor, elevator. Ideally suited for touring North West and North East Ireland and ideally located for golfing, fishing & beaches. Sligo 45km, Belfast 202km, Dublin 216km.

B&B from €55.00 to €85.00

BEN & MARY DORRIAN
PROPRIETORS

47 47

Closed 22 - 29 December

OSTAN GWEEDORE HOTEL & LEISURE COMPLEX

BUNBEG,
CO. DONEGAL

TEL: 074-953 1177 FAX: 074-953 1726
EMAIL: reservations@ostangweedore.com
WEB: www.ostangweedore.com

HOTEL ★★★ MAP 13 1 20

Luxury 3* hotel, all major guides approved, with 33 bedrooms & 3 executive suites. Facilities include leisure centre with 19m swimming pool, childrens' pool, sauna, steamroom, jacuzzi & gym. The Beauty & Body Spa offers a wide range of treatments from manicure to massage. Our award-winning Ocean Restaurant specialises in fresh local seafood and the Sundowner Wine Bar offers Tapas and fine wines from around the world. Live entertainment in the bar at weekends and most evenings during July and August.

B&B from €60.00 to €100.00

CHARLES BOYLE
MANAGING DIRECTOR

☺ Weekend specials from €150.00 pps

36 36

Closed 04 November - 13 February

OSTAN RADHARC NA MARA / SEA VIEW HOTEL

BUNBEG,
CO. DONEGAL

TEL: 074-953 1159 FAX: 074-953 2238
EMAIL: ostanradharcnamara@eircom.net

HOTEL ★★ MAP 13 1 20

In an area where nature remains untouched, the air is rich and pure, ensuring a heavy appetite. In the Seaview Hotel, guests are treated to wonderful food. The à la carte menu always includes a seasonal selection of fresh, local seafood dishes, with salmon, trout, lobster and oysters a speciality.

B&B from €50.00 to €60.00

JAMES BOYLE
GENERAL MANAGER

38 38

Closed 23 - 28 December

B&B Rates are per Person Sharing per Night incl. Breakfast
Room Rates are per Room per Night

HARBOUR INN HOTEL (THE)

DERRY ROAD,
BUNCRANA,
CO. DONEGAL
TEL: 074-932 1810 FAX: 074-932 1842
EMAIL: theharbourinn@eircom.net
WEB: www.harbourinnhotel.com

HOTEL P   MAP 14 K 20

The Harbour Inn Hotel is set against the beautiful hillside looking down over Lough Swilly. The accommodation comprises thirty spacious and luxurious bedrooms, all en suite with TV, tea/coffee making facilities, hairdyer and personal safe. We boast an excellent seventy-seater restaurant serving lunch and evening meals daily. Directions: As you enter Buncrana, Lisfannon Beach and the Northwest Golf Club are on the left. Top filling station is on the right and we are the next building on the right.

B&B from €40.00 to €50.00

KATHLEEN & HUGH DOHERTY

29 29

Open all Year

INISHOWEN GATEWAY HOTEL

RAILWAY ROAD,
BUNCRANA, INISHOWEN,
CO. DONEGAL
TEL: 074-936 1144 FAX: 074-936 2278
EMAIL: info@inishowengateway.com
WEB: www.inishowengateway.com

HOTEL ★★★   MAP 14 K 20

This elegant three star hotel has 79 bedrooms and is situated on the sandy shores of Lough Swilly, on the Inishowen Peninsula of North Donegal. The Gateway offers superb leisure facilities including the luxurious Gateway Health & Fitness Club and brand new health and beauty spa, Seagrass Wellbeing Centre. The Hotel's excellent Peninsula Restaurant serves the finest local produce overlooking sea, sand and golf courses.

B&B from €55.00 to €65.00

PATRICK DOHERTY
PROPRIETOR

79 79

IRISH HOTELS FEDERATION

Closed 24 - 26 December

B&B Rates are per Person Sharing per Night incl. Breakfast
Room Rates are per Room per Night

GREAT NORTHERN HOTEL

BUNDORAN,
CO. DONEGAL

TEL: 071-984 1204 FAX: 071-984 1114
EMAIL: reservations@greatnorthernhotel.com
WEB: www.greatnorthernhotel.com

HOTEL ★★★★ MAP 13 I 17

Great Northern Hotel, Conference & Leisure Centre Bundoran. The hotel is situated in the middle of an 18 hole championship golf course overlooking Donegal Bay. 4**** hotel with 96 bedrooms with top leisure facilities for all the family. This hotel has all en suite bedrooms, a restaurant, grill room, lounge, ballroom and syndicate rooms. Leisure centre with swimming pool, gymnasium, private jacuzzi, sauna, steamroom, plunge pool, beauty salon and hairdressing salon. We now offer a new state of the art conference centre.

Member of Brian McEniff Hotels

B&B from € 100.00 to € 115.00

PHILIP MCGLYNN
GENERAL MANAGER

96 96

Closed 19 - 26 December

MCGRORYS OF CULDAFF

CULDAFF,
INISHOWEN,
CO. DONEGAL

TEL: 074-937 9104 FAX: 074-937 9235
EMAIL: info@mcgrorys.ie
WEB: www.mcgrorys.ie

GUESTHOUSE ★★★ MAP 14 L 21

This popular premises offering quality accommodation, award-winning bar and restaurant is the ideal base for exploring the Inishowen Peninsula or golf at Ballyliffin. Our stylish restaurant serves excellent seafood, steaks, lamb and vegetarian choices. The front bar, Black and White Ulster Hotel Bar 2001, serves food daily. Macs Backroom Bar, famous music venue, features acts such as Altan, Albert Lee, Brian Kennedy, Peter Green and many more.

B&B from € 50.00 to € 65.00

JOHN & NEIL MCGRORY/
ANNE DOHERTY

10 10

Closed 23 - 27 December

ARD NA BREATHA

DRUMROOSKE MIDDLE,
DONEGAL TOWN

TEL: 074-972 2288 FAX: 074-974 0720
EMAIL: info@ardnabreatha.com
WEB: www.ardnabreatha.com

GUESTHOUSE P MAP 13 I 18

Ard na Breatha Restaurant & Guesthouse is located 1.5km from Donegal Town just off the road to lovely Lough Eske. You will be assured of a warm welcome in our cosy lounge, complete with open hearth, which has magnificent views of the Bluestack Mountains. Our en suite bedrooms (all with bath) have tea/coffee facilities, TV, phone and hairdryer. Our fully licensed restaurant specialises in modern French/Irish cuisine with an emphasis on local seafood and an extensive wine list. Restaurant and bar closed Tuesdays.

B&B from € 35.00 to € 45.00

AOIFE AND PHILIPPE PETRANI
PROPRIETORS

Weekend specials from €119.00 pps

6 6

Closed 12 January - 12 February

B&B Rates are per Person Sharing per Night incl. Breakfast
Room Rates are per Room per Night

DOWNINGS BAY HOTEL

DOWNINGS,
LETTERKENNY,
CO. DONEGAL

TEL: 074-915 5586 FAX: 074-915 4716
EMAIL: info@dowingsbayhotel.com
WEB: www.dowingsbayhotel.com

HOTEL N   MAP 13 J 19

Situated on Sheephaven Bay and the picturesque Atlantic Drive. Newly built to 3*** standards. Spacious bedrooms, many of them interconnecting, are luxuriously finished. The Sheephaven Suite available for 20-350 people. JC's Bar and The Haven dining room serving locally sourced fresh food daily. Secrets Beauty Salon for those who wish to pamper themselves. Local activities include golf, fishing, horseriding & water activities. Within driving distance of Glenveagh National Park.

B&B from €40.00 to €75.00

EILEEN ROCK
MANAGER

😊 Weekend specials from €125.00 pps

🛏🐾☎🗄🅲↩CMU♪🎵🅿🔒alc
40 40
💻 Inet

Open All Year

GLENEANY HOUSE

PORT ROAD,
LETTERKENNY,
CO. DONEGAL

TEL: 074-912 6088 FAX: 074-912 6090
EMAIL: gleneanyhouse@eircom.net
WEB: www.gleneany.com

GUESTHOUSE ★★★   MAP 13 J 19

Gleneany House TOWN CENTRE location opposite bus station in the heart of Letterkenny, offers both corporate and leisure clientele an excellent level of personal and friendly service. Renowned for its consistency in excellent cuisine, food is served all day. Our 19 en suite bedrooms have satellite TV and direct dial telephone. Our Lounge bar the ideal place for a quiet relaxing drink. An ideal base for touring beautiful Donegal, private car parking available. A warm welcome awaits all to the Gleneany House. So when next in town call and experience for yourself our hospitality.

B&B from €49.00 to €75.00

PAUL KELLY

😊 Special offers available

🛏🐾☎🗄T CM♪🅿🆂🔒alc
19 19

Closed 22 - 28 December

Lifford Old Courthouse
Award Winning Heritage Centre & Restaurant

A captivating experience of the 18th Century

Your tour of the historic Courthouse begins with a captivating audio-visual history lesson delivered by Manus, Chief of the O'Donnell clan. Then, in one of Ireland's oldest Courtrooms, you can witness re-enactments of famous cases such as the Napper Tandy Trial and the Lord Leitrim Murder, after which you will be taken into custody by the prison warden who will march you off to the dungeons to be charged and processed as a common criminal. Your fingerprints will be taken and added to the charge sheet, which you can keep as a momento of your visit.

After your release you will be free to relax in the Courthouse Restaurant, serving Full Irish Breakfasts, Sandwiches, Salads and homemade scones all day. A Carvery Lunch is served daily from 12.30 – 2pm with snacks served from 2 – 4pm. Our speciality Sunday Lunch is served from 12.30 – 4pm.

Opening Hours:

Monday - Friday 9am – 4.30pm
Sunday 12.30pm – 4.30pm
Last Tour at 4pm
Late Opening for groups available on request.
Concessionary rates given for families, OAP's, groups and children.

Lifford, Co Donegal.
Tel. (0035374) 9141733

B&B Rates are per Person Sharing per Night incl. Breakfast
Room Rates are per Room per Night

HOLIDAY INN LETTERKENNY CONFERENCE & LEISURE CENTRE

DERRY ROAD,
LETTERKENNY,
CO. DONEGAL
TEL: 074-912 4369 FAX: 074-912 5389
EMAIL: info@holidayinnletterkenny.net
WEB: www.holidayinnletterkenny.net

HOTEL ★★★ MAP 13 J 19

Conveniently located on the outskirts of Letterkenny Town, the Holiday Inn Letterkenny is the ideal stopover for exploring County Donegal and the North West region of Ireland. All 121 superbly appointed en suite guest bedrooms are fully equipped and decorated to exceptionally high standards. Experience the latest leisure facilities at our health and fitness club. Our Aileach Restaurant serves a wide range of International cuisine while the Tara Bar and Lounge serves light meals and live music can be enjoyed at weekends.

B&B from €60.00 to €140.00

MICHAEL NAUGHTON
GENERAL MANAGER

Midweek specials from €185.00 pps

121 121

Closed 23 - 27 December

MOUNT ERRIGAL HOTEL, CONFERENCE & LEISURE CENTRE

BALLYRAINE,
LETTERKENNY,
CO. DONEGAL
TEL: 074-9122 700 FAX: 074-9125 085
EMAIL: infor@mounterrigal.com
WEB: www.mounterrigal.com

HOTEL ★★★ MAP 13 J 19

A superior 3 star hotel and part of McEniff Hotels, one of Ireland's leading hotel groups, The Mount Errigal combines state-of-the-art facilities, superb accommodation, fine cuisine, with a warm and professional environment. Spacious bedrooms, a beautiful restaurant and a fashionable café serving a selection of delicious dishes, as well as the newly built leisure centre, all guarantee a comfortable and enjoyable stay. Free car parking available. Any special offer is subject to availabilty and only applies to specific dates.

B&B from €70.00 to €95.00

TERRY & LORETTO MC ENIFF

Family specials, 2 adults & 2 children from €120.00 per room.

82   82

Closed 23 - 27 December

QUALITY HOTEL LETTERKENNY

MAIN STREET,
LETTERKENNY,
CO. DONEGAL
TEL: 1850-746 8357 FAX: 021-427 1489
EMAIL: info@qualityhotelletterkenny.com
WEB: www.qualityhotelletterkenny.com

HOTEL ★★ MAP 13 J 19

Prime location in the heart of Letterkenny Town. Quality Hotel comprises 83 luxurious en suite bedrooms, 25 of which are 1 & 2 bedroom apartment-style luxury suites. Its tastefully decorated bistro style restaurant offers its patrons a delicately selective menu to suit all tastes. Quality Hotel has also gained its reputation with its famous bar "Dillons". Other facilities include meeting room & business centre suite. Telephone hotel directly at 074-912 2977.

Member of Quality Hotels

B&B from €39.00 to €119.00

STEPHEN ANDERSON
GENERAL MANAGER

Weekend specials from €89.00pps

83   83

Closed 25 December

B&B Rates are per Person Sharing per Night incl. Breakfast
Room Rates are per Room per Night

AISLEIGH GUEST HOUSE

**DUBLIN ROAD,
CARRICK-ON-SHANNON,
CO. LEITRIM**

TEL: 071-962 0313 FAX: 071-962 0675
EMAIL: aisleigh@eircom.net
WEB: www.aisleighguesthouse.com

GUESTHOUSE ★★★ MAP 10 I 14

A warm welcome awaits you at our family-run guest house situated 1km from the centre of the picturesque town of Carrick-on-Shannon, Ireland's best kept secret. Facilities include en suite bedrooms with TV, direct dial telephones (fax also available) games room and sauna. Local genealogy a speciality. Nearby there is golfing, swimming, tennis, squash, cruising, fishing (tackle & bait supplies) horseriding, walking, cycling, etc.

B&B from €35.00 to €50.00

SEÁN & CHARLOTTE FEARON
OWNERS

10 10

Open All Year

BUSH HOTEL

**CARRICK-ON-SHANNON,
CO. LEITRIM**

TEL: 071-967 1000 FAX: 071-962 1180
EMAIL: info@bushhotel.com
WEB: www.bushhotel.com

HOTEL ★★★ MAP 10 I 14

An hotel of ambience, style and comfort, The Bush Hotel (one of Ireland's oldest) has just completed a major refurbishment and extension whilst still retaining its olde world charm and character. Centrally located in the town centre, the hotel has 50 modern bedrooms with all facilities, theme bars, coffee shop and restaurant. New state of art business and banqueting centre. Attractions: Arigna Mining Museum, Strokestown House, King House, etc.

B&B from €59.00 to €79.00

JOSEPH DOLAN
MANAGING DIRECTOR

50 50

Closed 24 - 27 December

ABBEY MANOR HOTEL

**DROMAHAIR,
CO. LEITRIM**

TEL: 071-9164 202 FAX: 071-9164 570
EMAIL: sales@abbeymanorhotel.ie
WEB: www.abbeymanorhotel.ie

HOTEL P MAP 10 I 16

The Abbey Manor Hotel is situated in the picturesque village of Dromahair which is just 12km from Silgo and overlooking the salmon fished Bonet River. The hotel itself was built in the latter part of the 19th Century and is full of history and charm. The old stone building has been completely restored and its unique Victorian conservatory replaced in every detail. Our 26 bedrooms are of high quality as is our restaurant, bar lounge and fuction room. We also cater for conferences, weddings and private functions. Private car park available.

B&B from €40.00 to €70.00

MICHELLE HEALY
GENERAL MANAGER

Midweek specials from €120.00 pps

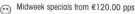

26 26

Open all Year

B&B Rates are per Person Sharing per Night incl. Breakfast
Room Rates are per Room per Night

RAMADA HOTEL & SUITES AT LOUGH ALLEN

DRUMSHANBO,
CO. LEITRIM

TEL: 071-964 0100 FAX: 071-964 0101
EMAIL: info@loughallenhotel.com
WEB: www.loughallenhotel.com

HOTEL N   MAP 10 I 15

Close to picturesque town of Drumshanbo, located on the shores of Lough Allen. Many rooms with balconies, decking area with stunning view of the lake. The best base for touring surrounding countryside. Yeat's Country, Verdant County Fermanagh, rocky coastline of Co. Mayo, the many lakes of County Leitrim. In a word IDYLLIC !

B&B from €66.50 to €120.00

ERIK SPEEKENBRINK
RESORT GENERAL MANAGER

Midweek specials from €170.00 pps

64 64

Open All Year

GLEBE HOUSE

BALLINAMORE ROAD,
MOHILL,
CO. LEITRIM

TEL: 071-963 1086 FAX: 071-963 1886
EMAIL: glebe@iol.ie
WEB: www.glebehouse.com

GUESTHOUSE ★★★   MAP 11 J 14

At the end of a sweeping driveway this lovely Georgian former Rectory dating to 1823, is set on 50 acres of mature trees and farmland and has been carefully restored by the Maloney Family. Enjoy the tranquillity of this unspoilt part of Ireland. Ideal touring base. Assistance given with genealogy. 2/3 bedroom suite available which is suitable for groups or families. Internet/computer for visitor use. Discount on bookings if more than one night.

B&B from €40.00 to €50.00

LAURA MALONEY
MANAGER

Weekend specials from €105.00 pps

8 8

Closed 20 November - 31 December

SHANNON KEY WEST HOTEL

THE RIVER EDGE,
ROOSKEY,
CO. LEITRIM

TEL: 071-963 8800 FAX: 071-963 8811
EMAIL: shnkywst@iol.ie
WEB: www.keywest.firebird.net

HOTEL ★★★   MAP 11 J 13

Situated on N4 Dublin Sligo route. Rooskey is an elegant marina village nestling between Carrick-On-Shannon and Longford Town. Dromod Train Station only 2km from Hotel. This beautiful 39 bedroom hotel with Greek, Georgian and modern architecture offers panoramic views of the River Shannon from both bedrooms and roof gardens. Excellent cuisine and personal service. Facilities include gymnasium, steamroom, jacuzzi, sunbed and outdoor tennis/basketball. Rooskey is a stress free comfort zone.

Member of Best Western Hotels

B&B from €62.50 to €70.00

JOHN LIKELY
MANAGING DIRECTOR

Midweek specials from €47.50 pps
per night B&B only

39 39

Closed 24 - 26 December

B&B Rates are per Person Sharing per Night incl. Breakfast
Room Rates are per Room per Night

CAWLEY'S

**EMMET STREET,
TUBBERCURRY,
CO. SLIGO**
TEL: 071-918 5025 FAX: 071-918 5963
EMAIL: cawleysguesthouse@eircom.net

GUESTHOUSE ★★ MAP 10 G 15

Cawley's is a large 3 storey family-run guesthouse with full bar license. We offer high standards in accommodation with tastefully decorated rooms. Our home cooking & personal service make this premises your home for the duration of your stay. Private parking, landscaped gardens, easily accessed by air, rail & bus. Local amenities include fishing, 9 hole golf course & horse riding. Seaside resorts close by. Major credit cards accepted. For further information please contact a member of the Cawley family on 071-918 5025.

B&B from €25.00 to €35.00

TERESA CAWLEY/PIERRE KREBS

17 10

IRISH
HOTELS
FEDERATION

Closed 23 - 26 December

B&B Rates are per Person Sharing per Night incl. Breakfast
Room Rates are per Room per Night

Map of North Region

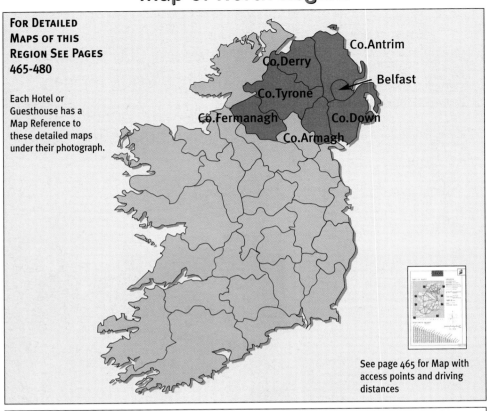

For Detailed Maps of this Region See Pages 465-480

Each Hotel or Guesthouse has a Map Reference to these detailed maps under their photograph.

Co.Antrim
Co.Derry
Belfast
Co.Tyrone
Co.Fermanagh
Co.Down
Co.Armagh

See page 465 for Map with access points and driving distances

Locations listing

ANTRIM
Ballymena
Bushmills
Carnlough
Portrush
Stoneyford
Templepatrick

ARMAGH
Armagh City
Lurgan

BELFAST
Belfast City

DERRY
Aghadowey
Coleraine
Derry City
Limavady

DOWN
Bangor
Castlewellan
Newcastle
Newry
Portaferry

FERMANAGH
Belcoo
Belleek
Enniskillen
Irvinestown

TYRONE
Cookstown
Omagh

irelandhotels.com INCLUDES DETAILED MAPS & GREAT VALUE SPECIAL OFFERS.
log on and book in

ADAIR ARMS HOTEL

BALLYMONEY ROAD,
BALLYMENA,
CO. ANTRIM BT43 5BS
TEL: 028-2565 3674 FAX: 028-2564 0436
EMAIL: reservations@adairarms.com
WEB: www.adairarms.com

HOTEL ★★★ MAP 15 O 19

A warm welcome awaits you at The Adair Arms Hotel, which is owned and run by the McLarnon Family Group. The hotel is situated in the heart of Ballymena and is ideally located for touring the Glens of Antrim, Slemish Mountain and the North Antrim Coast. The Adair Arms Hotel offers 44 en suite bedrooms providing guests with every comfort and convenience. The hotel is decorated to a high standard and luxuriously furnished. It is the ideal destination for conferencing, golfing, business, incentive travel and leisure.

B&B from £37.50 to £45.00

G MCLARNON
MANAGER/PROPRIETOR

Weekend specials from £85.00 pps

44 44

Closed 25 - 26 December

LEIGHINMOHR HOUSE HOTEL

LEIGHINMOHR AVENUE,
BALLYMENA,
CO. ANTRIM BT42 2AN
TEL: 028-2565 2313 FAX: 028-2565 6669
EMAIL: info@leighinmohrhotel.com
WEB: www.leighinmohrhotel.com

HOTEL U MAP 15 O 19

In a quiet and convenient location in the prestigious Galgorm Road area, with an unrivalled reputation for its food & service, Leighinmohr House Hotel is owned and run by the McLarnon family. Our 3*** standard hotel has 20 en suite bedrooms with all newly refurbished facilities. The hotel is ideally located for touring the Glens of Antrim, Slemish Mountain and the North Antrim Coast, or for some town centre shopping. Whether business or pleasure a warm welcome awaits.

B&B from £37.50 to £45.00

GERALDINE DOHERTY
MANAGER

20 20

Open All Year

B&B Rates are per Person Sharing per Night incl. Breakfast
Room Rates are per Room per Night

BAYVIEW HOTEL

2 BAYHEAD ROAD,
PORTBALLINTRAE,
BUSHMILLS, BT57 8RZ
TEL: 028-2073 4100 FAX: 028-2073 4330
EMAIL: info@bayviewhotelni.com
WEB: www.bayviewhotelni.com

HOTEL ★★★ MAP 14 N 21

Opened 2001, the Bayview Hotel is situated in the heart of the picturesque village of Portballintrae, one mile from Bushmills. Overlooking the Atlantic Ocean and close to the Giant's Causeway and Old Bushmills Distillery, with 25 luxurious bedrooms, standard, superior, premier, interlinking and ambulant disabled rooms available. Excellent conference facilities, Porthole Restaurant and Bar. Lift and private car park. This small luxury hotel is the ideal destination for conferencing, golfing, business, incentive travel and leisure.

Member of North Coast Hotels Ltd.

B&B from £40.00 to £55.00

MARY O'NEILL
GROUP MARKETING MANAGER

☺ Weekend specials from £125.00 pps

25 25

BUSHMILLS INN HOTEL

9 DUNLUCE ROAD,
BUSHMILLS,
CO. ANTRIM BT57 8QG
TEL: 028-2073 3000 FAX: 028-2073 2048
EMAIL: mail@bushmillsinn.com
WEB: www.bushmillsinn.com

HOTEL ★★★ MAP 14 N 21

"A living museum of Ulster Hospitality". This multi award-winning hotel with turf fires, oil lamps, nooks, crannies and even a secret room presents an extensive range of intriguing bedrooms, an atmospheric restaurant (new Irish cuisine), a turf fired old kitchen and a Victorian bar still lit by gas light - you're welcome. Location: at the world's oldest distillery, by the River Bush between the Giant's Causeway and Royal Portrush Golf Club.

Member of Ireland's Blue Book

B&B from £69.00 to £79.00

STELLA MINOGUE & ALAN DUNLOP
MANAGERS

32 32

CAUSEWAY HOTEL

40 CAUSEWAY ROAD,
BUSHMILLS,
CO. ANTRIM BT57 8SU
TEL: 028-2073 1226 FAX: 028-2073 2552
EMAIL: reception@giants-causeway-hotel.com
WEB: www.giants-causeway-hotel.com

HOTEL ★★ MAP 14 N 21

Situated on the North Antrim Coast at the entrance to the world famous Giant's Causeway. This old family hotel established in 1836 has been tastefully renovated and restored to provide modern facilities while retaining its old grandeur and charm. The 28 centrally heated bedrooms have TV, tea/coffee making facilities and bathrooms en suite.

B&B from £35.00 to £35.00

JOHANNA ARMSTRONG
MANAGER

☺ Weekend specials 2 nights Dinner and B&B from £90.00 pps

28 28

Open All Year

B&B Rates are per Person Sharing per Night incl. Breakfast
Room Rates are per Room per Night

LONDONDERRY ARMS HOTEL

GLENS OF ANTRIM, 20 HARBOUR ROAD,
CARNLOUGH,
CO. ANTRIM BT44 0EU

TEL: 028-2888 5255 FAX: 028-2888 5263

EMAIL: lda@glensofantrim.com
WEB: www.glensofantrim.com

HOTEL ★★★ MAP 15 P 20

This beautiful Georgian hotel was built in 1847. Once owned by Sir Winston Churchill, it is now owned and managed by Mr Frank O'Neill. With its open log fires, private lounges and award-winning restaurant, this premier hotel in the Glens of Antrim is the perfect place to stay and discover the north eastern part of Ireland. Member of Irish Country Hotels.

Member of Irish Country Hotels

B&B from £35.00 to £50.00

FRANK O'NEILL
PROPRIETOR

Weekend specials from £79.00 pps

35 35

Closed 24 - 26 December

AARANMORE LODGE

14 COLERAINE ROAD,
PORTRUSH,
CO. ANTRIM BT56 8EA

TEL: 028-7082 4640 FAX: 028-7082 4640

EMAIL: aaranmore@talk21.com
WEB: www.accommodation-northernireland.com

GUESTHOUSE ★★ MAP 14 N 21

Aaranmore Lodge, Portrush, offers superior accommodation in its spacious refurbished guest rooms. Situated on the A29 from Coleraine, close to the A2, it offers off-street parking and is the ideal choice for exploring the renowned Causeway Coast. Just minutes from Royal Portrush Golf Course, and with seven superb courses close by, Aaranmore attracts a world-wide golfing clientele. Pubs, restaurants and entertainment within walking distance. Internet facilities.

B&B from £25.00 to £30.00

J & F DUGGAN

4 4

Closed 20 - 30 December

COMFORT HOTEL PORTRUSH

73 MAIN STREET,
PORTRUSH,
CO. ANTRIM BT56 8BN

TEL: 028-7082 6100 FAX: 028-7082 6160

EMAIL: info@comforthotelportrush.com
WEB: www.comforthotelportrush.com

HOTEL ★★★ MAP 14 N 21

The award-winning 3*** Comfort Hotel Portrush opened 2001, situated overlooking the Atlantic Ocean in the centre of Portrush. 50 en suite bedrooms with interlinking and ambulant disabled rooms and lift. Ideal base for golfing, walking, cycling, angling, sightseeing, families, tour parties and conferences. Golf at Royal Portrush, Portstewart, Castlerock, Ballycastle and Galgorm Castle Golf Courses. Sister hotel "Bayview Hotel Portballintrae, Bushmills".

Member of Choice Hotels Europe

B&B from £35.00 to £50.00

MARY O'NEILL
GROUP MARKETING MANAGER

50 50

Open All Year

B&B Rates are per Person Sharing per Night incl. Breakfast
Room Rates are per Room per Night

PENINSULA HOTEL

15 EGLINTON STREET,
PORTRUSH,
CO. ANTRIM BT56 8DX
TEL: 028-7082 2293 FAX: 028-7082 4315
EMAIL: reservations@peninsulahotel.co.uk
WEB: www.peninsulahotel.co.uk

HOTEL ★★ MAP 14 N 21

The Peninsula Hotel, situated in the centre of Portrush is ideally located to allow you to enjoy the delights of the Causeway Coast including the world famous Giant's Causeway. Our bedrooms are warmly decorated with the finest of fittings to ensure comfort for all our guests. The hotel is wheelchair friendly throughout with a passenger lift to all floors. Excellent food served in our Galley Bistro. Less than 10 minutes walk to Royal Portrush Golf Club.

B&B from £35.00 to £50.00

KAY WADE
GENERAL MANAGER

24 24

inet

N I H F

Open All Year

BALLYMAC

7A ROCK ROAD,
STONEYFORD,
CO. ANTRIM BT28 3SU
TEL: 028-9264 8313 FAX: 028-9264 8312
EMAIL: info@ballymachotel.co.uk
WEB: www.ballymac.com

HOTEL ★★ MAP 15 O 18

The Ballymac Hotel set amid tranquil surroundings. Spectacularly reincarnated, the contemporary designed 15 en suite bedrooms with excellent facilities including DD phones, modem facilities, hairdryers, TVs and hospitality trays. Our Grill Bar/Lounge and à la carte restaurant feature outstanding cuisine along with an extensive wine list. The Ballymac also boasts well-equipped function suites suitable for weddings, parties, trade shows and conferences. Extensive private parking is available in our grounds.

B&B from £50.00 to £80.00

CATHY MULDOON
GENERAL MANAGER

15 15

inet

N I H F

Closed 25 December

TEMPLETON HOTEL

882 ANTRIM RD, TEMPLEPATRICK,
BALLYCLARE,
CO. ANTRIM BT39 0AH
TEL: 028-9443 2984 FAX: 028-9443 3406
EMAIL: reception@templetonhotel.com
WEB: www.templetonhotel.com

HOTEL ★★★ MAP 15 O 18

This privately owned hotel, 5 minutes from Belfast International Airport, 20 minutes from Belfast City Centre and Belfast and Larne Ports, offers total quality for all tastes. With the choice of Raffles à la carte restaurant, the Upton Grill Room and the spacious lounge bar, you are guaranteed an enjoyable dining experience. Sam's Bar hosts a pub quiz every Monday evening and offers a late bar at weekends. Our 24 en suite bedrooms, including executive suites, are ideal for a relaxing and comfortable stay.

B&B from £37.50 to £55.00

ALISON MCCOURT/CLAIRE KERR
GEN MANAGER/MRKTG MANAGER

☺ Weekend specials from £90.00 pps

24 24

N I H F

Closed 25 - 26 December

B&B Rates are per Person Sharing per Night incl. Breakfast
Room Rates are per Room per Night

LA MON HOTEL & COUNTRY CLUB

41 GRANSHA ROAD,
CASTLEREAGH,
BELFAST BT23 5RF
TEL: 028-9044 8631 FAX: 028-9044 8026
EMAIL: info@lamon.co.uk
WEB: www.lamon.co.uk

HOTEL ★★★★ MAP 15 P 18

This modern 4 star hotel offers 90 en suite bedrooms, excellent banqueting & conference facilities in a tranquil setting just 8 miles southeast of Belfast City centre. Guests will enjoy the superb luxury and leisure facilities including 15 metre swimming pool, childrens' pool, sauna, jacuzzi, steam room, gymnasium, hair studio & beauty salon. A wide range of dining options is available with table d'hôte and à la carte menus in the Shakespeare Restaurant. Casual dining with a cosmopolitan flavour is also available in our lively bistro. An ideal venue for business or leisure.

B&B from £47.50 to £70.00

FRANCIS BRADY
MANAGING DIRECTOR

Weekend specials from £89.00 pps

90 90

Open All Year

MALONE LODGE HOTEL & APARTMENTS

60 EGLANTINE AVENUE,
MALONE ROAD,
BELFAST BT9 6DY
TEL: 028-9038 8000 FAX: 028-9038 8088
EMAIL: info@malonelodgehotel.com
WEB: www.malonelodgehotel.com

HOTEL ★★★★ MAP 15 P 18

In the leafy suburbs of the university area of South Belfast, discover one of Northern Ireland's finest 4**** hotels. The centre piece of a beautiful Victorian terrace, the Malone Lodge Hotel offers you an oasis of calm and quiet elegance. The hotel offers luxury en suite accommodation, an award-winning restaurant, bar with big screen, conference & banqueting facilities and a fitness suite & sauna.

Member of Select Hotels of Ireland

B&B from £44.50 to £59.50

BRIAN & MARY MACKLIN

51 51

Open All Year

PARK AVENUE HOTEL

158 HOLYWOOD ROAD,
BELFAST BT4 1PB
TEL: 028-9065 6520 FAX: 028-9047 1417
EMAIL: frontdesk@parkavenuehotel.co.uk
WEB: www.parkavenuehotel.co.uk

HOTEL ★★★ MAP 15 P 18

The Park Avenue Hotel has recently been refurbished. 56 rooms with en suite facilities, including TV with satellite channels. Disabled facilities. Free parking. The Griffin Restaurant offers an extensive menu to suit all tastebuds. Alternatively our bistro menu is served daily in Gelston's Corner Bar. 5 minutes from Belfast City Airport. 10 minutes from city centre. Also in close proximity to the Odyssey Arena and Waterfront Hall. Excellent links to outer ring roads and all transport stations and ferry terminals.

Member of The Independents

B&B from £35.00 to £47.50

ANGELA REID
FRONT OFFICE/CONFERENCE MANAGER

56 56

Closed 25 December

B&B Rates are per Person Sharing per Night incl. Breakfast
Room Rates are per Room per Night

RADISSON SAS HOTEL, BELFAST

THE GASWORKS, 3 CROMAC PLACE,
ORMEAU ROAD,
BELFAST BT7 2JB

TEL: 028-9043 4065 FAX: 028-9043 4066
EMAIL: info.belfast@radissonsas.com
WEB: www.radissonsas.com

HOTEL N MAP 15 P 18

Radisson SAS Hotel, Belfast is an architecturally striking new 120 bedroomed hotel, located at the epicentre of regeneration in Belfast. The hotel has seven one bedroom suites and one impressive penthouse suite, a stylish all-day restaurant and bar, offering both traditional and international cuisine and five meeting rooms equipped with an impressive range of technical facilities.

B&B from £45.00 to £60.00

STUART GRANT
GENERAL MANAGER

120 120

Open All Year

RAMADA BELFAST

117 MILLTOWN ROAD,
SHAWSBRIDGE,
BELFAST BT8 7XP

TEL: 028-9092 3500 FAX: 028-9092 3600
EMAIL: mail@ramadabelfast.com
WEB: www.ramadabelfast.com

HOTEL ★★★★ MAP 15 P 18

The Ramada Belfast is situated in one of the most picturesque areas in Belfast, the Lagan Valley Regional Park approximately 10 minutes from the city centre. This 4* de luxe hotel has 120 luxurious bedrooms all equipped with the international traveller in mind. This newly built hotel offers guests the use of a fully equipped health club with a 20 metre swimming pool, along with the Omni Health and Beauty cente. Guests can enjoy a choice of three restaurants. The hotel also has the biggest conference facilities in Belfast.

B&B from £35.00 to £45.00

CLAIRE SUMMERS
SALES MANAGER

120 120

Open All Year

WELLINGTON PARK HOTEL

21 MALONE ROAD,
BELFAST BT9 6RU

TEL: 028-9038 1111 FAX: 028-9066 5410
EMAIL: info@wellingtonparkhotel.com
WEB: www.mooneyhotelgroup.com

HOTEL ★★★★ MAP 15 P 18

Located in the fashionable Malone Road area, this family owned & managed hotel is a Belfast institution. The hotel offers guests the ultimate experience in hospitality & modern comfort with 75 bedrooms. Guests can unwind & relax on the overstuffed sofas of the Arts Café or sample the finest local cuisine in the Piper Bistro. Attractions such as museums, theatres, public gardens & golf clubs are close by. Large conference facilities. Free parking. Families welcome. Only 5 mins from city centre & 10 mins from Belfast City Airport.

Member of Best Western Hotels

B&B from £40.00 to £80.00

ARTHUR MOONEY
GENERAL MANAGER

2 nights B&B +1 Dinner from
£75.00 pps

75 75

Closed 24 - 26 December

B&B Rates are per Person Sharing per Night incl. Breakfast
Room Rates are per Room per Night

BROWN TROUT GOLF & COUNTRY INN

209 AGIVEY ROAD,
AGHADOWEY, COLERAINE,
CO. DERRY BT51 4AD

TEL: 028-7086 8209 FAX: 028-7086 8878
EMAIL: bill@browntroutinn.com
WEB: www.browntroutinn.com

HOTEL ★★★ MAP 14 N 20

The Brown Trout Golf and Country Inn nestles near the River Bann only 12.8km from the picturesque Causeway Coast. This old inn with 15 rooms, and four 5 star cottages, is Northern Ireland's first golf hotel. Gerry, Jane or Joanna will happily organise golf, horseriding and fishing packages with professional tuition if required or you can just enjoy a relaxing break and the craic with the locals. The warm hospitality and 'Taste of Ulster' restaurant will make your stay enjoyable.

Member of Irish Country Hotels

B&B from £35.00 to £45.00

JANE O'HARA
OWNER

15 15

Open All Year

LODGE HOTEL & TRAVELSTOP

LODGE ROAD,
COLERAINE,
CO. LONDONDERRY

TEL: 028-7034 4848 FAX: 028-7035 4555
EMAIL: info@thelodgehotel.com
WEB: www.thelodgehotel.com

HOTEL ★★★ MAP 14 M 20

Conveniently situated for shopping, golfing, horseriding or sight seeing. A choice of 7 golf courses, one for each day of the week, all within 30 minutes drive. Relaxing conservatory & reception areas. Choice of two restaurants serving superb food. Entertainment at the weekends. Renowned for friendly hospitality. Don't take our word for it, come and try for yourself.

B&B from £35.50 to £40.50

NORMA WILKINSON
MANAGING DIRECTOR

56 56

Open all Year

BEECH HILL COUNTRY HOUSE HOTEL

32 ARDMORE ROAD,
DERRY BT47 3QP

TEL: 028-7134 9279 FAX: 028-7134 5366
EMAIL: info@beech-hill.com
WEB: www.beech-hill.com

HOTEL ★★★★ MAP 14 L 20

Beech Hill is a privately owned country house hotel, 2 miles from Londonderry. It retains the elegance of country living and has been restored to create a hotel of charm, character and style. Its ambience is complemented by the surrounding grounds, planted with a myriad trees, including beech. Superb cuisine using local produce and homemade specialties. NITB Highly Commended Marketing Excellence Award 2004. Sauna, steam room, jacuzzi and gym available. Relaxation weekends, aromatherapy, reiki, massage & beauty therapies. Booking advisable.

Member of Manor House Hotels

B&B from £45.00 to £55.00

SEAMUS DONNELLY
PROPRIETOR

Weekend specials from £99.00 pps

27 27

Closed 24 - 26 December

B&B Rates are per Person Sharing per Night incl. Breakfast
Room Rates are per Room per Night

BEST WESTERN WHITE HORSE HOTEL

**68 CLOONEY ROAD,
DERRY BT47 3PA**

TEL: 028-7186 0606 FAX: 028-7186 0371
EMAIL: info@whitehorsehotel.biz
WEB: www.whitehorsehotel.biz

HOTEL ★★★ MAP 14 L 20

A luxury family-run hotel with 56 bedrooms including 16 executive rooms and leisure complex. The hotel is ideal for pleasure and business with 4 conference suites. The leisure complex consists of 22m swimming pool, childrens' pool, sauna, steam room, jacuzzi, aerobics studio & state of the art gymnasium. Only 10 minutes from the historic city of Londonderry and on the main route to the Giant's Causeway. Award winning restaurant and bar, very keen room rates. AA selected. Horseriding, golf and fishing close by. Children welcome.

B&B from £35.00 to £60.00

SHEILA HUNTER
GENERAL MANAGER

Weekend specials from £69.00 pps

56 56

Open All Year

CITY HOTEL

**QUEENS QUAY,
DERRY BT48 7AS**

TEL: 028-7136 5800 FAX: 028-7136 5801
EMAIL: res@derry-gsh.com
WEB: www.gshotels.com

HOTEL ★★★★ MAP 14 L 20

The City Hotel is a stylish modern 4 star hotel in the heart of the city centre. Ideally located on Queen's Quay, it has magnificent views of the River Foyle and the Guildhall. Leisure facilities include indoor swimming pool, jacuzzi, steam room and gym. Thompson's on the River, the hotel's restaurant, is one of Derry's finest. The hotel has conference facilities for up to 450 delegates. A Great Southern Hotel. Bookable through UTELL International or central reservations in Dublin at: 01-214 4800.

Room Rate from £88.00 to £120.00

JASON FOODY
GENERAL MANAGER

Weekend specials from £93.00 pps

145 145

Closed 24 - 26 December

RAMADA AT DA VINCI - LONDONDERRY

**15 CULMORE ROAD,
DERRY BT48 8JB**

TEL: 028-7127 9111 FAX: 028-7127 9222
EMAIL: info@davincishotel.com
WEB: www.davincishotel.com

HOTEL ★★★ MAP 14 L 20

Da Vincis Hotel Complex is the recent winner of the NITB Hotel of the Year Award 2003/2004. The Complex boasts 70 luxurious bedrooms, 21 five star apartments, award winning bar, The Grillroom Restaurant, Style Bar and Spirit Bar. Located only one mile from city centre with private car parking. Corporate and leisure guests welcome. Base yourself in Derry and visit the famous Derry Walls, short drive to Donegal and Giant's Causeway.

Room Rate from £55.00 to £80.00

CIARAN O'NEILL
GENERAL MANAGER

70 70

Closed 24 - 26 December

B&B Rates are per Person Sharing per Night incl. Breakfast
Room Rates are per Room per Night

TOWER HOTEL DERRY

OFF THE DIAMOND,
DERRY CITY

TEL: 028-7137 1000 FAX: 028-7137 1234
EMAIL: reservations@thd.ie
WEB: www.towerhotelderry.com

HOTEL ★★★★ MAP 14 L 20

Located just inside the historic Walls of Derry, this is a truly stylish hotel in a city becoming more and more popular as a base from which to explore the spectacular Northern Coast. Spacious and comfortable guest rooms come well equipped and guests can relax in the leisure suite complete with sauna and steam room. The Bistro at the Tower has been awarded an AA rosette and a passion for good food is evident. The Lime Tree Bar regularly hosts live music, a fitting tribute to a city renowned for its musical tradition.

Member of Tower Hotel Group

B&B from £30.00 to £55.00

IAN HYLAND
GENERAL MANAGER

Weekend specials from £69.00 pps

93 93

Closed 24 - 26 December

WATERFOOT HOTEL & COUNTRY CLUB

CAW ROUNDABOUT,
14 CLOONEY ROAD,
DERRY BT47 6TB

TEL: 028-7134 5500 FAX: 028-7131 1006
EMAIL: info@thewaterfoothotel.co.uk
WEB: www.thewaterfoothotel.co.uk

HOTEL ★★★ MAP 14 L 20

A superbly appointed family-run hotel including indoor leisure centre guaranteeing a luxurious & restful stay. Located on the banks of the River Foyle and only a 5 minute drive to city centre. The hotel restaurant is renowned for its excellent cuisine and this reputation for fine food and drink has been an integral part of the Waterfoot philosophy. Mid-week and weekend breaks available throughout the year.

Member of Holiday Ireland Hotels

B&B from £25.00 to £35.00

JOHANNE FERGUSON
GENERAL MANAGER

Weekend specials from £79.00 pps

48 48

Closed 25 - 27 December

RADISSON SAS ROE PARK RESORT

ROE PARK,
LIMAVADY,
CO. LONDONDERRY BT49 9LB

TEL: 028-7772 2222 FAX: 028-7772 2313
EMAIL: sales@radissonroepark.com
WEB: www.radissonroepark.com

HOTEL ★★★★ MAP 14 M 20

One of the North Coast's only 4 **** de luxe resorts. Old and new combine to create a world class resort and featuring 118 bedrooms and suites, indoor heated pool, unrivalled leisure spa with extensive range of treatments, an excellent 18 hole parkland Golf Course, Driving Range and Indoor Golf Academy. The award winning Greens Restaurant serves classic fare with Irish flair and the Coach House Brasserie has a relaxed charm.

Member of Radisson SAS Hotels and Resorts

B&B from £49.00 to £65.00

JOHN O' CARROLL

Weekend specials from £99.00 pps

118 118

Open All Year

B&B Rates are per Person Sharing per Night incl. Breakfast
Room Rates are per Room per Night

CAIRN BAY LODGE

THE CAIRN, 278 SEACLIFF ROAD,
BANGOR,
CO. DOWN BT20 5HS
TEL: 028-9146 7636 FAX: 028-9145 7728
EMAIL: info@cairnbaylodge.com
WEB: www.cairnbaylodge.com

GUESTHOUSE ★★★ MAP 15 Q 18

Award-winning guesthouse set in extensive gardens directly overlooking Ballyholme Bay. Bangor Business Award -"Best Tourist Accommodation" - 3rd year in succession. The lodge is family-run, offering the highest standards of food, accommodation and service in luxurious surroundings. An oasis of calm yet only 5 minutes walk from Bangor Town Centre and marina. 50m from Ballyholme Yacht Club, 5 golf courses within 5 miles, in-house Guinot appointed beauty salon. Off street parking.

Member of Kingdoms of Down

B&B from £27.50 to £35.00

CHRIS & JENNY MULLEN
PROPRIETORS

3   3

Open all year

ROYAL HOTEL

26/28 QUAY STREET,
BANGOR,
CO. DOWN BT20 5ED
TEL: 028-9127 1866 FAX: 028-9146 7810
EMAIL: royalhotelbangor@aol.com
WEB: www.royalhotelbangor.com

HOTEL ★★ MAP 15 Q 18

Overlooking Bangor Marina this family-run hotel is probably the best known landmark on Bangor's seafront. All rooms en suite include 7 executive suites. Satellite TV, direct dial phone, courtesy tray and hairdryer are all standard throughout. Renowned for our food, Café Royal servery for lunch, Quays Restaurant for evening dining. Weddings our speciality, also conferences and functions. 15 minutes from Belfast City Airport. Direct rail link from Dublin and Derry.

B&B from £30.00 to £40.00

PAUL DONEGAN
PROPRIETOR

Weekend specials from £55.00 pps

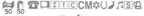

50   50

Closed 25 - 26 December

SHELLEVEN HOUSE

61 PRINCETOWN ROAD,
BANGOR BT20 3TA,
CO. DOWN
TEL: 028-9127 1777 FAX: 028-9127 1777
EMAIL: shellevenhouse@aol.com
WEB: www.shellevenhouse.com

GUESTHOUSE ★★★ MAP 15 Q 18

Two large Victorian houses converted into a substantial guesthouse, in a leafy conservation area, 5 mins walk from Bangor Centre. Shelleven has been run by Philip and Mary Weston for the past six years. The comfort & well-being of their guests is most important to them. 11 en suite bedrooms are tastefully decorated, some with sea views. Breakfasts, with a wide choice of dishes, are served in the elegant dining room. Several golf courses nearby, tee-off times can be arranged. Train/Bus station 5 mins away, with direct link to Dublin & Belfast City Airport.

Member of Kingdoms of Down

B&B from £28.00 to £32.00

MARY WESTON

Weekend specials from £72.00 pps

11   11

Open All Year

B&B Rates are per Person Sharing per Night incl. Breakfast
Room Rates are per Room per Night

CHESTNUT INN

28/34 LOWER SQUARE,
CASTLEWELLAN,
CO. DOWN BT31 9DW
TEL: 028-437 78247 FAX: 028-437 78247

GUESTHOUSE ★ MAP 12 P 16

In the old market town of
Castlewellan, the Chestnut Inn (King's
Hotel) is ideally situated to take
advantage of the Mournes, the
seaside town of Newcastle and all the
amenities of South Down. Royal
County Down is only 5 minutes away
as are the forest parks and the
beaches of Dundrum Bay. The Inn is
renowned for excellent bar food,
friendly atmosphere and also boasts
a superb à la carte restaurant.
World's biggest maze close by.

B&B from £25.00 to £35.00

JOHN & FIONNUALA KING
PROPRIETORS

🛏️ 🍴 📺 T C ♨ C M ∪ ♪ ♪ P 🔒 abc ▪
7   7

Open All Year

BURRENDALE HOTEL AND COUNTRY CLUB

51 CASTLEWELLAN ROAD,
NEWCASTLE,
CO. DOWN BT33 0JY
TEL: 028-4372 2599 FAX: 028-4372 2328
EMAIL: reservations@burrendale.com
WEB: www.burrendale.com

HOTEL ★★★ MAP 12 P 16

At the foot of the Mournes, the
Burrendale is the ideal location for
your family, golfing holiday or short
break. The hotel comprises a Country
Club, Beauty Salon, à la carte Vine
Restaurant, bistro style Cottage
Kitchen Restaurant, Cottage Bar and
excellent banqueting / conference
facilities. In close proximity are 15
golf courses including Royal County
Down, golden beaches, nature walks,
forest parks and pony trekking.
Superb hospitality awaits you.

B&B from £50.00 to £65.00

DENIS ORR
GENERAL MANAGER

✓ 🍴

😊 Weekend specials from £105.00 pps

🛏️ 🍴 ☎ ❄️ T C ♨ C M ✳️ 👤 🏠
🔌 ♪ P S 🔒 abc ▪ 👥 🐕
69   69

Open All Year

B&B Rates are per Person Sharing per Night incl. Breakfast
Room Rates are per Room per Night

CANAL COURT HOTEL

MERCHANTS QUAY,
NEWRY,
CO. DOWN BT35 8HF
TEL: 028-3025 1234 FAX: 028-3025 1177
EMAIL: manager@canalcourthotel.com
WEB: www.canalcourthotel.com

HOTEL ★★★★ MAP 12 O 15

This fabulous 4 star hotel is located in the heart of Newry City. The perfect location for a special break. With 51 beautiful bedrooms and suites and an extensive leisure complex it is the ideal location to relax and unwind. Enjoy the shopping opportunities or visit the wealth of visitor and tourist attractions this city has to offer

B&B from £65.00 to £120.00

MICHELLE BARRETT
GENERAL MANAGER

Weekend specials from £99.00 pps

51 51

Closed 25 December

NARROWS (THE)

8 SHORE ROAD,
PORTAFERRY,
CO. DOWN BT22 1JY
TEL: 028-4272 8148 FAX: 028-4272 8105
EMAIL: reservations@narrows.co.uk
WEB: www.narrows.co.uk

GUESTHOUSE ★★★ MAP 15 Q 17

Since it opened in 1996, The Narrows has taken the Northern Ireland hospitality industry by storm. With numerous awards and reviews for its architecture, cuisine, accommodation, accessibility and conference facilities, you will see why our guests keep coming back. Our 13 en suite rooms, restaurant and conference room all have stunning views of Strangford Lough. British Airways Tourism Award for Best Catering in Northern Ireland. Residents' bar and walled garden for your relaxation.

Member of Kingdoms of Down

B&B from £42.50 to £49.00

WILL & JAMES BROWN

13 13

Open All Year

PORTAFERRY HOTEL

10 THE STRAND,
PORTAFERRY,
CO.DOWN BT22 1PE
TEL: 028-4272 8231 FAX: 028-4272 8999
EMAIL: info@portaferryhotel.com
WEB: www.portaferryhotel.com

HOTEL ★★★ MAP 15 Q 17

Loughside hotel in spectacular setting. Award-winning cuisine and fine wines. Explore or simply relax and do nothing; just peace and tranquillity. BA Tourism Endeavour Award, RAC Restaurant of the Year Award, AA Rosette, Taste of Ulster, Good Hotel Guide. 29 miles from Belfast.

Member of Northern Ireland's Best Kept Secrets

B&B from £47.50 to £55.00

JOHN & MARIE HERLIHY
PROPRIETORS

Weekend specials from £109.00 pps

14 14

Closed 23 - 26 December

B&B Rates are per Person Sharing per Night incl. Breakfast
Room Rates are per Room per Night

ARLINGTON HOTEL

23/25 BACHELORS WALK,
O'CONNELL BRIDGE,
DUBLIN 1

TEL: 01-804 9100 FAX: 01-804 9152

EMAIL: info@arlington.ie
WEB: www.arlington.ie

HOTEL ★★★ MAP 8 O 11

The most central hotel in Dublin, overlooking the River Liffey at O'Connell Bridge. Dublin's top attractions and shopping districts on your doorstep. 116 en suite bedrooms, free underground parking, meeting room. Magnificent mediaeval Knightsbridge Bar with live Irish music and dancing 7 nights a week all year round (free admission). Carvery lunch and à la carte bar menu available, candle lit Knights Bistro. Perfect base for business or pleasure.

B&B from €65.00 to €120.00

PAT GEOGHEGAN
OPERATIONS MANAGER

116 116

Closed 24 - 26 December

ASHFIELD HOUSE

5 CLONSKEAGH ROAD,
DUBLIN 6

TEL: 01-260 3680 FAX: 01-260 4236

EMAIL: ashfieldguesthouse@eircom.net
WEB: www.guesthouse-dublin.com

GUESTHOUSE U MAP 8 O 11

One of Dublin's friendliest family run guesthouses. Providing comfort and service of a very high standard to the tourist and business sector. Rooms are en suite with TV, direct dial phones, tea/coffee facilities, hairdryer etc. A fax service is available. 10 mins from city centre, RDS, Lansdowne Road, Leopardstown Racecourse, ferry ports etc. Many top class pubs and restaurants adjacent to Ashfield House. We provide off street parking. There is an excellent bus service directly to city centre. Air coach direct to airport is a mere 5 min walk.

B&B from €50.00 to €65.00

FRANK AND OLIVE TAYLOR

10 10

Closed 24 - 27 December

ASHLING HOTEL

PARKGATE STREET,
DUBLIN 8

TEL: 01-677 2324 FAX: 01-679 3783

EMAIL: info@ashlinghotel.ie
WEB: www.ashlinghotel.ie

HOTEL ★★★ MAP 8 O 11

Why choose us? Stylish refurbishment. Spacious en suite bedrooms, secure parking, conference/meeting rooms. Under 8 mins by taxi/bus to city centre/Temple Bar. Lovely quaint pubs, Guinness Brewery, Phoenix Park, other attractions nearby. Easily found location by car/rail/bus. By car take city centre route & briefly follow River Liffey westward. Taxi/airlink bus from airport, Heuston Intercity rail station opposite. For onward journeys we are within easy access of all major roads. Adjacent to "LUAS" tram line.

Member of Best Western Hotels

B&B from €54.00 to €120.00

ALAN MOODY
GENERAL MANAGER

☺ Midweek specials from €147.00 pps

147 147

Closed 23 - 27 December

B&B Rates are per Person Sharing per Night incl. Breakfast
Room Rates are per Room per Night

ASTON HOTEL

7/9 ASTON QUAY,
DUBLIN 2

TEL: 01-677 9300 FAX: 01-677 9007
EMAIL: stay@aston-hotel.com
WEB: www.aston-hotel.com

HOTEL U   MAP 8 O 11

A warm welcome awaits you at the Aston Hotel, located in Temple Bar and overlooking the River Liffey. Friendly staff and pleasant surroundings will make your stay a memorable one. All our 27 rooms are en suite and offer every guest comfort including direct dial phone, colour TV, hairdryer and tea/coffee making facilities. A leisurely stroll from the Aston brings you to all Dublin's top attractions and amenities and makes it an ideal base for exploring the capital.

B&B from €45.00 to €90.00

ANN WALSH
MANAGER

27 27

Closed 24 - 26 December

BARRY'S HOTEL

1-2 GREAT DENMARK STREET,
DUBLIN 1

TEL: 01-874 9407 FAX: 01-874 6508

HOTEL ★★   MAP 8 O 11

Barry's Hotel is one of Dublin's oldest hotels built in the later part of the Georgian Period, the hotel has 32 en suite rooms with colour TV, direct dial phone, tea/coffee making facilities, 24 hour reception and resident's bar, entertainment is free for residents. The hotel is within walking distance of the Abbey and Gate Theatres, National Wax Musuem, Croke Park and principal shopping districts and major tourist attractions.

B&B from €50.00 to €60.00

SINÉAD FAHY
MANAGER

32 32

Closed 24 - 26 December

BELGRAVE GUESTHOUSE

8-10 BELGRAVE SQUARE,
RATHMINES,
DUBLIN 6

TEL: 01-496 3760 FAX: 01-497 9243
EMAIL: info@belgraveguesthouse.com
WEB: www.belgraveguesthouse.com

GUESTHOUSE ★★★   MAP 8 O 11

The Belgrave consists of two interconnecting early Victorian buildings overlooking a well matured square. While retaining all the character and charm of its era, the Belgrave has all the conveniences of a modern 3*** guesthouse, each room is en suite and has colour TV, direct dial telephone, tea making facilities. Private car park. Ideally located. We look forward to hosting you and according you a warm welcome for which we are renowned. Completely renovated in November 2004. We are 3 minutes walking distance from the new LUAS line.

B&B from €45.00 to €80.00

PAUL AND MARY O'REILLY
OWNERS

24 24

Closed 22 December - 02 January

B&B Rates are per Person Sharing per Night incl. Breakfast
Room Rates are per Room per Night

BERESFORD HALL

2 BERESFORD PLACE,
DUBLIN 1

TEL: 01-801 4500 FAX: 01-801 4501
EMAIL: stay@beresfordhall.ie
WEB: www.beresfordhall.ie

GUESTHOUSE ★★★★ MAP 8 O 11

Beresford Hall is a city centre, Gandon designed, listed Georgian townhouse overlooking the historic Customs House, adjacent to the financial services centre and close to the Point Depot, Temple Bar, shopping districts and cultural attractions. Enjoy both the elegance and charm of this authentically restored townhouse with splendidly decorated spacious rooms. We offer a friendly and premier guest service to ensure a memorable experience.

B&B from €70.00 to €160.00

COLLETTE SCHEER
MANAGER

16 16

Closed 23 December - 03 January

BERKELEY COURT (THE)

LANSDOWNE ROAD,
BALLSBRIDGE,
DUBLIN 4

TEL: 01-665 3200 FAX: 01-661 7238
EMAIL: berkeleycourt@jurysdoyle.com
WEB: www.jurysdoyle.com

HOTEL ★★★★★ MAP 8 O 11

The Berkeley Court is a premium hotel, offering discreet and personal service in intimate and warm surroundings. Part of the fabric of life, business and success in the locality, contemporary Ireland comes here for the Berkeley Court's brand of personal service and discreet but active networking, business, entertainment and meeting facilities. Set on its own grounds, behind a stand of fine trees, in the prestigious Georgian location of Ballsbridge, the city centre is a leisurely short walk or a 5 minute drive away.

Member of Jurys Doyle Hotel Group

Room Rate from €280.00 to €390.00

GERALDINE DOLAN
GENERAL MANAGER

188 188

Open All Year

BEWLEY'S HOTEL BALLSBRIDGE

MERRION ROAD,
BALLSBRIDGE,
DUBLIN 4

TEL: 01-668 1111 FAX: 01-668 1999
EMAIL: bb@BewleysHotels.com
WEB: www.BewleysHotels.com

HOTEL ★★★ MAP 8 O 11

Bewley's Hotel, Ballsbridge is situated next to the RDS and minutes away from the attractions of the city centre. Accommodating you in style with 304 de luxe bedrooms and 9 well-equipped meeting rooms. Award winning O'Connell's Restaurant offers a wide range of wonderful dining options. Bewley's Hotel provides a setting that is contemporary, relaxed and informal, at a fixed room rate - Every Room Every Night. The hotel is serviced by Aircoach. Real time on line reservations and availability at www.bewleyshotels.com

Room Rate from €99.00 to €99.00

CAROL BURKE
GENERAL MANAGER

304 304

Closed 24 - 26 December

B&B Rates are per Person Sharing per Night incl. Breakfast
Room Rates are per Room per Night

BEWLEY'S HOTEL LEOPARDSTOWN

CENTRAL PARK,
LEOPARDSTOWN ROAD, LEOPARDSTOWN,
DUBLIN 18
TEL: 01-293 5000 FAX: 01-293 5099
EMAIL: Leop@BewleysHotels.com
WEB: www.BewleysHotels.com

HOTEL N MAP 8 O 11

Situated in Central Park, this contemporary new hotel is located 6 miles from the city centre, and just off the extended M50 and N11. Leopardstown Racecourse and Luas tram station (22 minutes to St. Stephen's Green) are a short walk away, while Aircoach links the hotel with the airport. Real-time online reservations and availability at www.BewleysHotels.com

Room Rate from €79.00 to €79.00

DAMIEN MOLLOY
GENERAL MANAGER

357 357

Closed 24 - 26 December

BEWLEY'S HOTEL NEWLANDS CROSS

NEWLANDS CROSS,
NAAS ROAD (N7),
DUBLIN 22
TEL: 01-464 0140 FAX: 01-464 0900
EMAIL: res@BewleysHotels.com
WEB: www.BewleysHotels.com

HOTEL ★★★ MAP 8 O 11

A unique blend of quality, value and flexibility for independent discerning guests. Located just off the N7, minutes from the M50, Dublin Airport and the city centre. Our large spacious family size rooms are fully equipped with all modern amenities. Our Bewley's Restaurant offers you a range of dining options, from traditional Irish breakfast to full table service à la carte. Real time on line reservations and availability at www.BewleysHotels.com

Room Rate from €79.00 to €79.00

JENNIE HUSSEY
GENERAL MANAGER

258 258

Closed 24 - 26 December

BLOOMS HOTEL

6 ANGLESEA STREET,
TEMPLE BAR,
DUBLIN 2
TEL: 01-671 5622 FAX: 01-671 5997
EMAIL: info@blooms.ie
WEB: www.blooms.ie

HOTEL ★★★ MAP 8 O 11

Blooms Hotel is situated at the centre of Dublin's cultural and artistic heart - Temple Bar. The hotel itself is only a few minutes stroll from Grafton Street's shopping and most of the city's best sights. And for those who want to set the town alight, Blooms is on the doorstep of Dublin's most famous nightlife - not least of which is its own nightclub, Club M. Blooms Hotel is a perfect choice for everyone looking to experience Temple Bar and Dublin's city centre.

B&B from €50.00 to €100.00

BARRY O'SULLIVAN
GENERAL MANAGER

⊙ Midweek specials from €135.00 pps

86 86

Open All Year

B&B Rates are per Person Sharing per Night incl. Breakfast
Room Rates are per Room per Night

CLARA HOUSE

23 LEINSTER ROAD,
RATHMINES,
DUBLIN 6
TEL: 01-497 5904 FAX: 01-497 5580
EMAIL: clarahouse@eircom.net
WEB: www.clarahouse.com

GUESTHOUSE ★★★ MAP 8 O 11

Clara House is a beautifully maintained listed Georgian house with many original features skillfully combined with modern day comforts. Each bedroom has en suite bathroom, remote control colour TV, direct dial telephone, radio/alarm clock, tea/coffee making facilities, hair dryer and trouser press. Clara House is a mile from downtown Dublin with bus stops for Ballsbridge/RDS and city centre 200 metres away. Secure parking at rear of house.

B&B from €40.00 to €60.00

DAVE PEARCE
PROPRIETOR

13 13

Closed 24 - 26 December

CLARENCE HOTEL

6-8 WELLINGTON QUAY,
DUBLIN 2

TEL: 01-407 0800 FAX: 01-407 0820
EMAIL: reservations@theclarence.ie
WEB: www.theclarence.ie

HOTEL U MAP 8 O 11

Located on the River Liffey, in the heart of the city, The Clarence Hotel was built in 1852 and was transformed into a boutique hotel in 1996. Owned by Bono and The Edge of the rock group U2 and member of 'Leading Small Hotels of the World', the Clarence has 50 individually designed bedrooms and suites. A treatment room, fitness room and valet parking are available. The renowned Tea Room Restaurant and Octagon Bar, famous for its cocktails, are located here.

Member of Leading Small Hotels of the World

Room Rate from €330.00 to €350.00

ROBERT VAN EERDE
GENERAL MANAGER

50 50

Closed 24 - 27 December

CLARION HOTEL DUBLIN
IFSC

EXCISE WALK,
INTERNATIONAL FINANCIAL SERVICES CENTRE,
DUBLIN 1
TEL: 01-433 8800 FAX: 01-433 8801
EMAIL: info@clarionhotelifsc.com
WEB: www.clarionhotelsireland.com

HOTEL ★★★★ MAP 8 O 11

Designed to redefine the idea of what a four star hotel should be. Superbly located in the city centre. Unwind at Sanovitae Health and Fitness Club including 18m pool, complimentary to guests. Bedrooms with every modern facility to a 5***** hotel standard including broadband plug and play. Enjoy a choice of dining experiences in our Sinergie Restaurant, or an exciting twist of Eastern fare in Kudos Bar. uperbly appointed meeting rooms for small and large conferences and private events.

Member of Choice Hotels Ireland

B&B from €127.50 to €192.50

STEPHEN HANLEY
GENERAL MANAGER

163 163

Open all year

B&B Rates are per Person Sharing per Night incl. Breakfast
Room Rates are per Room per Night

CLARION STEPHENS HALL HOTEL AND SUITES

THE EARLSFORT CENTRE,
LOWER LEESON STREET,
DUBLIN 2

TEL: 01-638 1111 FAX: 01-638 1122
EMAIL: stephens@premgroup.com
WEB: www.stephens-hall.com

HOTEL ★★★ MAP 8 O 11

De luxe all-suite hotel located on Lower Leeson Street, in the heart of Georgian Dublin, just around the corner from St. Stephen's Green and only minutes walk to fashionable Grafton Street, Trinity College, National Art Gallery, National Concert Hall and the National Museum. Clarion Stephens Hall "all suite" Hotel is a home away from home as each room consists of a spacious living room, fully equipped kitchen, in room fax, modem point, CD player and TV with movie channels.

Member of Choice Hotels

Room Rate from €99.00 to €350.00

HEATHER WIKTORSKI
GENERAL MANAGER

33 33

Inet

HOTELS
FEDERATION

Open All Year

CLIFDEN GUESTHOUSE

32 GARDINER PLACE,
DUBLIN 1

TEL: 01-874 6364 FAX: 01-874 6122
EMAIL: bnb@indigo.ie
WEB: www.clifdenhouse.com

GUESTHOUSE ★★★ MAP 8 O 11

A refurbished city centre Georgian home. Our private car park provides security for guests' cars, even after check-out. All rooms are non - smoking and have shower, WC, WHB, TV, direct dial phone and tea making facilities. We cater for single, twin, double, triple and family occupancies. Convenient to airport, ferryports, Bus Aras (bus station) and DART. We are only 5 minutes walk from O'Connell Street. AA approved.

Room Rate from €55.00 to €180.00

JACK & MARY LALOR

15 15

HOTELS
FEDERATION

Closed 20 - 27 December

CLONTARF CASTLE HOTEL

CASTLE AVENUE,
CLONTARF,
DUBLIN 3

TEL: 01-833 2321 FAX: 01-833 0418
EMAIL: info@clontarfcastle.ie
WEB: www.clontarfcastle.ie

HOTEL ★★★★ MAP 8 O 11

A magnificent historic castle, dating back to 1172, is today a luxurious 4**** de luxe 111 room hotel. Ideally located only 10 minutes from the city centre and 15 minutes from Dublin Airport, complimentary car parking also available. Superb bedrooms, equipped with all the modern facilities, featuring wireless broadband access. Templar's Bistro specialising in modern international cuisine, 2 unique bars and state of the art conference and banqueting facilities.

B&B from €70.00 to €155.00

DERMOT HENNESSY
GENERAL MANAGER

111 111

HOTELS
FEDERATION

Closed 24 - 25 December

B&B Rates are per Person Sharing per Night incl. Breakfast
Room Rates are per Room per Night

FITZWILLIAM

41 UPPER FITZWILLIAM STREET,
DUBLIN 2

TEL: 01-662 5155 FAX: 01-676 7488
EMAIL: fitzwilliamguesthouse@eircom.net
WEB: www.fitzwilliamguesthouse.ie

GUESTHOUSE ★★★ MAP 8 O 11

Centrally located in the heart of elegant Georgian Dublin, minutes walk from St. Stephen's Green, National Concert Hall and Galleries. Enjoy the charm of this spacious townhouse. Rooms with en suite facilities, colour TV, direct dial telephone, clock/radios and hair dryers. Overnight car parking available. Excellent restaurants nearby. Our friendly staff will ensure your stay is a relaxed and memorable one.

B&B from €50.00 to €65.00

LAURENCE REDDIN
MANAGER

13 13

Closed 21 December - 04 January

FITZWILLIAM HOTEL

ST. STEPHEN'S GREEN,
DUBLIN 2

TEL: 01-478 7000 FAX: 01-478 7878
EMAIL: enq@fitzwilliamhotel.com
WEB: www.fitzwilliamhotel.com

HOTEL U MAP 8 O 11

A modern classic uniquely positioned on St. Stephen's Green, paces away from Grafton Street, Ireland's premiere shopping location. Understated luxury, a fresh approach & impeccable service make it the perfect retreat for business and pleasure. Dine in the highly acclaimed Thornton's Restaurant or the fashionable Citron. Recent additions include free unlimited broadband in bedrooms & 3 conference rooms. Wi-Fi available in our bar. Beauty salon and fitness centre. Stunning new 2,000 sq. foot penthouse.

Member of Summit Hotels & Resorts

Room Rate from €195.00 to €430.00

JOHN KAVANAGH
GENERAL MANAGER

138 138

Open All Year

FOUR SEASONS HOTEL DUBLIN

SIMMONSCOURT ROAD,
BALLSBRIDGE,
DUBLIN 4

TEL: 01-665 4000 FAX: 01-665 4099
EMAIL: reservations.dublin@fourseasons.com
WEB: www.fourseasons.com/dublin

HOTEL ★★★★★ MAP 8 O 11

The charms of Irish tradition and hospitality combine to provide the stage for Four Seasons Hotel Dublin. Set within the showgrounds of the historic Royal Dublin Society, the hotel brings together 259 exceptional guestrooms and suites with the finest facilities for business and relaxation. Residential in style, the hotel features 15,000 sq ft of meeting and banquet space, fine dining in Seasons Restaurant and an 11,000 sq ft full service spa.

Room Rate from €255.00 to €485.00

JOHN BRENNAN
GENERAL MANAGER

259 259

Open All Year

B&B Rates are per Person Sharing per Night incl. Breakfast
Room Rates are per Room per Night

GEORGE FREDERIC HANDEL HOTEL

16-18 FISHAMBLE STREET,
CHRISTCHURCH, TEMPLE BAR,
DUBLIN 8
TEL: 01-670 9400 FAX: 01-670 9410
EMAIL: info@handelshotel.com
WEB: www.handelshotel.com

HOTEL U   MAP 8 O 11

Our secret is out! Centrally located, while situated in the heart of Dublin's vibrant Temple Bar area, the George Frederic Handel Hotel is also within easy walking distance of the city's main tourist attractions and financial districts. We offer a high standard of accommodation combined with a warm Irish welcome - all at a great price. Live online booking system at www.handelshotel.com

B&B from € 37.50 to € 77.50

JONATHAN HYNES
OPERATIONS MANAGER

40 40

IRISH
HOTELS
FEDERATION

Closed 24 - 27 December

GEORGIAN HOTEL

18-22 BAGGOT STREET LOWER,
DUBLIN 2
TEL: 01-634 5000 FAX: 01-634 5100
EMAIL: info@georgianhotel.ie
WEB: www.georgianhotel.ie

HOTEL ★★★   MAP 8 O 11

This very comfortable 200 year old house with new extension in the heart of Georgian Dublin, next to St. Stephen's Green and a 5 minute walk to the major sites including Trinity College, galleries, museums, cathedrals, theatres and to fashionable shopping streets and pubs. Bathrooms en suite, TV, ISDN. Perfect location for business or holiday travellers and offers all the amenities of an exclusive hotel. Private car park.

Room Rate from € 99.00 to € 165.00

ANNETTE O'SULLIVAN
MANAGING DIRECTOR

47 47

IRISH
HOTELS
FEDERATION

Open All Year

GLASNEVIN MAPLES HOTEL

IONA ROAD,
GLASNEVIN,
DUBLIN 9
TEL: 01-830 4227 FAX: 01-830 3874
EMAIL: info@mapleshotel.com
WEB: www.mapleshotel.com

HOTEL ★★   MAP 8 O 11

The friendly and welcoming Glasnevin Maples Hotel is a beautifully newly refurbished 20th century Edwardian building situated north of the city centre just 15 minutes from Temple Bar. Croke Park is just 1 mile while international football/rugby grounds, concert venues, airport and golf courses are easily accessible. Our 22 bedrooms are of high quality as is our restaurant, bar, lounge and function room. We also cater for conferences, weddings, funerals and banquets.

B&B from € 45.00 to € 75.00

KEN & DEREK MURPHY

22 22

IRISH
HOTELS
FEDERATION

Closed 24 - 27 December

B&B Rates are per Person Sharing per Night incl. Breakfast
Room Rates are per Room per Night

GLENOGRA HOUSE

64 MERRION ROAD,
BALLSBRIDGE,
DUBLIN 4
TEL: 01-668 3661 FAX: 01-668 3698
EMAIL: glenogra@indigo.ie
WEB: www.glenogra.com

GUESTHOUSE ★★★★ MAP 8 O 11

Located opposite the RDS and Four Seasons Hotel, close to city centre, bus, rail, embassies, restaurants, car ferries. Glenogra provides luxury and elegance in a personalised, family-run environment. The cosy drawing room is perfect for a restoring afternoon tea. En suite bedrooms are decorated in harmony with a period residence, are all non-smoking with phone, TV, coffee making facilities. Private car parking. AA, RAC ♦♦♦♦♦.

Member of Premier Guesthouses

Room Rate from €90.00 to €100.00

JOSEPH DONOHOE
MANAGER

🛏🔥☎🖥TC✿PS▪
12 12

Closed 20 - 31 December

GRAFTON CAPITAL HOTEL

STEPHENS STREET LOWER,
DUBLIN 2
TEL: 01-648 1100 FAX: 01-648 1122
EMAIL: info@graftoncapital-hotel.com
WEB: www.capital-hotels.com

HOTEL ★★★ MAP 8 O 11

Ever just feel you're 'at home'? In the heart of Dublin's most fashionable & cultural area, your first experience of the Grafton Capital Hotel is that of its traditional Georgian townhouse façade. Guests will enjoy the luxury of superb accommodation, with a wealth of comforts for the discerning guest. Make the most of this prime central location - Grafton St, St Stephens Green & the colourful Temple Bar area, are all a short stroll from the hotel. Restaurants, cafés, bars & a host of visitor attractions all nearby. Complimentary admission to all Capital Bars/Clubs in Dublin.

Member of Capital Hotel Group

B&B from €60.00 to €119.00

FRANCES DEMPSEY
GENERAL MANAGER

☺ 2 nights B&B weekend special from €159.00 pps

🛏🔥☎🖥TC▾CM♫S🔲a|c▪
75 75

Inet

Closed 24 - 26 December

GRAFTON HOUSE

26/27 SOUTH GREAT GEORGES STREET,
DUBLIN 2
TEL: 01-679 2041 FAX: 01-677 9715
EMAIL: graftonguesthouse@eircom.net
WEB: www.graftonguesthouse.com

GUESTHOUSE ★★★ MAP 8 O 11

A recently refurbished (2004) city centre guesthouse in a beautiful Victorian Gothic redbrick building. 16 comfortable rooms (plus an apartment), all en suite & all designed in a contemporary but fun style (check out the wallpaper) with friendly staff & tasty breakfasts (with vegetarian option). This is definitely one of the best places to stay in downtown Dublin with restaurants, bars, nightclubs, theatres & cinemas all just a short walk away, (Temple Bar is at the end of the street). Secure car parking just around the corner.

B&B from €50.00 to €70.00

GABRIELA ANTHONI
DUTY MANAGER

🛏🔥☎🖥TY Inet 🐕
16 16

Open All Year

B&B Rates are per Person Sharing per Night incl. Breakfast
Room Rates are per Room per Night

GRESHAM (THE)

**23 UPPER O'CONNELL STREET,
DUBLIN 1**

TEL: 01-874 6881 FAX: 01-878 7175
EMAIL: info@thegresham.com
WEB: www.gresham-hotels.com

HOTEL ★★★★ MAP 8 O 11

The Gresham, a landmark building in Dublin City centre, is a 4**** hotel that has undergone a dramatic transformation. Relax over afternoon tea in our airy lobby, or enjoy an excellent dining experience in our award winning Restaurant '23'. 289 bedrooms including the executive Lavery Wing. Penthouse suites with views over the city individually redesigned in a range of superb styles. Car parking (charge applies). AA and RAC approved.

Member of Gresham Hotel Group

B&B from € 85.00 to € 200.00

PAUL MCCRACKEN
OPERATIONS DIRECTOR

Midweek specials 2 nights B&B from € 139.00 pps

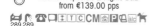
289 289

Open All Year

HARCOURT HOTEL

**60 HARCOURT STREET,
DUBLIN 2**

TEL: 01-478 3677 FAX: 01-478 1557
EMAIL: reservations@harcourthotel.ie
WEB: www.harcourthotel.ie

HOTEL ★★★ MAP 8 O 11

The Harcourt Hotel's Georgian exterior conceals its contemporary interior. The boutique style hotel is famous for once being home to George Bernard Shaw. Facilities include a convivial Bar D-Two, a landscaped year-round beer garden (heated), restaurant; Little Ceasers, traditional music bar; Barney's & a nightclub (Thurs to Sun). At the weekends if you are a light sleeper ask for a quiet room (as most rooms fit this category). Local secure car parking available @ €5.00 a night. The new LUAS tram service (serving Grafton Street to Sandyford) is adjacent.

B&B from € 44.00 to € 115.00

DANIELLE MCGILL
OPERATIONS MANAGER

51 51

Closed 24 - 26 December

HARDING HOTEL

**COPPER ALLEY,
FISHAMBLE STREET,
DUBLIN 2**

TEL: 01-679 6500 FAX: 01-679 6504
EMAIL: harding.hotel@kinlaygroup.ie
WEB: www.hardinghotel.ie

HOTEL ★★ MAP 8 O 11

Harding Hotel is a stylish city centre hotel located within Dublin's Temple Bar. This historic area offers the visitor an unrivalled choice of restaurants, cafés, bars and traditional Irish pubs. All 53 en suite rooms have television, direct dial telephone, hairdryer and tea/coffee making facilities. Darkey Kelly's Bar and Restaurant offer an exciting array of food and entertainment. Groups and individuals welcome.

Member of Kinlay Group

Room Rate from € 64.00 to € 131.00

AINE HICKEY
MANAGER

53 53

Closed 23 - 26 December

B&B Rates are per Person Sharing per Night incl. Breakfast
Room Rates are per Room per Night

HARRINGTON HALL

70 HARCOURT STREET,
DUBLIN 2

TEL: 01-475 3497 FAX: 01-475 4544
EMAIL: harringtonhall@eircom.net
WEB: www.harringtonhall.com

GUESTHOUSE ★★★★ MAP 8 O 11

Harrington Hall with its secure private parking in the heart of Georgian Dublin, provides the perfect location for holiday and business visitors alike to enjoy the surrounding galleries, museums, cathedrals, theatres, fashionable shopping streets, restaurants and pubs. All rooms are equipped to today's exacting standards with en suite, direct dial phone, hospitality tray, trouser press and multi channel TV, access to fax facilities, e-mail and internet. All floors are serviced by elevator. AA ♦♦♦♦ and RAC ♦♦♦♦♦.

B&B from €86.50 to €100.00

HENRY KING
PROPRIETOR

☺ Midweek specials from €210.00 pps

28 28

Open All Year

HARVEY'S GUEST HOUSE

11 UPPER GARDINER STREET,
DUBLIN 1

TEL: 01-874 8384 FAX: 01-874 5510
EMAIL: info@harveysguesthouse.com
WEB: www.harveysguesthouse.com

GUESTHOUSE ★★★ MAP 8 O 11

This fully restored family run Georgian guesthouse provides a friendly atmosphere. Located in the heart of Dublin City and only 700m from O'Connell Bridge and Temple Bar. Conveniently reached by the No 41 or 16 airport bus to Dorset Street and our street, walk back around the corner and up to us on the right after the church. Our en suite facilities include bath/shower and hairdryers. Our car park is free. All rooms have TV and telephone.

B&B from €35.00 to €70.00

ROBERT FLOOD
MANAGER

15 15

Closed 23 - 27 December

B&B Rates are per Person Sharing per Night incl. Breakfast
Room Rates are per Room per Night

HERBERT PARK HOTEL

BALLSBRIDGE,
DUBLIN 4

TEL: 01-667 2200 FAX: 01-667 2595
EMAIL: reservations@herbertparkhotel.ie
WEB: www.herbertparkhotel.ie

HOTEL ★★★★ MAP 8 O 11

AA's Courtesy & Care Awarded Hotel for Ireland 2003 is located in Ballsbridge, five minutes from the city centre with spectacular views over 48 acres of Herbert Park. Bedrooms are comfortably appointed with modern features including air conditioning, mini bar, safe, interactive television with playstation, internet access and pay per view movies. Facilities include the award-winning Pavilion Restaurant overlooking Herbert Park, Exhibition Bar, cardiovascular gym, meeting rooms and complimentary car parking.

Member of Supranational Hotels

B&B from € 67.50 to € 156.50

EWAN PLENDERLEITH
DIRECTOR/GENERAL MANAGER

Weekend Special 2 nights B&B
from € 135.00 pps

153 153

Open All Year

HOLIDAY INN DUBLIN CITY CENTRE

99-107 PEARSE STREET,
DUBLIN 2

TEL: 01-670 3666 FAX: 01-670 3636
EMAIL: info@holidayinndublin.ie
WEB: www.holidayinndublincitycentre.ie

HOTEL ★★★ MAP 8 O 11

Located in heart of the city centre with Dublin's main tourist attractions and principal shopping areas within walking distance including the IFSC, Point Depot, RDS, Lansdowne Road and Temple Bar. Featuring 101 en suite bedrooms, car parking, resident's gym & business centre. Conferene facilities for up to 400. Our Green Bistro & Bar offers a full menu throughout the day helped along by one of the finest pints of Guinness in Dublin. Whether here for business or pleasure the Holiday Inn Dublin City Centre is the ideal location.

Member of Intercontinental Hotels Group

B&B from € 45.00 to € 120.00

TREVOR SMITH
GENERAL MANAGER

101 101

Open All Year

HOTEL ISAACS

STORE STREET,
DUBLIN 1

TEL: 01-813 4700 FAX: 01-836 5390
EMAIL: hotel@isaacs.ie
WEB: www.isaacs.ie

HOTEL ★★★ MAP 8 O 11

Situated in the heart of Dublin City, 5 mins by foot from O'Connell Street Bridge, Hotel Isaacs, a converted wine warehouse, is the perfect location for the visitor to Dublin, at the perfect price, close to the shopping & financial centres. All rooms are tastefully furnished & are en suite with telephone, TV, tea/coffee making facilities & iron/ironing board. The restaurant, Il Vignardo, serves great tasting Italian food 7 days a week. Nearby overnight parking available at special rates.

Room Rate from € 100.00 to € 240.00

JUSTIN LOWRY
GENERAL MANAGER

88 88

Closed 23 - 27 December

B&B Rates are per Person Sharing per Night incl. Breakfast
Room Rates are per Room per Night

MESPIL HOTEL

MESPIL ROAD,
DUBLIN 4

TEL: 01-488 4600 FAX: 01-667 1244
EMAIL: mespil@leehotels.com
WEB: www.leehotels.com

HOTEL ★★★ MAP 8 O 11

The Mespil boasts an ideal city centre location overlooking the banks of the Grand Canal and just 15 minutes walk to St. Stephen's Green and many major attractions including museums, theatres and shopping areas. All 255 en suite guest bedrooms are bright, spacious and tastefully furnished. Relax and unwind in our Terrace Bar or enjoy some tantalising dishes from the Glaze Restaurant. Wireless Internet service (WiFi) now available. A warm and friendly welcome awaits you at the Mespil Hotel.

Member of Lee Hotels

Room Rate from €99.00 to €195.00

MARTIN HOLOHAN
GENERAL MANAGER

☺ Room only rate from €99.00

255 255

Inet WiFi

Closed 24 - 27 December

MONT CLARE HOTEL

MERRION SQUARE,
DUBLIN 2

TEL: 01-607 3800 FAX: 01-661 5663
EMAIL: montclareres@ocallaghanhotels.ie
WEB: www.ocallaghanhotels.com

HOTEL ★★★ MAP 8 O 11

A traditional Dublin hotel, The Mont Clare is centrally located on Dublin's Merrion Square, just a few minutes walk to all major attractions including Trinity College, museums, theatres, business and shopping areas. The Mont Clare offers 74 newly refurbished, air conditioned bedrooms, a charming lounge bar, Goldsmith's Restaurant, convention facilities and parking. Reservations via UTELL International Worldwide. USA Toll Free Reservations 1800 5699983 and online at www.ocallaghanhotels.com

Member of O'Callaghan Hotels

B&B from €65.00 to €132.00

PATRICK LERNIHAN
GENERAL MANAGER

74 74

Inet

Closed from 24 - 26 December

MORGAN HOTEL

10 FLEET STREET,
TEMPLE BAR,
DUBLIN 2

TEL: 01-679 3939 FAX: 01-679 3946
EMAIL: sales@themorgan.com
WEB: www.themorgan.com

HOTEL U MAP 8 O 11

The Morgan is a boutique contemporary hotel offering a lifestyles elegance, with modern chic décor, located in the heart of Dublin's Temple Bar. The Morgan offers a cool modern interior that contrasts from the dynamic street life in the area and provides the ultimate in comfort and luxury for the discerning traveller. All bedrooms including de luxe rooms & suites are individually designed and are equipped with TV/video, mini Hi-Fi, mini bar & bathrobes. High speed internet available in all rooms. Online bookings, www.themorgan.com

Room Rate from €140.00 to €250.00

AINE MCGUINNESS
GENERAL MANAGER

66 66

Closed 24 - 26 December

B&B Rates are per Person Sharing per Night incl. Breakfast
Room Rates are per Room per Night

MORRISON (THE)

LOWER ORMOND QUAY,
DUBLIN 1

TEL: 01-887 2400 FAX: 01-878 3185
EMAIL: info@morrisonhotel.ie
WEB: www.morrisonhotel.ie

HOTEL ★★★★ MAP 8 O 11

One of the most luxurious and sophisticated hotels in Dublin, the Morrison is in the heart of the city overlooking the River Liffey. The 124 superior rooms, 16 stunning suites and the uniquely designed penthouse are decorated in a style which combines the use of natural Irish materials. Features include Halo Restaurant, offering modern European style cooking, the Morrison Bar, The Café Bar and 5 state of the art meeting and event venues.

Member of Sterling Hotels & Resorts

B&B from €80.00 to €140.00

ANDREW O'NEILL
GENERAL MANAGER

141 141

WiFi

IRISH HOTELS FEDERATION

Open All Year

MOUNT HERBERT HOTEL

HERBERT ROAD,
LANSDOWNE ROAD,
DUBLIN 4

TEL: 01-668 4321 FAX: 01-660 7077
EMAIL: info@mountherberthotel.ie
WEB: www.mountherberthotel.ie

HOTEL U MAP 8 O 11

A rare gem of a hotel located in Dublin city's most exclusive residential area, steeped in the literary tradition of James Joyce and W.B. Yeats. Guests can relax in comfort, and enjoy all of the hotel's modern facilities, including 177 bedrooms, bar, restaurant, internet room, conference rooms and private car park.It's outstanding value has made it one of Dublin's most popular hotels for many years.

Room Rate from €75.00 to €199.00

MICHELLE SWEENEY
MANAGER

☺ Midweek specials from €150.00 pps

177 177

WiFi

IRISH HOTELS FEDERATION

Closed 23 - 29 December

NORTH STAR HOTEL

AMIENS STREET,
DUBLIN 1

TEL: 01-836 3136 FAX: 01-836 3561
EMAIL: norths@regencyhotels.com
WEB: www.regencyhotels.com

HOTEL ★★★ MAP 8 O 11

City centre location directly opposite I.F.S.C., beside Connolly Rail Station & Busarus. Trinity College, St. Stephen's Green, main shopping areas & Temple Bar all within walking distance. Newly appointed, air-cond. executive bedrooms and luxurious suites. Rooms are en suite with colour TV, DD phone, hairdryer & trouser press. The hotel has been enhanced by a new reception, lobby & restaurant and has excellent meeting facilities with ISDN lines & video conferencing. We have a fully equipped gym with sauna/changing rooms. 24hr supervised car park.

B&B from €65.00 to €140.00

DAVID KIELY
GENERAL MANAGER

☺ Weekend specials from €105.00 pps

130 130

Inet WiFi

IRISH HOTELS FEDERATION

Open All Year

B&B Rates are per Person Sharing per Night incl. Breakfast
Room Rates are per Room per Night

OLD DUBLINER GUESTHOUSE

**62 AMIENS STREET,
DUBLIN 1**

TEL: 01-855 5666 FAX: 01-855 5677
EMAIL: dublinerbb@aol.com
WEB: www.olddubliner.com

GUESTHOUSE ★★★ MAP 8 O 11

The Old Dubliner is a listed Georgian town house that has been completely refurbished to a high standard. All rooms are en suite with TV, phone, hairdryers and tea/coffee making facilities. Situated in the heart of the city close to Connolly Station and central bus station, 10 minutes walk from O'Connell Street and vibrant Temple Bar. Convenient to Point Theatre. Secure car park (limited availability). Our professional and friendly service will ensure a memorable stay.

B&B from €45.00 to €65.00

JOHN O'NEILL/SUSAN GARD
PROPRIETOR/MANAGER

14 14

Closed 21 - 27 December

ORMOND QUAY HOTEL

**7-11 UPPER ORMOND QUAY,
DUBLIN 7**

TEL: 01-872 1811 FAX: 01-872 1362
EMAIL: ormondqh@indigo.ie
WEB: www.ormondquayhotel.net

HOTEL ★★★ MAP 8 O 11

Perfectly located overlooking the River Liffey in Dublin City centre, minutes from Temple Bar and O'Connell Street, the Ormond Quay Hotel is the ideal base for any visitor to Dublin. With 62 en suite rooms, excellent conference & banqueting facilities, stylish Sirens Bar and the Gallery Restaurant, the Ormond Quay Hotel offers you small world charm in the heart of one of Europe's most vibrant capitals.

B&B from €65.00 to €150.00

VERONICA TIMLIN
GENERAL MANAGER

☺ Midweek specials from €100.00 pps

62 62

Closed 24 - 26 December

O'SHEAS HOTEL

**19 TALBOT STREET,
DUBLIN 1**

TEL: 01-836 5670 FAX: 01-836 5214
EMAIL: osheashotel@eircom.net
WEB: www.osheashotel.com

HOTEL U MAP 8 O 11

O'Sheas Hotel renowned the world over for its close association with Irish music, song & dance, it's this that provides the theme for the hotel, with its typical Irish pub and restaurant serving the best in Irish cuisine with a healthy sprinkling of international dishes. O'Sheas Hotel has 34 recently refurbished en suite bedrooms, the hotel also has function and conference room facilities for up to 180 people and provides live entertainment seven nights. We look forward to welcoming you.

B&B from €50.00 to €60.00

JOHN MCCORMACK
MANAGER

34 34

Closed 24 - 25 December

**B&B Rates are per Person Sharing per Night incl. Breakfast
Room Rates are per Room per Night**

OTHELLO HOUSE

74 LOWER GARDINER STREET, DUBLIN 1

TEL: 01-855 4271 FAX: 01-855 7460
EMAIL: othello1@eircom.net
WEB: www.othelloguesthouse.com

GUESTHOUSE ★★ MAP 8 O 11

Othello is 150m from Abbey Theatre, 200m from Dublin's main O'Connell Street, 50m from central bus station. Number 41 bus direct from Dublin Airport stops outside door. 150m to Connolly Railway Station, 1 mile to ferry terminal, 800m to Point Theatre. Lock up secure car park. All rooms en suite with TV, telephone, tea/coffee making facilities. Trinity College, National Museum, National Library all within walking distance.

B&B from €45.00 to €55.00

JOHN GALLOWAY
MANAGER

🛏️ 🏠 ☎️🖥️ T C P S 🔌
22 22

Closed 24 - 28 December

PALMERSTOWN LODGE

PALMERSTOWN VILLAGE, DUBLIN 20

TEL: 01-623 5494 FAX: 01-623 6214
EMAIL: info@palmerstownlodge.com
WEB: www.palmerstownlodge.com

GUESTHOUSE ★★★ MAP 8 O 11

Prime location adjacent to all amenities and facilities this superb purpose-built property adjoins the N4/M50 motorway. Minutes from the city centre and a mere 12 minutes drive to the airport we offer all the features and standards of a hotel. Each elegant en suite bedroom has individual temperature control, ambient lighting, automated door locking system, phone, TV, etc. Separate tea/coffee and iron/trouser press facilities. Private car park. Golf packages available.

B&B from €48.00 to €75.00

GERRY O'CONNOR
OWNER

🛏️ 🏠 ☎️🖥️C 🐕 J P S 🔌 Inet 🐴
19 19

Open All Year

PARAMOUNT HOTEL

PARLIAMENT STREET & ESSEX GATE, TEMPLE BAR, DUBLIN 2

TEL: 01-417 9900 FAX: 01-417 9904
EMAIL: sales@paramounthotel.ie
WEB: www.paramounthotel.ie

HOTEL ★★★ MAP 8 O 11

Set in Temple Bar's quieter west end, Paramount Hotel is one of the city's most trendy and cosmopolitan. The hotel boasts 66 en suite bedrooms, tastefully decorated in the very elegant style of the 1930s. The hotel's bar, the Turks Head, is a stylish bar renowned for its extravagant design, & vibrant colours. Bistro dishes are served daily, and the bar turns into a late bar with club at the weekend. Email: info@turkshead.ie or Web: www.turkshead.ie

Room Rate from €80.00 to €240.00

RITA BARCOE
GENERAL MANAGER

☺ Midweek specials from €100.00 pps

🛏️ 🏠 ☎️🖥️ 💡 T C 🔌 a|c 🔌 Inet
66 66

Closed 22 - 29 December

B&B Rates are per Person Sharing per Night incl. Breakfast
Room Rates are per Room per Night

PHOENIX PARK HOUSE

38-39 PARKGATE STREET,
DUBLIN 8

TEL: 01-677 2870 FAX: 01-679 9769
EMAIL: info@dublinguesthouse.com
WEB: www.dublinguesthouse.com

GUESTHOUSE ★★ MAP 8 O 11

This friendly AA listed family-run guesthouse directly beside the Phoenix Park with its many facilities is ideally located 2 minutes walk from Heuston Station with direct bus service to ferry ports, Dublin Airport, Connolly Train Station and central bus station. Close to the Guinness Brewery, Whiskey Corner, the re-located National Museum and Kilmainham Museum of Modern Art, the popular Temple Bar and numerous pubs and restaurants. Secure car parking available nearby.

B&B from €35.00 to €65.00

MARY SMITH & EMER SMITH
PROPRIETORS

25 25

Closed 22 - 28 December

PLAZA HOTEL

BELGARD ROAD,
TALLAGHT,
DUBLIN 24

TEL: 01-462 4200 FAX: 01-462 4600
EMAIL: reservations@plazahotel.ie
WEB: www.plazahotel.ie

HOTEL ★★★★ MAP 8 O 11

120 bedrooms, 2 suites. Convenient location on Belgard Road, just off the M50 motorway, 8 miles from the city centre. Secure underground car parking. Extensive conference & banqueting facilities for up to 220 people. Floor One serving food from 9.00am - 10.00pm daily. Obar1 music bar. The Playhouse Nightclub. Grumpy McClafferty's traditional pub. 20 minutes from Dublin Airport.

Room Rate from €110.00 to €187.00

JIM LAVERY
GENERAL MANAGER

122 122

WiFi

Closed 24 - 31 December

PORTOBELLO HOTEL & BAR

33 SOUTH RICHMOND STREET,
DUBLIN 2

TEL: 01-475 2715 FAX: 01-478 5010
EMAIL: portobellohotel@indigo.ie
WEB: www.portobellohotel.ie

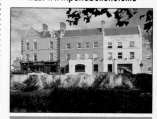

HOTEL U MAP 8 O 11

This landmark building is located in the heart of Dublin City along the Grand Canal. First opened in 1793, the Portobello Hotel & Bar boasts a long tradition in hospitality and provides guests with luxury en suite accommodation with tea/coffee making facilities, TV, radio, iron & board, direct dial phone & hair dryer. Temptation Night Club popular with all ages. A friendly welcome and service is guaranteed.

B&B from €50.00 to €70.00

CIARA DARCY
MANAGER

24 24

Open All Year

B&B Rates are per Person Sharing per Night incl. Breakfast
Room Rates are per Room per Night

PRINCIPAL HOTEL

19/20 FLEET STREET,
TEMPLE BAR,
DUBLIN 2
TEL: 01-670 8122 FAX: 01-670 8103
EMAIL: principalhotel@eircom.net
WEB: www.principalhotel.com

HOTEL ★★★ MAP 8 O 11

The Principal Hotel is ideally located in the Temple Bar area of the city. We offer the finest traditions of quality and service. We are ideally based for both business and leisure, walking distance from Trinity College, Grafton Street and all the local bars and restaurants. All rooms are en suite with tea and coffee facilities, direct dial telephone, hair dryer and trouser press. T.V. in all bedrooms.

B&B from €55.00 to €110.00

PATRICK CARNEY
OPERATIONS MANAGER

71 71

Closed 24 - 27 December

QUALITY HOTEL DUBLIN

CARDIFF LANE,
SIR JOHN ROGERSON'S QUAY,
DUBLIN 2
TEL: 1850-746 8357 FAX: 021-4271489
EMAIL: info@qualityhoteldublin.com
WEB: www.qualityhoteldublin.com

HOTEL P MAP 8 O 11

Superbly situated on Dublin's trendy South Bank, the new Quality Hotel is perfectly placed in the heart of Dublin's vibrant city centre, overlooking the River Liffey & within a short walk of main city centre shopping, Temple Bar, sightseeing & business districts. The Quality Hotel Dublin features 217 superior 3-star standard bedrooms, Lannigans Restaurant & Club Vitae Leisure Centre, all the facilities you would expect from one of Ireland's leading hotel groups.

Member of Choice Hotels International

Room from €89.00 to €189.00

ADRIAN SHERRY
SALES AND MARKETING DIRECTOR

217 217

Open All Year

RAGLAN LODGE

10 RAGLAN ROAD,
BALLSBRIDGE,
DUBLIN 4
TEL: 01-660 6697 FAX: 01-660 6781

GUESTHOUSE ★★★★ MAP 8 O 11

Raglan Lodge is a magnificent Victorian residence dating from 1861. It is just ten minutes from the heart of Dublin in a most peaceful location. There are 7 guest rooms, all of which have bathrooms en suite, colour TV, radio/alarm, telephone & tea/coffee facilities. Several of the rooms are noteworthy for their fine proportions and high ceilings. National winner of the Galtee Irish Breakfast Award. Also, received Breakfast Award in Georgina Campbell's Jameson Guide 2001. Secure car parking facilities. Recommended by RAC, AA & Egon Ronay.

B&B from €50.80 to €69.85

HELEN MORAN
PROPRIETRESS

7 7

Closed 18 December - 07 January

B&B Rates are per Person Sharing per Night incl. Breakfast
Room Rates are per Room per Night

RED COW MORAN HOTEL

**RED COW COMPLEX,
NAAS ROAD,
DUBLIN 22**
TEL: 01-459 3650 FAX: 01-459 1588
EMAIL: redcowres@moranhotels.com
WEB: www.moranhotels.com

HOTEL ★★★★ MAP 8 O 11

4**** Red Cow Moran Hotel combines classic elegance with modern design, situated at the Gateway to the Provinces, convenient to city centre, minutes drive from Dublin Airport. Easy access into the City Centre via the LUAS Light Rail Service! Bedrooms are fully air-conditioned with colour teletext TV, direct dial phones/fax, hairdryer, trouser press & tea/coffee facilities. The complex boasts a choice of lively bars and features two superb restaurants and a carvery restaurant, conference facilities. Night Club. Free carparking. AA 4****. A Moran Hotel.

Member of Moran Hotels

B&B from €60.00 to €130.00

TOM & SHEILA MORAN
PROPRIETORS

123 123

Closed 24 - 26 December

REGENCY AIRPORT HOTEL

**SWORDS ROAD,
WHITEHALL,
DUBLIN 9**
TEL: 01-837 3544 FAX: 01-836 7121
EMAIL: regency@regencyhotels.com
WEB: www.regencyhotels.com

HOTEL ★★★ MAP 8 O 11

The Regency Hotel is located 3km north of Dublin City centre on main route to Dublin's International Airport and Northern Ireland. All rooms have recently been refurbished to a high standard and have colour TV, DD phone and tea/coffee making facilities. The hotel incorporates 70 executive rooms with hairdryers and trouser press as standard. The hotel features the Shanard Restaurant, the Appian Lounge. Seasons Theme Restaurant is renowned for its steaks, chicken and pasta dishes with seating for 200. The hotel has ample parking.

B&B from €75.00 to €140.00

BRIAN MCGETTIGAN
GENERAL MANAGER

 Weekend specials from €109.00 pps

206 206

Open All Year

RIVER HOUSE HOTEL

**23/24 EUSTACE STREET,
TEMPLE BAR,
DUBLIN 2**
TEL: 01-670 7655 FAX: 01-670 7650
EMAIL: reservations@riverhousehotel.com
WEB: www.riverhousehotel.com

HOTEL ★★ MAP 8 O 11

A city centre hotel located in Dublin's colourful and exciting Temple Bar area. With its cobbled streets, shops, art galleries, bars, restaurants and lively night life, Temple Bar has become a tourist attraction itself. All of our 29 bedrooms are en suite and have tea/coffee making facilities, remote control TV, radio, hairdryer and direct dial telephone. Hotel facilities include 'The Mezz' Bar and sound proofed 'The Hub' Nightclub, the best live music venues in Dublin. Family run, friendly staff.

B&B from €49.00 to €72.50

SHEELAGH CONWAY
PROPRIETOR

Midweek specials from €125.00 pps

29 29

Closed 24 - 27 December

B&B Rates are per Person Sharing per Night incl. Breakfast
Room Rates are per Room per Night

ROXFORD LODGE HOTEL

46 NORTHUMBERLAND ROAD,
BALLSBRIDGE,
DUBLIN 4

TEL: 01-668 8572 FAX: 01-668 8158
EMAIL: reservations@roxfordlodge.ie
WEB: www.roxfordlodge.ie

HOTEL U   MAP 8 O 11

Luxury family-run boutique style hotel located in the heart of Ballsbridge, Dublin's most exclusive area. Just 10 minutes walk from the city centre and all the major attractions such as Trinity College and Grafton Street. All of our en suite bedrooms have the added luxury of saunas, and most also have jacuzzi baths. Our executive suite offers the ultimate in luxury. Secure car parking. Public transport at front door.

B&B from €40.00 to €125.00

DESMOND KILLORAN
PROPRIETOR

20 20

IRISH
HOTELS
FEDERATION

Closed 24 - 26 December

ROYAL DUBLIN HOTEL

O'CONNELL STREET,
DUBLIN 1

TEL: 01-873 3666 FAX: 01-873 3120
EMAIL: enq@royaldublin.com
WEB: www.royaldublin.com

HOTEL ★★★   MAP 8 O 11

Located in the heart of the city on Dublin's most famous street, O'Connell Street. Perfect base from which to explore shops, theatres, museums and galleries. Guest rooms include hairdryer, tea/coffee making facilities, direct dial telephone and all are en suite. Relax in the elegant Georgian Room or enjoy the lively Raffles Bar. Excellent food available all day in the Café Royale Brasserie. Secure car park available.

Room Rate from €140.00 to €270.00

DARRAGH BRADY
GENERAL MANAGER

117 117

Inet

IRISH
HOTELS
FEDERATION

Open All Year

SCHOOL HOUSE HOTEL

2-8 NORTHUMBERLAND ROAD,
BALLSBRIDGE,
DUBLIN 4

TEL: 01-667 5014 FAX: 01-667 5015
EMAIL: reservations@schoolhousehotel.com
WEB: www.schoolhousehotel.com

HOTEL ★★★★   MAP 8 O 11

Without doubt, one of the most unique and beautiful properties in the city. Do not miss an opportunity to stay at this charming 4**** hotel conversion. All 31 de luxe bedrooms are individually named and furnished to the highest international standard. The original classrooms now host the award-winning Canteen @ The Schoolhouse and the lively and popular Schoolhouse Bar. Just a short stroll to Grafton Street, Lansdowne Road, The RDS and all of Dublin's major visitor attractions.

Member of Sweeney Hotels

B&B from €99.50 to €150.00

MAUREEN CAFFERKEY
GENERAL MANAGER

31 31

Inet WiFi

IRISH
HOTELS
FEDERATION

Closed 24 - 26 December

B&B Rates are per Person Sharing per Night incl. Breakfast
Room Rates are per Room per Night

SHELBOURNE HOTEL (THE)

27 ST. STEPHEN'S GREEN,
DUBLIN 2

TEL: 01-663 4500 FAX: 01-661 6006
EMAIL: michelle.quinn@renaissancehotels.com
WEB: www.shelbourne.ie

HOTEL U MAP 8 O 11

The Shelbourne Hotel, an institution in Irish hospitality, with a distinguished address, offering the ultimate in luxury & service. Located within walking distance of Dublin's main shopping thoroughfare & cultural life. 190 rooms, 2 bars & 2 restaurants and the renowned Lord Mayor's Lounge serving afternoon tea since 1824. Shelbourne Club - 18m pool, sauna, jacuzzi, 50 pieces of gym equipment - strictly over 18s. Under restoration. Managed by Marriott International.

Room Rate from €210.00 to €250.00

PHILIP SPENCER
GENERAL MANAGER

190 190

alc Inet

IRISH HOTELS FEDERATION

Open All Year

SHELDON PARK HOTEL & LEISURE CENTRE

KYLEMORE ROAD,
DUBLIN 12

TEL: 01-460 1055 FAX: 01-460 1880
EMAIL: info@sheldonpark.ie
WEB: www.sheldonpark.ie

HOTEL N MAP 8 O 11

The Sheldon Park is ideally situated just off the N7 and M50. City centre is just 10 minutes by bus or LUAS. Liffey Valley Shopping Centre only minutes away. All rooms have tea & coffee making facilities. Relax in our superb leisure centre with fully equipped gym, sauna, steamroom, 20m pool, jacuzzi and beauty salon. Extensive bar food menu in Minnie McCabes Bar all day. Award winning Houstons Restaurant open for dinner nightly. Live entertainment Friday - Sunday. Extensive conference and banqueting facilities.

B&B from €67.00 to €75.00

RON MARKS
DEPUTY GENERAL MANAGER

105 105

P S alc

IRISH HOTELS FEDERATION

Closed 24 - 26 December

ST. AIDEN'S GUESTHOUSE

32 BRIGHTON ROAD,
RATHGAR,
DUBLIN 6

TEL: 01-490 2011 FAX: 01-492 0234
EMAIL: staidens@eircom.net
WEB: www.staidens.com

GUESTHOUSE ★★★ MAP 8 O 11

Charming guesthouse located in the up-market village suburb of Rathgar. Numerous bus routes to city centre. 10 minutes from M50. Orbital link to Airport and country. Several restaurants within 10 minutes walk. Discounted local health club access (swimming/gym), car hire and restaurant bookings by arrangement at reception. Family friendly.

B&B from €40.00 to €55.00

MARIE MC DONAGH
PROPRIETRESS

☺ Midweek special from €120.00 pps

8 8

IRISH HOTELS FEDERATION

Closed 22 December - 02 January

B&B Rates are per Person Sharing per Night incl. Breakfast
Room Rates are per Room per Night

STAUNTONS ON THE GREEN

**83 ST. STEPHEN'S GREEN,
DUBLIN 2**

TEL: 01-478 2300 FAX: 01-478 2263
EMAIL: info@stauntonsonthegreen.ie
WEB: www.stauntonsonthegreen.ie

GUESTHOUSE ★★★ MAP 8 O 11

Large Georgian house overlooking St. Stephen's Green, own private gardens. All rooms are en suite and fully equipped with direct dial telephone, TV and tea/coffee welcoming trays, trouser press and hairdryer. It is close to museums, galleries, Grafton Street shopping area and many other major tourist attractions. Stauntons On the Green occupies one of Dublin's most prestigious locations, close to many corporate headquarters and government buildings.

B&B from €70.00 to €83.00

JOANNE GROVES

30 30

Closed 24 - 27 December

STEPHEN'S GREEN HOTEL

**ST. STEPHEN'S GREEN,
DUBLIN 2**

TEL: 01-607 3600 FAX: 01-661 5663
EMAIL: stephensgreenres@ocallaghanhotels.ie
WEB: www.ocallaghanhotels.com

HOTEL ★★★★ MAP 8 O 11

Stephen's Green is a warm modern boutique style hotel, located within minutes walk of Grafton Street and the main shopping and business districts. The hotel beautifully marries two refurbished Georgian houses and contemporary style with a four story glass atrium overlooking St.Stephen's Green. 75 luxurious air conditioned bedrooms, gymnasium, business centre, fashionable Magic Glasses Bar and Pie Dish Bistro. Wireless broadband throughout and excellent meeting facilities. USA toll free reservations 1800 569 9983 or www.ocallaghanhotels.com

Member of O'Callaghan Hotels

B&B from €84.00 to €185.00

DARA MCENEANEY
GENERAL MANAGER

75 75

Inet WiFi

Closed 24 - 30 December

TARA TOWERS HOTEL

**MERRION ROAD,
DUBLIN 4**

TEL: 01-269 4666 FAX: 01-269 1027
EMAIL: info@taratowers.com
WEB: www.taratowers.com

HOTEL ★★★ MAP 8 O 11

A first-class hotel overlooking Dublin Bay, just 3km from the city centre. The hotel is very personal, friendly and full of local charm. All guest rooms are well appointed with modern amenities, furnishings and décor and some rooms offer spectacular sea views. The hotel includes the Conservatory Restaurant for fine dining, a traditional Irish pub popular with our guests and locals, extensive conference/banqueting and private parking for all guests.

Member of Mercer Accommodation Group

Room Rate from €99.00 to €190.00

MARY CUNNINGHAM

☺ Weekend specials from €165.00 pps

111 111

Closed 23 - 27 December

B&B Rates are per Person Sharing per Night incl. Breakfast
Room Rates are per Room per Night

TAVISTOCK HOUSE

64 RANELAGH ROAD,
RANELAGH,
DUBLIN 6
TEL: 01-498 8000 FAX: 01-498 8000
EMAIL: info@tavistockhouse.com
WEB: www.tavistockhouse.com

GUESTHOUSE ★★★ MAP 8 O 11

Magnificent Victorian house, tastefully converted retaining all its original plasterwork - very homely. Situated on the city side of Ranelagh Village, on the corner of Ranelagh / Northbrook Roads. We are only 7 minutes walk from Stephen's Green in the heart of Dublin, near Helen Dillon's world famous garden. All rooms have colour TV, direct dial phone, hair dryer and tea/coffee making facilities. Private parking. There is a wide variety of restaurants locally. Internet facilities.

B&B from €55.00 to €85.00

MAUREEN & BRIAN CUSACK
CO-OWNERS

☺ 4 nights price of 3 excl. Hol W/e,
Rugby & special events

6 6

IRISH HOTELS FEDERATION

Open All Year

TEMPLE BAR HOTEL

FLEET STREET,
TEMPLE BAR,
DUBLIN 2
TEL: 01-677 3333 FAX: 01-677 3088
EMAIL: reservations@tbh.ie
WEB: www.templebarhotel.com

HOTEL ★★★ MAP 8 O 11

A Tower Group Hotel - situated in the heart of Dublin's Temple Bar, in close proximity to theatres, shops and restaurants, the Temple Bar Hotel features 129 en suite bedrooms fully equipped with modern facilities. Restaurant. Conference and meeting room facilities for up to 70 people. The Temple Bar Hotel is within easy access of train stations, airport and Dublin port. There is a multi storey car park nearby. Special online offers available on www.towerhotelgroup.com

Member of Tower Hotel Group

B&B from €75.00 to €110.00

JOHN CAFFREY
GENERAL MANAGER

129 129

WiFi

IRISH HOTELS FEDERATION

Closed 24 - 26 December

B&B Rates are per Person Sharing per Night incl. Breakfast
Room Rates are per Room per Night

TRAVELODGE CASTLEKNOCK

AUBURN AVENUE ROUNDABOUT,
NAVAN ROAD, CASTLEKNOCK,
DUBLIN 15
TEL: 01-820 2626 FAX: 01-820 2151

WEB: www.travelodge.ie

HOTEL U   MAP 8 O 11

On the N3 route only 5 miles from
Dublin City Centre, just off the M50
ring road & mins from the airport, this
superb hotel offers comfortable yet
affordable accommodation. 100
rooms en suite with the majority
sleeping 2 adults & 2 children. 5
rooms are designed for wheelchair
access & can sleep up to 2 adults.
Price is fixed per room regardless of
the number of occupants. Each room
has en suite bathroom, colour
satellite TV & DD phone. Situated next
to Little Chef restaurant. Freephone
from UK 0800 850 950. From
Ireland Freephone: 1800 709 709.

Room Rate from €49.00 to €99.00

BRID LUCKIE

🛏️📶☎️🖥️TC🚬CM❄️P🐕🚫alc🛒
100 100
🐕

IRISH
HOTELS
FEDERATION

Open All Year

TRINITY CAPITAL HOTEL

PEARSE STREET,
DUBLIN 2
TEL: 01-648 1000 FAX: 01-648 1010
EMAIL: info@trinitycapital-hotel.com
WEB: www.capital-hotels.com

HOTEL ★★★   MAP 8 O 11

A first visit to the Trinity Capital will
immediately confirm that this hotel
offers something rather special
indeed. At the very heart of Dublin's
city centre, the striking & unique
interior design will delight you in an
eye-catching way & instantly you will
feel relaxed, welcomed & thus
pleased by your hotel choice. Opened
in May 2000, this hotel features all
mod cons as required by today's
business & leisure guest.
Accommodation is modern, spacious
& of a high standard. Complimentary
admission to a variety of clubs
belonging to Capital Bars Group.

Member of Capital Hotels

B&B from €60.00 to €119.00

JOSEPHINE PEPPER

 Weekend specials from €180.00 pps

🛏️📶☎️🖥️TC🚬CM♪P🅂🔲alc
82 82
🖥️ Inet WiFi

IRISH
HOTELS
FEDERATION

Closed 24 - 26 December

UPPERCROSS HOUSE

26-30 UPPER RATHMINES ROAD,
DUBLIN 6
TEL: 01-497 5486 FAX: 01-497 5361
EMAIL: reservations@uppercrosshousehotel.com
WEB: www.uppercrosshousehotel.com

HOTEL ★★★   MAP 8 O 11

Uppercross House is a hotel providing
49 bedrooms of the highest standard
of comfort. All with direct dial phone,
TV, tea/coffee maker, central heating
and all en suite. Uppercross House
has its own secure parking and is
ideally situated in Dublin's south side
2km from St. Stephen's Green and
R.D.S., with excellent public transport
from directly outside the door. A fully
licensed restaurant and bar opens
nightly with a warm and friendly
atmosphere.

B&B from €50.00 to €79.50

DAVID MAHON
PROPRIETOR

🛏️📶☎️🖥️TC🚬CM❄️♪P🔲alc
49 49
🖥️ Inet

IRISH
HOTELS
FEDERATION

Closed 23 - 30 December

B&B Rates are per Person Sharing per Night incl. Breakfast
Room Rates are per Room per Night

MARINE HOTEL

SUTTON CROSS,
DUBLIN 13

TEL: 01-839 0000 FAX: 01-839 0442
EMAIL: info@marinehotel.ie
WEB: www.marinehotel.ie

HOTEL ★★★ MAP 12 P 11

The Marine Hotel overlooks the north shore of Dublin Bay with its lawn sweeping down to the sea shore. All bedrooms are en suite and have trouser press, TV, direct dial phone and tea/coffee facilities. The city centre is 6km away and the airport 25 minutes drive. Close by is the DART rapid rail system. The hotel has a heated indoor swimming pool and sauna. Nearby are the Royal Dublin and Portmarnock championship golf courses.

B&B from €90.00 to €117.50

SHEILA BAIRD
GENERAL MANAGER

48 48

Closed 25 - 27 December

AIRPORT MANOR

NAUL ROAD,
KNOCKSEDAN, SWORDS,
CO. DUBLIN

TEL: 01-840 1818 FAX: 01-870 0010
EMAIL: info@airportmanor.com
WEB: www.airportmanor.com

GUESTHOUSE ★★★★ MAP 12 O 12

Airport Manor offers the highest standards of services/facilities that can be expected in any 4 star property. Guestrooms are uniquely designed ensuring our guests luxury and comfort. Excellent conference facilities. The perfect location to enjoy the peace and tranquillity of the countryside yet only 5 minutes from Dublin Airport, 20 minutes from city centre and accessible from all major routes. Going on holidays? Private parking for up to 2 weeks included in rates.

B&B from €50.00 to €85.00

MICHELLE LYNCH

17 17

Closed 24 December - 02 January

B&B Rates are per Person Sharing per Night incl. Breakfast
Room Rates are per Room per Night

CARNEGIE COURT HOTEL

NORTH STREET,
SWORDS,
CO. DUBLIN
TEL: 01-840 4384 FAX: 01-840 4505
EMAIL: info@carnegiecourt.com
WEB: www.carnegiecourt.com

HOTEL ★★★ MAP 12 O 12

The Carnegie Court Hotel is a luxury accommodation hotel ideally situated in the town of Swords, 5 mins from Dublin airport and 20 mins from the city centre. The newly built hotel comprising 36 beautifully decorated & spacious bedrooms and a warm welcoming atmosphere is the perfect place of rest be it business or pleasure. Enjoy our award-winning Courtyard Restaurant or indulge in a night out in one of our five bars. Other facilities include conference & banqueting services and an extensive secure car-park.

B&B from €65.00 to €85.00

ALLEN HARRINGTON
GENERAL MANAGER

36 36

Closed 24 - 28 December

GLENMORE HOUSE

AIRPORT ROAD,
NEVINSTOWN, SWORDS,
CO. DUBLIN
TEL: 01-840 3610 FAX: 01-840 4148
EMAIL: rebeccagibney@eircom.net
WEB: www.glenmorehouse.com

GUESTHOUSE ★★★ MAP 12 O 12

Ideally situated just 1km from Dublin Airport and 20 minutes from the city centre, on the main airport/city bus routes, Glenmore House is a spacious family-run guesthouse set in 2 acres of gardens, lawns and private secure carparks. All rooms are beautifully decorated with bathroom, phone, TV, tea/coffee facilities and hairdryer. The warmest of welcomes at a very reasonable cost for business and leisure alike.

B&B from €42.50 to €65.00

REBECCA GIBNEY
PROPRIETOR

30 30

☺ Midweek specials from €120.00 pps

Closed 24 - 25 December

ROGANSTOWN GOLF & COUNTRY CLUB

ROGANSTOWN,
SWORDS,
CO. DUBLIN
TEL: 01-843 3118 FAX: 01-843 3303
EMAIL: info@roganstown.com
WEB: www.roganstown.com

HOTEL N MAP 12 O 12

Converted from the original Roganstown House, the spectacular Roganstown Golf & Country Club is a destination of relaxation, fine food and exceptional golf set among circa 300 acres. To compliment the magnificent 52 bedroom hotel, facilities also include leisure club, state of the art business and conference centre, and one of Ireland's most outstanding new golf courses. Located just 5 minutes from Dublin Airport and 25 minutes from city centre.

B&B from €85.00 to €150.00

CIARAN FOGARTY
GENERAL MANAGER

☺ Midweek specials from €180.00 pps

52 52

Open All Year

B&B Rates are per Person Sharing per Night incl. Breakfast
Room Rates are per Room per Night

BEAUFORT HOUSE

GHAN ROAD,
CARLINGFORD,
CO. LOUTH

TEL: 042-937 3879 FAX: 042-937 3878
EMAIL: michaelcaine@beauforthouse.net
WEB: www.beauforthouse.net

GUESTHOUSE ★★★ MAP 12 O 15

Beaufort House, AA ◆◆◆◆◆, listed in Bridgestone, Michelin BIB Hotel Award, Georgina Campbell, a magnificent shoreside residence with glorious sea and mountain views in mediaeval Carlingford Village. Your hosts, Michael & Glynnis Caine, Failte Ireland award winners of excellence, will ensure the highest standards. In-house activities include sailing school and yacht charter. Golfing arranged in any of five golf courses within 20 mins of Beaufort House. Private car parking. Dinner by prior arrangement. Small business conference facilities available.

Member of Premier Guesthouses

B&B from €39.00 to €43.00

MICHAEL & GLYNNIS CAINE

5   5

IRISH
HOTELS
FEDERATION

Open All Year

FOUR SEASONS HOTEL & LEISURE CLUB CARLINGFORD

CARLINGFORD,
CO. LOUTH

TEL: 042-937 3530 FAX: 042-937 3531
EMAIL: info@4seasonshotel.ie
WEB: www.4seasonshotel.ie

UNDER CONTRUCTION - OPENING APRIL 2005

HOTEL P MAP 12 O 15

Opening Spring 2005, our 59 bedroomed hotel is located in the mediaeval village of Carlingford, overlooking The Lough, with The Cooley Mountains as a backdrop, an ideal location for a short relaxing or activity based break. We have the most picturesque setting for your Conference or Banquet. Our 1st floor suite has dedicated facilities. The guest rooms have all modern facilities, & residents have unlimited use of the Leisure Club - swimming pool, sauna, jacuzzi, steamroom and gym. We look forward to welcoming you.

B&B from €75.00 to €95.00

FRANK MCKENNA

59   59

P alc Inet WiFi

Closed 25 - 26 December

Louth
Land of Legends

Welcome
TO LOUTH

Less than an hour away...

Whether you are looking for a quiet break or an action-packed holiday, the county abounds with interesting places to see and a myriad of things to do. Walk in the hills of Cooley, windsurf in Carlingford Lough, golf at your leisure, shop to your heart's content, dine like a King and be astounded at the history of Ireland's wee county.

For details on
Accommodation
& Visitor Attractions call:

042 933 5484

NDP

B&B Rates are per Person Sharing per Night incl. Breakfast
Room Rates are per Room per Night

MCKEVITT'S VILLAGE HOTEL

MARKET SQUARE,
CARLINGFORD,
CO. LOUTH

TEL: 042-937 3116 FAX: 042-937 3144
EMAIL: villagehotel@eircom.net
WEB: www.mckevittshotel.com

HOTEL ★★ MAP 12 O 15

McKevitt's Village Hotel is family owned and personally supervised by Kay & Terry McKevitt. At the hotel, pride of place is taken in the personal attention given to guests by owners and staff. Carlingford is one of Ireland's oldest and most interesting mediaeval villages. Beautifully situated on the shores of Carlingford Lough and half way between Dublin and Belfast.

B&B from €55.00 to €80.00

TERRY & KAY MCKEVITT
OWNERS

17 17

alc

IRISH
HOTELS
FEDERATION

Open All Year

BELLINGHAM CASTLE HOTEL

CASTLEBELLINGHAM,
CO. LOUTH

TEL: 042-937 2176 FAX: 042-937 2766
EMAIL: bellinghamcastle@eircom.net
WEB: www.bellinghamcastle.com

HOTEL ★★ MAP 12 O 14

Bellingham Castle Hotel is situated close to the pleasant little village of Castlebellingham, Co. Louth, resting in countryside enveloped in history, legend and engaged in beautiful scenery. In the hotel itself, which is an elegant refurbished 17th century castle, you will find all the facilities of a modern hotel, harmonising beautifully with the antique décor and atmosphere of old world splendour.

B&B from €65.00 to €75.00

PASCHAL KEENAN
MANAGER

19 19

alc

Closed 24 - 26 December

BOYNE VALLEY HOTEL & COUNTRY CLUB

DROGHEDA,
CO. LOUTH

TEL: 041-983 7737 FAX: 041-983 9188
EMAIL: reservations@boynevalleyhotel.ie
WEB: www.boynevalleyhotel.ie

HOTEL ★★★ MAP 12 O 13

Gracious country house on 16 acres beside Drogheda: from Dublin, 35km North on M1, turn off to N1 Julianstown & Drogheda South. Only 25km from Dublin Airport. From Belfast-south on M1, turn off at Drogheda North at N1. Nearby are sites on Newgrange, Dowth, Knowth and medieval abbeys of Melifont, Monasterboice and Slane. Full leisure Complex, 2 tennis courts, Cellar Bistro. Large and small conference rooms available.

Member of Best Western

B&B from €78.00 to €78.00

MICHAEL MCNAMARA
PROPRIETOR/MANAGER

72 72

inet

IRISH
HOTELS
FEDERATION

Open All Year

B&B Rates are per Person Sharing per Night incl. Breakfast
Room Rates are per Room per Night

MARRIOTT JOHNSTOWN HOUSE ENFIELD

ENFIELD,
CO. MEATH

TEL: 046-954 0000 FAX: 046-954 0001
EMAIL: info@johnstownhouse.com
WEB: www.johnstownhouse.com

HOTEL N MAP 11 M 11

Located on the main Dublin to Galway road, just 40 minutes from Dublin Airport and 45 minutes from Dublin City Centre. Luxurious bedrooms, with modern features. Enjoy a choice of eating experiences - Pavilion Restaurant, Atrium Brasserie and Coach House Bar. Well equipped meeting rooms catering for 2-900 people. The Spa opening in spring 2005. Facilities will include indoor heated swimming pool, steam rooms, saunas, 10 spa therapy rooms and hot thermal suite area.

B&B from €52.50 to €145.00

BRIAN THORNTON
GENERAL MANAGER

2 nights B&B & 1 Dinner from €130.00 pps

126 126

Closed 24 - 26 December

HEADFORT ARMS HOTEL

KELLS,
CO. MEATH

TEL: 046-924 0063 FAX: 046-924 0587
EMAIL: headfortarms@eircom.net
WEB: www.headfortarms.com

HOTEL U MAP 11 M 13

In the Duff family for 35 years the Headfort Arms represents old and new world. Located in the heritage town of Kells only 40 km from Dublin City on the main Derry/Donegal route. Café Therese offers an array of casual food from 7.30am - 10pm, the contemporary award-winning Vanilla Pod Restaurant serving from 5.30 - late, Early Bird Menu and Sunday lunch. Conference and banqueting facilities up to 400. The wedding destination of the North East. Golfing, fishing packages available. Headfort Golf Club nearby. 32 new de luxe bedrooms opening Spring 2005.

B&B from €60.00 to €90.00

VINCENT DUFF
GENERAL MANAGER

12 12

Closed 25 December

STATION HOUSE HOTEL

KILMESSAN,
CO. MEATH

TEL: 046-902 5239 FAX: 046-902 5588
EMAIL: info@thestationhousehotel.com
WEB: www.thestationhousehotel.com

HOTEL U MAP 12 N 12

Step off the fast track into a relaxed rural setting where peace and tranquillity exude. Set on 5 acres of gardens. This first class hotel offers many amenities we appreciate today along with much of yesterday's charm. The Signal Suite is unique with four poster bed and whirlpool bath. The award-winning Signal Restaurant is open 7 days a week for lunch and dinner. A short drive from Dublin, Trim or Navan. It is a haven at the end of a journey.

B&B from €65.00 to €95.00

CHRIS & THELMA SLATTERY
PROPRIETORS

20 20

Open All Year

B&B Rates are per Person Sharing per Night incl. Breakfast
Room Rates are per Room per Night

CROFTON BRAY HEAD INN

STRAND ROAD,
BRAY,
CO. WICKLOW
TEL: 01-286 7182 FAX: 01-286 7182

GUESTHOUSE ★★ MAP 8 P 10

This 140 year old building is situated on the seafront, under the Bray Head Mountain. A 10 minute walk away from an excellent commuter train to Dublin, but also ideally located for touring Wicklow - The Garden of Ireland. The Bray Head Inn has ample car-parking and is fully licensed. It has a lift, en suite bedrooms with TV and telephone. Our prices include full Irish breakfast.

B&B from €50.00 to €60.00

ENA REGAN CUMMINS

30   30

Closed 02 October - 02 June

ESPLANADE HOTEL

STRAND ROAD,
BRAY,
CO. WICKLOW
TEL: 01-286 2056 FAX: 01-286 6496
EMAIL: info@esplanadehotel.ie
WEB: www.esplanadehotel.ie

HOTEL ★★★ MAP 8 P 10

Stylish hotel with magnificent views, 12 miles from Dublin. Located on the seafront in Bray, the hotel retains many of its splendid Victorian features whilst offering modern day luxury and comfort. Comfortable lounges, excellent menu choices and exceptional value for money. Fully equipped and staffed fitness centre. Close to Bray DART station. A member of the Strandwood Hotel Group.

Member of Strandwood Hotel Group

B&B from €50.00 to €140.00

DANIEL CORBETT
OPERATIONS MANAGER

40   40

Open All Year

HEATHER HOUSE HOTEL

STRAND ROAD,
BRAY,
CO. WICKLOW
TEL: 01-286 8000 FAX: 01-286 4254
EMAIL: info@heatherhousehotel.com
WEB: www.heatherhousehotel.com

HOTEL N MAP 8 P 10

A Family-run hotel with spectacular seaviews. Catering for the business or leisure guest, with well appointed en suite accommodation, as well as self catering apartments. The Martello Bar offers a superb carvery and bar food menu or dine in the Tower Bistro from our select menu and fine wines. Conference and banqueting facilities. Ideally located for touring Dublin City and County Wicklow. Located 5 minutes from all public transport and N11 Motorway.

B&B from €50.00 to €60.00

JOHN DUGGAN
GENERAL MANAGER

25   25
Inet

Closed 24 - 26 December

B&B Rates are per Person Sharing per Night incl. Breakfast
Room Rates are per Room per Night

PORTERHOUSE INN (THE)

STRAND ROAD,,
BRAY,
CO. WICKLOW
TEL: 01-286 0668 FAX: 01-286 1171
EMAIL: bray@porterhousebrewco.com

HOTEL U MAP 8 P 10

Located on Bray's seafront The Porterhouse Inn commands a panoramic view over the sea. Ideally situated for golfing (there are twelve courses within a short distance), hillwalking, fishing and sightseeing, it is the ideal spot for the outdoor enthusiast. The recently renovated hotel has sixteen luxurious rooms, some availiable with a stunning sea view. The busy bar and restaurant serve a full range of drinks including ten of our own signature beers.

B&B from €45.00 to €70.00

LYNDSEY BYRNE

16 16

Closed 24 - 25 December

RAMADA WOODLAND COURT HOTEL

SOUTHERN CROSS,
BRAY,
CO. WICKLOW
TEL: 01-276 0258 FAX: 01-276 0298
EMAIL: info@woodlandcourthotel.com
WEB: www.woodlandcourthotel.com

HOTEL ★★★ MAP 8 P 10

Located just minutes from the N11 motorway and 12 miles from Dublin City Centre the Ramada Woodland Court Hotel has much to offer the tourist and business traveller. 65 well-appointed en suite rooms, state of the art conference/business centre and excellent meals in our restaurant. An ideal venue for touring Dublin City and County Wicklow. Special group and business rates available on request. Self catering serviced apartments also available. A haven of relaxation. A member of the Strandwood Hotel Group.

Member of Ramada Hotels

B&B from €75.00 to €130.00

MARK FITZGIBBON
GENERAL MANAGER

65 65

Open All Year

ROYAL HOTEL AND LEISURE CENTRE

MAIN STREET,
BRAY,
CO. WICKLOW
TEL: 01-286 2935 FAX: 01-286 7373
EMAIL: royal@regencyhotels.com
WEB: www.dublin-hotel-wicklow.com

HOTEL ★★★ MAP 8 P 10

Located in the coastal resort of Bray, ideally positioned at the gateway to the garden county of Ireland & yet only 30 mins DART journey from Dublin. Leisure facilities include a pool, childrens' pool, sauna, steamroom, whirlpool spa, jacuzzi & gym. Other facilities include massage & beauty clinic, stand-up sunbed & creche. The hotel has a newly built ballroom for up to 400 persons for conferences, weddings and corporate banquets. The hotel features The Heritage Restaurant & à la carte menus & Quinn's Lounge with live musical entertainment most nights.

B&B from €65.00 to €130.00

MAUREEN MCGETTIGAN-O'CONNOR
GENERAL MANAGER

Weekend specials from €95.00 pps

98 98

Open All Year

B&B Rates are per Person Sharing per Night incl. Breakfast
Room Rates are per Room per Night

WESTBOURNE HOTEL

QUINSBORO ROAD,
BRAY,
CO. WICKLOW
TEL: 01-286 2362 FAX: 01-204 0074

WEB: www.westbournehotelbray.com

HOTEL ★★ MAP 8 P 10

The Westbourne Hotel is ideally located on the north east coast of the 'Garden of Ireland' in the charming town of Bray. Only minutes from exceptional scenery, beaches and has fast access to Dublin via the DART. Newly refurbished bedrooms en suite, direct dial phone, TV and tea/coffee making facilities. Clancy's Traditional Irish Bar, craic agus ceol. Food served all day. Dusty's contemporary style bar is recently refurbished and offers comfortable and stylish surroundings in a very relaxed atmosphere.

B&B from € 40.00 to € 55.00

DEBBIE TIERNAN
GENERAL MANAGER

13 13

Closed 25 - 26 December

RATHSALLAGH HOUSE, GOLF AND COUNTRY CLUB

DUNLAVIN,
(WEST WICKLOW),
CO. WICKLOW
TEL: 045-403112 FAX: 045-403343
EMAIL: info@rathsallagh.com
WEB: www.rathsallagh.com

GUESTHOUSE ★★★★ MAP 8 N 9

Winner of the Irish Country House Restaurant of the year Award 2002, & a member of Irelands Blue Book, & Small Luxury Hotels of the World, Rathsallagh is a large country house converted from Queen Anne stables in 1798. Rathsallagh, with its own 18 hole Championship Golf Course, described by the press as "Augusta without the Azalea", is set in a peaceful oasis of 530 acres of rolling parkland with thousands of mature trees, lakes & streams. On the West side of the Wicklow Mountains close to Punchestown & Curragh racecourses.

Member of Ireland's Blue Book

B&B from € 130.00 to € 150.00

THE O'FLYNN FAMILY
PROPRIETORS

29 29

alc Inet

Open All Year

POWERSCOURT ARMS HOTEL

ENNISKERRY,
CO. WICKLOW

TEL: 01-282 8903 FAX: 01-286 4909

WEB: www.powerscourtarmshotel.com

HOTEL ★ MAP 8 O 10

You will always find a warm welcome at the Powerscourt Arms Hotel situated in the beautiful picturesque Village of Enniskerry. It is an ideal base for touring expeditions, an intimate family-run hotel with 12 bedrooms furnished to include direct dial telephone, ensuite bathrooms and multi channel TV, ample car parking. The restaurant seats up to 45 people, our lounge with strong features of American white ash, serves bar food daily. The public bar has its own atmosphere complete with open fire.

B&B from € 50.00 to € 55.00

CHARLES MCTERNAN
GENERAL MANAGER

12 12

Closed 24 - 27 December

B&B Rates are per Person Sharing per Night incl. Breakfast
Room Rates are per Room per Night

SUMMERHILL HOUSE HOTEL

**ENNISKERRY,
CO. WICKLOW**

TEL: 01-286 7928 FAX: 01-286 7929
EMAIL: info@summerhillhousehotel.com
WEB: www.summerhillhousehotel.com

HOTEL ★★★ MAP 8 O 10

This charming hotel is just a short walk to the quaint village of Enniskerry, and the famous Powerscourt Gardens. Located on the N11, 19km south of Dublin City & 15km to Dunlaoire Ferryport. 57 spacious bedrooms, private free car parking, traditional Irish breakfast, hill walking & nature trails, local golf courses, family rooms (2 adults and 3 children). Enjoy a rare blend of the Wicklow countryside close to Dublin City. A member of the Strandwood Hotel Group.

Member of Strandwood Hotel Group

B&B from € 100.00 to € 140.00

ANDREW NOLAN
GENERAL MANAGER

57 57

Open All Year

GLENVIEW HOTEL

**GLEN-O-THE-DOWNS,
DELGANY,
CO. WICKLOW**

TEL: 01-287 3399 FAX: 01-287 7511
EMAIL: sales@glenviewhotel.com
WEB: www.glenviewhotel.com

HOTEL U MAP 8 O 10

Only 30 minutes from Dublin City Centre, the AA/RAC 4 star Glenview Hotel & Leisure Club is the unique environment for business and pleasure. Facilities include 70 deluxe bedrooms, leisure centre with indoor pool, award-winning Woodlands Restaurant, Conservatory Bar, conference facilities for up to 200 pax. Recent developments include beauty treatment and therapy room, snooker room, childrens' playroom and woodland walks. Golf nearby.

B&B from € 85.00 to € 115.00

LEE GREGSON
GENERAL MANAGER

Weekend specials from €185.00 pps

70 70

Open All Year

GLENDALOUGH HOTEL

**GLENDALOUGH,
CO. WICKLOW**

TEL: 0404-45135 FAX: 0404-45142
EMAIL: info@glendaloughhotel.ie
WEB: www.glendaloughhotel.ie

HOTEL ★★★ MAP 8 O 9

The Glendalough Hotel, built in the early 1800s, is a family run hotel situated in the heart of Wicklow's most scenic valley and within the Glendalough National Park. The hotel has recently been extended offering 40 beautifully decorated en suite bedrooms with satellite TV and direct dial phone. The hotel's restaurant offers superb cuisine and wines in a tranquil environment overlooking the Glendasan River. The Tavern Bar serves good pub food and offers entertainment at weekends.

B&B from € 68.00 to € 88.00

PATRICK CASEY

Weekend specials from €130.00

40 40

Closed 01 - 31 January

B&B Rates are per Person Sharing per Night incl. Breakfast
Room Rates are per Room per Night

LYNHAM'S HOTEL

**LARAGH,
GLENDALOUGH,
CO. WICKLOW**

TEL: 0404-45345 FAX: 0404-45514
EMAIL: info@lynhamsoflaragh.ie
WEB: www.lynhamsoflaragh.ie

HOTEL N   MAP 8 O 9

Family owned Lynham's Hotel Laragh
is situated in the heart of Wicklow
National Park, just a few minutes
from the beautiful historic
Glendalough. The warm welcoming
atmosphere of Jake's Bar lends a
traditional air to Lynham's. Famous
for its superb bar food, you can also
enjoy candlelight dining in our old
world restaurant. Lynham's also offer
special concessions to the world
famous Druids Glen and Druids Heath
Golf Courses.

B&B from €75.00 to €95.00

JOHN & ANNE LYNHAM
MANAGERS

Weekend specials from €155.00 pps

16 16

Inet

Closed 21 - 28 December

MARRIOTT DRUIDS GLEN HOTEL & COUNTRY CLUB

**NEWTOWNMOUNTKENNEDY,
CO. WICKLOW**

TEL: 01-287 0800 FAX: 01-287 0801
EMAIL: mhrs.dubgs.reservations@marriotthotels.com
WEB: www.marriott.ie/dubgs

HOTEL ★★★★   MAP 8 P 9

Situated within Druids Glen Golf
Resort, lies the luxurious Druids Glen
Marriott Hotel & Country Club - the
perfect venue to escape, relax and
enjoy, championship golf, holistic spa
treatments, excellent cuisine and
absolute comfort in the most beautiful
countryside setting. Two 18-hole golf
courses, Druid's Glen & Druids Heath,
on-site. Winner of Business Hotel of
the Year 2003, Georgina Campbell's
Jameson Guide.

B&B from €75.00 to €125.00

BJ SCHREUDER
GENERAL MANAGER

148 148

Open All Year

B&B Rates are per Person Sharing per Night incl. Breakfast
Room Rates are per Room per Night

HUNTER'S HOTEL

NEWRATH BRIDGE,
RATHNEW,
CO. WICKLOW
TEL: 0404-40106 FAX: 0404-40338
EMAIL: reception@hunters.ie
WEB: www.hunters.ie

HOTEL ★★★ MAP 8 P 9

One of Ireland's oldest coaching inns, its award winning gardens along River Vartry provide a haven from the world at large. Restaurant provides the very best of Irish food, fresh fish. Local amenities include golf, tennis, horseriding and fishing. Beautiful sandy beaches and sightseeing in the Garden of Ireland. Dublin 44.8km. Rosslare 115.2km. Off N11 at Rathnew or Ashford. Irish Country Houses and Restaurant Association. Refurbished 1995-1996. 1996 new conference room added.

Member of Ireland's Blue Book

B&B from € 90.00 to € 100.00

GELLETLIE FAMILY
PROPRIETORS

16 16

Closed 24 - 26 December

TINAKILLY COUNTRY HOUSE AND RESTAURANT

WICKLOW,
(RATHNEW),
CO. WICKLOW
TEL: 0404-69274 FAX: 0404-67806
EMAIL: reservations@tinakilly.ie
WEB: www.tinakilly.ie

HOTEL ★★★★ MAP 8 P 9

This Victorian mansion was built for Captain Halpin, who laid the world's telegraph cables. The bedrooms, some with 4 posters, are furnished in period style and most overlook the Irish Sea. Award winning cuisine is prepared from garden vegetables, local fish and Wicklow lamb. The family welcome ensures a relaxing, memorable stay. Available locally - golf, horse riding, Powerscourt, Mount Usher Gardens and Wicklow Mountains. Dublin 46km. Awarded RAC Blue Ribbon for Excellence. Blue Book member.

B&B from € 106.00 to € 131.00

JOSEPHINE & RAYMOND POWER
PROPRIETORS

51 51

Closed 24 - 26 December

GRAND HOTEL

WICKLOW TOWN,
CO. WICKLOW

TEL: 0404-67337 FAX: 0404-69607
EMAIL: grandhotel@eircom.net
WEB: www.grandhotel.ie

HOTEL ★★★ MAP 8 P 9

This charming hotel is the perfect base for touring the beautiful Garden of Ireland. Situated in Wicklow Town, it is only a 40 minute drive from Dublin on the N11. Enjoy golf, fishing, hill walking, sandy beaches and sightseeing locally. 33 large, bright, comfortable bedrooms all en suite with direct dial telephone, multi channel TV and tea/coffee making facilities. Fine food served in the restaurant and bar all day. Lively lounge bar. Conference facilities.

B&B from €45.00 to €62.50

ADRIAN FLYNN
HOTEL DIRECTOR

33 33

Closed 24 - 26 December

B&B Rates are per Person Sharing per Night incl. Breakfast
Room Rates are per Room per Night

NEW VALLEY INN

WOODENBRIDGE,
AVOCA,
CO. WICKLOW
TEL: 0402-35200 FAX: 0402-35542
EMAIL: info@newvalleyinn.com
WEB: www.newvalleyinn.com

HOTEL U MAP 8 O 8

Quaint country family-run hotel.
Ideally located for touring County
Wicklow. 1.5 miles from
Ballykissangel. 1 hour to Dublin and
Rosslare. Surrounded by woodlands
and forest and goldminer stream
running by hotel. Walking distance to
Woodenbridge Golf Club. Our
restaurant offers excellent food and
our bars are lively with good
atmosphere. Hill walking, fishing,
beaches are all within minutes of the
hotel.

B&B from €40.00 to €50.00

GAVIN MORAN
DIRECTOR

🖊️/

🛏️ 🛎️ ☎️ 🖥️ ⒶⒸ CM✹Ⓤ 🎵 🅿️ 🆂 ◧
14 14
ⓐⓘⓒ ☕

IRISH
HOTELS
FEDERATION

Open All Year

WOODENBRIDGE HOTEL

VALE OF AVOCA,
ARKLOW,
CO. WICKLOW
TEL: 0402-35146 FAX: 0402-35573
EMAIL: wbhotel@iol.ie
WEB: www.woodenbridgehotel.com

HOTEL ★★★ MAP 8 O 8

Family owned and run with 23
ensuite rooms, including rooms with
balconies overlooking Woodenbridge
golf course. Dating from 1608 the
hotel is the oldest in Ireland. Our
restaurant and bar service quality
Irish food: Bord Bia accredited.
Tourism menu award winner, bar
food served all day. Horse riding,
fishing, golfing, fine beaches and
walking available locally. Near Avoca
film location for Ballykissangel.

Member of MinOtel Ireland Hotel Dublin

B&B from €45.00 to €60.00

ESTHER O'BRIEN & BILL O'BRIEN
PROPRIETORS

🖊️/

😊 2 nights B&B + 2 rounds of golf
from €158.00 pps

🛏️ 🛎️ ☎️ 🖥️ Ⓣ ⒶⒸ ◧ CM✹Ⓤ 🎵 🅿️
23 23
🆂 🖥️ ⓐⓘⓒ

IRISH
HOTELS
FEDERATION

Closed 25 December

WOODENBRIDGE LODGE

VALE OF AVOCA,
ARKLOW,
CO WICKLOW
TEL: 0402-35146 FAX: 0402-35573
EMAIL: wbhotel@iol.ie
WEB: www.woodenbridgehotel.com

HOTEL N MAP 8 O 8

Sheltered by Wicklow's rolling hills
and nestling sleepily in the
picturesque Vale of Avoca you will
find Woodenbridge Lodge. Situated on
the banks of the Avoca River, this 40
bedroomed hotel, is the perfect setting
for golfing breaks, family reunions, or
relaxing peaceful weekends for two.

B&B from €45.00 to €60.00

ESTHER O'BRIEN & BILL O'BRIEN
PROPRIETORS

🖊️/

😊 2 nights B&B + 2 rounds of golf
from €158.00 pps

🛏️ 🛎️ ☎️ 🖥️ ⬚ Ⓣ Ⓒ ✦CM✹ 🎵 🅿️ 🆂
40 40
🔲 ⓐⓘⓒ 🖥️ Inet 🐾

IRISH
HOTELS
FEDERATION

Closed 25 December

B&B Rates are per Person Sharing per Night incl. Breakfast
Room Rates are per Room per Night

Map of Midlands & Lakelands Region

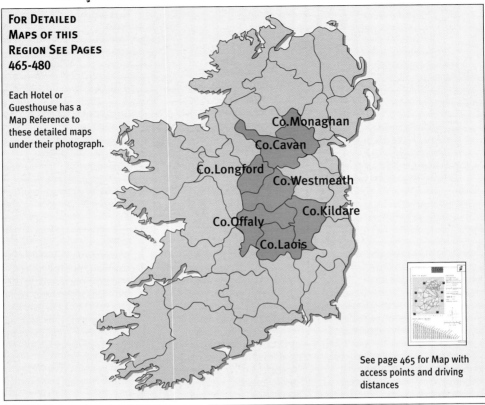

FOR DETAILED MAPS OF THIS REGION SEE PAGES 465-480

Each Hotel or Guesthouse has a Map Reference to these detailed maps under their photograph.

Co.Monaghan

Co.Cavan

Co.Longford

Co.Westmeath

Co.Kildare

Co.Offaly

Co.Laois

See page 465 for Map with access points and driving distances

Locations listing

CAVAN
Arvagh
Bailieborough
Ballinagh
Ballyconnell
Cavan Town
Kingscourt
Virginia

KILDARE
Athy
Ballymore Eustace
Castledermot
Celbridge
Curragh (The)
Kildare Town
Kill
Leixlip
Maynooth
Monasterevin
Naas
Newbridge
Straffan

LAOIS
Abbeyleix
Durrow
Portarlington
Portlaoise

LONGFORD
Clondra
Longford Town

MONAGHAN
Carrickmacross
Monaghan Town

OFFALY
Banagher
Birr
Tullamore

WESTMEATH
Athlone
Mullingar
Multyfarnham

irelandhotels.com *log on and book in* INCLUDES DETAILED MAPS & GREAT VALUE SPECIAL OFFERS.

LAKESIDE MANOR HOTEL

DUBLIN ROAD,
VIRGINIA,
CO. CAVAN

TEL: 049-854 8200 FAX: 049-854 8279
EMAIL: info@lakesidemanor.ie
WEB: www.lakesidemanor.ie

HOTEL N   MAP 11 L 13

This luxurious hotel located on the shores of Lough Ramor offers a tranquil retreat from your hectic schedule. With our restaurant and banqueting room overlooking the lake it provides an idyllic romantic setting for that special wedding day, catering for 20-250 people. The relaxed and friendly atmosphere leaves this hotel hard to leave and as is evident a return visit will be on the cards.

B&B from €50.00 to €60.00

MEABH & JIM BRADY
PROPRIETORS

30 30

Closed 24 - 26 December

B&B Rates are per Person Sharing per Night incl. Breakfast
Room Rates are per Room per Night

PARK HOTEL

VIRGINIA,
CO. CAVAN

TEL: 049-854 6100 FAX: 049-854 7203
EMAIL: virginiapark@eircom.net
WEB: www.parkhotelvirginia.com

HOTEL ★★★   MAP 11 L 13

Beautifully restored hotel set in its own 100 acre historic estate. Located on the shores of Lough Ramor and nestled among some of the country's most beautifully landscaped gardens. Guests can avail of our 9 hole golf course, 15 miles of walking trails and excellent fishing locally. Dine in the beautiful surroundings of our AA award-winning restaurant. Our conference facilities can cater for up to 100 delegates.

B&B from €55.00 to €65.00

MICHAEL KELLY
GENERAL MANAGER

☺ Weekend specials from €135.00 pps

29 29

IRISH
HOTELS
FEDERATION

Open All Year

RIVER FRONT HOTEL (THE)

MAIN STREET,
VIRGINIA,
CO. CAVAN

TEL: 049-854 7561 FAX: 049-854 7761
EMAIL: info@riverfront.ie
WEB: www.riverfront.ie

HOTEL ★★ MAP 11 L 13

Nestled in the heart of the picturesque village of Virginia, this boutique Hotel was tastefully transformed while upholding the traditions of seasonal fresh food and a warm welcome. Situated on the doorstep of some of Ireland's best angling and golfing, the individually appointed bedrooms enjoy all the facilities the modern traveller expects. Our recently refurbished banqueting suite boasts private landscaped gardens with exclusive frontage to the Rampart River. Private parking available.

B&B from €40.00 to €55.00

JIMMY & ANTOINETTE MURRAY
PROPRIETORS

Midweek specials from €120.00 pps

13 13

Closed 24 - 26 December

CLANARD COURT HOTEL

DUBLIN ROAD,
ATHY,
CO. KILDARE

TEL: 059-864 0666 FAX: 059-864 0888
EMAIL: info@clanardcourt.ie
WEB: www.clanardcourt.ie

UNDER CONSTRUCTION - OPENING APRIL 2005

HOTEL P MAP 7 M 9

Opening April 2005, Clanard Court is a family-run hotel. Built to 4**** international specifications. It is set in 8 acres of magnificent grounds, just 40 miles from Dublin and 1 mile from Athy town. Facilities include 38 luxurious guest rooms featuring state of the art facilities, The Court Yard Bistro, Baileys Bar, extensive conference and banqueting facilities catering for 2 to 400 delegates. 250 free car parking spaces. It is the ideal place from which to enjoy the charms of the midlands and surroundings.

B&B from €55.00 to €130.00

MARY FENNIN BYRNE
GENERAL MANAGER/DIRECTOR

Weekend specials from €130.00 pps

38 38

Open All Year

TONLEGEE HOUSE AND RESTAURANT

ATHY,
CO. KILDARE

TEL: 059-863 1473 FAX: 059-863 1473
EMAIL: marjorie@tonlegeehouse.com
WEB: www.tonlegeehouse.com

GUESTHOUSE ★★★★ MAP 7 M 9

Tonlegee House is situated on its own grounds, just outside Athy and only an hour from the bustle of Dublin. Our guests' relaxation is assured in the tranquil comfort of this lovingly restored Georgian Country House and Restaurant. With its antique furnishings and open fires it is an ideal place to stay for either an activity filled or leisurely break. Recommended by the Bridgestone Guide's Best 100 Places to Stay in Ireland.

Member of Premier Guesthouses of Ireland

B&B from €65.00 to €75.00

MARJORIE MOLLOY
PROPRIETOR

12 12

Closed 24 December - 10 January

B&B Rates are per Person Sharing per Night incl. Breakfast
Room Rates are per Room per Night

ARDENODE HOTEL

BALLYMORE EUSTACE,
CO. KILDARE

TEL: 045-864198 FAX: 045-864139
EMAIL: info@ardenodehotel.com
WEB: www.ardenodehotel.com

HOTEL U   MAP 8 N 10

The ultimate holiday setting, the Ardenode Hotel takes advantage of Kildare's most convenient and beautiful setting. Views of the Wicklow Mountains and manicured grounds are enjoyed from all public rooms and outdoor areas. At the Ardenode Hotel you can be assured of graceful and relaxing surroundings, professional service from a vibrant team. Dining is a truly magical experience in our award-winning Garden Restaurant.

B&B from €65.00 to €150.00

GEORGINA BROWNE
GENERAL MANAGER

17 17

Open All Year

KILKEA CASTLE

CASTLEDERMOT,
CO. KILDARE

TEL: 059-914 5156 FAX: 059-914 5187
EMAIL: kilkea@iol.ie
WEB: www.kilkeacastle.ie

HOTEL ★★★★   MAP 7 M 8

Kilkea Castle is the oldest inhabited Castle in Ireland. Built in 1180, offering the best in modern comfort while the charm and elegance of the past has been retained. The facilities include de luxe accommodation, a fine dining room, d'Lacy's Restaurant, restful bar/lounge area, full banqueting and conference facilities and full on-site leisure centre with an indoor heated swimming pool, sauna, jacuzzi, steamroom and fully equipped gym. 18 hole golf course encircles the Castle.

B&B from €110.00 to €175.00

SHANE CASSIDY
GENERAL MANAGER

36 36

Closed 23 - 27 December

SETANTA HOUSE HOTEL

CLANE ROAD,
CELBRIDGE,
CO. KILDARE

TEL: 01-630 3200 FAX: 01-627 3387
EMAIL: setantahousehotel@eircom.net
WEB: www.setantahousehotel.com

HOTEL U   MAP 8 N 11

Built in 1737, this former school situated in the historic Heritage Town of Celbridge combines elegance and tranquillity with modern facilities. Set in mature landscaped gardens with 65 newly refurbished spacious bedrooms including luxurious suites. Setanta House is ideal for business and leisure alike. Only 20 minutes from Dublin City and Airport with easy access off the N4 and M50. Renowned golf and racecourses nearby. A warm welcome is always assured.

B&B from €65.00 to €150.00

ARTHUR MCDANIEL
GENERAL MANAGER

Midweek specials from €195.00 pps

65 65

Closed 24 -26 December

B&B Rates are per Person Sharing per Night incl. Breakfast
Room Rates are per Room per Night

STANDHOUSE HOTEL LEISURE & CONFERENCE CENTRE

CURRAGH (THE),
CO. KILDARE

TEL: 045-436177 FAX: 045-436180
EMAIL: reservations@standhousehotel.com
WEB: www.standhousehotel.com

HOTEL U MAP 7 M 10

Standhouse Hotel has a tradition which dates back to 1700. Situated beside the Curragh Racecourse it has become synonymous with The Classics. The premises has been restored to its former elegance and offers the discerning guest a fine selection of quality restaurants, bars, leisure facilities, including 20 metre pool, state of the art gym, jacuzzi, steam room, sauna and plunge pool. Conference facilities cater for 20 to 500 delegates.

B&B from €95.00 to €140.00

PAT KENNY
GENERAL MANAGER

Weekend specials from €125.00 pps

63 63

Closed 25 - 26 December

CURRAGH LODGE HOTEL

DUBLIN STREET,
KILDARE TOWN,
CO KILDARE

TEL: 045-522144 FAX: 045-521247
EMAIL: clhotel@iol.ie

HOTEL U MAP 7 M 10

A friendly and warm welcome is assured at The Curragh Lodge Hotel, which is situated off the M7 from Dublin. Conveniently located in the town centre this popular hotel offers comfortable well equipped en suite rooms. Very close to the famous Curragh Race Course, Japanese Gardens, also local fishing available, Mondello Park, Greyhound Racing and great golf courses including The K Club, Kilkea, Knockanally, Craddockstown, to name but a few. Also local fishing available.

B&B from €50.00 to €50.00

BERNIE CULLEN
GENERAL MANAGER

20 20

Closed 24 - 27 December

AMBASSADOR HOTEL

KILL,
CO. KILDARE

TEL: 045-877064 FAX: 045-877515
EMAIL: reservations@ambassadorhotelkildare.com
WEB: www.ambassadorhotelkildares.com

HOTEL ★★★ MAP 8 N 10

Situated just 20km from Dublin City, this 36 bedroomed hotel is ideally located for those travelling from the south or west. Our restaurants boast excellent cuisine and our bar provides music 4 nights per week. Local amenities include 3 race courses, The Curragh, Naas and Punchestown, four golf courses, Goffs Horse Sales, (just across the road) and plenty of horseriding. The Ambassador has something for everybody.

B&B from €70.00 to €90.00

RITA GLEESON
GENERAL MANAGER

36 36

Open All Year

B&B Rates are per Person Sharing per Night incl. Breakfast
Room Rates are per Room per Night

K CLUB (THE)

AT STRAFFAN,
CO. KILDARE

TEL: 01-601 7200 FAX: 01-601 7298
EMAIL: resortsales@kclub.ie
WEB: www.kclub.ie

HOTEL ★★★★★ MAP 8 N 11

Ireland's only AA 5 Red Star Hotel, located 30 minutes from Dublin Airport. Leisure facilities include 2 18 hole championship golf courses designed by Arnold Palmer, home to the Smurfit European Open & venue for the Ryder Cup in 2006. Two bona fide championship courses side by side offering a distinctive and different experience for the golfer. In addition, both river & coarse fishing are available with full health & leisure club and sporting activities. Meeting & private dining facilities also available.

Room Rate from €295.00 to €445.00

RAY CARROLL
CHIEF EXECUTIVE

94 94

Open All Year

ABBEYLEIX MANOR HOTEL

ABBEYLEIX,
CO. LAOIS

TEL: 0502-30111 FAX: 0502-30220
EMAIL: info@abbeyleixmanorhotel.com
WEB: www.abbeyleixmanorhotel.com

HOTEL ★★★ MAP 7 L 8

Situated on the N8 halfway between Dublin and Cork. The Abbeyleix Manor boasts a prime location with 23 superbly appointed en suite bedrooms and conference centre which caters for up to 400 people. Malachi's Bar with live entertainment and food served daily or you can fine dine in Knaptons Restaurant. The friendly rural atmosphere will revive the most faded traveller, with golf fishing and walking locally, there is plenty to see and do.

B&B from €55.00 to €75.00

EILEEN O'CONNOR & TIM JOHNSON
& CLAIRE McGUIRE

☺ Weekend specials from €110.00 pps

23 23

Inet

Closed 25 - 26 December

CASTLE ARMS HOTEL

THE SQUARE,
DURROW,
CO. LAOIS

TEL: 0502-36117 FAX: 0502-36566
EMAIL: info@castlearmshotel.ie
WEB: www.castlearmshotel.ie

HOTEL ★ MAP 7 L 8

The Castle Arms Hotel is a family-run hotel situated in the award-winning picturesque village of Durrow. We are situated 1.5 hours from Dublin, two hours from Cork & three hours from Belfast. Our reputation is for good food, service & friendliness. Local amenities include fishing, Granstown Lake is described as being the best coarse fishing lake in Europe. Trout can be fished from the local Rivers Erkina and Nore, horse trekking & many golf courses within easy reach. Brand Central designer outlet is 10 minutes drive away. Ideal for a weekend away shopping.

B&B from €50.00 to €50.00

SEOSAMH MURPHY
GENERAL MANAGER

14 14

Open All Year

B&B Rates are per Person Sharing per Night incl. Breakfast
Room Rates are per Room per Night

CASTLE DURROW

DURROW,
CO. LAOIS

TEL: 0502-36555 FAX: 0502-36559
EMAIL: info@castledurrow.com
WEB: www.castledurrow.com

HOTEL U MAP 7 L 8.

Shelly & Peter fill this stunning place with so much informal warmth that it feels more family home than hotel. Everyone mucks in here. They want you to lounge and enjoy yourself rather than pay homage to the magnificent surroundings. Twinkly chandeliers drip from high ceilings, leather sofas, modern art, wooden floors and a dining room looking over a terrace towards the hills of Laois. A warm welcome awaits.

Member of Ireland's Blue Book

B&B from €90.00 to €150.00

SHELLY & PETER STOKES
OWNERS

😊 Special offers on web page

24 24

P

IRISH
HOTELS
FEDERATION

Closed 24 December - 19 January

HERITAGE @ KILLENARD

KILLENARD, PORTARLINGTON,
CO. LAOIS

TEL: 0502-45994 FAX: 0502-45052
EMAIL: info@theheritage.com
WEB: www.theheritage.com

UNDER CONSTRUCTION - OPENING JUNE 2005

HOTEL P MAP 7 L 10

The Heritage @ Killenard is due to open June 2005. Situated just off the main Dublin - Cork motorway (N7) - only 45 minutes drive to Dublin's City Centre. This luxury hotel/resort is surrounded by the renowned Heritage Golf Club - host to the the 2005 AIB Seniors. Open and world class destination spa. Sister property: The Heritage Hotel - Portlaoise, Co. Laois.

B&B from €120.00 to €200.00

EOIN O'SULLIVAN
MANAGING DIRECTOR

97 97

Open All Year

HERITAGE - PORTLAOISE (THE)

PORTLAOISE,
CO. LAOIS

TEL: 0502-78588 FAX: 0502-78577
EMAIL: res@theheritagehotel.com
WEB: www.theheritagehotel.com

HOTEL U MAP 7 L 9

The Heritage Hotel is fast becoming Ireland's leading conference & leisure venue. Offering 110 luxury bedrooms, bars, restaurants, Health and Fitness Club, Beauty Spa. We are situated in the town centre just off the main motorway. Throughout the year we offer special offers; please check our website. Sister property: The Heritage @ Killenard, Co. Laois.

Member of Select Hotels of Ireland

B&B from €75.00 to €175.00

EOIN O'SULLIVAN
MANAGING DIRECTOR

110 110

IRISH
HOTELS
FEDERATION

Closed 24 - 27 December

B&B Rates are per Person Sharing per Night incl. Breakfast
Room Rates are per Room per Night

MALTINGS GUESTHOUSE

CASTLE STREET,
BIRR,
CO. OFFALY
TEL: 0509-21345 FAX: 0509-22073
EMAIL: themaltingsbirr@eircom.net

GUESTHOUSE ★★★ MAP 7 J 9

Secluded on a picturesque riverside setting beside Birr Castle, in the centre of Ireland's finest Georgian town. Built circa 1810 to store malt for Guinness, and converted in 1994 to a 13 bedroom guesthouse with full bar and restaurant. All bedrooms are comfortably furnished with bath/shower en suite, colour TV and phones.

B&B from €32.00 to €35.00

MAEVE GARRY
MANAGERESS

13 13

Closed 24 - 27 December

BRIDGE HOUSE HOTEL & LEISURE CLUB

TULLAMORE,
CO. OFFALY
TEL: 0506-25600 FAX: 0506-25690
EMAIL: info@bridgehousehotel.com
WEB: www.bridgehousehotel.com

HOTEL U MAP 7 K 10

A warm welcome awaits you at the Bridge House Hotel. Enjoy the best of Irish Hospitality renowned for good food, service and great atmosphere. State of the art leisure club & swimming pool and a unique outdoor hot spa. Play golf in the virtual reality golf facility. Five minutes away are two of Ireland's golfing treasures, Esker Hill and Tullamore Golf Club, both 18 hole golf courses. Winner of the Best Hotel Bar in Ireland. This is one of Ireland's most luxurious hotels with 72 rooms incl. 4 executive suites and superb presidential suite. Céad míle fáilte, Be our guest.

B&B from €85.00 to €160.00

COLM MCCABE
MANAGER

72 72

Closed 24 - 26 December

B&B Rates are per Person Sharing per Night incl. Breakfast
Room Rates are per Room per Night

Castle Barna Golf Club.

Daingean, Co. Offaly
Tel: 0506 53384 • Fax: 0506 53077
Email: info@castlebarna.ie
Web: www.castlebarna.ie

A fantastic 18 hole parkland course built on the banks of the Grand Canal. Renowned for its excellent greens and lush fairways, mature trees and natural streams. It's a course that suits all levels of golfers. Castle Barna was host to the G.U.I. Pierce Purcell Shield in 2000 and 2002.

Members, Green Fees and Societies always welcome.

Located 8 miles off Dublin to Galway Road at Tyrellspass

The 19th hole is an old stone clubhouse with full bar and catering facilities and modern changing rooms.

Castle Barna is a course you would love to play again.

DAYS HOTEL

MAIN STREET,
TULLAMORE,
CO. OFFALY
TEL: 1890-776 655
EMAIL: info@dayshoteltullamore.com
WEB: www.dayshoteltullamore.com

HOTEL P   MAP 7 K 10

Days Hotel Tullamore, opened in November 2004, and is located just five minutes walk from the town centre. The hotel boasts first class accommodation in contemporary style. Each of the 62 guest rooms has king size bed, interactive TV with pay movies, high speed internet access, laptop size safe, tea/coffee station and iron/ironing board. Upgrade to an executive room with separate work desk and en suite jacuzzi bath. The hotel has 2 spacious air conditioned conference rooms with capacity from 5 to 50 delegates.

Member of Days Inn Ireland

Room Rate from €69.00 to €199.00

BRIAN PIERSON
GENERAL MANGER

62 62
inet WiFi

IRISH
HOTELS
FEDERATION

Closed 24 - 28 December

GRENNANS COUNTRY HOUSE

AHARNEY,
TULLAMORE,
CO. OFFALY
TEL: 0506-55893 FAX: 0506-55893
EMAIL: deirdregrennan@iol.ie
WEB: www.grennanscountryhouse.ie

GUESTHOUSE P   MAP 7 K 10

Situated in the heart of the Midlands 1 mile off N.80, 1.5 hours from Dublin Airport, Grennans Country House is a purpose built luxury guest house; golfers paradise - 10 golf courses within 1/2 hour's drive. Rural setting, ample car parking, All rooms en suite, tastefully furnished super king beds. With DD phone, TV, tea/coffee facilities, spring water, clock radio, hairdryer, iron/ironing board. Guest TV lounge, home baking. Access for wheelchair user. Ideal touring base, golfing, fishing, equestrian, walking - your choice is our pleasure.

B&B from €40.00 to €55.00

PAT & DEIRDRE GRENNAN

6   6

IRISH
HOTELS
FEDERATION

Open All Year

MOORHILL HOUSE HOTEL

MOORHILL,
CLARA ROAD, TULLAMORE,
CO. OFFALY
TEL: 0506-21395 FAX: 0506-52424
EMAIL: info@moorhill.ie
WEB: www.moorhill.ie

HOTEL U   MAP 7 K 10

Moorhill is a unique experience in the best possible ways. Combining the classic quality of a Victorian country house with the informal ambience of a modern hotel. In Moorhill, we have placed particular emphasis on marrying the elegant surroundings and atmosphere of the hotel with a warm Irish welcome and friendly efficient service. Centrally located and ideal for a relaxing break from daily life or to conduct business at a quiet and efficient pace.

B&B from €50.00 to €80.00

DAVID AND ALAN DUFFY

10 10

alc inet

IRISH
HOTELS
FEDERATION

Closed 24 - 26 December

B&B Rates are per Person Sharing per Night incl. Breakfast
Room Rates are per Room per Night

WHERE TO STAY WHEN YOU PLAY!

ACCOMMODATION

CORK Continued

COURSES

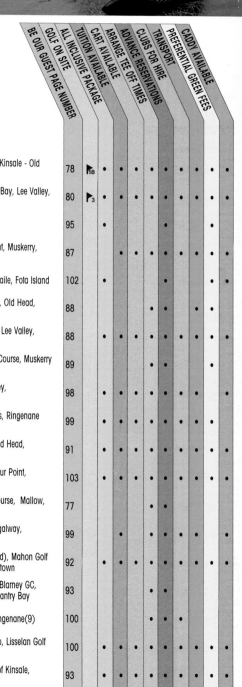

Accommodation	Courses	Page	Golf on Site	All Inclusive Package	Tuition Available	Cart Available	Arrange Tee Off Times	Advance Reservations	Clubs for Hire	Transport	Preferential Green Fees	Caddy Available
Fernhill Golf & Country Club	Douglas, Monkstown, Harbour Point, Kinsale - Old Head, Cork, Fota	78	18 •	•	•	•	•	•	•	•	•	•
Fernhill House Hotel	Skibbereen, Bandon, Lisselan, Bantry Bay, Lee Valley, Dunmore	80	3 •	•	•	•	•	•	•	•	•	•
Glengarriff Eccles Hotel	Bantry Bay, Glengarriff, Ring of Kerry	95	•				•				•	
Gresham Metropole	Fota Island, Little Island, Harbour Point, Muskerry, Kinsale	87		•	•	•	•	•	•	•	•	•
Hibernian Hotel and Leisure Centre	Mallow, Lee Valley, Charleville, Doneraile, Fota Island	102	•				•				•	•
Hotel Isaacs	Lee Valley, Fota Island, Harbour Point, Old Head, Muskerry	88				•	•	•		•	•	•
Imperial Hotel	Fota Island, Douglas, Cork, Muskerry, Lee Valley, Monkstown	88	•	•	•	•	•	•	•	•	•	•
Jurys Cork Hotel	Lee Valley Golf Course, Douglas Golf Course, Muskerry Golf Course	89				•	•				•	
Kierans Folkhouse Inn	Kinsale, Farrangalway, Fota, Lee Valley, Harbour Point, Old Head of Kinsale	98	•	•	•	•	•	•	•	•	•	•
Long Quay House	Kinsale Golf Club, Old Head Golf Links, Ringenane (Kinsale)	99	•	•	•	•	•	•	•	•	•	•
Maryborough House Hotel	Douglas, Fota Island, Cork, Kinsale Old Head, Harbour Point, Monkstown	91	•	•	•	•	•	•	•	•	•	•
Midleton Park Hotel & Spa	Fota Island, Cork - Little Island, Harbour Point, Water Rock, East Cork	103	•	•	•	•	•	•	•	•	•	•
Muskerry Arms	Muskerry Golf Course, Blarney Golf Course, Mallow, Harbour Point and Lee Valley	77					•	•				
Old Bank House	Old Head of Kinsale, Kinsale - Farrangalway, Fota Golf Course	99		•			•	•			•	•
Rochestown Park Hotel	Fota Island, Harbour Point (Little Island), Mahon Golf Club, Douglas G.C, Lee Valley, Monkstown	92	•	•	•	•	•	•	•	•	•	•
Silver Springs Moran Hotel	Old Head Kinsale, Harbour Point GC, Blarney GC, Water Rock GC, Fota Island GC and Bantry Bay	93					•	•				
Tierney's Guest House	Farrangalway(18), Old Head(18), Ringenane(9)	100					•	•				
Trident Hotel	Old Head Golf Links, Kinsale Golf Club, Lisselan Golf Club, Fota Island, Lee Valley	100	•	•	•	•	•	•	•	•	•	•
Vienna Woods Hotel	Cork, Harbour Point, Fota, Old Head of Kinsale, Water Rock	93	•	•	•	•	•	•	•	•	•	•

 = Full 18 Hole   = 9 Hole   ▶3 = Par 3

WHERE TO STAY WHEN YOU PLAY!

ACCOMMODATION	COURSES	BE OUR GUEST PAGE NUMBER	GOLF ON SITE	ALL INCLUSIVE PACKAGE	TUITION AVAILABLE	CART AVAILABLE	ARRANGE TEE OFF TIMES	ADVANCE RESERVATIONS	CLUBS FOR HIRE	TRANSPORT	PREFERENTIAL GREEN FEES	CADDY AVAILABLE
CORK Continued												
Walter Raleigh Hotel	Youghal GC, Fota Island GC, Water Rock GC, West Waterford GC, Harbour Point GC, Little Island	108						•	•			
WatersEdge Hotel	Fota Island, Harbour Point, Cobh, Water Rock, East Cork, Old Head of Kinsale, Cork	83			•	•	•	•	•	•	•	•
West Cork Hotel	Skibbereen, West Carbery	106						•	•		•	•
Westlodge Hotel	Arrangement with Bantry Bay Golf Club. Guaranteed times. 18 hole Championship Course	76	•		•	•	•	•	•		•	•
White House	Kinsale (18) and (9), Old Head, Bandon, Carrigaline, Muskerry	100						•	•	•		•
KERRY												
Abbey Gate Hotel	Tralee, Ballybunion, Killarney, Dooks, Waterville, Kerries	150	•		•	•	•	•	•	•	•	•
Aghadoe Heights Hotel & Spa	Waterville, Ballybunion, Kenmare, Killarney, Beaufort, Ring of Kerry	128					•	•	•	•	•	•
Arbutus Hotel	Killarney, Ballybunion, Waterville, Dooks, Tralee, Ring of Kerry	129	•		•	•	•	•	•	•	•	•
Ard-Na-Sidhe	Dooks, Killorglin, Waterville, Beaufort, Killarney, Tralee	112	•		•	•	•	•	•	•	•	•
Ashville Guesthouse	Killarney, Ross, Dunloe, Beaufort, Waterville, Dooks, Ballybunion	129	•		•	•	•	•	•	•	•	•
Bianconi	Killarney, Beaufort, Dunloe, Killorglin, Dooks, Waterville	147	•		•	•	•	•	•	•	•	•
Brehon (The)	Killarney, Ross, Beaufort	129	•				•	•		•	•	•
Butler Arms Hotel	Waterville, Dooks, Killarney, Tralee, Ballybunion, Ring of Kerry	156	•		•	•	•	•	•		•	•
Carrig House	Dooks, Killarney, Beaufort, Killorglin, Waterville, Tralee	112	•				•	•		•	•	•
Cashen Course House	Ballybunion Old Course, Ballybunion Cashen Course, Listowel GC, Tralee (Barrow), Lahinch GC, Doonbeg	109	•		•	•	•	•	•	•	•	•
Castlelodge Guesthouse	Killarney Golf Course, Ross Golf Course	130						•		•	•	•
Castlerosse Hotel & Leisure Centre	Killarney (3 courses), Beaufort, Dooks	131	♪9	•	•	•	•	•	•	•	•	•

♪18 = Full 18 Hole ♪9 = 9 Hole ♪3 = Par 3

WHERE TO STAY WHEN YOU PLAY!

Accommodation	Courses	Be Our Guest Page Number	Golf On Site	All Inclusive Package	Tuition Available	Cart Available	Arrange Tee Off Times	Advance Reservations	Clubs For Hire	Transport	Preferential Green Fees	Caddy Available
KERRY Continued												
Derrynane Hotel	Ring of Kerry, Kenmare, Waterville, Parknasilla, Beaufort, Dooks	111						•	•		•	
Dingle Benners Hotel	Dingle Golf Links, Ceann Sibeal, Castlegregory Golf Club	117	•			•	•	•	•	•	•	
Dingle Skellig Hotel	Dingle Golf Links, Ceann Sibeal, Castlegregory	117	•			•	•	•	•	•	•	
Earls Court House	Killarney, Waterville, Ballybunion, Tralee, Beaufort, Dooks, Old Head	132		•	•	•	•	•	•	•		•
Eviston House Hotel	Ballybunion, Beaufort, Killarney, Waterville, Dooks, Tralee	133	•	•		•	•	•	•	•		
Fairview Guesthouse	Killarney, Waterville, Tralee, Dooks, Ballybunion, Beaufort	134	•	•		•	•	•	•	•	•	•
Foley's Townhouse	Killarney, Barrow, Beaufort, Dooks, Ballybunion, Waterville	134						•	•			
Fuchsia House	Killarney, Tralee, Ballybunion, Waterville, Dooks, Beaufort.	135		•		•	•	•	•	•		•
Gleann Fia Country House	Killarney, Beaufort, Tralee, Ballybunion, Dooks, Waterville, Ring of Kerry Golf Course, Kenmare	135	•	•	•	•	•	•	•	•	•	•
Glencar House Hotel	Dooks, Beaufort, Waterville, Ring of Kerry and Killarney (3)	121	•	•		•	•	•	•	•		•
Gleneagle Hotel	Killarney, Ross, Beaufort, Ring of Kerry, Dooks, Ballybunion	136	•					•	•		•	
Grand Hotel	Tralee, Ballybunion, Waterville, Dingle, Dooks, Killarney	154	•	•		•	•	•	•	•	•	•
Grove Lodge Riverside Guesthouse	Waterville, Tralee, Ballybunion, Beaufort, Killarney, Killorglin, Dooks, Gap of Dunloe, Dingle	148	•	•		•	•	•	•	•	•	•
Harty Costello Town House	Ballybunion, Tralee, Listowel, Ballyheigue, Killarney	109	•			•	•	•	•			•
Hotel Dunloe Castle	Dunloe, Dooks, Beaufort, Killarney, Ross, Killorglin	137	•	•		•	•	•	•	•		•
Hotel Europe	Killarney Mahony's Point, Killeen, Lackabane, Beaufort, Dooks, Killorglin	137	•	•		•	•	•	•	•		•
Inveraray Farm Guesthouse	Beaufort, Dunloe, Killarney, Ross, Killorglin, Dooks	138		•		•	•	•	•	•		•
Iragh Ti Connor	Ballybunion, Tralee, Dooks, Doonbeg, Lahinch, Waterville	110	•				•	•	•	•		•
Kathleens Country House	Killarney, Waterville, Tralee, Dooks, Ballybunion, Beaufort	138		•		•	•	•	•	•	•	•

 = Full 18 Hole   = 9 Hole   = Par 3

WHERE TO STAY WHEN YOU PLAY!

ACCOMMODATION	COURSES	BE OUR GUEST PAGE NUMBER	GOLF ON SITE	ALL INCLUSIVE PACKAGE	TUITION AVAILABLE	CART AVAILABLE	ARRANGE TEE OFF TIMES	ADVANCE RESERVATIONS	CLUBS FOR HIRE	TRANSPORT	PREFERENTIAL GREEN FEES	CADDY AVAILABLE
KERRY Continued												
Killarney Avenue Hotel	Killarney, Ballybunion, Tralee, Waterville, Beaufort, Castleisland	139		•	•	•	•	•	•	•	•	•
Killarney Oaks	Waterville, Ballybunion, Kenmare, Killarney, Beaufort, Ring of Kerry	140						•	•			
Killarney Park Hotel	Killarney, Ballybunion, Tralee, Waterville, Dooks, Ring of Kerry	141		•		•	•	•	•	•	•	
Killarney Plaza Hotel & Spa	Killarney Golf & Fishing Club, Waterville, Ballybunion, Dooks, Tralee, Old Head Kinsale	141				•	•	•	•		•	•
Killarney Royal	Killarney, Tralee, Dooks, Waterville, Beaufort, Ross	141		•		•	•	•	•	•	•	
Killeen House Hotel	Killarney, Waterville, Tralee, Dooks, Ballybunion, Beaufort	142		•	•	•	•	•	•	•	•	•
Kingfisher Lodge Guesthouse	Beaufort, Dunloe, Castlerosse, Killarney, Ross, Killorglin	142		•	•	•	•	•	•	•	•	•
Lake Hotel	Killarney (3 courses), Beaufort, Dooks, Ballybunion, Waterville, Tralee, Ross, Castlerosse	142		•	•	•	•	•	•	•	•	•
Lansdowne Arms Hotel	Ring of Kerry Golf Club, Kenmare Golf Club	124		•		•	•	•	•	•	•	•
McSweeney Arms Hotel	Killarney, Waterville, Tralee, Ballybunion, Ring of Kerry, Dooks	143		•	•	•	•	•	•	•	•	•
Meadowlands Hotel	Ballybunion, Tralee (Barrow), Killarney, Dooks, Killorglin, Waterville	154		•		•	•	•	•			•
Moorings (The)	Waterville Golf Links	148		•	•	•	•	•	•	•	•	•
Muckross Park Hotel & Garden Suites	Beaufort, O'Mahony's Point, Killeen, Ross, Tralee, Ballybunion, Waterville, Dooks	144		•	•	•	•	•	•	•	•	•
Old Weir Lodge	Killarney, Waterville, Ballybunion, Tralee, Dooks, Beaufort	144		•		•	•	•	•	•	•	•
Parknasilla Great Southern Hotel	Ring of Kerry, Waterville, Killarney, Dooks	149	⧏9	•		•	•	•	•	•	•	•
Randles Court Clarion Hotel	Killarney, Tralee, Beaufort, Dooks, Ring of Kerry	145		•		•	•	•	•	•	•	
Rivermere	Killarney (O'Mahony's Point and Killeen), Dooks, Ballybunion, Waterville, Tralee, Ring of Kerry	145		•	•	•	•	•	•	•	•	•
Riverside Hotel	Ross GC, Killarney GC, Dooks GC, Dunloe GC, Beaufort GC, Tralee GC	146		•			•	•				•
Scarriff Inn	Waterville, Kenmare, Sneem, Killorglin, Tralee, Ballybunion	111		•	•	•	•	•	•	•	•	•

412

 = Full 18 Hole   = 9 Hole   ⧏3 = Par 3

WHERE TO STAY WHEN YOU PLAY!

ACCOMMODATION	COURSES	BE OUR GUEST PAGE NUMBER	GOLF ON SITE	ALL INCLUSIVE PACKAGE	TUITION AVAILABLE	CART AVAILABLE	ARRANGE TEE OFF TIMES	ADVANCE RESERVATIONS	CLUBS FOR HIRE	TRANSPORT	PREFERENTIAL GREEN FEES	CADDY AVAILABLE
KERRY Continued												
Sheen Falls Lodge	Kenmare, Ring of Kerry	126	•	•	•	•	•	•	•	•	•	•
Smugglers Inn	Waterville, Killarney, Dooks, Tralee, Ballybunion, Kenmare, Parknasilla	157	•	•	•	•	•	•	•	•		•
Tuscar Lodge	Killarney Golf Club, Beaufort, Dooks, Killorglin, Waterville, Tralee	146	•	•	•	•	•	•	•	•		•

Shannon

ACCOMMODATION	COURSES	BE OUR GUEST PAGE NUMBER	GOLF ON SITE	ALL INCLUSIVE PACKAGE	TUITION AVAILABLE	CART AVAILABLE	ARRANGE TEE OFF TIMES	ADVANCE RESERVATIONS	CLUBS FOR HIRE	TRANSPORT	PREFERENTIAL GREEN FEES	CADDY AVAILABLE
CLARE												
Aran View House Hotel & Restaurant	Lahinch Links Course, Lahinch Castle Course, Doonbeg Greg Norman Course, Woodstock, Ennis Golf Club	164					•	•	•			
Ballinalacken Castle Country House & Restaurant	Lahinch, Lahinch Castle, Woodstock, Galway Bay, Dromoland Castle, Doonbeg	164				•	•	•	•	•	•	•
Bellbridge House Hotel	Spanish Point, Lahinch, Doonbeg	178	•			•						
Dough Mor Lodge	Lahinch Golf Club (36 holes), Doonbeg Golf Club, Kilrush, Kilkee	174					•	•	•			
Falls Hotel	Lahinch, Doonbeg, Woodstock, Dromoland	169						•				
Fitzpatrick Bunratty	Dromoland, Shannon, Adare Manor Golf Resort, Limerick County Golf Club, Castletroy, Ballyneety	163	•				•	•	•	•	•	•
Greenbrier Inn Guesthouse	Lahinch Championship Links, Lahinch Castle Links, Doonbeg Championship Links, Woodstock (Ennis)	174			•	•						•
Grovemount House	Lahinch, Spanish Point, Doonbeg, Ennis, Dromoland	170				•	•	•	•	•	•	
Halpin's Townhouse Hotel	Ballybunion, Lahinch, Kilkee, Doonbeg, Woodstock, Shannon	170	•	•	•	•	•	•	•	•		•
Kilkee Bay Hotel	Kilkee, Kilrush, Doonbeg	170	•			•	•	•	•		•	•
Kincora Hall Hotel	East Clare, Lahinch, Limerick County Golf & Country Club, Adare Manor	172	•	•	•	•	•	•	•	•	•	•
Magowna House Hotel	Woodstock, Ennis, Lahinch, Dromoland Castle, Shannon, Doonbeg	168	•	•	•	•	•	•	•	•	•	•
Mountshannon Hotel	Bodyke - East Clare Golf Club, Portumna	179	•	•		•	•	•	•	•	•	•
Old Ground Hotel	Doonbeg, Lahinch, Woodstock, Ennis, Dromoland, Shannon, East Clare	168	•			•	•	•	•	•	•	•

🏌 18 = Full 18 Hole   🏌 9 = 9 Hole   🏌 3 = Par 3

WHERE TO STAY WHEN YOU PLAY!

Accommodation	Courses	Be Our Guest Page Number	Golf On Site	All Inclusive Package	Tuition Available	Cart Available	Arrange Tee Off Times	Advance Reservations	Clubs For Hire	Transport	Preferential Green Fees	Caddy Available
CLARE Continued												
Sancta Maria Hotel	Lahinch Championship Golf Links, Lahinch Castle, Doonbeg, Woodstock, Dromoland, Spanish Point	175		•	•	•	•	•	•			•
Temple Gate Hotel	Woodstock, Ennis, Lahinch, East Clare, Doonbeg, Dromoland	168		•	•	•	•	•	•	•	•	•
LIMERICK												
Adare Manor Hotel & Golf Resort		181	18	•	•	•	•	•	•	•	•	•
Carrabawn House	Adare Manor Golf Resort, Limerick Golf & Country Club, Newcastle West, Ballybunion, Lahinch	181						•				
Courtenay Lodge Hotel	Newcastle West, Adare Manor, Adare Golf Club, Ballybunion, Charleville, Dingle (Ceann Sibeal)	188		•	•	•	•	•		•	•	•
Fitzgeralds Woodlands House Hotel, Health and Leisure Spa	Adare Manor Golf Club, Adare Golf Club, Newcastle West, Charleville, Limerick County Golf Club	182		•	•	•	•	•	•	•	•	
Rathkeale House Hotel	Adare, Adare Manor, Newcastle West, Charleville, Ballybunion	189		•	•	•	•	•	•	•	•	•
TIPPERARY NORTH												
Abbey Court Hotel and Trinity Leisure Club	Nenagh, Roscrea, Birr, Portumna, Thurles, Castletroy	189		•	•	•	•	•	•	•	•	•
Anner Hotel & Leisure Centre	Thurles, Dundrum, Templemore	191		•	•	•	•	•	•	•	•	•
Racket Hall Country House Golf & Conference Hotel	Roscrea, Birr, Mountrath, Rathdowney, Portumna, The Heritage	190		•	•	•	•	•	•	•	•	•

West

Accommodation	Courses	Be Our Guest Page Number	Golf On Site	All Inclusive Package	Tuition Available	Cart Available	Arrange Tee Off Times	Advance Reservations	Clubs For Hire	Transport	Preferential Green Fees	Caddy Available
GALWAY												
Adare Guest House	Galway Bay, Oughterard	204		•	•	•	•	•	•	•	•	•
Anno Santo Hotel	Glenlo, Athenry, Galway, Oughterard, Galway Bay, Barna	205		•		•	•	•	•	•	•	
Ardagh Hotel & Restaurant	Connemara	199			•	•	•	•			•	•
Ben View House	Connemara	199				•	•	•	•	•		
Boat Inn (The)	Oughterard, Barna, Ballyconneely	223		•		•	•	•		•		

18 = Full 18 Hole   9 = 9 Hole   3 = Par 3

WHERE TO STAY WHEN YOU PLAY!

Accommodation	Courses	Be Our Guest Page Number	Golf on Site	All Inclusive Package	Tuition Package	Cart Available	Clubs Available	Arrange Tee Off Times	Advance Reservations	Clubs for Hire	Transport	Preferential Green Fees	Caddy Available
GALWAY Continued													
Carrown Tober House	Oughterard, Galway, Connemara, Westport	224	•	•	•	•	•		•	•	•	•	•
Connemara Country Lodge	Connemara GC, Ballyconneely, Hazel Wood, Oughterard, Westport	201					•	•		•			
Connemara Gateway Hotel	Oughterard, Barna Golf and Country Club	224	•				•	•				•	
Dun Ri Guesthouse	Connemara, Westport, Oughterard	201		•	•	•	•	•		•	•	•	•
Erriseask House Hotel & Restaurant	Connemara Golf Course (only 4km)	202			•	•	•	•	•				
Forster Court Hotel	Galway, Barna, Galway Golf & Country, Athenry	209						•	•				
Galway Bay Hotel, Conference & Leisure Centre	Galway, Galway Bay, Athenry, Bearna, Gort	209	•	•	•	•	•	•	•	•	•	•	•
Glenlo Abbey Hotel	Glenlo Abbey, Galway, Bearna, Oughterard, Galway Bay, Connemara	211 (18)	•	•	•	•	•	•	•			•	
Inishmore Guesthouse	Barna, Galway Bay, Oughterard, Athenry, Galway, Gort	212	•	•	•	•	•	•	•	•	•	•	•
Lady Gregory Hotel	Gort	218	•	•	•	•	•	•	•	•	•	•	•
Mountain View Guest House	Oughterard, Galway, Connemara, Westport	225	•	•	•	•	•	•	•	•	•	•	•
O'Deas Hotel	Loughrea, Curragh, Gort, Galway Bay	222	•		•	•	•	•	•	•	•	•	•
Peacockes Hotel & Complex	Oughterard, Ballyconneely, Glenlo Abbey, Barna, Westport	222	•			•	•	•	•	•	•	•	•
Ross Lake House Hotel	Oughterard, Barna, Galway Bay, Connemara	226	•	•	•	•	•	•	•	•	•	•	•
Shannon Oaks Hotel & Country Club	Portumna, Galway Bay, Birr, Glasson, Gort, Lahinch	226	•	•	•	•	•	•	•	•	•	•	•
Westwood House Hotel	Barna, Oughterard, Ballyconneely, Galway Bay Golf and Country Club	218	•			•	•	•	•	•	•	•	•
Zetland Country House Hotel	Connemara Golf Club, Westport Golf Club, Oughterard Golf Club	197	•	•			•	•	•	•	•		•
MAYO													
Atlantic Coast Hotel	Westport, Enniscrone, Carne, Ballyconneely, Castlebar, Ballinrobe	237	•	•	•	•	•	•	•	•	•	•	•

 = Full 18 Hole   = 9 Hole = Par 3

ACCOMMODATION / COURSES

Accommodation	Courses	Be Our Guest Page Number	Golf On Site	All Inclusive Package	Tuition Available	Cart Available	Arrange Tee Off Times	Advance Reservations	Clubs For Hire	Transport	Preferential Green Fees	Caddy Available
MAYO Continued												
Castlecourt Hotel Conference and Leisure Centre	Westport, Ballinrobe, Castlebar, Belmullet, Clew Bay, Enniscrone	238		•	•	•	•	•	•	•	•	•
Downhill House Hotel	Ballina, Enniscrone, Carne (Belmullet), Rosses Point, Strandhill, Westport, Claremorris, Ballinrobe	231		•	•	•	•	•	•	•	•	•
Healys Restaurant & Country House Hotel	Castlebar, Ballina, Westport, Enniscrone, Carne, Swinford, Ballinrobe, Mulranny	236		•	•	•	•	•	•	•	•	•
Hotel Westport, Conference & Leisure Centre	Westport, Castlebar, Ballinrobe, Carne	238		•	•	•	•	•	•	•	•	•
Knockranny House Hotel	Westport, Castlebar, Ballinrobe, Clew Bay, Mulranny	239		•	•	•	•	•	•	•	•	•
Ostan Oilean Acla	Achill, Mulranny, Westport, Castlebar, Ballinrobe, Carne	230		•	•	•	•	•	•	•	•	•
Stella Maris Country House Hotel	Carne/Belmullet, Enniscrone, Bartra Island, Ballina, Rosses Point, Westport, Castlebar	232		•	•	•	•	•	•	•	•	•
Teach Iorrais	Carne Links Golf Course, Ballina, Enniscrone, Westport, Castlebar	234		•				•	•	•	•	•
TF Royal Hotel & Theatre	Castlebar, Westport, Three Oaks, Ballinrobe, Belmullet, Enniscrone	233		•	•	•	•	•	•	•	•	•
Westport Woods Hotel & Leisure Centre	Westport, Castlebar, Ballinrobe, Clew Bay, Carne (Belmullet)	240		•	•	•	•	•	•	•	•	•
Wyatt Hotel	Westport Golf Club, Castlebar Golf Club, Ballinrobe Golf Club, Carne Golf Links	241		•	•	•	•	•	•	•	•	•
ROSCOMMON												
Abbey Hotel, Conference and Leisure Centre	Glasson 18 hole, Carrick-on-Shannon 18 hole, Ballinasloe 18 hole, Longford 18 hole	242		•			•	•			•	
O'Gara's Royal Hotel	Roscommon, Glasson, Longford, Athlone	242		•			•	•			•	

North West

Accommodation	Courses	Be Our Guest Page Number	Golf On Site	All Inclusive Package	Tuition Available	Cart Available	Arrange Tee Off Times	Advance Reservations	Clubs For Hire	Transport	Preferential Green Fees	Caddy Available
DONEGAL												
Arnolds Hotel	Dunfanaghy 18 Hole Links, Cloughaneely 9 Hole Parkland, Rosapenna 36 Hole Links, St. Patricks 18	252		•		•	•	•	•	•	•	•
Bay View Hotel & Leisure Centre	Murragh (Donegal), Narin, Portnoo	254		•			•	•	•	•		•
Castle Grove Country House Hotel	Portsalon, Letterkenny, Rosapenna, Ballyliffin	254		•		•	•	•	•		•	•

 18 = Full 18 Hole   9 = 9 Hole   3 = Par 3

416

WHERE TO STAY WHEN YOU PLAY!

ACCOMMODATION	COURSES	BE OUR GUEST PAGE NUMBER	GOLF ON SITE	ALL INCLUSIVE PACKAGE	TUITION AVAILABLE	CART AVAILABLE	ARRANGE TEE OFF TIMES	ADVANCE RESERVATIONS	CLUBS FOR HIRE	TRANSPORT	PREFERENTIAL GREEN FEES	CADDY AVAILABLE
DONEGAL Continued												
Dorrians Imperial Hotel	Murragh (Donegal), Bundoran	248			•	•		•		•	•	
Downings Bay Hotel	Rosapenna Links, St. Patricks Carrigart Links, Dunfanaghy, Portsalon	255	•		•	•	•	•	•	•	•	
Fort Royal Hotel	Portsalon, Letterkenny, Otway	259 ▶3	•		•	•	•	•	•		•	
Great Northern Hotel	Donegal, Strandhill, Rosses Point	250 ▶18	•		•	•	•	•	•		•	
Inishowen Gateway Hotel	Buncrana, North West Golf Course, Ballyliffin Old Course, Ballyliffin Glashedy Course	249	•			•	•			•		
Malin Hotel	Ballyliffin Golf Club - Clashedy Links, The Old Course, Greencastle Golf Club and North West Golf Club.	258	•			•	•			•		
McGrorys of Culdaff	Ballyliffin Golf Club	250	•		•	•	•	•	•	•	•	
Milford Inn Hotel	Portsalon, Rosapenna, Letterkenny, Dunfanaghy, Ballyliffin	258	•		•	•	•	•		•		
Mill Park Hotel, Conference Centre & Leisure Club	Murragh (Donegal Golf Course)	251	•			•	•			•		
Ostan Na Tra (Beach Hotel)	Rosapenna Hotel (2 courses-36 holes), Carrigart Hotel St.Patricks (2 courses-36 holes)	252	•	•	•	•	•	•	•	•	•	
Rosapenna Hotel and Golf Links	Old Tom Morris Course, Sandy Hills Links	252 ▶18	•		•	•	•		•		•	•
Sandhouse Hotel	Donegal Murvagh, Bundoran, Rosses Point, Castle Hume, Ballyliffin and Portnoo	259	•		•	•	•	•	•	•	•	•
Silver Tassie Hotel	Portsalon, Letterkenny, Rosapenna, Dunfanaghy, Ballyliffin	257	•		•	•	•	•	•	•	•	•
LEITRIM												
Abbey Manor Hotel	County Sligo Golf Course - Rosses Point, Strandhill Golf Course, Carrick-on-Shannon Golf Course	261	•		•	•	•	•	•	•	•	•
Ramada Hotel & Suites at Lough Allen	Carrick-on-Shannon, County Sligo Golf Club	262	•			•	•		•		•	
Shannon Key West Hotel	Longford, Carrick-on-Shannon, Roscommon	262		•		•	•	•				
SLIGO												
Castle Arms Hotel	Enniscrone, Ballina, Strandhill, Rosses Point	263	•		•	•	•	•	•	•	•	•

▶18 = Full 18 Hole   ▶9 = 9 Hole   ▶3 = Par 3

WHERE TO STAY
WHEN YOU PLAY!

ACCOMMODATION	COURSES	BE OUR GUEST PAGE NUMBER	GOLF ON SITE	ALL INCLUSIVE PACKAGE	TUITION AVAILABLE	CART AVAILABLE	ARRANGE TEE OFF TIMES	ADVANCE RESERVATIONS	CLUBS FOR HIRE	TRANSPORT	PREFERENTIAL GREEN FEES	CADDY AVAILABLE
SLIGO Continued												
Sligo's Southern Hotel & Leisure Centre	Rosses Point, Strandhill, Bundoran, Enniscrone	266		•	•	•	•	•	•	•	•	•
Yeats Country Hotel and Leisure Club	Co. Sligo, Strandhill, Enniscrone, Bundoran	264		•	•	•	•	•		•	•	•
North												
ANTRIM												
Bayview Hotel	Royal Portrush, Portstewart, Castlerock, Ballycastle, Bushfoot, Gracehill, Galgorm Castle	270		•	•	•	•	•	•	•	•	•
Bushmills Inn Hotel	Royal Portrush, Portstewart, Castlerock, Ballycastle, Bushfoot, Gracehill	270		•	•	•	•	•	•	•	•	•
Comfort Hotel Portrush	Royal Portrush, Portstewart, Castlerock, Ballycastle, Bushfoot, Gracehill, Galgorm Castle	271		•	•	•	•	•		•	•	•
DERRY												
Radisson SAS Roe Park Resort	Roe Park Golf Club, Radisson SAS Roe Park Resort	281	🏌18	•	•	•	•	•	•	•	•	•
DOWN												
Burrendale Hotel and Country Club	Royal County Down, Kilkeel, Downpatrick, Ardglass, Spa, Bright	283							•	•		
Royal Hotel	Bangor, Clandeboye, Blackwood	282		•								
Dublin & East Coast												
DUBLIN												
Aberdeen Lodge	St. Margaret's, Portmarnock, K Club, Elm Park, Carton House, Druids Glen	295		•		•	•	•	•	•	•	•
Academy Hotel	Portmarnock, Royal Dublin, K Club, St. Margaret's, The Island, St. Anne's	295		•	•	•	•	•	•		•	•
Ardagh House	Milltown, Rathfarnham, The Grange	298						•	•	•		
Carriage House	St. Margarets, Portmarnock, Skerries, Balbriggan, Hollywood, Luttrellstown, The Island	344		•	•	•	•	•	•	•	•	•
Castleknock Hotel and Country Club	Luttrellstown, Carton House and Citywest	305	🏌18			•	•	•	•		•	•

🏌18 = Full 18 Hole   🏌9 = 9 Hole   🏌3 = Par 3

WHERE TO STAY WHEN YOU PLAY!

ACCOMMODATION

COURSES

DUBLIN Continued

Accommodation	Courses	BE OUR GUEST PAGE NUMBER	GOLF ON SITE	ALL INCLUSIVE PACKAGE	TUITION AVAILABLE	CART AVAILABLE	ARRANGE TEE OFF TIMES	ADVANCE RESERVATIONS	CLUBS FOR HIRE	TRANSPORT	PREFERENTIAL GREEN FEES	CADDY AVAILABLE
Charleville Lodge	St. Margaret's, Luttrellstown, The Links, Portmarnock, The Island Golf Links	306		•	•	•	•	•	•	•	•	•
Citywest Hotel & Golf Resort		346	18	•		•	•		•		•	
Deer Park Hotel and Golf Courses		342	18	•		•	•	•	•		•	
Grand Hotel	Portmarnock GC, Malahide GC, The Island GC, Swords GC, St. Margaret's, Royal Dublin	344					•	•		•		
Gresham (The)	Royal Dublin, Portmarnock, St. Margaret's, The Island, St. Anne's, Malahide	316				•	•	•	•		•	
Holiday Inn Dublin City Centre	Elm Park, Clontarf, St. Margaret's, Royal Dublin, The Castle, The Island	318		•								
King Sitric Fish Restaurant & Accommodation	Deerpark, Howth, Royal Dublin, Portmarnock, St. Margaret's, The Island	342					•	•	•	•	•	•
Marine Hotel	Portmarnock Hotel & Golf Links, Howth GC, Sutton GC, Royal Dublin GC, St. Anne's	347					•	•			•	
Merrion Hall	Portmarnock, Royal Dublin, Elm Park, Castle, K Club, Druid's Glen	326		•	•	•	•	•	•	•	•	•
Portmarnock Hotel & Golf Links	Portmarnock, St. Margaret's, Royal Dublin, Malahide, The Island	345	18	•	•	•	•	•	•	•	•	•
Redbank House Guesthouse & Restaurant	Skerries, Laytown, Bettystown, Baltray, Portmarnock, St. Margaret's, Donabate	346		•	•	•	•	•	•	•	•	•
Regency Airport Hotel	Malahide, Clontarf, Hollystown, St. Anne's, Royal Dublin	333		•			•	•	•	•	•	
Roganstown Golf & Country Club		348	18	•		•	•	•	•	•	•	
Stillorgan Park Hotel	Druid's Glen, Portmarnock, Woodbrook, Powerscourt, Edmondstown, Glen of the Downs.	290		•			•	•	•	•	•	
Waterside Hotel	Donabate, Turvey, Beaverstown, Balcarrick, The Island, Corballis	292		•			•	•	•	•	•	•
White Sands Hotel	Malahide, St. Margaret's, Royal Dublin, Portmarnock Golf Links, Donabate, Balcarrick	345		•		•	•	•	•	•	•	•

LOUTH

Accommodation	Courses	BE OUR GUEST PAGE NUMBER	GOLF ON SITE	ALL INCLUSIVE PACKAGE	TUITION AVAILABLE	CART AVAILABLE	ARRANGE TEE OFF TIMES	ADVANCE RESERVATIONS	CLUBS FOR HIRE	TRANSPORT	PREFERENTIAL GREEN FEES	CADDY AVAILABLE
Ballymascanlon House Hotel		351	18	•		•	•	•	•		•	•
Boyne Valley Hotel & Country Club	Baltray-Seapoint, Laytown/Bettystown, Dundalk, Headfort (2 courses), Kells, Ardee, St. Margarets	350		•	•	•	•	•	•	•	•	•

 = Full 18 Hole   = 9 Hole   ⛳3 = Par 3

419

WHERE TO STAY WHEN YOU PLAY!

ACCOMMODATION	COURSES	BE OUR GUEST PAGE NUMBER	GOLF ON SITE	ALL INCLUSIVE PACKAGE	TUITION AVAILABLE	CART AVAILABLE	ARRANGE TEE OFF TIMES	ADVANCE RESERVATIONS	CLUBS FOR HIRE	TRANSPORT	PREFERENTIAL GREEN FEES	CADDY AVAILABLE
LOUTH Continued												
Clanbrassil Hotel	Carron Beg, Greenore, Ballymascanlon, Killen	352	•	•	•	•	•	•	•	•		•
Derryhale Hotel	Killen Park, Blackrock, Ardee, Greenore, Carnbeg	352	•	•		•	•	•	•	•	•	•
Fairways Hotel & Conference Centre	Ballymascalon, Carnbeg, Killen, Dundalk, Seapoint, Greenore	353	•	•	•	•	•			•	•	
Hotel Imperial	Ballymascanlon, Dundalk, Greenore, Carnbeg	353	•		•	•	•	•	•		•	•
McKevitt's Village Hotel	Greenore	350	•				•				•	•
MEATH												
Castle Arch Hotel (Formerly Wellington Court)	Trim, Keegans, Glebe, Royal Tara Golf Club	358	•				•	•	•	•		
Conyngham Arms Hotel	Tara Golf Course, Navan, Baltray Golf Course, Ardee Golf Course, Ardee, Bettystown Golf Course, Moorepark	358	•	•	•	•	•	•	•	•	•	
Headfort Arms Hotel	Headfort Golf Course - 36 Holes, Royal Tara	356	•				•		•			
Neptune Beach Hotel & Leisure Club	Laytown & Bettystown, Sea Point, County Louth/Baltray, Royal Tara	355		•		•	•	•	•	•		•
Station House Hotel	Royal Tara, Blackbush, Headfort	356	•	•		•	•	•		•		
WICKLOW												
Arklow Bay Conference and Leisure Hotel	European, Arklow, Woodenbridge, Blainroe, Seafield	358	•	•	•	•	•	•	•	•	•	•
Ballyknocken Country House	Druid's Glen, European Club, Woodenbridge, Wicklow Town, Blainroe, Powerscourt	360	•	•	•	•	•	•	•	•	•	
Chester Beatty Inn	Druid's Glen, Woodenbridge, Blainroe, European, Glen of the Downs, Charlesland	361	•		•	•	•	•	•	•		
Glendalough Hotel	The European Club, Woodenbridge, Charlesland, Druid's Glen, Blainroe, Roundwood	366	•				•	•	•	•		
Glenview Hotel	Glen O' The Downs, Powerscourt, Druid's Glen, The European Club, Charlesland, Delgany	366	•		•	•	•	•	•	•	•	•
Grand Hotel	Blainroe, Wicklow, Druid's Glen, European Golf Course	368	•	•	•	•	•	•	•	•		•
Heather House Hotel	Bray, Woodbrook, Old Conna, Powerscourt, Greystones, Druid's Glen	363					•	•	•	•	•	

 = Full 18 Hole   = 9 Hole   = Par 3

WHERE TO STAY WHEN YOU PLAY!

ACCOMMODATION	COURSES	BE OUR GUEST PAGE NUMBER	GOLF ON SITE	ALL INCLUSIVE PACKAGE	TUITION AVAILABLE	CART AVAILABLE	ARRANGE TEE OFF TIMES	ADVANCE RESERVATIONS	CLUBS FOR HIRE	TRANSPORT	PREFERENTIAL GREEN FEES	CADDY AVAILABLE
WICKLOW Continued												
Hunter's Hotel	Druid's Glen, European, Blainroe, Powerscourt, Woodenbridge, Delgany	368		•	•	•	•	•	•	•	•	•
Lawless's Hotel	Woodenbridge, Coolattin, European, Blainroe, Arklow, Druid's Glen, Tulfarris	361					•	•	•	•	•	•
Marriott Druids Glen Hotel & Country Club	Druid's Glen, Druid's Heath	367	🏴18	•	•	•	•	•	•	•	•	•
New Valley Inn	Woodenbridge, Arklow	369		•	•	•	•	•	•		•	
Porterhouse Inn (The)	Bray Golf Club, Druid's Glen Golf Club, Glen of the Downs Golf Club, Woodbrook G.C, Powercourt G.C	364		•			•	•	•		•	
Rathsallagh House, Golf and Country Club	Mount Juliet, K Club, Druid's Glen, Powerscourt, Portmarnock and Carton	365	🏴18	•	•	•	•	•	•	•	•	•
Royal Hotel and Leisure Centre	Woodbrook, Charlesland, Delgany, The European Club, Druid's Glen, Dargle View Golf	364					•	•	•	•	•	•
Summerhill House Hotel	Powerscourt, Druid's Glen, Kilternan, Old Conna	366		•	•	•	•	•	•	•	•	•
Tinakilly Country House and Restaurant	European, Druid's Glen, Blainroe, Woodenbridge, Wicklow, Delgany	368		•	•	•	•	•	•	•	•	•
Wingate Tulfarris Hotel & Golf Resort	K Club, Druid's Glen, Citywest, Rathsallagh	362	🏴18	•	•	•	•	•	•	•	•	•
Woodenbridge Hotel	Woodenbridge, Blainroe, Arklow, European Club, Coollattin, Seafield	369		•		•	•	•	•	•	•	•
Woodenbridge Lodge	Woodenbridge GC, Arklow GC, Seafield GC, Coollattin GC, Blainroe GC, European Club	369		•		•	•	•	•	•	•	•

Midlands & Lakelands

ACCOMMODATION	COURSES	BE OUR GUEST PAGE NUMBER	GOLF ON SITE	ALL INCLUSIVE PACKAGE	TUITION AVAILABLE	CART AVAILABLE	ARRANGE TEE OFF TIMES	ADVANCE RESERVATIONS	CLUBS FOR HIRE	TRANSPORT	PREFERENTIAL GREEN FEES	CADDY AVAILABLE
CAVAN												
Breffni Arms Hotel	Cavan, Longford, Carrick on Shannon, Slieve Russell	372		•	•	•	•	•	•	•	•	•
Cavan Crystal Hotel	Co. Cavan Golf Club, Belturbet, Virginia, Clones	374		•	•	•	•	•	•		•	•
Park Hotel	Cavan Golf Club, Headfort Golf Club, Kells	375	🏴9	•			•	•			•	
River Front Hotel (The)	Headfort, Slieve Russell, Park Virginia	376		•	•	•	•	•	•	•	•	•
Slieve Russell Hotel, Golf & Country Club		373	🏴18	•	•	•	•	•	•	•	•	•

🏴18 = Full 18 Hole   🏴9 = 9 Hole   🏴3 = Par 3

ACCOMMODATION	COURSES	BE OUR GUEST PAGE NUMBER	GOLF ON SITE	ALL INCLUSIVE PACKAGE	TUITION AVAILABLE	CART AVAILABLE	ARRANGE TEE OFF TIMES	ADVANCE RESERVATIONS	CLUBS FOR HIRE	TRANSPORT	PREFERENTIAL GREEN FEES	CADDY AVAILABLE
KILDARE												
Barberstown Castle	K Club, Carton House, Rathsallagh House	382						•	•		•	
Courtyard Hotel Leixlip (The)	K Club - 18 x 2 hole course, Carton - 18 x 2 hole course, Hertiage - 18 hole course, Lucan - 18 hole	379	18	•								
Glenroyal Hotel, Leisure Club & Conference Centre	Knockanally, K Club, Killeen, Castlewarden, Bodenstown, Citywest, Carton	380		•				•	•	•		
Hazel Hotel	Cill Dara, Portarlington, Curragh, The Heath, Athy	380		•	•	•	•	•	•	•	•	•
K Club (The)	Luttrellstown Castle, Druid's Glen, Portmarnock Links, Rathsallagh, Hermitage, Heritage	383	18	•	•	•	•	•	•	•	•	•
Setanta House Hotel	Carton House GC, K Club, Citywest GC, Millicent GC	377		•	•	•	•	•	•	•	•	•
Standhouse Hotel Leisure & Conference Centre	Killeen, Cill Dara, The Curragh, Castlewarden, Naas, Craddockstown	378		•	•	•	•	•	•	•	•	•
LAOIS												
Castle Durrow	Abbeyleix, Mountrath, Rathdowney, The Heath Portlaoise, Heritage Killenard	384						•	•		•	
Heritage - Portlaoise (The)	The Heritage@Killenard, The Heath, Abbeyleix	384		•	•	•	•	•	•	•	•	•
Heritage @ Killenard		384	18	•	•	•	•	•	•	•	•	•
LONGFORD												
Annaly Hotel	Longford, Ballyconnell, Glasson, Mullingar, Roscommon	385		•	•	•	•	•	•	•	•	•
Longford Arms Hotel	Longford, Glasson, Ballyconnell, Carrick-on-Shannon, Roscommon, Mullingar	386		•	•	•	•	•	•	•		•
MONAGHAN												
Four Seasons Hotel & Leisure Club	Rossmore, Nuremore, Armagh, Clones, Slieve Russell	386		•	•		•	•			•	•
Hillgrove Hotel	Rossmore GC, Clones GC, Nuremore Country Club, Castle Hume GC, Mannan Castle GC, Co. Armagh GC	387		•	•	•	•	•	•	•	•	•
Nuremore Hotel & Country Club	Nuremore, Baltray, Headfort, Dundalk, Greenore, Royal County Down	386	18	•	•	•	•	•	•	•	•	•

 18 = Full 18 Hole   9 = 9 Hole 3 = Par 3

422

WHERE TO STAY WHEN YOU PLAY!

Accommodation	Courses	BE OUR GUEST PAGE NUMBER	GOLF ON SITE	ALL INCLUSIVE PACKAGE	TUITION AVAILABLE	CART AVAILABLE	ARRANGE TEE OFF TIMES	ADVANCE RESERVATIONS	CLUBS FOR HIRE	TRANSPORT	PREFERENTIAL GREEN FEES	CADDY AVAILABLE
OFFALY												
Bridge House Hotel & Leisure Club	Esker Hills, Tullamore Golf Club both 5 mins away. Virtual Reality Golf Facility on site	389		•	•	•	•	•	•	•	•	•
Brosna Lodge Hotel	Birr, Esker Hills, Tullamore, Glasson, Portumna, Ballinasloe	387		•		•	•	•	•		•	•
County Arms Hotel	Birr, Portumna, Roscrea, Glasson, Tullamore, Esker Hills	388		•	•	•	•	•	•	•	•	•
Moorhill House Hotel	Esker Hills, Tullamore, Daingean, Mount Temple, Birr, Glasson	390		•	•	•	•	•	•	•	•	•
Tullamore Court Hotel Conference & Leisure Centre	Tullamore, Esker Hills, Castle Barna, Mount Temple, Glasson, Birr	391		•	•	•	•	•	•	•	•	•
WESTMEATH												
Bloomfield House Hotel	Mullingar, Glasson, Mount Temple, Esker Hills, Athlone, Tullamore	394		•	•	•	•	•	•	•	•	•
Glasson Golf Hotel and Country Club	Glasson Golf Hotel & Country Club, Athlone Golf Club, Mount Temple Golf Club	392 ▶18	•	•	•	•	•	•	•	•	•	•
Greville Arms Hotel	Mullingar, Glasson, Mount Temple, Tullamore, Longford, Esker Hills	395		•	•	•	•	•	•	•	•	•
Hodson Bay Hotel	Athlone, Glasson, Mount Temple, Ballinasloe, Roscommon, Esker Hills	392 ▶18	•	•	•	•	•	•	•	•	•	•
Mullingar Park Hotel	Mullingar, Glasson, Tullamore, Delvin, Mount Temple, Athlone	396		•	•	•	•	•	•	•	•	•
Newbury Hotel	Mullingar, Mount Temple, Moate, Delvin, Esker Hills, Dangain, Castlebarna	396		•	•	•	•	•	•	•	•	•
Prince of Wales Hotel	Glasson Golf, Mount Temple, Athlone, Esker Hills, Tullamore, Birr	392		•		•	•	•	•	•	•	•
Radisson SAS Hotel	Glasson Golf Club, Athlone Golf Club, Esker Hills, Moate Golf Club, Mullingar GC, Tullamore GC	393		•			•	•			•	

▶18 = Full 18 Hole   ▶9 = 9 Hole   ▶3 = Par 3

THE BANTER IS FLOWING
THE GUINNESS IS GREAT

IRELAND FOR
FISHING
HOTELS & GUESTHOUSES

Ireland is accepted as being the outstanding angling holiday resort in Europe. Whether you are a competition angler, a serious specimen hunter, or just fishing while on holiday, you are sure to enjoy yourself here. With over 14,000km of rivers feeding over 4,000 lakes and with no part of Ireland over 112km from sea. Ireland can, in truth, be called an angler's dream.

So come on and get hooked!

ANGLING FOR A PLACE TO STAY!

We invite you to sample the fishing, the countryside and the friendship of the Irish people and then to stay in some of Ireland's most charming accommodation. We have listed a range of hotels and guesthouses which are either situated with or near angling facilities. Your host will assist you in arranging your angling itinerary. A full description of the hotels and guesthouses can be had by looking up the appropriate page number. Premises are listed in alphabetical order in each county.

ACCOMMODATION	TYPES OF FISH	BE OUR GUEST PAGE NUMBER	COARSE FISHING	GAME FISHING	SEA FISHING	BAIT AND TACKLE	BOATS FOR HIRE	DRYING ROOM	PACKED LUNCHES	GILLIE	TACKLE ROOM	FREEZER	PERMITS REQUIRED
South East													
CARLOW													
Seven Oaks Hotel	Bream, Perch, Roach, Pike, Eel, Salmon, Trout	24	•	•		•		•	•			•	•
KILKENNY													
Butler House	Brown Trout, Salmon	27		•		•		•	•	•	•	•	•
Mount Juliet Conrad	Salmon, Trout	34		•		•		•	•	•	•	•	
TIPPERARY SOUTH													
Cahir House Hotel	Perch, Pike, Trout, Salmon	35	•	•		•		•	•	•		•	•
Cashel Palace Hotel	Perch, Salmon, Brown Trout, Grilse	37	•	•		•		•	•	•	•	•	•
WEXFORD													
Millrace Hotel (The)	Bass, Small Wild Brown Trout, Sea Trout, Black Pennell	57	•	•	•		•		•				•
Quay House	Cod, Ling, Tope, Bass, Blue Shark	62			•	•	•		•			•	•
South West													
CORK													
Aherne's Townhouse & Seafood Restaurant	Trout, Salmon, Monkfish, Ling, Cod, Pollock, Mackerel, Shark	107	•	•		•		•	•	•			•
Blue Haven Hotel and Restaurant	Salmon, Sea Trout, Brown Trout, Ling, Blue Shark, Sea Bass, Conger, Cod	97	•	•	•	•		•			•	•	•
Celtic Ross Hotel Conference & Leisure Centre	Bream, Roach, Tench, Trout, Salmon, Cod, Shark, Wrasse, Flat Fish	104	•	•	•	•		•	•		•	•	•
Commodore Hotel	Ling, Cod, Pollock, Conger, Blue Shark	82			•	•	•	•				•	

ANGLING FOR A PLACE TO STAY!

ACCOMMODATION	TYPES OF FISH	BE OUR GUEST PAGE NUMBER	COARSE FISHING	GAME FISHING	SEA FISHING	BAIT AND TACKLE	BOATS FOR HIRE	DRYING ROOM	PACKED LUNCHES	GILLIE	TACKLE ROOM	FREEZER	PERMITS REQUIRED
ROSCOMMON Continued													
Whitehouse Hotel	Pike, Perch, Rudd, Bream, Tench, Brown Trout	241	•	•					•	•	•	•	•

North West

ACCOMMODATION	TYPES OF FISH												
DONEGAL													
Arnolds Hotel	Brown Trout, Salmon, Sea Trout, Mackerel, Pollock, Haddock, Cod, Ling	252		•	•		•	•	•	•	•	•	•
Bay View Hotel & Leisure Centre	Salmon, Sea Trout, Brown Trout, Tuna, Shark, Pollock, Cod, Ling	254	•	•	•	•	•	•	•	•		•	•
Dorrians Imperial Hotel	Bream, Pike, Eel, Trout, Salmon, Cod, Sea Trout, Sole	248	•	•	•		•	•	•	•		•	•
Downings Bay Hotel	Pollock, Mackerel, Tuna, Ling, Skate, Cod, Haddock	255		•		•							
Great Northern Hotel	Pike, Perch, Salmon, Trout, Pollock, Cod, Ling, Plaice, Shark, Sole	250	•	•	•	•	•	•	•	•		•	•
Ostan Na Tra (Beach Hotel)	Shark, Cod, Haddock, Ling, Conger, Gurnard, Pollock	252		•	•	•			•			•	
Silver Tassie Hotel	Brown Trout, Sea Trout, Salmon, Shark, Tope, Ling, Mackerel	257		•	•	•		•		•		•	•
LEITRIM													
Abbey Manor Hotel	Pike, Bream, Perch, Salmon, Trout	261	•	•			•	•		•		•	•
Ramada Hotel & Suites at Lough Allen	Pike, Bream, Perch, Rudd, Tench, Hybrids	262	•			•	•	•		•			•

North

ACCOMMODATION	TYPES OF FISH												
DOWN													
Royal Hotel	Cod, Skate, Mackerel, Haddock, Whiting	282			•	•	•		•			•	

Dublin & East Coast

ACCOMMODATION	TYPES OF FISH												
MEATH													
Castle Arch Hotel (Formerly Wellington Court)	Trout, Salmon	358		•					•			•	•

ANGLING FOR A PLACE TO STAY!

Accommodation	Types of Fish	Be Our Guest Page Number	Coarse Fishing	Game Fishing	Sea Fishing	Bait and Tackle	Boats for Hire	Drying Room	Packed Lunches	Gillie	Tackle Room	Freezer	Permits Required
WICKLOW													
Arklow Bay Conference and Leisure Hotel	Trout	358		•		•			•				
Glendalough Hotel	Trout	366		•		•	•	•	•				
Lawless's Hotel	Wild Brown Trout, Rainbow Trout, Codling, Dab, Bass, Dogfish	361		•	•	•	•		•			•	•
Porterhouse Inn (The)	Pike, Perch, Salmon, Sea Trout, Brown Trout, Cod, Mackerel, Sea Bass, Pollock	364	•	•	•	•			•			•	•
Royal Hotel and Leisure Centre	Trout, Salmon, Cod, Plaice, Pollock	364		•	•	•	•		•			•	•
Midlands & Lakelands													
CAVAN													
Breffni Arms Hotel	Bream, Tench, Pike, Roach, Hybrids, Trout	372	•	•		•	•	•	•			•	•
Lakeside Manor Hotel	Bream, Hybrids, Roach, Perch, Pike, Trout	375	•	•		•	•	•	•			•	•
River Front Hotel (The)	Bream, Perch, Hybrid	376	•			•	•		•			•	•
KILDARE													
Hazel Hotel	Pike, Rudd, Roach, Eel, Tench, Perch, Salmon, Trout	380	•	•		•			•			•	•
K Club (The)	Salmon, Trout, Carp, Tench, Bream, Rudd	383	•	•		•	•	•	•	•	•	•	
LAOIS													
Heritage - Portlaoise (The)	Trout, Salmon	384		•		•	•		•		•	•	•
OFFALY													
Brosna Lodge Hotel	Bream, Tench, Rudd, Roach, Perch, Brown Trout, Pike, Salmon	387	•	•		•	•	•	•	•	•	•	•
Moorhill House Hotel	Bream, Roach, Perch, Brown Trout, Pike	390	•			•	•	•	•			•	

SELECT A VENUE FOR YOUR AGENDA

ACCOMMODATION	CONTACT PERSON	BE OUR GUEST PAGE NUMBER	500+	400+	300+	200+	100+	50+	8+	BLACK OUT FACILITIES	AIR CONDITIONING	INTERPRETING EQUIPMENT	AUDIO VISUAL EQUIPMENT
WATERFORD													
Clonea Strand Hotel, Golf & Leisure	Mark Knowles or Ann McGrath	45			2	2	3	4	5	•	•	H	H
Dooley's Hotel	Margaret Darrer	52		1	1	2	1	3		•	•	H	O
Faithlegg House Hotel and Golf Club	Suzanne Molloy	48			1		1	3		•	•	H	O
Grand Hotel	Annie Friel	49			1	1	1	1		•	•	H	O
Granville Hotel	Richard Hurley	52				1	2	1		•		H	H
Lawlors Hotel	Frank Treyvaud & Lucy McEnery	45		1		2	3	4	5	•	•	H	O
McEniff Ard Ri Hotel	Eileen Barry	53	1			2	2	2		•	•	H	H
Tower Hotel & Leisure Centre	Catherina Hurley	55	1			3	1	2		•	•		H
WEXFORD													
Ashdown Park Hotel Conference & Leisure Centre	Louise Ryan	61	1				1	2		•	•	H	O
Millrace Hotel (The)	Jean O'Connell	57		1	1	1		2		•	•	O	O
Newbay Country House	Fiona Giess	67					1	1	2				
Rosslare Great Southern Hotel	Colin Ahern	66				1		1		•	•	H	H
Talbot Hotel Conference and Leisure Centre	Niamh Lambert	68			1	1	2	3	4	•	•	H	O
South West													
CORK													
Actons Hotel	Anne Marie Cross	96		1				2		•	•	H	H
Aherne's Townhouse & Seafood Restaurant	John Fitzgibbon	107						2		•	•	H	H
Ambassador Hotel	Sile Ni Dhonaile / Dudley Fitzell	84			1	1	2	1		•	•		O

H = Can Arrange Hire   O = Available On Premises

SELECT A VENUE FOR YOUR AGENDA

ACCOMMODATION — CONTACT PERSON

CORK Continued

Accommodation	Contact Person	Be Our Guest Page Number	Number of Rooms of Various Seating Capacities							Black Out Facilities	Air Conditioning	Interpreting Equipment	Audio Visual Equipment
			500+	400+	300+	200+	100+	50+	50-				
Ballymaloe House	Natasha Harty	105						2					H
Blarney Castle Hotel	Una Forrest	76					1	1	1			H	H
Blarney Park Hotel and Leisure Centre	Josephine Noonan	77				1		3	2	•	•	H	H
Celtic Ross Hotel Conference & Leisure Centre	David Harney	104				1		1	1	•	•	H	H
Commodore Hotel	Robert Fitzpatrick	82			1				1			H	O
Commons Inn	Ashley Colson	86			1			1	3	•	•		O
Glengarriff Eccles Hotel	Geraldine Owens	95			1			1	1	•	•	H	H
Great Southern Hotel	Rose O'Donovan	83				1			5	•	•	H	O
Gresham Metropole	Fiona Keohane	87	1	1	1	2	2	6	11	•	•	H	H
Hibernian Hotel and Leisure Centre	Catherine Gyves	102				1		2	4	•			O
Hotel Isaacs	Paula Lynch	88							2	•	•	H	H
Imperial Hotel	Lorna Murphy	88				1	2	5	1	•	•	H	H
Inchydoney Island Lodge & Spa	Peter Lehoybe	80			1				4	•	•	H	O
Jurys Cork Hotel	Janice Casey	89	1	1	1	2	2	4	6	•		H	H
Maryborough House Hotel	Mary Bernard	91			1	1	2	2	5	•	•	H	O
Midleton Park Hotel & Spa	Ruth Vaughan	103			1		1		3	•		H	H
Rochestown Park Hotel	Liam Lally/Jim Casey	92	2	2	2	2	4	9	9	•	•	H	H
Silver Springs Moran Hotel	Sales & Conference Co-ordinator	93	2		4	4	7	11	6	•	•	H	H
Springfort Hall Hotel	Mags Brazzill	102			1			1	3			H	O

H = Can Arrange Hire   O = Available On Premises

SELECT A VENUE FOR YOUR AGENDA

ACCOMMODATION   CONTACT PERSON

Accommodation	Contact Person	Page Number	500+	400+	300+	200+	100+	50+	30+	Black Out Facilities	Air Conditioning	Interpreting Equipment	Audio Visual Equipment
CORK Continued													
Trident Hotel	Hal McElroy/Una Wren	100				1			5	•	•	H	O
Walter Raleigh Hotel	Therese Donnelly	108			1	1	1	1	2	•	•	H	H
Westlodge Hotel	Eileen M. O'Shea	76			1	1	1	1	1	•	•	H	H
KERRY													
Abbey Gate Hotel	Patrick Dillon	150		1	1	1	2	3	3	•	•	H	O
Aghadoe Heights Hotel & Spa	Emma Phillips	128					1		2	•	•		H
Brandon Hotel Conference and Leisure Centre	Aine Brosnan	152	1	1	2	3	4	7	8	•	•	H	O
Brehon (The)	Anthony Palmer	129					1		4	•	•	H	H
Castlerosse Hotel & Leisure Centre	Michael O'Sullivan	131					1		1	•		H	H
Dingle Skellig Hotel	Karen Byrnes	117					1		2	•	•	H	O
Dromhall Hotel	Bernadette Randles	132			1	1	1	1	1	•	•	H	H
Gleneagle Hotel	Cara Fuller	136	2	2	3	3	4	4	4	•	•	H	O
Grand Hotel	Eileen Egan	154				1	1	6	6	•	•	H	H
Hotel Dunloe Castle	Suzanne Ennis	137				1	2	2	2			H	H
Hotel Europe	Suzanne Ennis	137		1	1	1	3	2			•	O	H
Killarney Avenue Hotel	Mary Hartnett	139		1	1	1	1			•	•	H	O
Killarney Great Southern Hotel	Emer Smyth	139	1			1		2	2	•	•	H	H
Killarney Park Hotel	Niamh O'Shea / Marie Carmody	141					1	1	3	•	•	H	O
Killarney Plaza Hotel & Spa	Mary Hartnett	141					1		2	•	•		O

NUMBER OF ROOMS OF VARIOUS SEATING CAPACITIES

H = Can Arrange Hire   O = Available On Premises

SELECT A VENUE FOR YOUR AGENDA

Accommodation	Contact Person	Be Our Guest Page Number	500+	400+	300+	200+	100+	50+	50-	Black Out Facilities	Air Conditioning	Interpreting Equipment	Audio Visual Equipment
KERRY Continued													
Killarney Royal	Nicola Duggan	141						1			•	H	H
Lake Hotel	Tony Huggard/Marie O'Shea/Majella Steinbeck	142						1	2		•	H	O
Manor West Hotel	James Feeney	154			1				2	•	•	H	H
Meadowlands Hotel	Mairead Harnett	154				1	2	1	2	•	•	H	H
Muckross Park Hotel & Garden Suites	Louise O' Flaherty/Bryan O' Sullivan	144			1			4		•	•	H	H
Parknasilla Great Southern Hotel	Pat Cussen	149						1	1	•		H	H
Randles Court Clarion Hotel	Tom Randles	145						1		•	•	H	O
Sheen Falls Lodge	Aoife Colligan	126					1	1	2	•	•	H	O

Shannon

Accommodation	Contact Person	Be Our Guest Page Number	500+	400+	300+	200+	100+	50+	50-	Black Out Facilities	Air Conditioning	Interpreting Equipment	Audio Visual Equipment
CLARE													
Bunratty Castle Hotel	Kathleen McLoughlin	162					1	1	2	•	•	H	H
Falls Hotel	Therese O'Connor	169		1	1	1		2	4			H	O
Fitzpatrick Bunratty	Kevin Crampsie	163	1							•	•	H	H
Great Southern Hotel	Louise O'Hara	180				1			3	•	•	H	O
Kilkee Bay Hotel	Stephanie Smyth	170					1	1		•	•	H	H
Kincora Hall Hotel	Matt Sherlock	172					1				•	H	O
Mountshannon Hotel	Pauline Madden	179					1				•	H	H
Old Ground Hotel	Phil Spellissy	168					1	1	1	•	•	H	O
Temple Gate Hotel	Paul Madden	168				1	1	2	1	•	•	H	O

H = Can Arrange Hire   O = Available On Premises

SELECT A VENUE FOR YOUR AGENDA

Accommodation	Contact Person	Be Our Guest Page Number	500+	400+	300+	200+	100+	50+	50-	Black Out Facilities	Air Conditioning	Interpreting Equipment	Audio Visual Equipment
LIMERICK													
Adare Manor Hotel & Golf Resort	Yvette Kennedy	181			1	1	1	1		•		H	O
Castletroy Park Hotel	Ursula Cullen	183	1	2	2	2	2	9		•	•	H	O
Clarion Hotel Limerick	Veronica Edwards	184				1	2	9		•	•	H	H
Fitzgeralds Woodlands House Hotel, Health and Leisure Spa	David or Michael	182	1	1	1	2	3	3		•	•	H	H
Greenhills Hotel Conference/Leisure	Daphne Greene	185	1	1	1	1	2	3	4	•	•	H	O
Old Quarter Lodge	Carole Kelly	186						1					H
Ramada Kilmurry	Ciara Hogan	187		1		1	2	3			•	H	
Rathkeale House Hotel	Gerry O'Connor	189		1		1		1		•	•	H	O
Woodfield House Hotel	Ken or Majella	188					1	1		•	•		O
TIPPERARY NORTH													
Abbey Court Hotel and Trinity Leisure Club	Clodagh McDonnell	189		1	1	1	2	6	4		•	H	H
Anner Hotel & Leisure Centre	Joan Brett-Moloney	191		1	1	1	2	3			•	H	O
Racket Hall Country House Golf & Conference Hotel	Edel Holland	190			1	1	2	4	3	•	•	H	O
Templemore Arms Hotel	Julie Tarrant	190				1		1	1		•		H

West

GALWAY													
Anglers Rest Hotel	Frank Heneghan	219					1	1		•	•	H	H
Connemara Coast Hotel	Paul O'Meara/Michelle Cremin	203		1	1	2	2	5	8	•		H	O
Doonmore Hotel	Aileen Murray	220						2					

H = Can Arrange Hire   O – Available On Premises   441

SELECT A VENUE FOR YOUR AGENDA

ACCOMMODATION	CONTACT PERSON	BE OUR GUEST PAGE NUMBER	500+	400+	300+	200+	100+	50+	5+	BLACK OUT FACILITIES	AIR CONDITIONING	INTERPRETING EQUIPMENT	AUDIO VISUAL EQUIPMENT
GALWAY Continued													
Galway Bay Hotel, Conference & Leisure Centre	Virginia Connolly	209	1	1	2	2	2	5	5	•	•	H	O
Galway Great Southern Hotel	Tina Kelly	210				1	1	3		•	•	H	O
Galway Radisson SAS Hotel	Fiona Keys	210	1				3	8		•	•	H	O
Glenlo Abbey Hotel	Brian Bourke	211					1	2	9	•	•	H	H
Lady Gregory Hotel	Yvonne McNamara	218			1			2		•	•	H	O
Meadow Court Hotel	Tom Corbett Jnr	222			1			1		•	•		H
Oranmore Lodge Hotel, Conference & Leisure Centre	Mary O'Higgins	223			1		1	1	1	•	•	H	H
Peacockes Hotel & Complex	Eimear Killian	222	1				1	1		•	•	H	O
Salthill Court Hotel	Pauline Griffin	215					1	1		•	•	O	O
Shannon Oaks Hotel & Country Club	Mary Broder	226	1				1	1	2	•	•	H	O
Victoria Hotel	Reception	216						1			•	H	H
Westwood House Hotel	Declan Curtis	218			1	1	1	3	3	•	•	H	O
MAYO													
Atlantic Coast Hotel	Suzanne O'Brien	237					1		3	•	•	H	O
Castlecourt Hotel Conference and Leisure Centre	Ciara Joyce	238	1	1	1	2	2	3	3	•	•	H	O
Downhill House Hotel	Kay Devine / Rachael Moylett	231		1	1	1	1	2	4		•	H	O
Hotel Westport, Conference & Leisure Centre	Gerry Walshe/Ruth Farrell/Rhona Chambers	238		1			1	3	1	•	•	H	O
Knock House Hotel	Brian Crowley	235					1	1	1				O
Knockranny House Hotel	Patricia Crowley/Fergal Harte	239	1	1	1	1	2	3	3	•	•	H	O

H = Can Arrange Hire   O = Available On Premises

SELECT A VENUE FOR YOUR AGENDA

ACCOMMODATION	CONTACT PERSON	BE OUR GUEST PAGE NUMBER	500+	400+	300+	200+	100+	50+	8+	BLACK OUT FACILITIES	AIR CONDITIONING	INTERPRETING EQUIPMENT	AUDIO VISUAL EQUIPMENT
MAYO Continued													
Ostan Oilean Acla	Michael McLoughlin	230			1			1	1	•	•	0	0
Pontoon Bridge Hotel	Breta Geary / Noel Cafferkey	236				1	1	1	2			H	H
Teach Iorrais	Sean Gaughan	234				2				•	•	H	H
TF Royal Hotel & Theatre	Michelle O'Brien	233	1	1	2	2	3	3	4	•	•	H	0
Westport Woods Hotel & Leisure Centre	Margaret Mulchrone	240		1	1	1	2	1	2	•	•	H	H
Wyatt Hotel	Chris McGauley	241		1				2	3	•	•		0
ROSCOMMON													
Abbey Hotel, Conference and Leisure Centre	Ann Mannion	242				2		1	3	•			H
O'Gara's Royal Hotel	Larry O'Gara	242	1	1	1	1	1	2	1	•	•		0

North West

ACCOMMODATION	CONTACT PERSON	BE OUR GUEST PAGE NUMBER	500+	400+	300+	200+	100+	50+	8+	BLACK OUT FACILITIES	AIR CONDITIONING	INTERPRETING EQUIPMENT	AUDIO VISUAL EQUIPMENT
DONEGAL													
Castle Grove Country House Hotel	Mary Sweeney	254							1				H
Dorrians Imperial Hotel	Mary Dorrian	248				1		1	1	•	•		H
Downings Bay Hotel	Eileen Rock	255			1		1	1			•	H	0
Great Northern Hotel	Philip McGlynn	250	1	1	1	1	1	1	1	•	•	H	0
Holiday Inn Letterkenny Conference & Leisure Centre	Roisin McGuinness	256	1	2				1	2	•	•	H	H
Mill Park Hotel, Conference Centre & Leisure Club	Karen Timoney/Mary McGowan	251			1				4		•	H	0
Mount Errigal Hotel, Conference & Leisure Centre	Marie Di Bartolo	256	2	2	1	1	1	2	4	•	•	H	H
Radisson SAS Hotel	Emer Sweeney	257		1				1	4	•	•	H	0

H = Can Arrange Hire   0 = Available On Premises   443

SELECT A VENUE FOR YOUR AGENDA

Accommodation	Contact Person	Be Our Guest Page Number	500+	400+	300+	200+	100+	50+	5-	Black Out Facilities	Air Conditioning	Interpreting Equipment	Audio Visual Equipment
DONEGAL Continued													
Sandhouse Hotel	Paul Diver	259						1	3	•	•	H	H
Silver Tassie Hotel	Rose Blaney / Siobhan Barrett	257			1	1	1	2	3	•			O
LEITRIM													
Abbey Manor Hotel	Bridie Gallagher	261				1	1	1	2	•	•	H	O
Bush Hotel	Joseph Dolan	261			1		2	3	5	•	•	H	O
Ramada Hotel & Suites at Lough Allen	G. Aldwell	262					1		1	•	•	H	
Shannon Key West Hotel	Ann Marie Frisby	262			1				1	•	•		O
SLIGO													
Radisson SAS Hotel Sligo	Emma Nevin	265	1	1	1	3	3	5	11	•	•	H	O
Sligo's Southern Hotel & Leisure Centre	Kevin McGlynn/Jackie McLoughlin	266			1	1	1	2	4			H	H
Yeats Country Hotel and Leisure Club	Breda O'Dwyer	264					1	2	3			H	H
North													
ANTRIM													
Ballymac	Cathy Muldoon	272				1			1	•			O
Bayview Hotel	Mary O'Neill	270						1	1	•	•	H	H
Comfort Hotel Portrush	Mary O'Neill	271						1	1	•	•	H	H
Londonderry Arms Hotel	Frank O'Neill	271					1	2	2	•		H	H
ARMAGH													
Armagh City Hotel	Gary Hynes	273	2	2	2	4	4	5	10	•	•	H	O

444

H = Can Arrange Hire   O = Available On Premises

SELECT A VENUE FOR YOUR AGENDA

ACCOMMODATION	CONTACT PERSON	BE OUR GUEST PAGE NUMBER	500+	400+	300+	200+	100+	50+	30+	BLACK OUT FACILITIES	AIR CONDITIONING	INTERPRETING EQUIPMENT	AUDIO VISUAL EQUIPMENT
BELFAST													
Dukes Hotel	Christine Cardwell	275					1	2	3	•	•	H	H
Dunadry Hotel and Country Club	Sheree Davis	276			1	1	1	3	4	•	•		O
Jurys Inn Belfast	Susan Black	276							6	•	•		H
La Mon Hotel & Country Club	Duty Manager	277	1	1	1	3	4	5	5	•	•		H
Park Avenue Hotel	Angela Reid	277	1	1	1	3	4	8	11	•	•	H	O
Ramada Belfast	Louise Donnelly	278	1			1	1	4	7		•	H	O
Wellington Park Hotel	Gerardo Jimenez	278		1	1	2	3	4	9	•	•	H	O
DERRY													
City Hotel	Colette Brennan	280		1	1	1					•	H	H
Tower Hotel Derry	Elaine Ferguson	281				1			3	•	•	H	H
DOWN													
Burrendale Hotel and Country Club	Fiona O'Hare	283					1	1	6	•	•	H	O
Royal Hotel	Glenda Feeney	282					1		2	•			O
Dublin & East Coast													
DUBLIN													
Aberdeen Lodge	Pat Halpin	295							1	•	•	H	O
Academy Hotel	Peter Collins	295							5	•	•	H	O
Alexander Hotel	Sharon Joyce	296		1	1	2	4	5	1	•	•	H	O
Arlington Hotel	Ruth McGann	299						1	1		•	H	H

H = Can Arrange Hire   O = Available On Premises   445

SELECT A VENUE FOR YOUR AGENDA

Accommodation	Contact Person	Be Our Guest Page Number	Number of Rooms of Various Seating Capacities							Black Out Facilities	Air Conditioning	Interpreting Equipment	Audio Visual Equipment
			500+	400+	300+	200+	100+	50+	5+				
DUBLIN Continued													
Ashling Hotel	Pauline or Eugene	299				1	1	1	5	•	•	H	H
Beresford Hall	Sarah O'Sullivan	301						1		•	•	H	H
Brooks Hotel	Paul O'Neill	303							3	•	•	H	H
Burlington (The)	Michelle Spain	303	1	1	3	4	7	10	14	•	•	H	H
Buswells Hotel	Julie McCole	303						1	5	•	•	H	O
Camden Court Hotel	Denise Corboy	304					1	1	3				H
Carnegie Court Hotel	Teresa Long	348					1	1	2	•	•	H	O
Cassidys Hotel	Carol/Maeve	304						1	3	•	•		H
Castleknock Hotel and Country Club	Conference and Banqueting Manager	305	1	1	1	2	4	4	6	•	•	H	O
Chief O'Neill's Hotel	Triona Thornton	306				1	2	3	2	•	•	H	H
Citywest Hotel & Golf Resort	Fiona Killilea	346	4	5	5	9	12	16	9	•	•	H	H
Clarence Hotel	Sean McDonald	307						1		•	•	H	H
Clarion Hotel Dublin IFSC	Jane Hurley	307					2	2	7	•	•		O
Clontarf Castle Hotel	Valerie Burns	308		1			3	2	1	•	•	H	H
Conrad Dublin	Bernadette McKeogh	309				1	1	4	9	•	•	H	H
Crowne Plaza, Dublin Airport	Judith Graham	292				1			12	•	•	H	H
Davenport Hotel	Karen O'Sullivan	310			1	2	2	2	7	•	•	H	O
Dublin Hilton Airport	David Webster	292	1			2		1	8	•	•	H	H
Finnstown Country House Hotel	Jenny Holmes	343			1	1	1	2	4	•		H	O

446

H = Can Arrange Hire   O = Available On Premises

SELECT A VENUE FOR YOUR AGENDA

ACCOMMODATION	CONTACT PERSON	BE OUR GUEST PAGE NUMBER	NUMBER OF ROOMS OF VARIOUS SEATING CAPACITIES							BLACK OUT FACILITIES	AIR CONDITIONING	INTERPRETING EQUIPMENT	AUDIO VISUAL EQUIPMENT
			500+	400+	300+	200+	100+	50+	5+				
DUBLIN Continued													
Fitzpatrick Castle Dublin	Brenda Killeen	342			1	1		3	6	•	•	H	O
Four Seasons Hotel Dublin	Robin Stewart	313	1			1		3	1	•	•	H	H
Georgian Hotel	Hazel Boyle	314							3			H	H
Grand Hotel	Bernadette Joyce	344		1		1	1	6	6	•	•	H	O
Great Southern Hotel	Louise Maguire	293			1	1	3		8	•	•	H	O
Gresham (The)	Ian Craig	316			1	2	3	8	22	•	•	H	H
Herbert Park Hotel	Sorcha Moore	318					2	1	2	•	•	H	H
Holiday Inn Dublin City Centre	Helena Sands	318		1	1	1	2	5	6	•	•	H	O
Hotel Isaacs	Evelyn Hannigan	318						1	4	•		H	H
IMI Residence	Adrian Hughes	319			1	2	3	10	30	•	•	O	O
Jurys Ballsbridge Hotel	Angela Cody	320	1			1	2	4	12	•	•	H	H
Jurys Inn Parnell Street	Mark Roche Garland	321							3	•			H
Jurys Montrose Hotel	Conor O'Kane	321					2		6			H	H
Kingston Hotel	Marge Daly	341					1	1	1	•	•	H	H
Lucan Spa Hotel	Betty Dolan	343	1	1	1	1	1	1	2	•	•		O
Marine Hotel	Louise O'Reilly	347					1		6	•	•	H	H
McEniff Grand Canal Hotel	Gillian Nevin	325					1	1	3	•	•	H	H
McEniff Skylon Hotel	Andrew Hyland	325						1	1	•	•		H
Mercer Hotel	Carien Veldman	326					1				•	H	H

H = Can Arrange Hire   O = Available On Premises   447

SELECT A VENUE FOR YOUR AGENDA

Accommodation	Contact Person	Be Our Guest Page Number	500+	400+	300+	200+	100+	50+	8+	Black Out Facilities	Air Conditioning	Interpreting Equipment	Audio Visual Equipment
DUBLIN Continued													
Merrion Hall	Pat Halpin	326							2	•	•	H	H
Mont Clare Hotel	Claire Walker	327					1	2	9	•	•	H	H
North Star Hotel	Lynn Graham	328					1	1	1	•	•	H	H
Ormond Quay Hotel	Robert McClenaghan	329						1	3	•	•	H	H
Portmarnock Hotel & Golf Links	Nicola Cassidy	345				1	2	2	3	•	•	H	H
Radisson SAS St Helen's Hotel	Jennifer Patton	290				1		4	2			H	H
Red Cow Moran Hotel	Karen Moran	333	1	1	1	2	5	10	16	•	•	H	H
Regency Airport Hotel	Catherine McGettigan	333			2			1	3	•	•	H	O
Roganstown Golf & Country Club	Lynda Reilly	348				1			8	•	•	H	
Shelbourne Hotel (The)	Gwen McGauley	335		1			2	2	6	•		H	H
Stephen's Green Hotel	Tina Ward	336							6	•	•	H	O
Stillorgan Park Hotel	Cailin Keaney	290	1	1	1	2	5	7	12	•	•	H	O
Tara Towers Hotel	Caitriona Power	336					1					H	H
Temple Bar Hotel	Taryn Alcala	337						1	4	•		H	H
Waterside Hotel	Phillip O'Neill	292				1	1	1	3		•	H	H
West County Hotel	Aine Grogan	339					1	1	2	•	•	H	O
Westin Dublin	Hilary O'Connor	340				1	2	2	8	•	•	H	O
LOUTH													
Boyne Valley Hotel & Country Club	Noel Comer	350	2	2	1	2	1	2	4	•	•	H	H

H = Can Arrange Hire   O = Available On Premises

SELECT A VENUE FOR YOUR AGENDA

ACCOMMODATION	CONTACT PERSON	BE OUR GUEST PAGE NUMBER	500+	400+	300+	200+	100+	50+	3+	BLACK OUT FACILITIES	AIR CONDITIONING	INTERPRETING EQUIPMENT	AUDIO VISUAL EQUIPMENT
LOUTH Continued													
Fairways Hotel & Conference Centre	Killian O'Grady/Dara McCarthy	353	1	1	2	2	2	5	10	•	•	H	O
Four Seasons Hotel & Leisure Club Carlingford	Banqueting Manager	349			1	1	2	5	5		•	H	O
Hotel Imperial	Conference Co-Ordinator	353					1	2	2	•			O
McKevitt's Village Hotel	Terry and Kay McKevitt	350					1		1	•			H
Park Hotel	Harry O'Hare	353			1				1				O
MEATH													
Ardboyne Hotel	Richard Meehan	357			1		2	3	4	•	•	H	O
Conyngham Arms Hotel	Gallina Koeva	358				1			1	•	•	H	H
Headfort Arms Hotel	Olivia Duff	356		1	1	1	1	3	4		•	H	O
Marriott Johnstown House Enfield	Patsy Mooney	356	1	1	2	2	2	2	13	•	•	H	O
Neptune Beach Hotel & Leisure Club	Philip Lee	355				1			2	•		H	O
Newgrange Hotel	Lorraine Cunningham	357	1			2	1	1	3	•	•	H	O
Station House Hotel	Chris Slattery/Denise Slattery	356		1		1	1	1	1	•	•	H	O
WICKLOW													
Arklow Bay Conference and Leisure Hotel	Sabine Luedke	358	1	1	1	2	2	4	5	•	•	H	O
Glendalough Hotel	Cormac O'Sullivan	366					1		2	•	•	H	O
Glenview Hotel	Tara Costello	366				1	1	2	2	•	•	H	O
Hunter's Hotel	Tom Gelletlie	368							3	•		H	H
Lawless's Hotel	Seoirse or Maeve O'Toole	361				1			1	•		H	O

H = Can Arrange Hire   O = Available On Premises

SELECT A VENUE FOR YOUR AGENDA

Accommodation	Contact Person	Be Our Guest Page Number	500+	400+	300+	200+	100+	50+	8-	Black Out Facilities	Air Conditioning	Interpreting Equipment	Audio Visual Equipment
WICKLOW Continued													
Marriott Druids Glen Hotel & Country Club	Aileen Strachan	367		1		2	1		7	•	•	H	O
Rathsallagh House, Golf and Country Club	Catherine Lawlor	365				1			4	•		H	O
Royal Hotel and Leisure Centre	Stephanie Curran / Anna Villota	364			1	1	1		1	•	•	H	O
Tinakilly Country House and Restaurant	Brenda Gilmore	368					1		3	•	•	H	O
Wingate Tulfarris Hotel & Golf Resort	Lillian Mahon	362					1	2	2	•		H	O
Midlands & Lakelands													
CAVAN													
Breffni Arms Hotel	Eamon Gray	372	1							•	•		O
Cavan Crystal Hotel	Lorraine Meegan	374	1	2	2	2	2	6	8	•	•	H	O
Hotel Kilmore	Deborah Egan	374	1			2	3	3	4	•	•	H	O
Lakeside Manor Hotel	Meabh Brady or Tracy Clarke	375		1		1		1	2	•	•		O
Park Hotel	Debbie Benn	375						2	2	•	•	H	O
River Front Hotel (The)	David Cahill	376			2	1	1	1	3	•	•	H	O
Slieve Russell Hotel, Golf & Country Club	Anne Barnes	373	2	2	3	4	4	4	7	•	•	H	O
KILDARE													
Barberstown Castle	Gretchen Ridgeway	382				1	1	1	2	•	•	H	O
Clanard Court Hotel	Diane Lynch	376		1		1	1		3	•	•	H	O
Courtyard Hotel Leixlip (The)	Mark O'Sullivan	379					2	4		•	•	O	O
Glenroyal Hotel, Leisure Club & Conference Centre	Clare Lyons	380	1	2	4	4	6	6	12	•	•	H	O

H = Can Arrange Hire   O = Available On Premises

LET US PAMPER YOU WHILE YOU STAY!

Accommodation	Types of Treatment	Types of Facilities	Be Our Guest Page Number	No. of Treatments	No. of Treatment Rooms
KERRY Continued					
Killarney Plaza Hotel & Spa Molton Brown Spa	Spring, Summer, Autumn and Winter Facial and Massage, Cloud Walking, Palm Pressure, Earth, Fire and Water Serial, Gulfstream Pool	Gulfstream Pool, Sauna, Steamroom, Jacuzzi	141	20	8
Manor West Hotel Hotel opening May 2005	Selection of treatments available	Floatation Tank, Hot Tubs, Vichy Shower, Razul, Laconium, Balneotheraphy Baths, Gym, Leisure Pool, Health Club	154	20	7
Park Hotel Kenmare SAMAS	Full Spa Facilities with Treatments - Ayurvedic, Deep Tissue, Aromatherapy etc.	Laconium, Rock Sauna, Steam, Tropical Mist Showers, Vitality Pool, Relaxation Rooms, Tai Chi	125	78	8
Parknasilla Great Southern Hotel	Massage - 1 hour & 1/2 hour, Reflexology - 45 minutes, Aromatherapy - 1 hour, Hydrotherapy Baths	Outdoor Canadian Hot Tub, Hydrotherapy Baths, Jacuzzi, Sauna, Steamroom, Indoor Heated Swimming Pool, Organised Walks	149	10	2
Sheen Falls Lodge The Sheen Spa	Facial, Body Wrap, Manicure, Massage, Aromastone, Pedicure, Indian Head Massage, Reiki, Body Detox Wrap, Seaweed Wrap	Jacuzzi, Sauna, Steamroom, Swimming Pool, Gymnasium, Sun Deck, Tennis, Jogging Trail	126	30	3

Shannon

CLARE					
Thomond Guesthouse & Kilkee Thalassotherapy Centre Kilkee Thalassotherapy Centre	Natural Seaweed Baths, Balneotherapy, Sweedish Massage, Body Scrub, Seaweed Body Wrap, Frigi-Thalgo, Facials, Manicures, Pedicures, Aromatherapy, Massage	Sauna, Steamroom, Manicure/Pedicure room, 6 Treatment rooms. Relaxation area. Winner, Best Day Spa 2004 (Irish Beauty Industry)	171	18	6
LIMERICK					
Fitzgeralds Woodlands House Hotel, Health and Leisure Spa Revas Hair Salon, Beauty & Relaxation Spa	Plantogen Hot Stone Massage Therapy, Thalgo Body Polish, Platinum Detox, Non-Surgical Lyposculpture, Ocean Chleir Seaweed Envelopment Wrap, Genesis Inch Loss Wrap, Stimulating & Oxygenating Facial, Lifting with Vitamin C, Acadespa Light Legs Treatment, Acadespa Tonic Treatment	Spray Tan, Balneotherapy, Hair Salon	182	60	9
TIPPERARY NORTH					
Abbey Court Hotel and Trinity Leisure Club The Spa Health and Beauty Sanctuary	Swedish Massage, Decléor Facials, Jessica Pedicure, Manicure, Make-up, Waxing, Self-Tan, Universal Contour Wrap	Stand Up Balneotherapy Bath, Sunroom	189	20	8

LET US PAMPER YOU WHILE YOU STAY!

ACCOMMODATION	TYPES OF TREATMENT	TYPES OF FACILITIES	BE OUR GUEST PAGE NUMBER	NO. OF TREATMENTS	NO. OF TREATMENT ROOMS
West					
GALWAY					
Benbaun House			200		
Galway Great Southern Hotel The Square Spa and Health Club	Hydrotherapy Baths, Waxing Treatments (various), Massage (various), Facials (various), Hand & Feet Treatments, Aromatherapy	Fitness Suite, Steamroom, Jacuzzi, Outdoor Canadian Hot Tub, Hydrotherapy Baths	210	20	3
Galway Radisson SAS Hotel Spirit One Spa	Massage, Facials, Hand Treatments, Foot Treatments, Floats, Wraps, Waxing, Reflexology, Exfoliation, Eye Teatments	Indoor Swimming Pool, Hot Tub, Gym, Slipper Bath, Laconium, Sabia Med, Heated loungers, Rock Sauna, Hammam, Snail Showers	210	60	16
Harbour Hotel	The Repêchage Four Layer Facial, Seaweed "on the go" Facial, Aromatherapy Purifying Facial, Back Facial, Repêchage Sea Body Treat, Repêchage New York Experience, Peppermint Sea Twist, Seaweed Body Treatment, Honey & Almond Body Polish, Manicure/Pedicure	Jacuzzi, Gym, Steamroom	211	21	2
MAYO					
Atlantic Coast Hotel Elysium Health and Beauty Spa	Holistic/Swedish Massage Therapy, Reflexology, Reiki Therapy, Aromatherapy, Indian Head Massage, Facials, Seaweed Bath, Enzymatic Sea Mud Pack Treatment	Swimming Pool, Steamroom, Sauna, Gymnasium, Childrens' Pool	237	21	4
Hotel Westport, Conference & Leisure Centre Hotel Westport, Health & Beauty Spa.	Hydrotherapy Bath, Serail Mud Treatment, Turkish Hammam Massage, Aromatherapy Massage, Swedish & Holistic Massage, Body Exfoliant Treatments, Body Moisturising Treatments, Facials, Pedicure/Manicure	Hydrotherapy Bath, Serail Mud Chamber, Hammam Wet Massage, Relaxation Suite, 20 Metre Pool, Lounger Pool, Jacuzzi, Steamroom, Sauna, Gym	238	35	10
Knockranny House Hotel	Elemis Deep Tissue Muscle Massage, Elemis Deep Tissue Back Massage, Elemis Oxygen SkinCalm Facial, Elemis S.O.S. Purifying Facial, Elemis Absolute Spa Ritual, Elemis Pro-Collagen Marine Facial - many other treatments available	Spa Pool, Gymnasium, Sauna & Steam Room, Hydrotherapy Baths, Calderium, Canadian Hot Tub - other facilities available	239	30	9

KEY TO MAPS

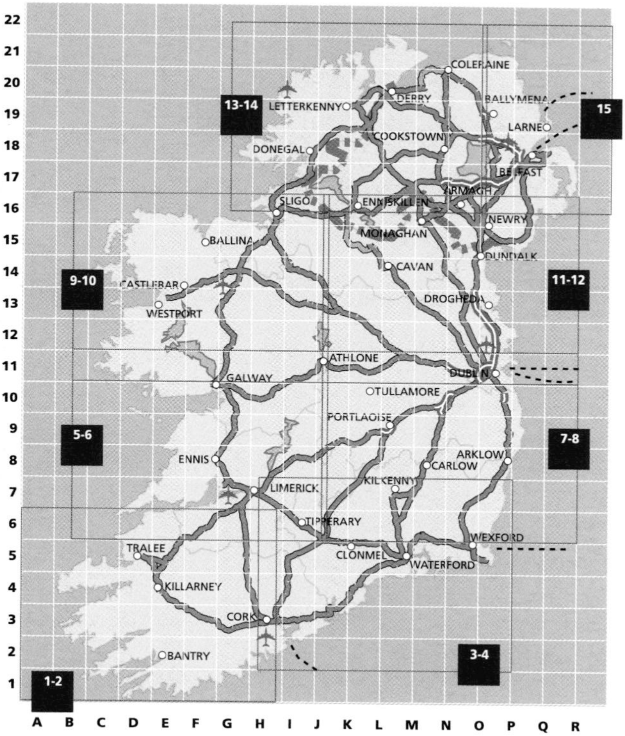

LEGEND

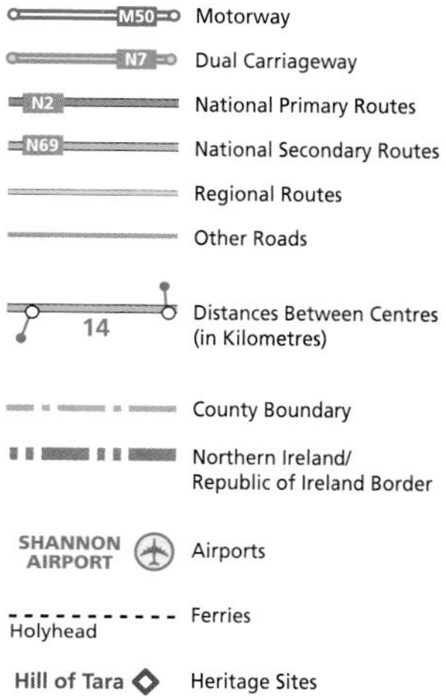

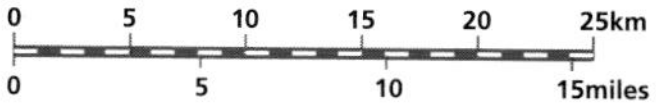

M50 Motorway	Motorway
N7 Dual Carriageway	Dual Carriageway
N2	National Primary Routes
N69	National Secondary Routes
	Regional Routes
	Other Roads
14	Distances Between Centres (in Kilometres)
	County Boundary
	Northern Ireland/ Republic of Ireland Border
SHANNON AIRPORT ✈	Airports
Holyhead	Ferries
Hill of Tara ◆	Heritage Sites

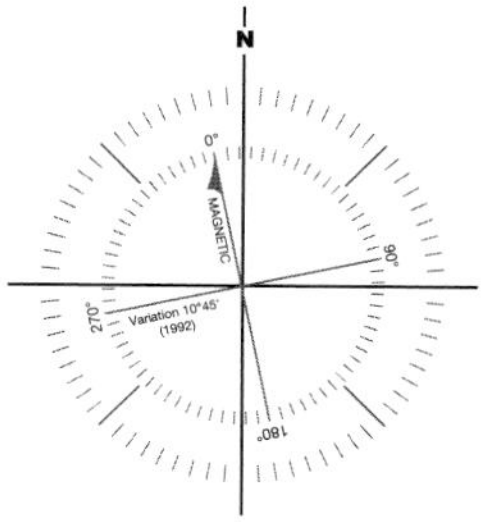

Map grid labels: 1–22 (rows), A–R (columns)

Map place names: COLERAINE, LETTERKENNY, DERRY, BALLYMENA, LARNE, COOKSTOWN, DONEGAL, BELFAST, SLIGO, ENNISKILLEN, ARMAGH, NEWRY, BALLINA, MONAGHAN, DUNDALK, CASTLEBAR, CAVAN, WESTPORT, DROGHEDA, ATHLONE, GALWAY, DUBLIN, TULLAMORE, PORTLAOISE, ENNIS, ARKLOW, CARLOW, LIMERICK, KILKENNY, TIPPERARY, WEXFORD, TRALEE, CLONMEL, WATERFORD, KILLARNEY, CORK, BANTRY

Map panel references: 13-14, 15, 9-10, 11-12, 5-6, 7-8, 1-2, 3-4

Compass: N, Variation 10°45' (1992)

DISTANCE CHART
in Kilometres

ARMAGH	ATHLONE	BELFAST	CARLOW	CLIFDEN	CORK	DERRY	DUBLIN	DUNDALK	ENNISKILLEN	GALWAY	KILKENNY	KILLARNEY	LARNE	LIMERICK	PORTLAOISE	ROSSLARE HARBOUR	SHANNON AIRPORT	SLIGO	TRALEE	WATERFORD	WEXFORD	WICKLOW
159																						
66	224																					
211	108	248																				
316	171	370	256																			
380	219	423	187	287																		
114	225	118	309	303	460																	
129	124	167	82	296	256	233																
45	142	82	166	314	340	158	84															
81	127	135	240	237	346	98	175	101														
238	92	303	177	79	206	277	216	233	192													
245	121	282	39	248	148	335	114	200	242	169												
388	229	430	235	295	480	303	348	356	214	196												
105	264	40	287	411	462	122	206	121	174	343	320	470										
279	119	320	138	184	101	369	192	238	245	105	114	109	356									
208	71	250	37	229	174	287	82	167	192	150	50	221	285	109								
282	201	320	93	348	151	237	324	269	100	272	356	204	130									
293	134	345	163	172	126	357	216	261	261	93	138	134	380	24	134	229						
148	116	203	224	167	336	134	213	171	68	142	237	345	240	235	187	319	224					
382	222	423	242	288	121	472	296	341	349	208	216	32	460	103	213	291	127	338				
285	167	324	74	296	126	383	156	240	290	217	48	192	359	124	97	81	148	283	211			
264	184	301	76	330	187	365	132	219	306	250	81	254	338	187	113	19	209	299	272	61		
185	138	222	61	311	256	293	56	140	221	232	100	303	259	193	82	118	216	238	296	135	100	

Scale: 0 5 10 15 20 25km / 0 5 10 15miles
SCALE 1 : 625 000

MAPS

465

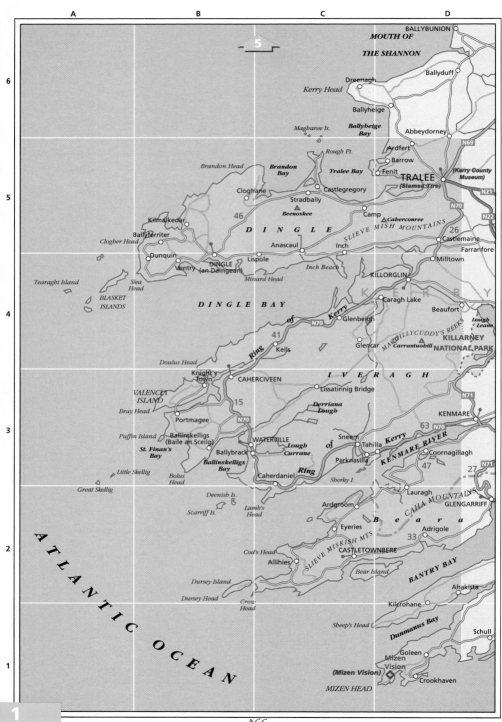

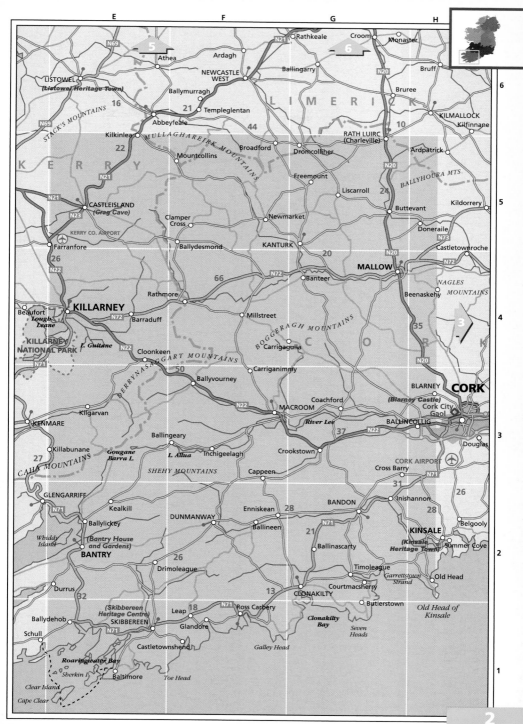

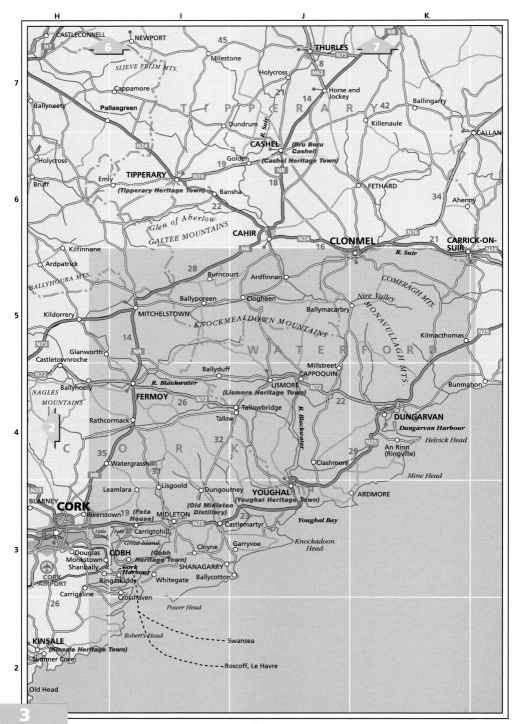

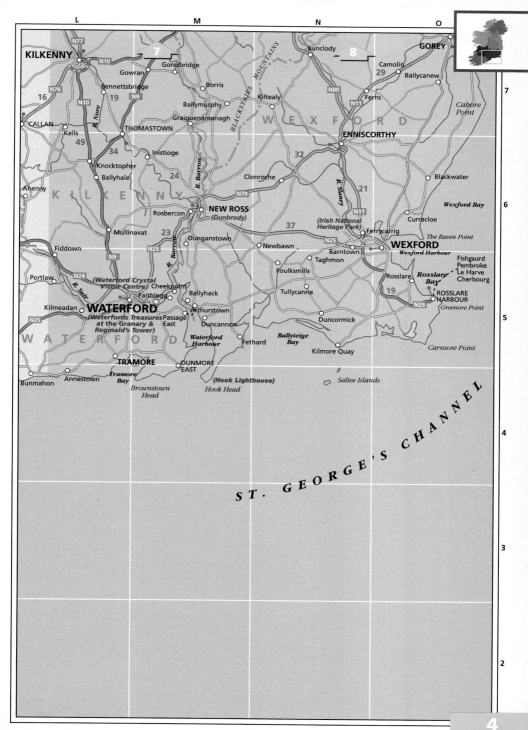

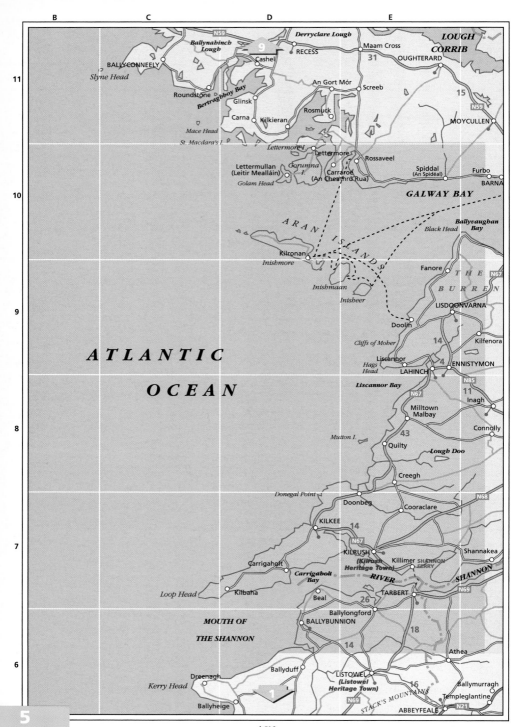

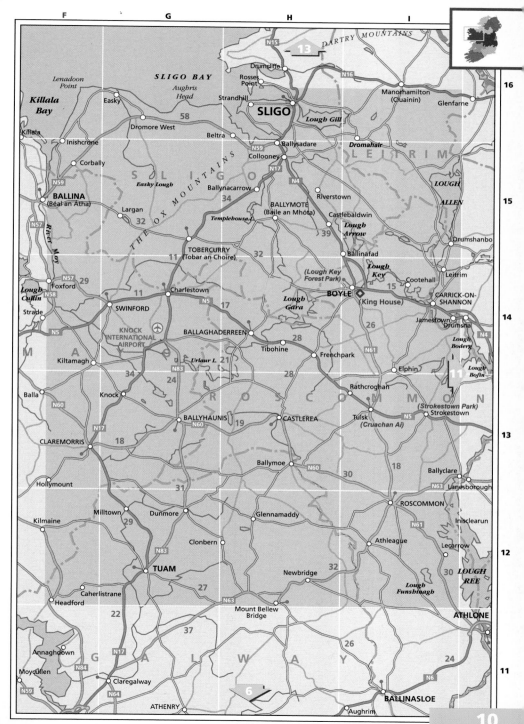

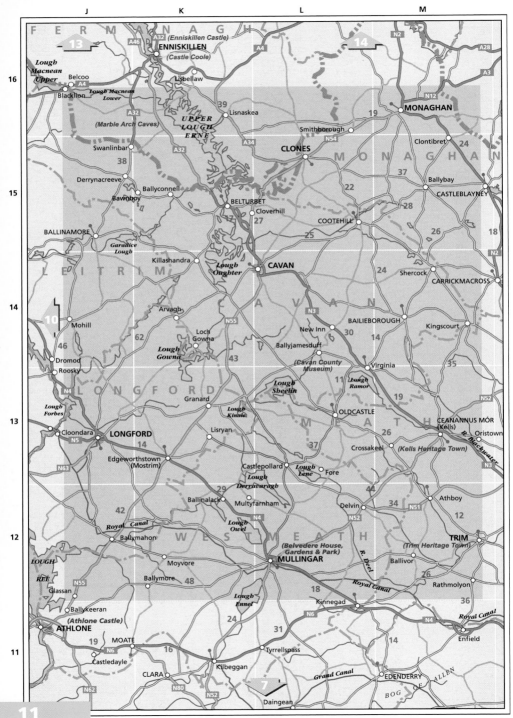

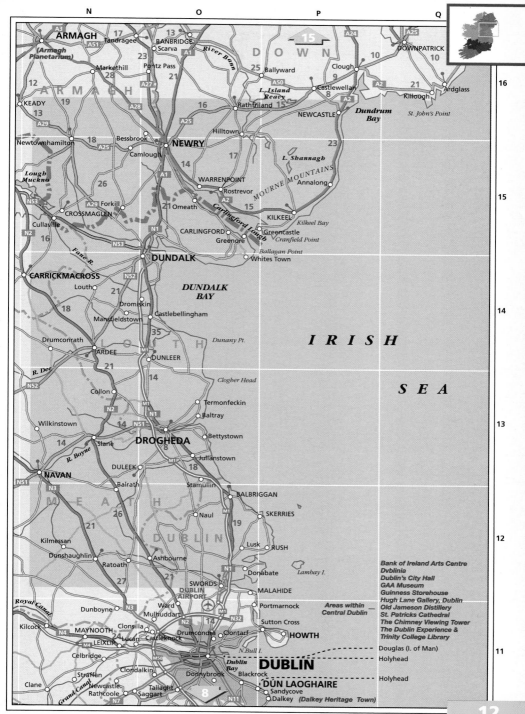

12

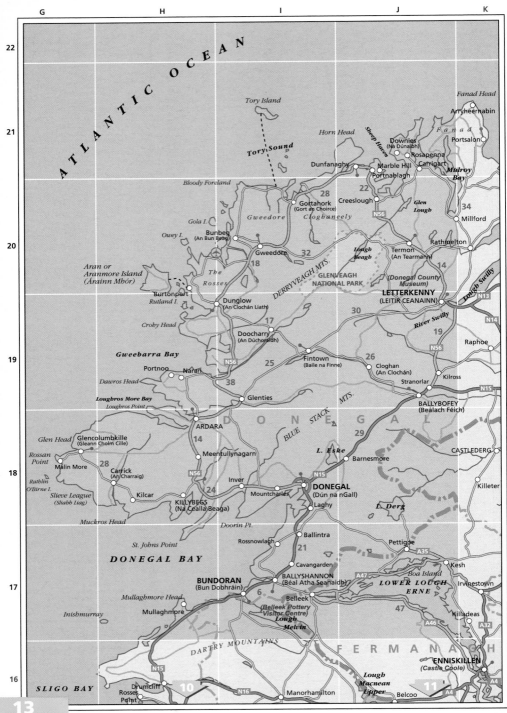

ASHLEY HOTEL
Cork City, Cork 85
☎ 021-450 1518

ASHLING HOTEL
Dublin City, Dublin 299
☎ 01-677 2324

ASHVILLE GUESTHOUSE
Killarney, Kerry 129
☎ 064-36405

ASTON HOTEL
Dublin City, Dublin 300
☎ 01-677 9300

ATHENAEUM HOUSE HOTEL
Waterford City, Waterford 50
☎ 051-833 999

ATLANTA HOUSE
Bantry, Cork 74
☎ 027-50237

ATLANTIC COAST HOTEL
Westport, Mayo 237
☎ 098-29000

ATLANTIC HOTEL
Lahinch, Clare 173
☎ 065-708 1049

ATLANTIC HOUSE
Dungloe, Donegal......................253
☎ 074-952 1061

ATLANTIC VIEW GUESTHOUSE
Galway City, Galway 206
☎ 091-582109

AUBURN LODGE HOTEL
Ennis, Clare 166
☎ 065-682 1247

AUGUSTA LODGE
Westport, Mayo 237
☎ 098-28900

AULBER HOUSE
Cashel, Tipperary South...............36
☎ 062-63713

AUSTIN FRIAR HOTEL
Mullingar, Westmeath................394
☎ 044-45777

B

BAILEYS OF CASHEL
Cashel, Tipperary South...............37
☎ 062-61937

BAILIE HOTEL
Bailieborough, Cavan 372
☎ 042-966 5334

BALLINALACKEN CASTLE COUNTRY HOUSE & RESTAURANT
Doolin, Clare 164
☎ 065-707 4025

BALLINSKELLIGS INN
Ballinskelligs, Kerry 108
☎ 066-947 9104

BALLYGARRY HOUSE HOTEL
Tralee, Kerry 150
☎ 066-712 3322

BALLYGLASS COUNTRY HOUSE
Tipperary Town, Tipperary South..42
☎ 062-52104

BALLYKNOCKEN COUNTRY HOUSE
Ashford, Wicklow 360
☎ 0404-44627

BALLYMAC
Stoneyford, Antrim 272
☎ 028-9264 8313

BALLYMALOE HOUSE
Shanagarry, Cork........................105
☎ 021-465 2531

BALLYMASCANLON HOUSE HOTEL
Dundalk, Louth 351
☎ 042-935 8200

BALLYNAHINCH CASTLE HOTEL
Ballynahinch, Galway 196
☎ 095-31006

BALLYROE HEIGHTS HOTEL
Tralee, Kerry 150
☎ 066-712 6796

BALLYSEEDE CASTLE HOTEL
Tralee, Kerry 151
☎ 066-712 5799

BALLYVARA HOUSE
Doolin, Clare 164
☎ 065-707 4467

BALLYVAUGHAN LODGE
Ballyvaughan, Clare....................160
☎ 065-707 7292

BALLYVERGAL HOUSE
Carlow Town, Carlow 22
☎ 059-914 3634

BALMORAL HOTEL
Belfast City, Belfast 274
☎ 028-9030 1234

BALTIMORE BAY GUEST HOUSE
Baltimore, Cork 73
☎ 028-20600

BALTIMORE HARBOUR HOTEL & LEISURE CENTRE
Baltimore, Cork 73
☎ 028-20361

BAMBURY'S GUEST HOUSE
Dingle, Kerry...............................114
☎ 066-915 1244

BANNER LODGE
Ennis, Clare 166
☎ 065-682 4224

BANTRY BAY HOTEL
Bantry, Cork 75
☎ 027-50062

BARBERSTOWN CASTLE
Straffan, Kildare.........................382
☎ 01-628 8157

BARNABROW COUNTRY HOUSE
Midleton, Cork 103
☎ 021-465 2534

BARNAWEE BRIDGE GUESTHOUSE
Dungarvan, Waterford.................45
☎ 058-42074

BARR NA SRAIDE INN
Dingle, Kerry..............................115
☎ 066-915 1331

BARROW COUNTRY HOUSE
Tralee, Kerry 151
☎ 066-713 6437

BARROWVILLE TOWN HOUSE
Carlow Town, Carlow 22
☎ 059-914 3324

BARRY'S HOTEL
Dublin City, Dublin 300
☎ 01-874 9407

BAY VIEW HOTEL
Waterville, Kerry 155
☎ 066-947 4122

BAY VIEW HOTEL & LEISURE CENTRE
Killybegs, Donegal 254
☎ 074-973 1950

INDEX OF HOTELS & GUESTHOUSES — GUINNESS.

DERGVALE HOTEL
Dublin City, Dublin 311
☎ 01-874 4753

DERRYHALE HOTEL
Dundalk, Louth 352
☎ 042-933 5471

DERRYNANE HOTEL
Caherdaniel, Kerry......................111
☎ 066-947 5136

DIAMOND HILL COUNTRY HOUSE
Waterford City, Waterford 52
☎ 051-832855

DINGLE BAY HOTEL
Dingle, Kerry..............................116
☎ 066-915 1231

DINGLE BENNERS HOTEL
Dingle, Kerry..............................117
☎ 066-915 1638

DINGLE SKELLIG HOTEL
Dingle, Kerry..............................117
☎ 066-915 0200

DOHERTY'S POLLAN BEACH HOTEL
Ballyliffin, Donegal 247
☎ 074-937 8840

**DOLMEN HOTEL AND
RIVER COURT LODGES**
Carlow Town, Carlow 23
☎ 059-914 2002

DONNYBROOK LODGE
Dublin City, Dublin 311
☎ 01-283 7333

DOOLEY'S HOTEL
Waterford City, Waterford 52
☎ 051-873531

DOOLYS HOTEL
Birr, Offaly.................................388
☎ 0509-20032

DOONMACFELIM HOUSE
Doolin, Clare 165
☎ 065-707 4503

DOONMORE HOTEL
Inishbofin Island, Galway............220
☎ 095-45804

DORRIANS IMPERIAL HOTEL
Ballyshannon, Donegal 248
☎ 071-985 1147

DOUGH MOR LODGE
Lahinch, Clare 174
☎ 065-708 2063

DOWNHILL HOUSE HOTEL
Ballina, Mayo 231
☎ 096-21033

DOWNHILL INN
Ballina, Mayo 231
☎ 096-73444

DOWNINGS BAY HOTEL
Letterkenny, Donegal 255
☎ 074-915 5586

DOWNSHIRE HOUSE HOTEL
Blessington, Wicklow 362
☎ 045-865199

**DOYLES SEAFOOD BAR &
TOWN HOUSE**
Dingle, Kerry..............................117
☎ 066-915 1174

DROMHALL HOTEL
Killarney, Kerry 132
☎ 064-39300

DROMOLAND CASTLE
Newmarket-on-Fergus, Clare......179
☎ 061-368144

DRUMCREEHY HOUSE
Ballyvaughan, Clare....................160
☎ 065-707 7377

DRURY COURT HOTEL
Dublin City, Dublin 311
☎ 01-475 1988

DUBLIN HILTON AIRPORT
Dublin Airport, Dublin 292
☎ 01-877 5400

DUKES HOTEL
Belfast City, Belfast 275
☎ 028-9023 6666

DUN RI GUESTHOUSE
Clifden, Galway 201
☎ 095-21625

**DUNADRY HOTEL AND
COUNTRY CLUB**
Belfast City, Belfast 276
☎ 028-9443 4343

**DUNBRODY COUNTRY HOUSE
HOTEL & COOKERY SCHOOL**
Arthurstown, Wexford 56
☎ 051-389600

DUNDRUM HOUSE HOTEL
Cashel, Tipperary South...............37
☎ 062-71116

DUNMORE HOUSE HOTEL
Clonakilty, Cork...........................79
☎ 023-33352

DUNRAVEN ARMS HOTEL
Adare, Limerick 182
☎ 061-396633

E

EAGLE LODGE
Ballybunion, Kerry......................109
☎ 068-27224

EARLS COURT HOUSE
Killarney, Kerry 132
☎ 064-34009

EAST VILLAGE HOTEL
Cork City, Cork 87
☎ 021-436 7000

EGAN'S GUESTHOUSE
Dublin City, Dublin 312
☎ 01-830 3611

ELDON HOTEL
Skibbereen, Cork........................106
☎ 028-22000

ELDONS HOTEL
Roundstone, Galway 227
☎ 095-35933

EMLAGH HOUSE
Dingle, Kerry..............................118
☎ 066-915 2345

EMMET HOTEL
Clonakilty, Cork...........................80
☎ 023-33394

**ERRISEASK HOUSE HOTEL
& RESTAURANT**
Clifden, Galway 202
☎ 095-23553

TF ROYAL HOTEL & THEATRE
Castlebar, Mayo 233
☎ 094-902 3111

THREE RIVERS GUEST HOUSE
Cheekpoint, Waterford 44
☎ 051-382520

TIERNEY'S GUEST HOUSE
Kinsale, Cork...............................100
☎ 021-477 2205

TIGH CHUALAIN
Spiddal, Galway 229
☎ 091-553609

TIGH FITZ
Aran Islands, Galway..................195
☎ 099-61213

TIMES HOTEL
Tipperary Town, Tipperary South..43
☎ 062-31111

TINAKILLY COUNTRY HOUSE AND RESTAURANT
Rathnew, Wicklow 368
☎ 0404-69274

TONLEGEE HOUSE AND RESTAURANT
Athy, Kildare..............................376
☎ 059-863 1473

TOWER GUESTHOUSE, BAR & RESTAURANT
Roscrea, Tipperary North............190
☎ 0505-21774

TOWER HOTEL & LEISURE CENTRE
Waterford City, Waterford 55
☎ 051-875801

TOWER HOTEL DERRY
Derry City, Derry 281
☎ 028-7137 1000

TOWERS HOTEL
Glenbeigh, Kerry 121
☎ 066-976 8212

TRALEE TOWNHOUSE
Tralee, Kerry 155
☎ 066-718 1111

TRAVELODGE CASTLEKNOCK
Dublin City, Dublin 338
☎ 01-820 2626

TREACY'S HOTEL
Enniscorthy, Wexford 60
☎ 054-37798

TRIDENT HOTEL
Kinsale, Cork..............................100
☎ 021-477 9300

TRINITY CAPITAL HOTEL
Dublin City, Dublin 338
☎ 01-648 1000

TULLAMORE COURT HOTEL CONFERENCE & LEISURE CENTRE
Tullamore, Offaly.......................391
☎ 0506-46666

TULLYLAGAN COUNTRY HOUSE HOTEL
Cookstown, Tyrone 286
☎ 028-8676 5100

TUSCAR LODGE
Killarney, Kerry 146
☎ 064-31978

UPPERCROSS HOUSE
Dublin City, Dublin 338
☎ 01-497 5486

VICKERY'S INN
Bantry, Cork 75
☎ 027-50006

VICTORIA HOTEL
Cork City, Cork 93
☎ 021-427 8788

VICTORIA HOTEL
Galway City, Galway 216
☎ 091-567433

VICTORIA HOUSE HOTEL
Killarney, Kerry 147
☎ 064-35430

VIENNA WOODS HOTEL
Cork City, Cork 93
☎ 021-482 1146

VIKING HOTEL
Waterford City, Waterford 55
☎ 051-876 133

VIRGINIA'S GUESTHOUSE
Kenmare, Kerry 127
☎ 064-41021

WALTER RALEIGH HOTEL
Youghal, Cork 108
☎ 024-92011

WARDS HOTEL
Galway City, Galway 216
☎ 091-581508

WATERFOOT HOTEL & COUNTRY CLUB
Derry City, Derry 281
☎ 028-7134 5500

WATERFORD CASTLE HOTEL & GOLF CLUB
Waterford City, Waterford 55
☎ 051-878203

WATERFORD MANOR HOTEL
Waterford City, Waterford 56
☎ 051-377 814

WATERFRONT HOTEL
Galway City, Galway 217
☎ 091-588100

WATERLOO HOUSE
Dublin City, Dublin 339
☎ 01-660 1888

WATERLOO LODGE
Dublin City, Dublin 339
☎ 01-668 5380

WATERSEDGE HOTEL
Cobh, Cork 83
☎ 021-481 5566

WATERSIDE
Graiguenamanagh, Kilkenny 25
☎ 059-972 4246

WATERSIDE HOTEL
Donabate, Dublin 292
☎ 01-843 6153

WELLINGTON PARK HOTEL
Belfast City, Belfast 278
☎ 028-9038 1111

WEST CORK HOTEL
Skibbereen, Cork........................106
☎ 028-21277

WEST COUNTY HOTEL
Dublin City, Dublin 339
☎ 01-626 4011

SEE ALSO INDEX TO LOCATIONS 503